GETTING ABOUT

TRAVEL WRITINGS OF
WILLIAM F. BUCKLEY JR.

GETTING ABOUT

EDITED BY
BILL MEEHAN

ENCOUNTER BOOKS · NEW YORK · LONDON

First American edition published in 2023 by Encounter Books,
an activity of Encounter for Culture and Education, Inc.,
a nonprofit, tax-exempt corporation.
Encounter Books website address: www.encounterbooks.com

Manufactured in the United States and printed on
acid-free paper. The paper used in this publication meets
the minimum requirements of ANSI/NISO Z39.48-1992
(R 1997) (*Permanence of Paper*).

FIRST AMERICAN EDITION

Library of Congress Cataloging-in-Publication Data is available
for this title under the ISBN: 978-1-64177-317-1

1 2 3 4 5 6 7 8 9 20 23

Contents

CHAPTER SIX: 1990-1994

Introduction

In your room there are problems. There is no air-conditioning in the tiny living room, and to go to the bedroom requires that you turn on the light that illuminates the dark stairway. But having reached the bedroom, you then need to turn off the light when it is time to sleep. But you cannot do that without descending the stairway; there is only the single switch. So, you climb up in the dark.

You need to telephone a companion staying in another room. You call the operator. It rings busy. You try off and on, for one hour. It is very important, so you descend to hotel reception and ask the woman at the desk: Where is Mr. Peter Samara staying?

What then happens is as if you asked your grandmother to come up with the picture of her high school graduation. The receptionist hauls up a lapful of yellow slips and begins to go over them one by one. At the end, she says: "He is not here." "Yes, he is here. He has been here for two days." "He is not here." At that moment, Peter shows up. You exchange intelligence, and ask for his room number, which is 601, so that you can dial him directly.

The next morning you wish to call 601. You follow the hotel dialing instructions. To call 601, you must dial 203-20-97. Well, you can manage that. Does that mean that to call 602 you would dial 203-20-98? No: 203-50-40.

*At 3:30 p.m., on your way out, you report to the concierge that your
toilet is stopped up. You come in at 11:00 p.m. and note that it is still
stopped up. At 9:00 a.m. it is still stopped up. It occurs to anyone scheduled
to check out of the hotel that morning that there is an obvious way to
leave the mark of one's displeasure.*

—"Moscow: Waiting for Mr. Hilton"
by William F. Buckley Jr., July 24, 1990

When it came to writing about travels, few journalists could rival William
F. Buckley Jr. Author of sixteen novels, Buckley was a master storyteller
who skillfully balanced the apparently conflicting devices of fiction with
the elements of reporting to create entertaining travel pieces suffused with
exuberance and authority. With a flair for literary journalism, a fondness
for friendship, and a passion for fun, Buckley was an elegant jet-setter
whose travel writings deserve compiling into a single volume. These selections—spanning nearly a lifetime of adventures on boats, trains, and planes
around the world for work or pleasure—broaden the scope and deepen the
significance of Buckley's *oeuvre*. The collection also helps preserve Buckley's
legacy as his centenary, in 2025, approaches.

But why *now* a book about travel and travel writing, when the landscape for the genre appears to be shifting? The *New York Times*, for example, dropped its thick travel section from the Sunday paper, then brought
it back as a weekly page. *National Geographic Traveler*, a reputable brand,
discontinued its US edition, and *Lonely Planet*, the most trusted name in
guide books, rethought its collection of newly offered titles. Perhaps the
most important development took place when the *Best American Travel
Writing*, an anthology published annually for twenty-two years, released
its final volume in 2021. Reacting to this news, Thomas Swick at Lithub
suggested that the genre has "mystifyingly lost its allure." But has it? I side
with author Carl Thompson, who believes, "Travel writing is currently a
flourishing and highly popular literary genre…[R]ecent decades have
undoubtedly witnessed a travel writing 'boom,' and this boom shows no
signs of abating in the near future." Although Thompson made those claims
more than a decade ago in his book *Travel Writing*, some evidence supports

embracing it today. Take the Lowell Thomas Travel Journalism Competition. Recognizing "excellence in the field" since 1985, and administered by the Society of American Travel Writers Foundation, this prestigious contest received 1,278 entries in thirty-seven categories for material produced in 2020—a year when travel was, to say the least, uncertain due to the worldwide pandemic.

Demonstrating the genre's resiliency, as well, technology has facilitated the growth of blogs, newsletters, multimedia presentations, and social-media platforms as vibrant outlets. What is more, travel writing has sustained a gradual ascent in academia arguably ever since the publication of Paul Fussell's 1980 pioneering book *Abroad: British Literary Travel Between the Wars*. Once thought too "popular" for legitimate Ivory Tower scholarship, travel writing is now an acceptable field of inquiry—although a) much of it is informed by trendy themes and b) a commercially successful author like Paul Theroux still might be thought lowbrow. Which brings up the travel writer's motivation. Jan Lukacs "travel[ed] to certain places because of their history" and later gathered the essays into a wonderful book, *Destinations Past*, which he maintains "is not really a travel book, and…not travel-writing." But it really is. In the soul of every travel writer resides the pedagogue, whose *wanderlust* inspires a personally fulfilling journey of discovery to be shared with readers. For the travel writing journalist, however, there's one measure of success: "A story," writes doyen of travel Tim Cahill, "is the essence of the travel essay. Readers want something that holds their attention. They want to be entertained and informed."

Besides one essay that appeared in a book ("A Beginner's Tribulations") and the review of Henry James' travel writings, the 101 articles by Buckley collected here fall into two categories: narratives and commentary. The narratives delight, holding a reader's attention with fast-paced plots similar to one of Buckley's best-selling Blackford Oakes spy novels. Typical of the autobiographical nature of travel writing, Buckley is an active participant in the action, bringing a talent for writing himself into the story but not dominating it, all while arranging a *mise-en-scène* that heightens atmosphere. On the other hand, the commentary, usually a syndicated column, represents Buckley's gimlet eye mainly on the airline and railroad industries, or on travel in general. Although some columns resemble a narrative, (see "Getting About in Italy" or "Moscow: Waiting for Mr. Hilton,") most of them are sensible judgments about something "that boils the blood of free men"—but not mean-spirited like Mark Twain's infamous letter to the head of Western Union. Buckley is good-natured, typically offering "alternative" (i.e., humorous) suggestions which, however, the head of Northeast Airlines thought "gratuitous" (see "Midsummer Fare"). But they are typically written in the style and tone of "Airplane Crosstalk":

> I tend to travel first class, thanks to the hospitality of my own clients, combined with hedonistic inclinations cultivated with great sweat over a period of many years. The primary difference between first class and tourist-class travel is the increasing differential in price. If the price increase were happening *pari passu,* with increased amenities, that would make economic sense.
>
> But exactly the opposite is happening. The quality of the food diminishes, legroom straitens, and scheduling is progressively bizarre.

If there's anything Buckley desired when he boarded a plane, besides some proper nourishment served at the proper time, it was plenty of room. So, when a *New York Times* editorial in 1986 proposed that airlines limit carry-ons, Buckley answered with a column titled "Worst Suggestion of the Year."

> There are lots of travelers who need with them on board the entire para-phernalia of their professional life. I (for instance) carry a briefcase. In it are the usual things (passport-type stuff, research material, speech port-folios); but, also a toilet bag, customized to individual requirements. Mine, for instance, includes Actifed, Afrin, and Ayr, without which I contract head colds. An altimeter, to check on the pressurization of the airplane, and a compass. I forget why I insist on carrying a compass, but I do, and would know sooner than anyone else if a hijacker had got hold of the controls and was heading toward Cuba while the passengers thought ourselves heading serenely toward Minneapolis.
>
> Then, of course, there is the laptop computer. These come in differ-

ent sizes. I have traveled with a Kaypro (about the size of a standard Royal typewriter), an Epson Geneva (about the size of a compact-disk player), and a Toshiba (about twice the size of the Epson). But more often than not you absolutely need such an instrument if you are, say, writing the speech you will deliver a few minutes after your arrival at Minneapolis.

Then, of course, there is the third bag, which is roughly designated as one's paperwork. Two hundred unanswered letters, manuscripts to read, copy to edit. For this one needs a clipboard and, of course, a dictating machine. I weigh 185 pounds, clothed. When I step onto an airplane, I weigh about 235 pounds.

The mystique of the sea is a prominent theme in Buckley's *oeuvre*, so it is no surprise that thirty-one articles in *Getting About* pertain to life fore and aft the mast. Buckley took up sailing as a teenager in 1938 and enjoyed a lifetime whirling across waters around the world. It wasn't long after Buckley started racing sailboats, however, that he discovered the pleasures of amateur *cruising* (see "An Amateur Skipper Talks Back" and "A Beginner's Tribulations"). What is more, being at sea awakens in Buckley an appreciation for nature, almost poetic in its sentiment. Indeed, a night landfall for Buckley was nothing less than "sublime" (see "Finale").

Buckley started skiing shortly after the inaugural issue of *National Review* hit the newsstands in November 1955 and found in the sport "a bit of paradise," his experience paralleling emotions aroused on a sailboat. Alta, nestled in Utah's Little Cottonwood Canyon at 8,500 feet, is the subject of two articles. It is in the second, in 1994 for *Ski* magazine, where Buckley describes twenty years of vacationing at Alta in late January for five days with economist Milton Friedman and attorney Lawry Chickering: "After so many years of total immersion in one another's company, over a period of time so brief, it is remarkable what confidences one finds oneself willing to share. It is to be compared with night watches on a sailing boat: the intimacy is of the kind that generates true pleasure in one another's company."

From an early age, Buckley navigated a course guided by an impatient search for truth, steered as much by his heart as his head. The people fortunate enough to have been acquainted with him understood this, as might others who became familiar with him through his life and work. The *New Yorker* editor William Shawn, for example, recognized the innate goodness he had come to meet when serializing several of Buckley's books. What is more, Buckley's literary voice is heightened by the genial tradition he so highly regarded at Yale, as well as by the school's polite custom to forget, and forgive. But there was an ornery side, his long-time secretary, Frances Bronson, told me one day over a long lunch at a French bistro in Murray Hill not far from the *National Review* offices. This fun-loving trait is on display in "The Angel of Craig's Point."

Buckley remarked in a magazine interview when *Miles Gone By*, his literary autobiography, hit the bookstores in 2005 that his intention was "to put it all together [and] to do so without any preaching at all." Buckley's was a high calling, debating ideas, defending the eternal verities, treating others decently, and being endlessly grateful for friends and the occasions that brought them together. Whether on land or at sea, he enjoyed life— with pizzazz. According to the headline for his 1980 article in *People*, Buckley "Braves the High Seas in High Fashion, with Champagne and Scarlatti." Similarly, in "Maritime Traveler" he envisions a more refined dining experience at 30,000 feet:

> I predict, on the matter of food and drink, that there is a future for the *really* good box lunch. It should be sold at major airports and contain maybe a little celery *remoulade*, a cold slightly breaded veal, a super chocolate pastry, a little cheese and maybe a fresh fig, plus a mini-bottle of an Alsatian white wine that you can drink even after the temperature rises, and a mini-bottle of good Bordeaux. Then ring for your coffee…

Buckley took his work but not himself seriously, and he writes candidly as much about the misadventures as he does the adventures while traveling. What is more, there's always Buckley's witty, playful side that furnishes subtle humor: "I forget who appointed me or when," he teases in the 1981 column about overweight baggage at the Pan Am check-in counter, "but somewhere along the line I emerged as unofficial journalistic protector of the traveling public in the Matter of Overweight. My commission is not disinterested, since I regularly travel with excess luggage, required as I am to carry the burdens of the world with me wherever I go."

In my 1996 interview with him for the *University Bookman*, Buckley commented that his four sailing books (*Airborne, Atlantic High, Racing Through Paradise*, and *Windfall*) appealed to an audience beyond the readers of *National Review*; they, he explained, were not so much conservative crusaders but instead were interested in stories about family, friendships, and festivities aboard a boat at sea. Similarly, the reader for *Getting About* is more the armchair traveler whose romantic reveries are enriched by appreciation for the aesthetic and intellectual qualities of fine literary journalism—and for a good story.

Buckley engages readers with his command of language. The structure of each piece in this collection varies, no two alike. Buckley composes for the well-tuned ear, so his sentences harmonize into a composition similar to a vigorous Bach concerto, with its magnificent blending of points and counterpoints. Pure enjoyment. To slur language, Buckley thought, is as painful to the well-tempered ear as to slur music. There are, he insisted, kind and less kind ways of treating the ear. And, as to punctuation: at first glance the comma appears unwieldy, but it is used, he says, "with intended effects."

Then there are the big words and foreign phrases scattered throughout his corpus. "It's an old complaint," Buckley wrote in defense of their usage. He explained that he did not invent the words and would not suppress any term that expresses exactly what he aims to express. And besides, he added, people should look up their meaning instead of complaining. (Note: Buckley served on the editorial board of the *American Heritage Dictionary*.) *Getting About* thus contains the following examples from what Buckley called his "working vocabulary": *a capella, anfractuosities*, annealed, *anni horribili*, antimacassar, attenuatedly, *aposiopesis, bel canto, belletristically, blasé*, capricious, chiliastic, contumacy, deliquescence, demisemiquaver, *élan*, encyst, *en passant, epigoni*, eponymous, eschatalogical, eschew, *et ux,* exasperating, exiguous, exultation, fastidiously, *gemütlichkeit*, gregarious, *hegira*, imperturbability, ineluctable, inveighed, jeremiad, jocular, laconically, *laissez passer, les petits*, lapidary, latitudinarian, licentious, lucabrations, lurid, *maladroit, mañana, mirabile dictu,* multifarious, numinous, obloquy, ombudsman, pallid, *par impossible,* periphrastic, *père, piquancy,* plenipotentiary, prehensile, *qua, querencia,* repristinated, ruminate, solecisms, solipsistic, somnambulistically, *sommelier,* soritical, *sotto voce,* supererogatory, sybaritic, sycophancy, synecdoche, *tout court,* and yclept. Additional foreign phrases include *force de frappe, Quam ad Antiguam pervenimus, secundum estimationem fori,* and *sub specie aeternitatis,* not to mention passages of dialogue where Buckley speaks Spanish and French.

To better illustrate Buckley's output over five decades and to juxtapose the theme and construction of the selections, I have organized *Getting About* chronologically. During the Sixties, when Buckley was launching *National Review,* commencing a syndicated column, running for mayor of New York City, and beginning the television program *Firing Line,* he stayed close to home. After that, however, Buckley was constantly in motion.

The selections—which include fifty-three *On the Right* columns, do not require introductory notes since the titles, except in a couple instances, convey the topic. In the spirit of Ernest Hemingway's *A Moveable Feast*—the author around town in local surroundings—I have included Buckley's story about a late-night dramatic incident at his apartment in New York City; and a paean to Paone's, his favorite restaurant. In addition to writing twice about skiing at Alta, UT, Buckley published two articles about cruising on *Club Med I* and riding the Orient Express. Excluded from the collection are the "Letters from Abroad" in 1957 and the pilgrimage to Lourdes in 1993—all written for *National Review*; the numerous revisions of articles that Buckley and his literary agent Lois Wallace resourcefully placed in multiple publications; three columns and introductory material for two books about the *Titanic* since they repeat parts of "Down to the Great Ship," written for the *New York Times Magazine*; and the *New Yorker's* lengthy excerpts from the sailing books *Atlantic High* and *Racing Through Paradise.* A few columns datelined overseas also are omitted because they pertain to economic or political conditions and not traveling *per se.*

Some pieces appeared in the anthologies Buckley published every five or ten years, but almost all selections are reprinted for the first time between the covers of a book. Besides the syndicated column reaching hundreds of newspapers across the country, outlets for Buckley's travel writings included *Life*; *New York Times* and its *Book Review*, *Magazine*, *Sophisticated Traveler*, and *Good Health Magazine*; *Condé Nast Traveler*; *National Geographic Traveler*; *New Yorker*; *People*; *House Beautiful*; *Architectural Digest*; *Esquire*; *Saturday Review*; *Atlantic*; *Town & Country*; and the premier boating magazines such as *Cruising World, Yachting, Motor Boating & Sailing,* and *Rudder.*

Furthering Buckley's professional prestige is the official approval he earned for achievement. Notably, he took first place in the Magazine Article on Foreign Travel category in the Lowell Thomas Travel Journalism Competition for eight reports written while "Concording Around the World" in 1989. He also was recognized with the University of Southern California's Distinguished Achievement Award in Journalism, American Friends of Haifa University Carmel Award for Journalism Excellence, National Institute of Social Sciences Gold Medal Award, American Book Award for Best Mystery (*Stained Glass*), the Union League's Lincoln Literary Award, and the Lifetime Achievement Award by the American Society of Magazine Editors; was selected a Fellow of the Society of Professional Journalists, Sigma Delta Chi; and received the Presidential Medal of Freedom, Living Legend Award from the Library of Congress, and thirty (!) honorary degrees.

Buckley telephoned me in April 2004 to let me know that he had written an important article coming out in the *Atlantic*. He explained to me that while skiing in Gstaad during his working vacation (see "Living and Working in Gstaad") he lost his balance a few times, which meant he no longer spent afternoons on the slopes, which resulted in a decision to sell his sailboat, *Patito* (*See* "Aweigh"). He passed away almost three years later.

I have, for twenty-six years, focused most of my scholarly activity on the dashing cosmopolitan who, with the publication of *God and Man at Yale,* entered the scene with uncommon *élan* in 1951. *Getting About,* which grew from a course in travel literature I recently taught at the University of Delaware and is informed partially by prior employment as an international guide with Maupintour, Inc., is my third (edited) book on Buckley. The first two opportunities came to me unexpectedly. *William F. Buckley Jr.:*

A Bibliography (ISI Books, 2002), occurred when I interviewed Buckley for my dissertation. After he graciously gave me ninety minutes of his time on a sunny December morning in 1995, Buckley asked if, when I completed my studies, would I consider compiling and editing his works into a bibliography. For *Conversations with William F. Buckley Jr.* (University Press of Mississippi, 2009), the publisher contacted me after Buckley's official biographer Sam Tanenhaus declined the project and recommended me. With Gary Gregg, I co-taught a seminar on Buckley's novel *Getting it Right* for the McConnell Center at the University of Louisville when I worked there in the library's special collections department. Supported by a grant from the Neal and Jane Freeman Foundation, I directed the cataloging of Buckley's personal library of 5,000 books, a multi-year project that involved three graduate assistants funded by Valdosta State University, where I was an assistant professor in the School of Information Science. My scholarship on Buckley's life and work also includes book reviews, conference papers, lectures, and an essay about the fictional spy Blackford Oakes. I even travelled to Alta in 2020 during the same week in January that Buckley went there and wrote about the trip for the *University Bookman*.

I have taken a few liberties, especially with numbers, but mostly followed the "house rules" at Encounter Books mixed with elements of the *Chicago Manual of Style* for editorial consistency. The only *ukase* Buckley ever issued at *National Review* made omission of the serial comma "a capital offense!"—so I have inserted it wherever it was needed. The provenance for each article includes dateline if provided, periodical title, and date of publication. For *On the Right* columns, only the date appears. Where no dateline appears, the place of origin is New York City.

Christopher T. Buckley, the executor of his father's estate, has generously allowed me to publish these articles with the *proviso* that one-half of the royalties be directed to the William F. Buckley Jr. Program at Yale. After reading my proposal, Roger Kimball, publisher at Encounter Books and one of Buckley's cruising mates, envisioned the volume a companion to *Athwart History: Half a Century of Polemics, Animadversions, and Illuminations*, a collection of Buckley's essays he and Linda Bridges coedited in

2010. Three of Buckley's *confrères* from *National Review*—Neal Freeman, Jack Fowler, and Jay Nordlinger—supported the idea for this collection when I mentioned it to them, as did Jeff Nelson, now at the Russell Kirk Center for Cultural Renewal. Two indispensable resources were my Buckley bibliography and Hillsdale College's "Buckley Online," a preservation project I helped create while employed there. In addition to the University of Delaware's interlibrary loan staff in Morris Library obtaining (within twenty-four hours) articles from out-of-print periodicals, undergraduate students Tad Glasscock and Braydon Moore converted the articles from PDF to Word. Denise Perez, my colleague at *Lewes History*, helped with manuscript preparation, while she and David Riddick, my classmate at Hampden-Sydney College, offered valuable suggestions for this introduction. Victoria Larson and Mary Lu Abbott at the Society of American Travel Writers Foundation promptly assisted with research in the organization's archives. For their personal interest in this book, my gratitude goes to David Lyons, Karen Medford, and Darlise DiMatteo. Finally, I thank the staff at Encounter Books who worked anonymously behind the scenes to bring this collection to print.

Bill Meehan

Lewes Beach, DE

May 1, 2022

CHAPTER ONE

1958–1965

An Amateur Skipper Talks Back

Motor Boating, April 1958

Very early in my very brief career as an ocean-going sailor I read with considerable interest the chapter in one of H. A. Calahan's *Learning How* series on selecting the ideal crew. The subject has continued to absorb me, both as an abstract problem, and as a practical matter. At about the time I was getting together a crew for the Newport-Annapolis Race I read a magazine article which posed the question: What are the proper qualifications for crew members on a transatlantic race?

The author's answer—he should be able to do (make?) a long splice from the masthead— struck me, at the time, as a perfectly serviceable symbolic requirement for the useful crew member; so drugged was I by the propaganda of cultism. I coasted along for several days at peace with that generalization until some devil prompted me, apropos nothing at all, to ask the crew of my boat, *The Panic*, at a moment when we were sprawled about the cockpit and deck having supper, "How many of you know how to do a long splice?"

Of the six persons I addressed, five did not know how. Two or three of them had once known how, but had forgotten. The sixth said that under perfect circumstances he probably could negotiate a long splice. What, I asked him, did he consider perfect circumstances to be? Well, he said, lots of time, nobody looking over his shoulder, nothing said about the aesthetic appearance of the splice once consummated, and maybe a sketch to refresh his memory in the event it should lapse.

Not, in a word, from the masthead.

I felt no embarrassment, I hasten to add, in putting the question to my crew, because I do not myself know how to do a long splice, or even a short one. I intend, one of these days, to learn, as I intend, one of these days, to read Proust. Just when, I cannot say; before or after Proust, I cannot say either.

I mean to make two points. The first is that the crew on the race in question was a perfectly competent crew *according to my standards*, the standards of an amateur; and the second, that the cultists are these days, as far as sailing is concerned, winning a creeping victory over us amateurs. And then, of course, I have an exhortation: let us amateurs refuse to yield further ground.

What are the standards I am here to defend? At this point I must be permitted an autobiographical word or two detailing my own experiences with, and knowledge of, sailing, data which are here relevant.

Sailing has always had an allure for me which I have found irresistible. At twelve, I persuaded my indulgent father to give me a boat. Cautiously, he gave me a boat and a full-time instructor. The boat was a sixteen-foot Barracuda (a class since extinct), and I joined the variegated seven-boat fleet in Lakeville, CT, as the only member under twenty-one.

The Wononscopomuc Yacht Club, whose only assets were a charter, an aluminum trophy donated by a local hardware store, and $2 per year from each of the boats, was fortunate enough at the time I joined it to be administered, or rather reigned over, by a retired commodore whose passion for ritual and discipline imposed upon the carefree fleet a certain order. From him we got a knowledge of, and respect for, the rudiments of yachting, and even some of the niceties. We learned, too, something about the rules of racing (although I infer from the animadversions of an adjacent skipper at the starting line at a recent race that some of those rules have since changed). After virtually every race (we raced three times a week) the Commodore would buzz around the fleet in a squat canoe propelled by four melancholy ten-year-old camp boys, informing us of the delinquency of our racing strategy, and of the size of the swath we had that day cut into the rule book.

Dutifully, we would file our protests. Having done so, we would meet some evening during the following week—never less than three days after the offense, for the Commodore required at least that much time to reflect on the enormity of the offense, and to weigh carefully the conflicting demands of justice and mercy. After an elaborate exposition of the problem, he would pronounce, ponderously, sentence.

This ranged from disqualification to, on the lenient days, a terrible warning to which, of course, was attached public obloquy.

So it went for three years; fifty races per season, rain or shine. The war interrupted all that, and I did not sail again until a few years ago, when I bought a fourteen-foot Sailfish.

The Sailfish pricked the curiosity of my six-foot-five, 250-pound brother-in-law, Austin Taylor, who had never sailed before.

Austin regulates his life on the philosophy that tomorrow we may die and hence he was soon urging that we buy a cruising boat and move around a little bit. In the summer of 1955, a persuasive yacht broker parlayed our ambition for a nice little cruising boat into *The Panic*. Austin's size provided the rationalization.

The Panic is a lovely forty-two-feet and one-half-inches, steel-hulled cutter, stiff, fast, built in Holland in brazen disregard of American handicap rules. Her CCA rating is a merciless and xenophobic 34.4, putting her up in the company of the racing machines, which she is not. Our first race was the Vineyard Race of that September. Our large genoa and spinnaker arrived two hours before the start. A crew was hastily put together by a friend who knew the race, and the rigors of ocean racing. We did not come in last, but that was not, the skipper commented ruefully, because we didn't try. We learned a great deal and resolved to enter, the following year, the exotic race to Bermuda.

What kind of a sailor, then, do I consider myself? I am perfectly at home in a small boat, and would, in a small boat race, more often than not come in if not this side of glory, surely this side of ignominy. I know enough of the elements of piloting to keep out of normal difficulties. I have a spectacularly defective memory, so that I am hopeless in recognizing even landmarks I may have set eyes on a thousand times, and therefore not a naturally talented pilot.

"High Enough for What?"

When my Radio Direction Finder works, I can work it. I am studying celestial navigation (how it works, not why). My instructor would classify me as a medium-apt student, though my attendance record has been erratic. I know my boat reasonably well and even know now why it suddenly sank at a slip a year or so ago, mystifying me (I was a thousand miles away when it happened) as well as the experts. I am reasonably calm, reasonably resourceful, and have reasonable resistance to adversities. Those are my credentials. And the question before the house: Are my credentials high enough? And the corollary, high enough for what?

Herewith my first collision with a cultist.

Second only to the fear of God, the beginning of wisdom is the knowledge of one's limitations. That much wisdom Austin Taylor and I exhibited in resolving to ask someone with considerably more experience than we to take command of *The Panic* on the race to Bermuda. The name of a highly experienced sailor known slightly to Austin Taylor suggested itself. Parkinson (let us call him) had met Taylor in the course of business in downtown New York, and identified himself as an enthusiastic and seasoned sailor. He had his own boat (I think it was an eight-meter) but it was ill-equipped and unsuited to the Bermuda ordeal. Parkinson had approached a mutual friend with the idea of getting a berth aboard *The Panic*. Instead, we offered him, and he promptly accepted, command.

There followed eight or so of the most hectic weeks of my life. Parkinson had not only got control of *The Panic*, he had got me and my wife and child and dogs in the bargain. (Austin Taylor fled to the Philippines and stayed away a year.) My life, I think it is accurate to say, was at his disposal. To begin with, the crew was seated at lunch; and before we knew it there had been duly constituted some one-dozen committees, each of which had three members and a chairman, meaning about four committees for each member of the seven-man crew.

Each committee had an area of responsibility. There was, for example, the Safety Committee (flares, life jackets, dye markers, etc.), the Navigation Committee (HO 211, six pencils, etc.), the Bermuda Reservations Committee, the Food Committee, the Supplies Committee—ten or twelve in all. Parkinson suggested I go to work on my backwardness by doing a little remedial reading. Without even glancing at the list he furnished me, I turned it over to my secretary and asked her to secure the books. A week later anyone gazing at my desk would have taken the occupant for the curator of a maritime library.

Moreover, I had the distinct feeling that, at Newport, Parkinson would examine me and, if I did not pass to his satisfaction, I would probably see the start of the race from the committee boat. Beginning that weekend in February, Parkinson and one or two of his associates (he had promptly filled out half of the crew with his expert friends) started coming to the Muzzio Brothers boatyard in Stamford to brood over *The Panic*.

Parkinson is a highly efficient and useful human being, and I do not mean to underrate the services he performed for *The Panic* in the succeeding six weekends: but I could not avoid getting the impression that he liked to fuss over the boat, and arriving at the conclusion, upon meditation, that in liking to do so, he is one of a breed.

An Early Race Start

I believe, to give an example, that my concern that the standing rigging in my own boat be sound is as lively as his own. But whereas I am satisfied to inspect the rigging cursorily, and otherwise repose my faith in professional riggers whom I retain to go over the rigging every year, Parkinson spent hours feeling every strand of wire, and fingering every screw and bolt for signs of wear, or fatigue, or restiveness of the subtlest kind. *The Panic* had no secrets left, when Parkinson was through with her. She might as well have been turned over to a psychoanalyst. I soon learned that the Bermuda race began the day we took on Parkinson: which meant, really, that it was too long a race.

We foundered, curiously, on a triviality, but one on which I decided, providentially, to take a stand.

Nothing, as I say, was being left to take care of itself. And, so, in one connection or other (probably the chairman of the Supplies Committee brought the matter up) the question arose what to take along in the way of liquor.

"There will be no liquor consumed during the race," Parkinson said, with rather arresting firmness. I rose to the bait, and said I thought it reasonable to permit members of the watch going off duty to have a drink, if they chose.

In races, Parkinson said patiently, one does not drink liquor until one crosses the finish line. I said: "One undoubtedly knows more about the traditions than I do. But," I added, warming a little bit to the subject, "some traditions are rational and some are not, and I think it reasonable, in such a case as this, to bring one's own intelligence to bear on the subject rather than submit unquestioningly, to doctrinaire propositions minted by our nautical forbears. Is it your assumption," I asked jocularly (it was a mistake to be jocular with Parkinson) "that the Battle of Trafalgar would have been won sooner had someone reminded Admiral Nelson of *Tradition* in time to recall the ration of rum he had recklessly dispensed to the fleet immediately before the engagement?"

Occasional Intemperance, Not a Drunk

Parkinson explained that crossing the Atlantic Ocean in a small boat requires an alert crew. I explained that I was aware of the fact, and was not suggesting a drunk, nor even, for those on watch, a drink; that I thought reasonable men could distinguish between a drink and a drunk. I suggested, as the subject began to carry me away, that his position was fetishistic, that unless he could defend it more reasonably, it must be written off either as superstition or as masochism or as neo-Spartanism, and that I was anti all three. Parkinson said that no boat of which he had charge would dispense liquor to the crew, and that was that. I told him liquor would be on board, and those who wanted it could have it.

Late that night he called me dramatically to say that he and his associates were pulling out of the crew, on the grounds that my attitude toward sailing was too frivolous. Parkinson's replacement, an engaging, highly skilled, and wonderfully permissive Middlewesterner, arrived for the trip two days before we set out from Newport. He was relaxed and competent and congenial. (There was liquor aboard, by the way; and, further by the way, in the four-day trip we probably averaged two drinks apiece.)

We did rather creditably, as a matter of fact; half way in our high-powered class. Parkinson, who had joined another boat, came in two days after we got to Bermuda, second to last in the fleet. I am not implying divine justification here, or even empirical corroboration of my theories. If Parkinson was in charge of his boat, I am certain things were tidier and better ordered than on *The Panic*, and that it was his boat's fault, or the cruelest ill luck, against which no committee however diligent could have shielded him, that we trounced him so decisively. I am merely saying that if I should be guaranteed the Bermuda Trophy, provided I race with Parkinson aboard, I should say thanks very much, but no thanks. I like to sail, and I like to sail well; and I'd love to win the Bermuda race. But when I step on a boat, I do not want to have the sensation of participating in a Hellenic gymnastic exhibition; we amateurs want to sail. Sail—remember?

Somewhat of a Handicap

I almost always end up with a crew one or two members of which have had very little sailing experience. This is some sort of handicap in a race, no doubt about it. When at the helm in a boat the novice will too often luff up, or bear away and lose position. Leading the jib sheet, he will at least once in the course of the race gird the winch counter-clockwise. Ask him to rig a preventer and he rushes forward with a boom vang. Almost surely, he will pronounce leeward *leeward*, and who knows the measure of Triton's vengeance on the boat where that enormity is perpetrated?

I have seen consternation on the faces of the more experienced members of the crew at such evidence of inexperience or even ignorance, and I do not myself pretend to imperturbability when they occur.

But shouldn't one bear in mind other factors? The annoyances, *sub specie aeternitatis*, are trivial. The mistakes seldom make a marginal difference, particularly in a long race. And there are other things to be weighed. You are introducing a friend to a magnificent sport. You see him learn his way about much faster than ever he would on a cruise. There is aboard a person or two upon whom the wonder of it all works sensations of a distinctive freshness; and there is vicarious pleasure to be had in bringing such pleasure to others. The novice is a friend, and to other common experiences you have shared, you now add that of sailing. One must make certain, of course, that there is enough aggregate experience aboard to cope with emergencies: so that the levy is not on the wellbeing of other crew members, but on their patience, and, to some extent, on their chances—so very remote, anyway, in the company *The Panic* keeps—for hardware.

Let us face it, the ocean-going race is largely an artificial contest. Will the best boat win? It is impossible to weigh the relative merits of different boats except by one standard at a time. In ocean races the boats are not alike; each boat represents an individually balanced set of concessions to speed, safety, comfort, and economy. A noble effort is made by ingenious statisticians and measurers to devise a Procrustean formula that will leave all boats identical; but it is a failure, and all of us, in our hearts, know it. The handicap rule is a Rube Goldberg contrivance designed to succeed in the kind of tank-test situation which Nature, in her sullen way, never vouchsafes us.

If *Cotton Blossom* and *Niña* were both manned by automatons and sailed around a given course a thousand times, on a thousand consecutive days, the chances are very good that the corrected times of the two would not once coincide. The contest, then, given differing characteristics and differing relative speeds of boats in different tacks and under different conditions, is not really between boats.

Is it between crews? Again, only if the boats are identical. A good crew will get more out of a boat than a poor crew, but the only generalization that this permits is that a given boat will do better with Crew A than it would have done with Crew B: meaning, if you want to make a contest out of it, that Crew A beat Crew B. But that is a hypothetical contest; in reality, a boat can only sail, at any given time, with a single crew. What, then, can be proved between competing crews on different boats? Not very much.

There is, finally, a feature of ocean racing that can make a shambles of the whole thing. The poorest judgment can, under capricious circumstances, pay the handsomest rewards. Crew A, out of an egregious ignorance and showing execrable judgment, elects to go around Block Island north to south while the seasoned and shrewd Crew B makes the proper choice under the circumstances, and goes south to north. The wind abruptly and inexplicably changes, and has the effect of whisking A in and stopping B dead in its tracks. Ridiculous, isn't it? What satisfaction am I entitled to feel if I beat Rod Stephens? I should feel an ass; for given the presumptions, there could be no clearer demonstration of my inexpertness. That a playful providence should have elected to reward folly and punish wisdom does not mitigate my offense against sound judgment.

It will be objected that, after all, the facts are that 10 percent of the boats win 75 percent of the hardware. True. But what does the statistic prove? Merely that fast boats with digestible handicaps, or slow boats with exorbitant handicaps, do best. Not more. One cannot set up, in the way that one can in class boat races, or in tennis or golf matches, a ladder which will reflect with reasonable accuracy the relative proficiency of ocean racers.

Wherein, then, does the contest lie, in the sport of ocean racing? It is, I think, a contest with oneself. It lies in the demands made upon the crew by the boat, the weather, and the crew itself. There is of course the formal race, within the general framework of which that contest takes place. And there is the delusive tendency to feel that one's position in the fleet exactly reflects the quality of one's response to the challenge. But that is false.

The challenge for all of us, in every boat, takes place in context of our total experience with, and our total preoccupation with, sailing. It is absurd to expect that the casual sailor whose mind, week in, week out, is very much on other things, shall have acquired the expertise of an Alan Villiers; and it is barbarous to suggest that that sailor, given the failure of meet the standards of a Villiers, is either presumptuous or impudent in participating in ocean racing. The challenge, I say then, lies in setting the sails as quickly as you know how, in trimming them as well as you know how; in handling the helm as well as you can; in getting as good a fix as you can; in devising the soundest and subtlest strategy given your own horizons; in keeping your temper, and your disposition; and above all things, in keeping your perspective, and bearing in mind, always, the essential beauty of the experience.

All these things are, by definition, since the standards are subjective and not objective, as "well" done by amateurs as by professionals. In one sense, better done. The amateur, though his failures will be more abysmal than the professional's, can also soar to greater heights. He is more often afraid, and therefore more often triumphant; more often in awe, hence more often respectful; more often surprised, hence more often grateful. When did the crew of *Finisterre* last experience the exultation that comes to the amateur crew on expertly jibing their spinnaker?

A Beginner's Tribulations
Ocean Racing, 1958

When we ducked inside the harbor at Newport, two hours after sundown, the sudden stillness was preternatural. The spinnaker was down for the first time in three full days. The wind stopped blowing on our necks and the water, finally, was calm for now we were shielded from the southwesterly that had lifted us out of Chesapeake Bay, and carried us on the long second leg of the race, right to Newport. That sudden stillness, the sudden relief, caused us, out of some sense of harmony, to quiet our own voices so that it was almost in whispers that we exchanged the necessary signals as we drew into an empty slip at Christie's Wharf. We tied up, doing our work in silence, dimly aware that the boat that had crossed the line a half mile behind us was groping its way to the slip opposite. A searchlight pierced the darkness and focused for an instant on our distinctive red bowsprit. "Oh my God," we heard a voice in muted anguish, "*The Panic*!" The man with the flashlight, aboard the famous *Golliwog*, deduced how poorly his boat must have done—behind *The Panic*! We felt very sorry for *Golliwog*. In reversed circumstances, we too would have felt ashamed.

I and *The Panic*, a glorious forty-two-foot, steel-hulled cutter I own jointly with my brother-in-law, are arrant beginners in the sport of ocean racing. We are bumptiously amateur, and appear to have a way of provoking the unreasoned and impulsive resentment of sailors whose view of ocean racing tends to be a little different from my own. That resentment is wholly spontaneous and, I like to feel, evanescent. I distinguish it sharply from the highly mobilized and systematic displeasure that I have here and there engendered in proud experts. I have even been scolded in public by one sailor who announced that he would take his stand by precisely these professionals, some of whose tendencies I have here and there criticized. We experts, my critic said, have made it possible for sub-amateurs to sail in ocean races without breaking your necks. Your corresponding obligations are 1) to stop being amateurs just as soon as you possibly can; and 2) to show a little reverence for the experts, to whom you are so solidly indebted.

I gather that my failure to proceed with satisfactory speed toward goal Number One above, and my inconsistent adherence to rule-of-the-road Number Two are, perversely, my qualifications (I have no others) to appear in this distinguished company where I am given a few moments to speak my little piece, on some of the problems of the amateur. I will make it as fast, and unobtrusive, as I can.

Let me begin by saying that I am a conservative, and that the worship of excellence is a part of the conservative creed. Indeed, I abhor the indifference to excellence which I suggest is, nowadays, the hottest pursuit of our society. Nor do I underestimate the importance of what the social scientists call "expertise"—that body of expert knowledge that is supposed to form the backbone of any field. It is hard for me to believe, therefore, that in declaiming so impassionately about the great contributions the experts have made toward ocean racing, anyone could understand himself to be arguing with me. How can *anyone* question the usefulness of such lives, or, particularly in the very act of putting that knowledge to practical use, speak lightly, or condescendingly of their attainments? I would not count it a life wasted that was consumed in the development of the definitive snatch block, heaven knows. I have merely, here and there, suggested that the principal difficulties of the beginning ocean sailor are 1) the mystifying *in*expertise in much of what goes into ocean sailing; and 2) the tendency, in some experts, to desiccate the entire experience by stripping it of spontaneity, of wonder; the tendency to demand the kind of reverence for the experts that belongs to the sea.

I have not made a study of the tribulations of novitiate sailors, and I pass off my own without any suggestion that I am writing about universal experience. If what I have to say turns out to be not at all useful to others, then I apologize for wasting their time. If it turns out that I have something useful to say, then I am pleased beyond words finally to have contrived a way to requite, in some small measure, my large debt to the sport of sailing.

One reads a great deal in primers on boat buying about the practices of unscrupulous men. I have no doubt that such men exist. It is natural that they should, for confidence men notoriously gather around the commodities that dreams are made of—money, power, women, boats. But I am singularly fortunate in never having been handled by one. From the outset, I have dealt with honest men, genuinely concerned to satisfy the desires of the owners of *The Panic* while, to be sure, making an honest living out of it. It is against such a framework that I discuss my first point above and, by lurid autobiographic detail, make my point about the perplexing inexpertness of experts.

The Panic is a looker. I would not know what to say to anyone who was not instantly captivated by her appearance. We fell in love with her at first sight, and decided, on second sight, to buy her. How much did the broker (remember: a wholly honest one) think we would have to spend to put it in racing shape? He thought and thought about it, and made careful notes. Five hundred dollars, he decided.

I am not sure how much we have spent on *The Panic* (and the experts would not even now designate her as being a racer. The original mistake most of them would say now was made on that Dutch drawing board), but it is not exaggeration to say that we have bought her, so to speak, two or three times. (I intend to will my boat bills to the museum at Mystic, so that future beginners can have a detailed idea of just where the mines are buried.)

Let us take one item. *The Panic* proved to have a terrible weather helm. When it began to blow, and particularly when we had to shorten headsails, we used to measure the force needed to keep the boat on course in terms of horsepower. Racing to Bermuda in 1956 we would wear out a helmsman every half hour, even with the aid of a becket made out of several strands of thick shock cord. We determined, that winter, to do something about it.

Now even beginners can figure out that a weather helm results when the center of effort is too far forward. Let me try to put that more intelligibly. A weather helm will result when a greater area of sail is exposed to the wind aft of the fulcrum point of the boat than forward of it. The obvious way to correct the situation is to move the mast back. But in large boats that is not feasible: so, I took the problem to the experts. What should I do? What would *you* recommend? (One minute of silence, while you think…) Well, the experts reasoned, let us increase the sail area forward, to compensate the pressure aft. How? No room on lop, because it's a masthead rig. What, then? A bowsprit. (*A bowsprit! A bowsprit! The cry rang out from consultant to consultant, from boatyard to rigger, gaining volume as it traveled through the echo chambers of expertise.*) We were so intoxicated by the proposal that we ordered it executed without regard to cost: on with the bowsprit.

Well, all it involved was constructing a thirty-nine-inch steel section with a couple of sheaves for the anchor chain and a bob stay, welding it on, yanking out the woodwork and pulpit, machining and installing two new stanchions and chocks: and there we were. But, of course, the headstay had to move forward. So, in came the riggers and moved it forward. The headstay, having moved forward, the forestay could not linger behind—so off it went—another stainless-steel cable and installation. Then, what do you know, the spinnaker pole—too short now. A new pole. But you couldn't have a bigger pole without a bigger spinnaker—so you just increase the size of your spinnaker, a matter of a couple of weeks' work by a couple of expert sailmakers. Then you find your headsails are hanging down, as what dope couldn't have figured out, now that the headstay being strung out, the angle is changed. So, you recut them. Having done so, you find that the deck plates are just plain no use where they are—they have to be changed, to reflect the new angle of descent of the head-sails. And then the horrible moment when, realizing we had increased the area of the foretriangle, we called in the Measurer. He surveyed the revised boat with the sadistic satisfaction of the headmaster of Dotheboys Hall confronting a refractory student: severe punishment was in order. Up soared our rating.

That's all there was to it.

It didn't work worth a damn. Before, the helm had only been bad in fresh air. Now when the wind freshened you had to reduce headsail, or luff the main, or both: and there went the advantage of the bowsprit. In light airs, the increase in comfort was barely noticeable; the increase in speed not notice able at all. Odd it shouldn't have been predicted by the experts.

The problem continued to be serious, so last winter we started at the other end. At the suggestion of the estimable Mr. Bill Muzzio of Muzzio Brothers Boatyard, we bade goodbye to the sails and journeyed below, to the keel. If we could not change the center of effort, we could change the center of lateral resistance. We proceeded to extend the keel *aft*, adding about twenty square feet. The operation involved virtually rebuilding the after half of the boat—new rudder pipe, new tiller, new lazarette. The result was miraculous. We now have no helm at all. The boat is beautifully balanced. Question: Could we not have been spared our first experience?

Take our radio-direction-finder. Our first one was Dutch. It sort of worked, but the signal was not really satisfactory. We asked a top firm of marine electricians to recommend and install the very best thing available. In came a Bendix loop and a war surplus airplane Bendix radio-direction-finder. That was three years ago. Every three months, that is to say, every time I have desperately needed it and it refused either to work at all, or to work well enough to yield an intelligible signal, I write a letter of complaint to the electricians. In response to my complaint, they bear down on *The Panic* and "fix" it. They will then demonstrate the quality of its performance as we sit in our slip in Stamford, and sure enough WOR turns out to be located in New York City. Three days later, surrounded by fog off Block Island, Point Judith turns out to be in Pennsylvania, and Montauk has begun to sail off toward Iceland at about forty miles per hour. I report my complaint. We repeat our performance. The same thing happens again. I repeat my complaint. This has gone on for three years. An exception? There's our radio telephone, never fear, I reassured my apprehensive wife on purchasing the boat, the Radio Corporation of America will never permit us to be truly separated. Ten percent of the time, I get through to the marine operator. The other times, she doesn't hear me—not a word. I'd much prefer it if the set didn't work at all, because then one could buy new tubes, or something. In come the electricians. We have tested the telephone they will report to me. "Got a check from the New York marine operator on four different stations. The perfect power effect is ten. Your set got three tens and a nine." Yes I know, I say. Only it doesn't work for *me,* when *I,* not *you,* want to use it. What should I do? I now have radio aerials that are the pride of the electronics industry. If I am on a port tack, I can switch to a port aerial, freeing the antenna of any leeward encumbrance. The aerial is exquisite. The telephone has been checked fifteen times. Only it doesn't work. Why? *I* don't know. *I* never said *I* was an expert."

In a piece I wrote for *Motor Boating*, I made the claim that unlike the fusspot sailors, I was prepared to repose my faith in professional riggers, to whom I would say, simply, "Please give me first-rate rigging"—and I would not insult them by following them around, making a strand-by-strand examination of their handiwork.

I am beginning to modify my views. Not because, as Norris Hoyt would have it, my respect for the expert increases; but rather because my faith in him having diminished, I begin to realize that though I am not inclined that way, I shall probably have to become, before I am done, not only an electronics engineer, but a rigger.

Here is what I mean: on the first race to Bermuda, coming back, the backstay parted where the stainless-steel cable fitted into an insulator which had to do with the aerial (in those days, before the alterations, the aerial didn't work on the backstay, whereas now it doesn't work on the shrouds). "What do you know!" the rigger exploded when I held the sundered pieces in my hand, "that aerial thing is tested for five million pounds' (or something) pressure." "Yes," I said, "only it didn't work."

In the most recent Bermuda race we were sailing along and, Bang—the headstay, no less, was gone, parted at the turnbuckle. We were sailing alongside *Finisterre* (a brief encounter). On the way back, in the airplane, where I had the honor to meet him, Carleton Mitchell asked what had gone wrong, that the entire crew should have rushed forward so excitedly to the bow. I told him. "Oh, yes," he said. "I had the same trouble once. Now I don't use a turnbuckle at the headstay at all. I do all the adjusting on the backstay turnbuckle. You do, of course, have a double toggle on your headstay, don't you?

Never in all my life was I so anxious to please, but I just couldn't pretend to know and get away with it. "What's a toggle?" I asked sheepishly. He explained (I assume the reader knows). Well, it turns out, we didn't have a double toggle, we had only a single toggle. Why? The people who rigged *The Panic* rigged one of the contestants for US representation in the America's Cup Race (come to think of it, the boat didn't qualify). If a double toggle is obviously the thing to do, why wasn't it done? Are there two points of view about double toggles? Why aren't they ventilated? Why don't some people come forward as single-toggle men, prepared to fight to the finish double-toggle men? But no. There appears to be no expertise in the making on the subject. Oh yes: on the way back from Bermuda, the topping lift parted.

And the main halyard parted. Seems there was a strain where the true lock fitting ran up against the sheave at the top of the mast. Why hadn't the experts caught that? Because they are inexpert? Or because there is inexpertise?

The point I labor so clumsily to make is that I suspect it is the latter, and that the beginner, buffeted as he especially is by the marauding experts, has the sharpest insight into the fact. The rigger who splices a wire around a thimble with loving care has a regard for, and takes a pride in, excellence. And, if he does it "correctly," he is an expert. But if the splice does not hold the wire around the thimble as it is designed to do, then there is insufficient expertise in the matter. It happens all about us. Masts break—for no very clear reason. Boats sink at the slip (mine did, and all the king's horses and all the king's men could not figure out why it happened) for no reason at all. This telephone will work every time—and that one won't. This paint works beautifully on this hull; and that hull, with the identical paint, gets to look as though it had impetigo.

But we are dealing, are we not, with laws of nature which, at this level can be assumed to be constant? Hume, dismissing miracles, said he would believe that human testimony had erred rather than that the laws of nature had been suspended. It is miraculous then that John's radio works and William's does not? I should consider it the most rational explanation yet offered if my electrician would inform me that my radio telephone does not work because of the absence of miraculous conditions. But he does no such thing, nor do the riggers, or painters, or engine makers (engines! What a temptation to write about my engine!), or sailmakers, or meteorologists, or ropemakers. The fact of the matter is they are half craftsmen (and excellent craftsmen, at that) and half medicine men who, due to the absence of experience in the design, manufacture and maintenance of boats, do not know what they are up against and hence traffic in sheer charlatanry.

My advice to the beginner? Read all those books and listen to all that advice with high skepticism. There is much there to learn, but there are many, many uncharted seas, and the man who tells you with that robust certitude that is characteristic of the expert's rhetoric (viz. Mr. Calahan's advertisements) that the way from A to C lies via B is very likely to be quite utterly wrong. There are compensations in the situation. Think how much the amateur can accomplish for himself. If anyone is of a mind to conquer, there is a great deal around to subdue. And, if anyone has the stomach for high adventure, I wish he would bear my radio telephone in mind.

The second point I have made before, and I do not want to be tiresome about it. Hilaire Belloc was driven to a rage at the very thought of racing a cruising boat. It was never very hard to drive Belloc into a rage, but in this case, he surely had a point, and if he had participated in some of today's races, he would have felt fully justified. Cruising boats, offshore boats of varying design, are made for cruising; and to race them, Belloc seems to feel, is like seeing how fast you can play a symphony: the very point is lost.

I disagree, obviously, for I race; and will race again and again, in all likelihood. But I do believe that the dangers that most horrified Belloc are preeminently there, that one has only to go down to a yacht club, survey the ministrations tendered to a twelve-foot racing dinghy, extrapolate, and you have an idea of the way you may find yourself spending your life if you race a forty-footer to win. I can understand an amateur's mothering a dinghy, or a Comet, or a Star—or even an International twelve-meter—with the kind of loving care necessary to eliminate those marginal seconds and half-seconds, but I do not understand why such a thing is done when disparate boats race each other under the colossal, though conscientious, hoax that is The Rule—I do not understand, because the contest, multiplications, square roots, and long divisions notwithstanding, is essentially a phoney.

I have witnessed cases where the obsession with high fidelity has displaced the appreciation of the music. I have known one or two persons of essentially bright disposition who developed into crashing bores as they transmute ocean racing into a neo-Spartan and neverending ordeal that, even when it gives pleasure, gives a pleasure that is totally unrelated to the generic source of pleasure in sailing which is the sea and the wind. I have a notion that the inertia of our age, the perfect expression of which is the Western paralysis in international affairs during the past half century, has had the effect of extravasating the natural physical and moral energies of some people into athletic channels. I can understand the lure of the total workout, expressed in sailing by the devotion of twenty hours a week, thirty weeks a year, toward the perfection of one's yacht and the forwarding of one's competitive position. Only I say such as they threaten the sport as surely as some of the new critics threaten the art of poetry. And I say to the beginner, don't let them tyrannize over you, or you may never recapture your romance.

I am solidly for amateurism in ocean sailing. I have lost, as I indicated above, faith in the very existence of the expertise before which, even did I know it to exist, I should not be disposed to humble myself in quite the manner that some deem appropriate. I am quite serious in saying that I idolize Carleton Mitchell because he is a professional who, one can tell by reading what he writes, derives an amateur's pleasure out of his trade. (Has anyone noticed that there is no rasp in Mitchell's writing? That is the sign.) He would never, I think, stultify the sport by discouraging its discovery by beginners, as so many people are likely to do. Of the eight or ten people who regularly race *The Panic* nowadays, it is fair to say that by contrast with the gold platers, our boat is crewed by rank beginners. And before the comment gets made that this is all too visible to any boat a half mile away from *The Panic*, let me say: Brother, think what you like. Let us go, amiably, our amiable ways. Just rescue me if I fall overboard, as I would you, and get out of my way when I'm on a starboard tack. I make no other demands.

Do I have advice for a beginner? Yes. If you intend to race, buy a racing boat. They are just as comfortable nowadays. But remember, they are much, much more expensive. If you buy a boat that is afflicted with an unviable rating, and then race it, you will—unless you exercise a solipsist's self-discipline—fret, and be unhappy. Do you know about the Law of Rusher's Lag? Well, it especially applies to ocean racers. Rusher's Lag is the lag *beyond* the lag that one normally anticipates. Apply it generously in your calculation of costs. Assume your upkeep will be five times what you first anticipated. Especially the first year or two. Assume no one has yet invented a radio telephone. Take four extra turnbuckles everywhere you go and a hundred cable clamps, to say nothing, of course, of a complete hardware store. Have your drink (singular) before dinner. The first couple of days out, take a sedative when your turn comes to go off watch, and take a stimulant when you get up. That will catapult you, rather than drag you slowly by the hair, into the new and very different rhythm of life aboard an ocean racer. Wear an eyeshade when trying to sleep during the day. Do not assume it is possible to stay dry when you go forward in a heavy sea.

(The only way to accomplish that, a friend of mine has observed, having tried every other way, is to strip naked and get completely vulcanized at the home port.) Race your boat hard. And pay no attention to the results.

Midsummer Fare
August 20, 1964

Recently I wrote that the American people, myself included, have apparently abandoned all hope of eliminating some of the minor irritations of life, and gave a few examples. I have been deluged by mail from readers raw with exasperation: the theme of which is, "it doesn't even pay to complain—it doesn't do any good, no one any longer cares." I come bearing hope. A week ago, I sent the following letter to the president of Northeast Airlines:

Dear Sir:

Last Saturday my wife and I breakfasted at 7:30, as is our custom. We arrived at Bangor Airport to take your 10:30 flight to New York one-half-hour before flight time, as requested. The airplane did not land until after eleven, as unannounced. It stopped at Portland, then Boston, then New York behind schedule. We arrived in New York at almost exactly three o'clock in the afternoon. During the period we flew with you we were offered not one cup of coffee, not one sandwich, not one stick of bread.

I mentioned to an agent, as I summoned my depleted strength at the end of the flight, that I found it odd that Northeast should ambush its passengers into traveling through the noon period, well into the middle of the afternoon, knowing that they would not be given any refreshments at all, nor time sufficient to get their own in the airports. He mumbled something about how low your fares are, and how impossible, under the circumstances, to give away any food or drink to your passengers.

I write to make a few alternative suggestions:

1) The price of my ticket, New York-Bangor round trip, was $65.00. Why not raise the price to $65.40, and provide passengers with one cup of coffee and one doughnut each, each way? I am sure the Civil Aeronautics Board would not object to the price rise under the circumstances.

Or 2) Advertise yourself, in the newspapers and airports, as the Low-Calorie Airline—"Fly With Us and Lose Weight." Those who elect not to combine weight reduction with flying will then have an opportunity to arrive at your airline with a thermos of coffee and a dinner pail with sandwiches.

Or 3) Keep a limited number of K Rations aboard and auction them during the flight time. I have no doubt Northeast could make a substantial profit by offering them at let us say 2:40 p.m., at prices beginning at $10.00 per ounce of hardtack.

Or 4) Persuade the Red Cross to maintain a St. Bernard dog at each of your stops, to administer first aid to those of your passengers who arrive giddy from hunger. (Motto: "Northeast Thinks of Everything," "What Other Airline Greets You with St. Bernards?").

My limited experience suggests that no airline anywhere in the entire world operates on so spartan a regimen. I remember getting a very adequate meal on a flight from Burundi to Rwanda. Granted, it is unsafe to starve Africans. If Northeast were ever to take over the management of air service between those two places, or others in Africa, you would no doubt find that fewer passengers arrived, than embarked. Come to think of it, your flights have been overcrowded lately. Could this be what you have in mind? Really, I can't think *what* you have in mind.

Yours faithfully,
Wm. F. Buckley Jr.

And what do you know, I have back a letter from the president of the airline, most of which was a grateful surprise. "I received your letter," he said, "I'm sorry your flight was off schedule, for I am sure the late arrival served as an aggravation to you. Further, I have asked our Passenger Service people to review our food and beverage policy with respect to this flight." How is that for progress? To be sure, the letter ended on a discouraging note: "I will make no comment with respect to your several gratuitous suggestions and comments." Well, the gentleman didn't think much of my suggestions, which makes me sad, but he will change the airline's policies, which makes me, and the farm surplus, glad. So, take heart. Say not the struggle naught availeth.

CHAPTER TWO

1970–1974

Railroad Reform
January 13, 1970

I do not know the particular situation elsewhere, but in New York the commuter railroads are a mess, and I for one do not believe that this was necessarily meant to be. This morning a friend began his telephone conversation, in reply to the routine question How are you? by muttering stoically that he had no complaint in the world except against the Penn Central Railroad.

What was it this particular morning? The "third track" wasn't working—on account of the bitter cold, the conductor had said. On the other hand, neither does the third track work regularly in the summertime, on account, presumably, of the bitter heat. Yesterday, on the line from Greenwich, Connecticut, the three, count 'em, three rear cars had absolutely no heat at all, so that the passengers had all to crowd in the forward cars passing an hour eyeball to eyeball, without space enough, even, to bide their tears with a copy of the *New York Daily News*.

My friend, who is a lawyer, waxed wrother and wrother, and reminded me that a year ago a passenger, protesting against some casual brutality of that morning's train, had refused to surrender his ticket. He was taken away and sentenced there and then by the judge for deprivation of service, which means that he deprived the railroad of money which belonged to the railroad in compensation for its services. What, my friend asked cogently, about the railroad's deprivation of its passenger's time? The gentleman in question is worth seventy-five dollars an hour on the open market. The figure is rough, but one can safely assume that in the course of a year, his commuter railroad costs him, in delays, oh, say $5,000.

I say it was not meant to be because I continue to believe that if no one had invented the railroad, and suddenly one were to call a press conference and divulge the idea of a track running in a straight line from city to city on which an enormous engine, an adaptation of an automobile, could pull enormous buses at speeds of 100 miles per hour, that the whole country would stop in amazement and every Congressman and Senator would rise in a chorus to appropriate money to make the dream come true. Yet, incredibly, railroads are grinding to a halt. Most of New England you cannot now reach by railroad.

I am in the mood to make a few practical proposals.

1) Is there any reason at all why the International Chamber of Commerce shouldn't be abolished? It was set up primarily to guard against excessive abuses by the railroads of their advantages as monopolies. To guard against such abuses in this day and age is the equivalent of protecting the public against American Motors' selling their cars at too high a price.

2) It is, in my judgment, too late to turn the railroads completely over to free enterprise, but not too late for first economic principles to come to our help. The railroads' two principal economic encumbrances are a) taxes, and b) union monopolies. I propose legislation under which the government would acquire the railroad beds. The sole reason for doing so would be in order to prevent the states and the municipalities from taxing the railroads, most particularly the land over which their trackage runs.

3) The government would then proceed to lease the railroad beds for fees only just large enough to attend to the maintenance of the railroad beds, even as the highways are publicly maintained. Anyone paying the fee could use the bed and provide public services, subject to observance of safety rules, and Eastern central coordination. So that, for instance, the Greyhound Company say, Eastern Airlines, or even the Buckley Syndicate, could offer services to commuters, or even to longer haul passengers at a price to be arrived at by competition, and by the quality of the service and equipment that they furnish. And, just as railway unions are covered under

special legislation, so would they be covered under special legislation in the future: no union shop.

A sensible set of proposals, with the compliments of a former patron of the railroads, who is a prospective patron of the new railroads.

Swiss Sojourn
March 24, 1970

ROUGEMONT, Switzerland—I have always thought that Switzerland is the way station to Paradise. I have been coming here for almost forty years. The first few winters, at age five or six, I would amuse myself by asking any old Swiss, any old time, "Excuse me, but could you please tell me the name of the president of Switzerland?" The record, thus far, is 100 percent: nobody has known the name of the president of Switzerland. Inevitably there is a nervous silence, and then a whisper to the neighboring partner, which whisper goes down the length of the room, the last man tiptoeing out to the telephone, or to an almanac, and eventually the name of the president is triumphantly divulged.

The reason nobody knows the name of the president of Switzerland is because it doesn't much matter who is the president of Switzerland. Switzerland is so well governed, the responsibilities are so diffused, the national sense of purpose is so explicit, that there simply isn't very much left over for the President to do, except to get very angry when a terrorist blows up one of his airplanes.

The other day, by mistake, a clerk in a little post office dropped a carton that contained emergency military summonses to duty for the male population of that town, everyone between the ages of twenty and fifty. The next morning the postman routinely stuck the summonses in the boxes, and by that afternoon all the men of the town had simply gone off—reporting for duty at the cantonal capital. All except two or three, who not having had news of any national emergency, thought to telephone to the capital to verify their summons. They were, of course, told that there was no summons, that it must have been a clerical mistake. Now, the interesting thing is that all the newspapers criticized not the gullible majority who had gone automatically off to duty, but the inquisitive minority. Switzerland expects that every man will do his duty unquestioningly, even if it is a clerical mistake.

That is true efficiency. Speaking of which, the Swiss Post Office is easily the most efficient in the world, the mail traveling faster between any part of Switzerland and the United States, than between Chicago and New York—even in non-strike conditions. To be sure, it needs to be efficient, if only to understand its own postage rates. If you desire to airmail a letter abroad, you must know, just to begin with, whether you are in category one or in category ten, twenty, twenty-five, thirty, forty, fifty, or seventy. Now reflect on the progression of those numbers. Crazy, isn't it? Why shouldn't the twenty-five be eliminated, and a sixty inserted?

The United States is in category twenty-five, and it costs 775 centimes to airmail a letter that weighs up to five grams. Up to ten grams, one franc. Up to fifteen grams, 1.25 francs. Up to twenty grams, 1.50 francs. Got it? Oh no you don't: in Switzerland, that's hubris. Up to twenty grams isn't the expected 1.75 francs, but—for reasons as obscure as the identity of the president of Switzerland—2.05 francs. You climb that scale at twenty-five centimes per five grams for four times, and then you skip again, to another interval of sixty centimes. It takes a first-class mathematical education to send a letter in Switzerland, which is a good way of cutting down on the post office load. And, oh yes, if you want to airmail a postcard to America, the postage is—a flat fifty-five centimes. But, of course, you can't buy a fifty-five-centime stamp—they just don't make them. You buy a fifty and a five. It all gets very expensive. I figured the other day that it would cost me about five times as much to wrap myself up and send myself airmail to the United States as it would to travel first-class on the *Queen Elizabeth*.

There is a price—and a penalty—for everything in Switzerland. Going up on a ski gondola a while ago it was very hot and I noticed that the window could be removed by prying it out of its rubber frame. This I did, and on reaching the top received a most royal and lengthy dressing down from the attending mechanic in a most flustered French, ending with a simple declarative, "That will be seven francs, fifty centimes." It was known exactly how much to charge even for so rogue an infraction.

I know. I know, that if, having established his identity, anyone were so foolish or so evil as to shoot the president of Switzerland, he would be most severely tried and tongue-lashed, and then told that the penalty for shooting presidents of Switzerland is 78,450 francs. It is a most glorious country and, after my own, I love it best, and do herewith, in the presence of witnesses, plight to it my troth.

A Week Aboard *Cyrano*
Rudder, May 1970

Friday, December 19

We arrive at Antigua airport, and that is an achievement. J. K. Galbraith says you shouldn't use pull unless you need to. Well, I needed to get to Antigua inasmuch as I decided to go there for Christmas aboard *Cyrano*—that was two months ago—only to find all the airlines booked solid for December 19, and for a day or two bracketing that day. I tried everybody I knew—or almost everybody I knew. One terribly helpful passenger agent wondered whether I wouldn't just as soon go to Antigua on January 19. I retorted that perhaps his airline could arrange to reschedule Christmas for January 25. I then asked whether, since he could not get me directly to Antigua, he might get me there if I consented to go via, say, the Canary Islands. He very nearly concluded the itinerary before feeling the steel of my sarcasm, which was rather poorly tempered that day. But it does suggest an interesting form of prospective commercial exploitation, namely, bidding up a ticket to where you want to go, when the traffic is dense, by routing you via remote places and demanding the full fare. I *know* that if I had volunteered to go via Buenos Aires, Eastern Airlines would have got me to Antigua even if its president had to give me the copilot's seat.

When all else fails in life, I usually call Mrs. Julie Nicholson, who with her husband and family dominate Antigua more firmly than Horatio Nelson ever did. She is a yacht and charter broker, whose descriptions of any boat you are considering will make it sound like the boat Onassis could not afford to make available to Jackie. Her husband can get you a ticket from anywhere to anywhere, anytime. It was only ordained that we should make a stop at San Juan, which is a bearable interruption. There, waiting for us, were the three Finucanes, who had come in from Los Angeles, joining three Buckleys and one Wagner, classmate of the younger Buckley, and the seven of us proceeded to Antigua. Without incident? Not quite. My son's .22 rifle caught the eye of Her Majesty's Customs. We explained that we keep the gun on board only for those occasions when it becomes necessary to talk back to sharks. Summit conference. An agent of H.M. Customs will accompany us to English Harbour, personally to deposit the rifle with the policeman there. Said policeman will turn over the rifle to us at the moment when we are actually ready to weigh anchor and head out. A satisfactory arrangement, and it is understood that I must pay the cost of the taxi to return the customs official to the airport, which is certainly reasonable: altogether a felicitous resolution of the occasional difficulty of traveling with a gun. At the dockside is our own Captain Killeen of the *Cyrano*, and a half-dozen partygoers, at the center of which is Mrs. Nicholson herself, who greets me warmly and, as I slip away in the tender, demands to know what comes after "*Gaudeamus Igitur.*" My memory fails me, and I feel dreadful, after all the Nicholsons have done for me. However, I did not forget to bring her Barricini Chocolates and Ribbon Candy, which you must not forget to do if ever you find yourself coming from where you can get Barricini Chocolates and Ribbon Candy to Antigua at Christmastime. I have made a mental note to let Mrs. Nicholson know what comes after "*Gaudeamus Igitur*" as soon as I find out. Let us therefore rejoice... What would follow naturally from that? At this point, I could only think: *Quam ad Antiguam pervenimus.*

Saturday, December 20

Cyrano is nowadays stationed in St. Thomas, and it was Ned Killeen's idea that it would make for a fun cruise if he "deadheaded" to Antigua, permitting us to cruise downwind back to St. Thomas. To deadhead, *v.i.*, means, I gather (I am afraid to ask Ned because that will once again remind him how much more he knows about sailing than I do and would make him positively unbearable)—to take a boat under power, without payload, against the wind. It took him two long nights, into midmorning, to deadhead from St. Thomas 220 miles to Antigua. Ned likes daytime landfalls. I like nighttime landfalls. Ned usually prevails. Ned always prevails when I am not aboard. Interesting thought. How much should we charge charterers to deliver them *Cyrano* in Antigua, should they so desire it? Ned suggests $200 for the two days, which is less than one half the $265 per day that we get for the use of *Cyrano*, but his point is that at $100 per day we are not actually losing money, and a little *noblesse oblige* on the high seas is always in order. I say something dour about how I wish the bankers would show a little *noblesse oblige* and acquiesce in the arrangement.

It is a beautiful morning, but I am feeling very blue. Because I learn, on arriving at dockside, that the Empress Julie is not in her office today; that she will not be coming into the office today; and that there is no telephone in her house. How can I show her my beautiful *Cyrano*? So I walk, dejectedly, to the police department and ask for my rifle, which is handed over to me a little apprehensively so palpable is my gloom, and I return to the boat to begin the cruise.

My beautiful *Cyrano*. I have owned her for two-and-one-half years. I bought her through Ned Killeen, who brokered the transaction. We had become friends after he volunteered, *qua* broker, to skipper a weekend aboard another yacht I was interested in, which turned out to be a disaster—not only the weekend but the yacht, which under full sail in a brisk breeze could only manage about five knots.

Then he wrote me about *Pinocchio*, as she was then called. Built in Abaco, in the Bahamas, to an old fishing boat design. Sixty feet overall, fifty-two feet on the waterline, with an extraordinary eighteen feet of bowsprit, seventeen feet of beam, tapering back to about thirteen feet at the transom where two stout davits hold up the tender. Acres and acres of deck space. And, below, an upright piano which the previous owner and skipper banged away at to the great delight of his passengers over the three years between the construction of the boat and my purchase of her.

What was needed, I thought on looking the boat over, was a great deal of impacted luxury plus complete equipment and instrumentation for ocean passages. The latter was obvious enough: running backstays, loran, radar, automatic pilot; that kind of thing. The former is I think less obvious. I had done a fair amount of chartering, not a great deal. But I had come to a few conclusions:

1) Sleeping quarters should be small and public quarters large. One needs only, in sleeping cabins, privacy and room to turn around in.

2) Every cabin should have a port, which should be situated at about eye level when your head is down on the pillow. Why the hell not? I have been on boats all my life which require that in order to see through the port—presumably there for you to see through—you need to stand on tiptoe, which is hard to do while going to sleep. The naval architect gulped the presumptive gulp that all naval architects gulp when you go about tampering with their beloved Integrity of the Hull. But I had along a friend, a plastics consultant, graduate of MIT, who stared him down and calmly reminded the architect that he could put into the port a polysyllabic-ethylene-whatever, which is stronger than the original wood, etc. Anyway, I got my ports. Three of them on the starboard side, one for each of the cabins, and three of them on the port side in the saloon—all this in addition to the picture windows in the deckhouse.

3) Color, color, and more color. More boats are ruined by monochromatic dullness than by careless seamanship. So, every room was decorated by my wife in a chintz of different color, of congruent patterns; so that we have the red cabin, the yellow cabin, and the green cabin, a green carpet, and a glazed cotton print for the settee and couches, a pattern taking off, in reds and blues, on an old Spanish sailing map.

4) Chairs, settees, and couches must be comfortable. I rebuilt the main settee three times, so as to make it finally slope back far enough and extend out far enough to make sitting in it truly comfortable for the slouchers of this world, who are my friends and clients. Opposite it, two club chairs, facing my three ports. Wall-to-wall carpeting, kerosene, and electric torches. Then I persuaded my friend Richard Grosvenor, the excellent New England artist who teaches at St. George's School, to do three original oil paintings of boat scenes which exactly fit the principal exposed areas I had wired to receive them. So that every picture is lit as in an art gallery, the three little overhead lights providing plenty of illumination for the entire saloon, unless you want to read, at which point you snap on one of the other lights. But the saloon now, with the oil paintings alone, lights up in color and comfort, a beautiful room of utter relaxation. When you are under way in a

breeze, the seas sometimes rise up covering the ports completely, for whole seconds at a time. (Sometimes the moonlight comes in to you right through the water.) Aft of the piano is the bar and refrigerator which the former owner so thoughtfully installed to keep charterers from having to go back and back to the galley quarters which are a whole engine room away.

5) The deck area should be—well, perfect. There was no deckhouse. I had one designed and built, with two six-foot-long cushions, usable as berths on either side. Between them, the companionway and then a well, where your feet can dangle while you navigate over an area larger than a standard card table and look into your radar, or your depth finder. Or at the compass, steering the ship electrically. That's when you want to come forward from the wheel to get out of the rain. Stepping aft, six or seven feet, an enormous settee. Once again, the accent on comfort. In the Mediterranean, many boats have main cockpit settees on which you can sprawl out in any direction. The trick was to accomplish this and also convert the new deckhouse into dining quarters for fair weather. Castro Convertible came to the rescue. The adaptation of his essential mechanism that permits the raising of a table. Then a custom-built tabletop which exactly fits the arc of the settee. So that when you are not eating, the table sinks down and three tailored cushions exactly cover the area, which now merges with the settee, giving you an enormous area of about four feet by twelve feet in which four or five people can stretch out and read, or merely meditate on the splendid achievements of the settee designer. At mealtimes, remove the three cushions, pull a lever and—*hesto!* a perfectly designed table rises elegantly into place, around which eight people can sit. At night, you can close off the entire area with canvas, giving you something of the feel of a large Arabian tent.

6) The crew must have living space. Under existing arrangements, it is almost never necessary to occupy the old dining quarters in the after section. There the crew has its privacy, adjacent to the captain's cabin, the main navigation table, the galley, and the lazaret, etc.

7) Noise. Somebody, somewhere along the line, told me that the biggest most expensive generators make the least noise. I consulted Ned, who had volunteered to oversee the entire remodeling—which he was uniquely

equipped to do, having at one point owned and operated a boat construction company—and he came up with an Onan so noiseless that you simply
are unaware that it is turned on. It provides all the power you need, including 110-volt AC outlets. And finally,

8) Coolness. I do not care how much it costs, or how difficult it is
to install. Air-condition, or die. I reason as follows: that if you live in the
Caribbean the year round, perhaps you can get used to hot temperatures.
But if you only *visit* the Caribbean, you plain get hot in the middle of the
day—just as you can get hot in the middle of Long Island Sound. Turn on
your air conditioner, and life changes for you; or it does for me, anyway. I
shall never be without my air conditioner. If the bankers one day descend
on me, I shall go on national TV and deliver a Checkers speech about my
air conditioner. They will never take it from me.

Now I also thought to dally with closed circuit TV and did so. I bought
one of those Sony jobs. The idea is that, at night in the islands, the children
might get bored; or you might think it fun to show a movie. So why not
stock an inventory of tapes of great movies pirated from the TV channels,
the commercials thoughtfully dubbed out. I do remember one night, 300
miles out toward Bermuda, lazy sailing conditions, a full moon, pleasant
company, and I thought to ask my companions had they heard Horowitz's Carnegie Hall concert which had been televised that season as a CBS
special. Well, no, they hadn't. Would they like to see it? The whole investment was worth that indelible memory of sipping brandy, smoking cigars,
sailing at about eight knots out in the middle of the ocean, and viewing
and listening to one hour of Horowitz doing Schubert, Chopin, and Liszt.
There was another occasion—come to think of it—when an old friend, an
official of the New York Yacht Club, arrived in full regalia late one evening
in Padanaram in an advanced state of decomposition, to take (yet another)
nightcap with us. He came upon us lounging around a television set. I solemnly informed him that I had requested the local television station to run
the *Wizard of Oz* for us, and they had just begun. "I'll phone and tell them
to start it again from the beginning for you," I said gravely. I disappeared
below for a few seconds, turned a couple of knobs surreptitiously, and *Oz*
quick-rewound and started again. I returned to see my friend clinging to

the mast in amazement at my extraordinary powers over the local station. On the other hand, he'd have been clinging to the mast in any case.

But I gave up my Sony. It was too often not working, and the stuff and bother of getting it to New York to be fixed was too much. Also, stowage was a problem. And, somehow, charterers seldom get around to asking for a movie on board *Cyrano*. I like that. And Ned is delighted. Stringing the machine together required a certain electrical coordination which only he possessed; and that meant standing by late at night, which can be a bore. Especially if the impulse to see the *Wizard of Oz* comes to a charterer at, say, midnight.

I am staring at the chart as we cruise out of the tight little entrance to English Harbour. What do you say we go to Nevis? I suggest to Ned. Nevis is about forty-five miles west, and it is already noon, what with the last-minute shopping one always has to do. The wind is as it should be, east-northeast. Ned, so wise, so seasoned, suggests that perhaps we would be better off just going west along the coastline of Antigua, instead of striking out for so distant a goal so late in the day. I am glad I gave in.

Sunday, December 21

I said I was glad I gave in, and I imagine that I gave the impression that where we did spend the night, which was in Mosquito Bay in Antigua, was unique. Not really. It is a very beautiful cove (there are no mosquitoes on it, by the way), shallow, and if you want to know when the tide changes, it changes exactly when it changes in Galveston, TX, for heaven's sake; and not even Ned knew instinctively how to figure *that* one out. I mean, if the *Tide Book* says: See Galveston, TX, and you find that the tide begins to ebb at Galveston, TX, at 19:00, what time does it begin to ebb at Mosquito Bay, Antigua? You will immediately see that conflicting hypotheses are plausible. You may find yourself reasoning that when it is 7:00 p.m. at Galveston, the tide also begins to change at Mosquito Bay, which means you have to figure out the time zone for Galveston. Well, figure Galveston is two hours behind New York and we are one hour ahead of New York; ergo it changes at Mosquito Bay at 10:00 p.m. Right? Not necessarily. Maybe it means that just as when it is 7:00 p.m. local time at Galveston the tide changes, so when it is 7:00 p.m. local time at Mosquito Bay the tide changes—what's implausible about that?

The time has come to note a further complication, which is that when I sail *Cyrano* in the Caribbean, I go on what we call Buckley Watch Time, the only eponymous enterprise I have ever engaged in. What you do is tell everybody on board to move their clocks up by one hour. The practical meaning of it all is that you can start the cocktail hour as the sun is setting, and eat dinner one hour later at eight o'clock, BWT. Otherwise, you start drinking at six o'clock and eat dinner at seven. The former offends the Calvinist streak in a Yankee, the latter the Mediterranean streak in a yacht owner. Anyway, in order to avoid digging into the fine print of the *Tide Book*, we decide to fasten on the fact that, after all, the tide is less than one foot anyway; so, we throw out the hook at 150 yards from the beach rather than crawl up farther as we might have done if we had been absolutely sure that Galveston had another hour or so to go before the ebb began. No matter. The sunset was beautiful, we swam, ate—ate very well, thanks to Rawle who is a superb cook, a native of St. Vincent, and has the prestige of a real-life shipwreck under his belt. Then we played 21, and I won consistently. The tape player is the arena of a subtle contest between the generations. When one of us goes by it, we glide into the tape cavity something melodic. When one of the seventeen-year-olds goes by, quite unobtrusively he, or she, will slip in The Creams, or The Peanut Butters, or whomever. I acknowledge to myself that the war will be formally declared by about tomorrow, lunchtime. ("Will you please get those screaming banshees off the air, children?" "Mother, can we put on something that isn't Marie Antoinette?") I am right. We go to bed, and my wife and I can see, outside our port, the full moon and the speckly light it casts on the waters—our waters, because there is no one else in sight.

Monday, December 22

I must make myself plain. I am glad I took the advice that we make the shorter rather than the longer run to Nevis, because I know enough now about other people to know what suits the general taste in a cruise. I come from a rather Spartan tradition, which is not what cruising/chartering is about. I remember talking with Art Kadey, who owned *Pinocchio*, and the disbelief with which I heard him say that the typical charterer travels approx-imately four hours every other day! I thought that (and still do) rather on the order of owning a Boeing 707 and operating it only every other day. It takes time to change your rhythm, if you have raced a boat in ocean races, getting accustomed to day-and-night running. Some come easily to the change and indeed find it easy to oscillate from furious, implacable racing-day after day, week after week, in such as the Transatlantic or Transpac races—to strolling about for a few hours on the same boat you often race, going perhaps no farther than ten or fifteen or twenty miles in a single day.

I remember announcing to Ned last summer that I desired to bring *Cyrano* from New York, to Bermuda, to St. Thomas. He showed me an article that described the dangers of that passage in November, said article recom-mending instead that a boat should go warily down the coastline, in and out of the waterway to Morehead City in North Carolina, at which point you are south of the North Atlantic gale area; then shoot across the 1,200 miles or so to the Virgins. But going from Morehead City to St. Thomas simply isn't like going from Bermuda to St. Thomas; indeed, going from Morehead City to any place isn't like going from Bermuda to any place. And I had in mind bringing six classmates from Yale to share the trip with me. Ned begged me to let him and the crew take *Cyrano* on down to Miami, whence he would dead-head to St. Thomas, and let the lot of us meet him there, and simply cruise— we would have a much better time, he persisted. But I thought: How can you have a better time than to take a 1,000-mile ocean voyage in a tough, comfort-able schooner in absolute isolation, taking your chance with the weather and the seas? So, Ned and the crew having brought *Cyrano* down to Bermuda, the rest of us flew in and we took off at midnight—not because midnight is a melodramatic time to take off, but because the sixth friend came in from South America at eleven. The weather reports were discouraging. The strat-egy outlined by Ned, after accepting my resolution as an immovable object, was to head south (St. Thomas, by the way, is exactly south of Bermuda) as fast as possible for the 200 miles necessary to get into the trades and out of the formal limits of the North Atlantic gale area. However, a largish front was even then passing just north of Bermuda causing heavy seas, estimated at twelve to sixteen feet, a *datum* that Ned gave me over the telephone with quite unseemly satisfaction, while I was still in New York, going on to suggest the advisability of postponing our departure until Thursday morning. I replied that unless there was every reason to suppose that everything would be pacific on Thursday morning, we might as well baptize the passengers into discomfort beginning at midnight, inasmuch as we had, but absolutely *had*, to get to St. Thomas by the following Wednesday at the latest. So, there we were, excited, tucked away, the shifts assigned (four hours on, eight hours off), headed out of the little cut at St. Georges—through which, coming the other way, I had passed so often before, exhausted, elated, at the end of the Bermuda race expecting the worst; and being most pleasantly surprised. Light winds from the northeast, quite moderate seas, and, darting in and out of the clouds, a moon that would be full in mid-passage.

Cyrano is a shoal-draft boat, built for the Bahamas. It hasn't even a centerboard: merely a long keel stretching the entire length of the hull, five-feet-one-half inches below the waterline. The result is a certain stodginess in coming about, as any boat has that isn't equipped with ballet shoes; but, with that great beam, and with whatever it is the designer did to those numinous lines, she achieves a glorious sea-kindliness that makes seagoing dry, fast, and stable. The storm front, unfortunately, kicked up most monstrous waves by the time it was several hundred miles northeast of Bermuda, and these rolled down on us the fourth and fifth days of our passage such as to give forty-eight hours of roller-coasting which severely taxed the equanimity of the passengers. As a matter of fact, what I felt one night at dinnertime and after was either seasickness, which I hadn't experienced since I was twelve years old on one of the early voyages of the *Normandie* before they put the stabilizers on her; or some sort of a stomach virus. I felt dreadful, as did most of the rest of us. During the worst of it we put on a storm trysail and the forward staysail. I wanted to put up at least a part of the Genoa (we have it on a roller-reefing fitting). But the fitting on the halyard having slipped overboard while I was making an adjustment, the substitute swivel proved too weak, and the sail came tumbling down after a few hours. I went theatrically up to the masthead to bring down the halyard and put on yet another swivel, but this one, too, gave way after a half day, and now it was really too rough to go up again. The result was a heavy weather helm, which was unpleasant, and which also put too great a strain on the automatic pilot, reducing us to the humility of having to steer our own boat—imagine, with only ten people aboard. It was especially galling to lose the extra knot or two from the rudder's brake action—like driving a sports car in second gear mile after mile, day after day. We had the sun and a full moon, though, and I could bring down Polaris even at midnight, and Ned got perfect star sights, and our landfall was within a half hour of when it was anticipated. But the wind and seas were relentless, and it wasn't until we got right into the harbor at St. Thomas that we got a little relief, and my friends poured gratefully into Pan American, first class, minutes after arriving in St. Thomas, bruised and strained, my *Cyrano* rather weather-beaten. The twelve-year-old daughter of one of my friends wrote me a letter a week or so later on some vexing political question and added the P.S., "What did you do to my daddy?" The wife of another of my friends, who is a very nice man even though he did run for Congress against Shirley Temple, recounted a week or so later when we came upon them in California that three times, at three in the morning, her husband has suddenly risen stiff out of bed, stared straight ahead, and declared somnambulistically, but firmly, "I have to go on deck!" whereupon he walks straight ahead into a closet, which sharply, but reassuringly, jolts him back into the knowledge that his nightmare is over. Ned would like that, and I'll tell him about it when I think of it.

It isn't easy for everybody to relax on a boat. I adore my boat: every boat I have ever had. But I feel, somehow, that I am always, in a sense, on duty; and that I must be going from here to there, and if there is a little weather or whatever, well, isn't that a part of the general idea? The point is, as Ned and others have patiently explained to me, there is the wholly other use for a boat, the use which is absolutely ideal for charterers, and that is the totally comfortable, totally unstrained cruise. So that if you decide this morning to go from Antigua to Nevis but the wind isn't right, why you simply go somewhere else, what the hell. You don't have any obligations to meet the New York Yacht Club Squadron at Nevis at 17:00, and nobody will tell Dooley Roosevelt if, instead, you ease off to St. Kitts—I mean, some people come to total relaxation in boats more easily than others, and they do not feel any constraint to harness their boats to an instrumental objective, like getting from here to exactly there, and there had better be a good distance way from here in order to give you the feeling that you have accomplished a good run and earned the quiet hours of anchorage. All I say is: There are those of us who are slightly driven, and if you are one of those, you will have to speak firmly to Ned. To say nothing of your wife.

St. Kitts is absolutely ravishing. We arrive latish and do not disembark, simply because we cannot be bothered to register the boat. Why, oh, why don't the islands issue a *triptyque*, or whatever the Europeans called that document with all the coupons that they used to issue which facilitated car travel in postwar Europe? Hunting down the immigrations and customs officer, giving him (on one occasion, at Virgin Gorda, six) copies of the crew and passenger list. Why not a bond, that every boat owner could buy, the possession of which would grant free passage everywhere during a season, with a severe penalty if you are caught smuggling or whatever, guaranteed by the bonder? How easy everything would be if I were given plenipotentiary power over these matters.

The run to St. Bartholomew (St. Barts) is quite long—forty miles or so—and I suggest to Ned that we take off early at nine o'clock and sail under the great fort which they call the Gibraltar of the Caribbean. Surely you mean after the crew has breakfast? says Ned. What the hell, I say, why not get started under power, and *then* have breakfast? We weigh anchor and proceed, and two days later I notice in the ship's log the stern entry, "Got underway before the crew had breakfast." A brilliant day, strong winds just abaft the beam, my poor son is seasick, the only time during the whole trip, but by two o'clock we have pulled in to the exemplary little harbor, so neat, so landlocked, so lackadaisical, where the rum is cheaper than the water, and the rhythm of life is such that the natives never go to work before breakfast, and not always after breakfast.

Tuesday, December 23

The proposal is to make a short run for St. Maartens, which my materialistic family favors, sight unseen, because the guidebook says that the prices there are even a little bit less than those at St. Barts. The sail is a mere fifteen miles. We considered dropping by St. Maartens and then proceeding four or five miles west to Anguilla, perhaps to decolonize it, now that history has taught us how easy it is to do. But the iron schedule (we must relinquish the boat to charterers in four days) makes this imprudent. I feel very keenly the loss, inasmuch as during the few months of Anguilla's independence, when the rebel government took a full-page ad in the *New York Times* asking for contributions to revolutionary justice, I slipped the government a five-dollar bill in the mail and got back a handwritten letter of profuse gratitude from the Prime Minister. Another day.

The idea is to spend a relaxed, few hours at St. Maartens and then make the longish (100-mile) sail to the Virgins, touching in at Virgin Gorda. St. Maartens is half Dutch (the lower half) and half French (the other half). A very large harbor, almost the size of Provincetown, with beaches, and calm, and lots of picturesque boats. We swim, and water-ski, and then head out for dinner at the Little Bay Hotel, which is a Hilton type, with casino, triple-air-conditioned bar, so-so restaurant, and better than so-so prices. We did not get to gamble because the casino opened at 9:00 p.m. and we forgot that Buckley Watch Time wiped out the gambling hour we had counted on, so that we went back to *Cyrano* and started out.

I insisted on hoisting all sails, in anticipation of wind (it was just a whisper from the east), and by the time we had lost sight of the light off Anguilla two hours out, we pulled them down, as Ned predicted we would be doing, and settled for a long motor run in preternaturally calm seas which, I might add, the Caribbean owed us.

I took the watch until 02:00, along with my sister-in-law, while my wife and her brother-in-law played gin rummy, and the boys and my niece lazed about on deck forward, discussing no doubt the depravities of their elders. I felt constrained (I am that way on a boat) to go forward every twenty minutes or so to make an aesthetic point—single out the moon, for instance, which was about as easy to miss at this point as the sun at dawn, and say casually, "Have you noticed the moon?" The Kids are so easy to ambush, because it never fails that they will look up from their conversation, stare about, focus eventually on the moon, and say, finally, "Uh."

It was a fine opportunity to write belletristically in the log. The man I admire most in the whole seafaring community is William Snaith, who lives a busy life as president of Raymond Loewy, and races his several Figaros strictly to win, which he usually does, although not often enough to satisfy his perfectionist appetites. In his enthralling book *Across the Western Ocean*, be writes, among other things, about the joys of entering the daily log. He takes a voluptuary delight from going on and on in his logbook with the most entertaining, descriptive, informative sea prose by anybody in memory, at once the business-like Joshua Slocum explaining just how it was, and the reflective Hilaire Belloc, explaining just how it ought to be. I remember, after reading Mr. Snaith, resolving to expand on my anemic entries into the log, bearing in mind the diffuser graces of rhetoric. But I am face-to-face with the unfortunate differences between Mr. Snaith and myself, every one of them in his favor. Writing is what I go to sea to get away from. But I did *try*, and a year ago, taking *Cyrano* from Miami to New York, I got pretty talkative in the log the first two or three entries, but by the third watch I found myself writing, "Nothing new. Proceeding as above. Wind speed down, two-to-five knots." Then, Remembering Snaith, I added, "Drank Coke." Six hours later, I observed that the intervening watch captain, who has sailed with me since he was twelve years old, had scrawled alongside my entry, "So why do you think we care if you drank a Coke?" He led with his chin, did my impudent colleague, because I was able to write down in headmasterish script to my beer-guzzling pal, "Go ye and do likewise." But, of course, that kind of thing really isn't what Mr. Snaith had in mind.

It was an uneventful overnight journey, except that at 3:00 a.m. I was roused from my cabin (Ned was still asleep, his watch scheduled for 4:00 a.m.) by my wife, who reported that my apprehensive brother-in-law desired me personally to confirm that the lights off at one o'clock were not (a) an uncharted reef; (b) an unscheduled island; or (c) a torpedo coming at us at full speed. I came on deck, peered out at the lights of what appeared to be a tanker going peacefully toward whatever it was going peacefully toward. A good chance, though, to show off my radar, which immediately picked him up at six-and-one-half miles away, heading toward, approximately, Dakar. I went back to sleep and awoke when Ned at the wheel was past the famous Anegada Passage, down which the Atlantic often sweeps bustily into the Caribbean, but which on this passage had acted like a wall-to-wall carpet;

and now we were surrounded by tall, hilly islands, such that by contrast we felt almost as though we were going through a network of rivers, calm, warm, but breeze enough (finally) to sail. And we put in, at eleven, at Spanish Town, in order to regularize ourselves with the government of the British Virgins which, on Christmas Eve, was most awfully obliging, after Robert Mauer, the first mate, and I completed the six forms registering the names and affirming the nonsubversive intentions of the tired but happy crew and passengers of *Cyrano*.

Wednesday, December 24

We head now for a bay particularly favored by Ned, in Virgin Gorda. Getting there is a minor problem, requiring a certain concentration so as to avoid Colquhon Reef. In nonnavigational language, you proceed like up, over, down, back, and up so as to avoid the long reef. Look it up in any of the books or guides, and it is abundantly charted. The rewards are great because when you nestle down you see, along the reef a few hundred yards away from the anchorage, the beautiful blues and greens that you have been missing thus far, the water having been deep. It is strictly Bahamian here. They say, by the way, that the Virgins are vastly to be preferred to the Bahamas "from the water level up." This is shorthand to communicate the following: the islands are infinitely more interesting in the Antilles—the Virgins, the Windwards, and the Leewards. Every island is strikingly interesting, and different, both topographically and culturally. St. Kitts, for instance, has Mount Misery, an enormous volcano rising to 4,300 feet. Nothing of the sort happens in the Bahamas, where the islands are almost uniformly low. But the Bahamian waters are uniquely splendid in coloration. The sand bars and reefs, which are so troublesome to the navigator, repay the bother to the swimmer, and to anyone who just wants to look. Anyway, Virgin Gorda is that way, and on shore is the Drake's Anchorage hostelry, which just that morning had changed hands. The previous owner of the little bar and inn has sold out to—would you believe—a professor at MIT. The bar and dining room is Somerset Maugham-tropical and was all dressed up for Christmas. The talk was of the necessity to persuade somebody to come down and take over the exciting underwater tours of the departing owner, who specializes in taking adventurous spirits for scuba diving in the Anegada Passage to poke about the wrecks at Horse Shoe Reef, not all of which by any means have reposed there since the eighteenth century. The flagpole at the hostelry is the corroded aluminum mast of the *Ondine* that foundered there just a few years ago, the navigator, or whoever, having been less lucky than we on the trip down from Bermuda.

Having reconnoitered, we went back to *Cyrano*, which at that point was almost alone in the anchorage, only just in time to see a smallish sloop come gliding toward us, brazenly avoiding the circumnavigatory imperatives of the guidebooks, treating the reef we had given such studied berth to as familiarly as if it were the skipper's bathroom. We watched in awe as a dignified lady with sunbonnet directed the tiller to conform with the directions given by the angular, robust old gentleman up forward handling the anchor. The landing was perfect, the motor never having been summoned to duty, and they edged down, fifty yards away from us. I discreetly manned the binoculars, peeked for a while, and said to my companions, "By God, I do believe that is Dr. Benjamin Spock."

I know the gentleman slightly, having sparred with him here and there in the ideological wars. I wondered what, under the circumstances, would be an appropriate way to greet him. I thought of sending Ned over to his sloop, instructed to say, "Dr. Spock, compliments of *Cyrano*, do you happen to have anything aboard for bubonic plague?" But the spirit of the season overcame me, and instead I wrote out an invitation: "Compliments of the military-industrial complex, Mr. and Mrs. William F. Buckley Jr., would be honored to have the company of Dr. and Mrs. Benjamin Spock and their friends for Christmas cheer at 6:00 p.m." The good doctor rowed over (I knew, I knew he wouldn't use an outboard) to say thanks, how was I, Mrs. Spock wasn't feeling very well, please forgive them, they were pulling out anyway within the hour, come back soon, once you've sailed the Virgins you can never sail anywhere else, and rowed back. We struck out in the glass hopper (all-glass dinghy) with the kids to explore the reef, which they did for hours on end. I returned to *Cyrano* (I enjoy skindiving, but a half hour of it is fine by me), mounted the easel and acrylic paint set my sister-in-law bought me for Christmas, and set about industriously to document, yet again, my extraordinary lack of talent—you would have to see it not to believe it; which, come to think of it, makes my stuff pretty valuable. The girls were working on the decorations, and by the time the sun went down we had a twinkling Christmas tree on deck and twinkling lights along the canvas of the dodger, and the whole forward section was piled with Christmas gifts and decorations; and when we sat down for dinner, with three kerosene lights along my supper table, the moon's beam, lambent, aimed at us as though we were the single target of the heavens, Christmas music coming in from the tape player, the wine and the champagne and the *flambéed* pudding successfully passed around, my family there, and friends, I persuaded myself that nowhere, on that evening, at that time of day, could anyone have asked for any kinder circumstances for celebrating the anniversary of the coming of the Lord.

Thursday, December 25

Intending to go to a church service on Christmas Day at Road Town, the capital of the British Virgins, we pull out earlyish, on the assumption that there is a mass at noon. We arrive at 11:45 and come in, European-style, at the yacht basin. European-style, by the way, involves dropping an anchor, sometimes two, about thirty yards ahead of where you intend finally to position your boat. Then you back up toward the pier (usually stone or concrete) while someone up forward, the anchor having kedged, is poised to arrest your backward movement the moment you give the signal. You back up the boat to about ten feet from the landing. At the right moment (Ned always knows just the right moment) you toss out the port stem line diagonally, and the starboard stern line ditto. Obliging passersby secure these lines on the pier, and you have—you can readily see—a very neat situation. The stem lines are acting as, in a way, spring lines, restricting the boat's sideward movement, sideward being where other boats are lined up, leaving, very often, no more than a foot or two of sea room. Then, when you are safely harnessed, you motion to the gentleman on the foredeck to ease the line to the anchor, while the two gentlemen aft take up on their lines, bringing the stem of *Cyrano* gently aft until the davits are banging quietly over the pier. You have now only to take a step over the taffrail, touch down easily on the ground and, without equilibratory gyration (something you should practice), stroll on toward the nearest *tavèrna*. I don't know why the custom isn't more widespread in American harbors, the economy of space and motion being so very obviously advantageous. Of course, you need to have a sheer situation off the pier, which isn't always the case, for instance, in many New England snuggeries. But even when there is water, the habit is not practiced by American yachtsmen. So much is it the drill in, for instance, Greece that pleasure craft of any size carry gangways that extend from the transom to the pier, including stanchions and lifelines to serve as banisters for milady to hang on to as she descends daintily to earth. I remembered a year ago in the Aegean seeing a hedonistic triumph called the *Blue Leopard*, an enormous yawl which, miraculously, ejected its gangway, it would appear electrically, from just beneath the deck level, where it is stowed—like a convair. Right down to the pier? No, dear. To six inches above the pier, contact with which it was protected from by two special halyards which quickly materialized and were quickly attached to the far comers. The purpose? Why, to spare the *Blue Leopard* the fetid possibility that a restive rat might amble up the companionway, it being a known fact that healthy rats crowd aboard a floating ship.

We linger only an hour or so. The gentleman who owns the bar, the Sir Francis Drake Pub, is moved by the spirit of the season and does not charge you, Merry Christmas, for your first drink, and we feel rather sneaky ordering only a single round, and then returning to *Cyrano* for lunch. Christmas lunch. Rawle, as I have said, is a splendid cook and would give us anything we asked for, beginning with lobster Newburg and ending with baked Alaska. We settle on a fish chowder, of which surely he is the supreme practitioner, and cheese and bacon sandwiches, grilled, with a most prickly Riesling picked up at St. Barts for peanuts or, more accurately, cashews. Then we wander off to the Fort Burt Hotel, which is built around the top of the old fort, providing a 300-degree view of the harbor and adjacent islands. There is another hotel there, dubbed the Judgment Day Hotel, which has not been completed, even though it has been a-building to these many years, and is therefore the butt of many local jokes, classic among them that it will finally open only on Judgment Day. The attitude toward progress in the Antilles is ambivalent. On the one hand, the natives recognize that "progress" is both ineluctable and commercially desirable. On the other hand, the agents of progress are the presumptive disrupters of the natural order, and when bad fortune befalls them, as with the builder of the phantom hotel, they take pleasure in their fugitive alliance with adversity.

Off we go, to swim, and spend the night off Norman Island, which is reputedly the island that Robert Louis Stevenson described when he wrote *Treasure Island*. It is, needless to say, just like any other island (except that it lies adjacent to fascinating grottoes, complete with bats, into which you row, Disneyland-like). On the other hand, needless to say, like the other islands it, too, is captivating: a beach, a fine protected cove. I remembered when a few years ago my son, age fourteen, having done well at school, I took him with me cross country to San Francisco, where I was bound to record some television programs. My son is the prodigy of the McLuhanite dogma, but I was determined not to raise my voice in criticism. But finally, after four hours of flight during which, earphones glued on, Christopher stared at the ceiling while his overworked father fussed fetishistically with all his briefcases and papers, I lost control, turned to him, and said acidly, "Christopher, just out of curiosity, have you *ever* read a book?" He moved his right hand slowly, with that marvelous impudence the rhythm of which comes so naturally to the goddamn Kids, dislodging his right earphone just enough to permit him to speak undistracted, not so much as to cause him to lose the musical narrative of whatever rock-rolling fustian he was listening to, and replied, "Yeah. *Treasure Island.*" Back went the earphone. The eyes did not need to revert to the ceiling of the plane. They had never left it.

It was our final night aboard *Cyrano*, and we felt, although we did not sentimentalize over it, the little pang one feels on approaching the end. The night was fine, calm, and peaceful. The moon made its appearance, although later, begrudgingly it seemed. I think that we all lingered, more than usual, before going below.

Friday, December 26

We stopped at Trunk Bay, St. John, to skin dive. St. John is the island most of which was given by the US government to the Rockefellers, or vice versa, I forget which. In any case, you must drop your anchor well out in the cove, because the lifeguards do not permit you to come too close. In fact, when you come in to the beach with your dinghy you must, if you have an outboard motor, anchor it fifty yards from the beach, and off to the right, away from the swimmers. If you don't have an outboard, you may beach your dinghy. But if you do beach your dinghy, you may not attach its painter to the palm tree up from the beach, because you will be told that people might stumble over it, which indeed people might do, if they are stone-blind. Then you walk to the east side of the beach, put on your face mask and fins, and follow the buoys, ducking down to read underwater quite marvelously readable descriptions of flora, fauna, and fish, the reading matter engraved on stone tablets which tilt up at a convenient angle and describe the surrounding situation and the fishes you are likely to come across. The tablets I saw did not describe the barracuda which took a fancy to me, whose visage was fascinatingly undistinguishable from David Susskind's, but then my eye mask was imperfectly fitted. We got back to *Cyrano* and sailed on down past the Rockefeller Hotel at Caneel Bay, to Cruz Bay, where we officially reentered the United States of America. Embarrassing point. My wife thought, it being the day after Christmas and all, that it would be pleasant if I took to the lady who transacts these official matters a bottle of cheer. I went to her with Ned and found her wonderfully efficient and helpful. She completed the forms and then, rather like David Copperfield making time with the Beadle, I surfaced a bottle of Ron Ponche and, with a flourish or two, presented it to her. She smiled benignly and then explained that she could not, under The Rules, accept such gifts. I am crestfallen, embarrassed, shaken, and return feistily to my wife to say, "See, that's what you get trying to bribe American authorities," to which she replied, "Trying to bribe them to do what?" Which stumped me, and I took a swig of the rejected Ron Ponche, which tasted like Kaopectate, perhaps explaining the lady's rectitude.

We travel under power to St. Thomas, a mere couple of hours. Yacht Haven at St. Thomas might as well be Yacht Haven at Stamford, CT, where *Cyrano* used to summer. Hundreds of boats, harried administrators, obliging officials, giving and taking messages, paging everybody over the loudspeaker, connecting pallid Northeasterners, with all their snowflaked baggage, with wizened boat captains. Only the bar, which opens at 8:00 a.m., made it obviously other than Yacht Haven, Stamford, and, of course, the weather. About eighty-two degrees, and sun, sun, sun. We had not been without it, except for an hour or two on either side of a squall, during the entire idyllic week. A charter was coming aboard the next afternoon, so the preparations were feverish. The adults obliged by taking a couple of rooms at the Yacht Haven Hotel. The boys stayed on board to help. We had yet to do a dinner cruise around the harbor, and our guests were my lawyer in New York, Mr. Charles Rembar, his wife, and son. They arrived (an hour late—a serious matter inasmuch as they had not been indoctrinated in Buckley Watch Time), and we slid out in the darkness (the moon would be very, very late) and cruised about, under power this time, bouncing off the lights of the five great cruise ships that lined the harbor and its entrance. St. Thomas is not unlike Hong Kong at night, except, of course, that it is less steep. But the lights are overwhelming, and the spirit of Christmas was everywhere, so that we cruised gently in the galaxy, putting down, finally, the anchor; had our dinner, pulled back into the slip, said our good-byes, and left my beautiful *Cyrano*, so firm and reliable, so strong and self-assured, so resourceful and copious, and made our way back, in stages, to New York, where for some reason—obscure after the passage of time—our ancestors left their boats, in order to settle down there, so that their children's children might dream, as I do, of reboarding a sailing boat, and cruising the voluptuous waters that Columbus hit upon in his crazy voyage, 500 years ago, because he did not have Ned aboard to tell him when enough was enough.

Path to Rome
March 27, 1971

ROME, Italy—Having business in Rome, I thought to go there by sleeping-car from Montreux, my wife having endorsed the conveyance as exemplary after using it a few years ago. I booked a double stateroom, inasmuch as my wife and I together with paraphernalia tend to overflow; and as we set out by car for Montreux, I thought our gesture particularly appropriate on the very day that the House of Representatives in Washington would decide the fate of supersonic travel.

We waited on the platform as a turbulent sky blackened over the still and misty lake that stretches eighty miles from Geneva to Montreux. The train pulled in dead on schedule at 19:05, as they call 7:05 p.m. in these parts, and we boarded. In the bustle of bags and porters and ticket-showing, the darkness of the sleeping car was unremarkable, but as the train slid out I lightheartedly asked the steward, who was wrestling with the bags while holding a mini-flashlight in his mouth, when ho-ho would the lights go on? He mumbled, like a patient trying to communicate to his dentist, something that sounded awfully like "when we get to Rome." He led us then to a minuscule cabin, the upper and lower bunks already made up, and heaved the bags onto the overhead rack until there was no more room, so that the last two were dumped on the floor, leaving the lower bunk to sit on provided you crouched forward at a forty-five-degree angle, else you bumped into space preempted by the upper bunk.

The steward explained that because of a recent strike in Rome the electrical system had not been repaired, and because of an administrative oversight we had not got the second cabin, and the car was full. I asked him in choked accents which way was the restaurant car, and he said there is no restaurant car on this train, hasn't been for three years, but that when we crossed the border into Italy three hours from now we could run out and buy a picnic basket. I overcame paralysis sufficiently to ask formally for a second flashlight, and he replied that there was only one available per cabin. My French was simply inadequate to the depths of my indignation. I mean, *"maintenant j'ai tout vu"* somehow doesn't accomplish what "now I've seen everything!" does.

Now I like to think that my wife and I, if summoned to rampart-watching by dawn's early light, could manage quite stoically along with everybody else. But we were not here forwarding any grand patriotic purpose. The little light was insufficient for reading anything except the larger headlines in the afternoon paper. I thought of reciting poetry, only to recognize that in my misspent youth I had managed to memorize a total of one poem by Ogden Nash, one couplet by Wordsworth, one sonnet by Sor Juana Inés de la Cruz, and one exhortation from *Paradise Lost*.

We thereupon resolved to take leave of the Geneva-Rome express, only to learn from the steward that the very next stop, forty-five minutes down the line, would leave us stranded in a remote and taxi-less part of Switzerland. So, we decided instead to laugh about it; but to pass along these lapidary lines for the benefit of future romantics who think, when headed from Switzerland to the Eternal City, to disdain jet travel.

That day in the life of William Buckleyvitch seems remote, twenty-four hours later. This morning there was high Mass at St. Peter's, a brilliant organist, absorbed in the beauty of his music and the purpose it served, transmuting the noisy tourists into soft-shoed pilgrims. And then, sipping coffee and reading the *Sunday Times* on the Square, we await the Pope, who will appear sharp at noon at his window in the Vatican apartment to deliver the weekly homily.

Five minutes before noon, the shutters open and the Papal banner, twenty feet long, is lowered. The wind, gusty and irreverent, hurls it back up, and over, and twists it here and there, and one wonders that after 2,000 years the Vatican has not learned how to deal with unruly winds. And then a fantasy: might it happen—just possibly!—that when the Pope appeared, suddenly the wind would quiet down, even as the seas of Galilee once did?

Quite the contrary. The Vicar of Christ appeared, to address the crowd of 50,000, his voice somewhat tired and uncertain, like the Church whose voice he is, and the banner revolted right into his face, smothering the microphone. I do not know what he said, not knowing Italian, but I must suppose that he acknowledged the sacrifices that some of those, pressed into the square, had made in coming there; and I recalled that Hilaire Belloc walked all the way to Rome from Paris before I was born, and that not so many lifetimes ago, a journey to Rome consumed a major part of the lifetime of many pilgrims; and now, the journey, in modern times, takes longer and longer, as the impediments multiply, and the flesh weakens.

The Sorry Conditions of the Airlines
November 16, 1971

SEATTLE—There is an air of resigned depression here, the assumption being that Boeing will never rise again. Boeing isn't out, but it is down, and it will be a while, longer than the economy of Seattle would like, before the supply of its airplanes wears so thin that it will need to reemploy the dozens of thousands of men and women who have been let go. Wernher von Braun was here the other day, and he reassured the community by saying that the Luddite spirit of the day will soon be spent, and before long, America will turn back to technology and go confidently forward. This would mean, among other things, the resumption of the SST (Supersonic Transport) program, and a happier economic future for Boeing.

The chances would appear to be happier even for Boeing, than for the American-run carriers. Figures recently published by *Aviation Daily* make the point with spectacular lucidity. The magazine made a study of five major employee categories at TWA, Pan Am, Air France, Lufthansa, and Alitalia. The statisticians studied the minimum and maximum wages paid to: mechanics, ramp servicemen, ticket agents, accountants, and captains.

Pan Am pays its captains a little more, its mechanics and ramp servicemen a little less than TWA, but the differences are, for these purposes, negligible. Air France pays a little more than Lufthansa, which in turn pays a little more than BOAC, but again the differences are, for these purposes, negligible,

The lesson, then, is conveniently communicated by comparing the figures for Pan Am and those for Lufthansa. Pan Am begins its mechanics at $11,000 (I round out the figures), and pays them a maximum of $12,000. Lufthansa's comparable figures are $4,000 and $5,000. Pan Am begins its ramp servicemen at $9,000, and pays them a maximum of $10,000. Lufthansa's comparable figures are $3,000 and $4,500. Pan Am begins its ticket agents at $9,000, and pays them a maximum of $10,500. Lufthansa's comparable figures are $4,000, and $6,000.

Pan Am begins its accountants at $9,000 and pays them a maximum of $13,000. Lufthansa's comparable figures are $4,000 and $6,000. Pan Am begins its 727 pilots at $40,000, and pays them a maximum of $49,000. Lufthansa's comparable figures are $20,000 and $27,000. Pan Am begins its 747 pilots at $48,000 and pays them a maximum of $71,000. Lufthansa's comparable figures are $20,500 and $33,000.

"Added together," the survey concludes, "the five maximum salary levels for Pan Am and TWA (an average of the two carriers at each level) total $118,500, while the same figure for the four European carriers is $58,500."

In other words, it costs the American carriers almost exactly double what it costs the European carriers to operate the airlines.

The classical concept of competition between nations with widely differing pay scales is that the richer nation will make up for the disparity by a higher capitalization per job, How does this apply to the aircraft industry? Here in Seattle, they will sell anyone a 747 for the same price. And when these carriers are put into operation between Europe and New York there is the identical vessel there for the passengers to fly on.

Manifestly, there is no way out. Unless…

Unless what? Well, unless the American carriers take on a lot more passengers than the European carriers. Here they have at least a temporary advantage. There are more Americans who want to go to Europe and can, than Europeans who want to come to America, and can. And when someone from Kansas City books a passage to London, he gravitates naturally towards an American carrier. But let Lufthansa offer a lower rate, and the Kansas City shopper will quickly shift, why not? That is the reason why the American carriers are so deeply disturbed by the rate war. In order to pay the much higher wages, the carriers have need of the extra business. Obviously, paying the wages they do, the foreign carriers can afford to transport passengers at lesser fares. And when the free market comes finally to the airplane companies, the American airlines are going to have to do one of three things: 1) lower their pay scales; 2) apply to the government for subsidies; or 3) go out of business, like the American ocean-going passenger lines. The likeliest of the three alternatives is the latter.

Frisking: The Social Dividend
November 30, 1972

The American Civil Liberties Union has expressed concern over the procedures by which airline travelers are being searched and, especially, the consequences of many of such searches. It is the ACLU's point that the hijacking problem is proving to be an invitation to lawlessness by federal agents.

The raw data are these. During the past twenty-two months, 6,000 airline travelers were arrested after being searched. But only 20 percent of these were arrested for carrying contraband related directly to hijacking. The federal regulations involving airplanes tell you that you cannot take aboard weapons which are related to the hijacking enterprise. For instance, you can't carry aboard a machine gun, or a mortar, or a pistol, or a Bowie knife.

But what if you carry aboard, say, a pound of heroin? It is unreasonable for the people who search you to contend that it was your intention to stick the pilot with a hypodermic needle, transfuse him with rapid joy, and in his transfixed condition coo him into taking you to Havana. In this sense the ACLU people are as a matter of fact quite plausible. The passengers who have been arrested, while in the process of boarding aircraft carrying drugs, can't legitimately be thought of as passengers interdicted from the act of hijacking.

The generic point is therefore raised: Should an arresting officer be permitted to opportunize on chance discoveries of contraband? The principal judicial finding, thus far, is that of Judge Jack Weinstein, federal judge of the eastern district of New York, who ruled eighteen months ago that a frisker is entitled to move against targets of opportunity. "If a 'frisk' for weapons is conducted in good faith to locate a weapon believed to be present on the basis of information generated by a well-administered federal anti-hijacking system and does not go beyond the limits of what is required to uncover such an object, seizure of evidence in crimes other than those involved in boarding aircraft with a weapon is justified. The officer need not close his eyes to evidence of other crimes which he may uncover."

The Fourth Amendment of the Constitution protects us against "unreasonable searches and seizures." It would be unreasonable—to reach for an example—for federal (or state) agents to search on boarding, say, the bus from Winnetka to Chicago: for the simple reason that there isn't a sufficient historical incidence, on the bus from Winnetka to Chicago, of busjackers. The need for airborne security, by contrast, is historically demonstrated.

But, admitting the constitutionality of search, what about the constitutionality of seizure: of unrelated contraband? The ACLU veers toward saying that you can't seize it. Technically the questions are various: a) Can you seize it? (Yes, is most people's answer); b) Can you offer it in evidence in order to prosecute the passengers from whom you seized it? (Yes, is Judge Weinstein's answer; No, the ACLU-types seem to be saying).

As regards the latter point, one runs into the generic precedent of *Weeks vs. United States*, which found in 1914 against the use as evidence of illegally *seized* material. It is not clear that the *Weeks* ban would apply in the disputed cases: because if John Jones is legally searched and found to have in his possession illegal goods, it hasn't been established that these are inadmissible. They are, one would think, a social dividend. If, on investigating Lizzie Borden's quarters in search of an axe, one finds instead a hand grenade, the operative judicial assumption is that you can not only seize it but also introduce it into whatever court is concerned with pressing anti-hand grenade laws.

The philosophical point gradually crystallizes, and it bears of course on the great socio-juridical question: How do you even up the disequilibrium now working in favor of the criminal? The ACLU-types are fanatically concerned with the defendant's rights. They are never around to suggest judicial or legislative reforms designed to strengthen the hand of the innocent. They are not even there to give him artificial respiration. The ACLU was eloquent in its indifference to the militants who interfered with the rights of professors and students who in recent years sought to express their own rights to free speech. They are now preparing to take a hijacking dilemma and run with it in the same old direction.

An Aborted Cruise
Yachting, January 1973

The wind would not budge from the east, but having powered for seven endless hours from Miami to Cat Cay and waited here a whole (pleasant) day for a change in the wind, so that we might turn off the motor and sail in the general direction of Nassau, we decided what the hell, let's accept the wind's obstinacy and move north to Grand Bahama, which we could do under sail, and then work our way, again under sail, south to the Berry Islands, and on into Nassau, which we didn't have to reach until Thursday, this being only Saturday—all the time in the world to complete a leisurely detour. But Grand Bahama is a good stretch from Cat Cay so we resolved, there and then in late afternoon, to get a leg up on the northerly before nightfall by coasting the eight miles to Bimini, to overnight there.

It was the kind of afternoon, with which the Bahamas are so frequently touched, which causes the heart and the memory to flutter: a steady balmy breeze, lengthening shadows on sugar-white beaches, ten shades of blue and green between my schooner *Cyrano* and the entrance to the little harbor, only forty yards away. We were on the leeward side of the dock, tied up alongside, and so we had only to release the lines to the pilings, float clear of the Hatteras behind us and the Hatteras ahead of us, back gently under power out into the channel, then hard right rudder, a lazy ninety-degree turn and on out by the inland passage to Bimini. We slid smoothly away from the dock and in due course I eased the gear stick into reverse and quickened the throttle by a few hundred rpm, and in seconds I found myself dreaming the dream where you are trying desperately to run away from the monster who is chasing you, only your legs, though they go furiously through the motions, fail to propel you. My beautiful sixty-foot schooner was proceeding slowly, majestically, toward the stone jetty, twenty yards down-wind.

(At the exhaustive postmortem I was told cheerily by an expert that a folding propeller sometimes disdains to engage immediately in reverse gear at low rpm speeds. I got myself a non-folding propeller.)

Danny Merritt was following us in the whaler under his own power, so as to be out of the way of our stern when we backed down. With the whaler as tug, in a few seconds we were laced back along the pier, and discovered that the drive shaft had disengaged from the coupling.

For those as ignorant of mechanical arrangements as I, this means that the rod to which the propeller is affixed, which rod must (obviously) itself be turned by something, had come loose from what turns it, namely, the engine. Frank Warren, the young professional captain of *Cyrano*, had had this difficulty under tame circumstances a few weeks earlier, whereupon he took the boat to a great shipyard in Miami which put it in dry-dock, aligned the engine, tested the shaft, repaired the coupling, for all I know prayed over it, and wished us happy cruising.

We examined the shaft and found that a stainless-steel through-pin binding the shaft to the engine had sheared, and that moreover the liberated member had rocketed aft, imbedding the propeller in the sternpost forward of the rudder. A local mechanic meditated laconically on the situation and in three hours, during which I had laboriously devised a beaching program so that we could at low tide hammer the shaft into position, pronounced it repaired. He used a galvanized pin and suggested that we exchange it for another stainless-steel pin, the collapsed one having been clearly defective, eventually, when the boat got back to Miami. The next day, approaching Lucayan Beach in Grand Bahama, we had the identical experience.

This time the local mechanic pronounced oracularly on the sources of our difficulty. The pin, he said, is not nearly strong enough to carry the load of the revolving drive shaft. To begin with, the shaft engages positively a key in the engine. This key had worn. We needed a new key. He would have one made up at the machine shop—perhaps that very Sunday afternoon!

Some thirty hours and $125.00 later, he pronounced us totally fit. Not only had he put in a fresh key, and a fresh pin, he had tapped in three set screws. There was no way for the drive shaft to give us any more trouble.

It was early afternoon, and the wind now was oscillating from south to southwest, in a dirtying sky, barometer, however, steady (at 30.02). It seemed reasonable, since we were edgy to move on, to sail the thirty-seven miles to the end of Grand Bahama, beyond which is the bight wherein Deep Water Cay beckons. The *Yachtsman's Guide to the Bahamas* describes it as "an anchorage [which will] carry six foot at L.W. while four feet can be taken in over the bar. The Deep Water Cay Club…[is] an attractive fishing camp with space for four boats, gas and diesel fuels, electricity, water and ice in small quantities. …The bone fishing is considered among the best in the Bahamas. There is a 2,200-ft. grass airstrip, but buzz the Club and make contact…before landing as it might be soft." Would that we had been airborne.

Chart 26320 shows the shallow water along the southern coast of Grand Bahama tapering off decisively ten or twelve miles before the entrance to Deep Water Cay, with glorious depths of not less than thirty feet (we draw only five feet) right up to the beaches approaching the bight.

Six hours later the wind was stiffening, so we pulled down the fisherman. I noticed then that two (of the seventeen) lugs that slide up the groove in the aluminum mast, holding the bolt rope of the mainsail to the mast, had pulled out. Strange, they have never done that before. They are tough, one-inch by half-inch, hard plastic. My son Christopher tightened the halyard with all his strength, another half inch, to take the strain off the remaining members, but within minutes the rest of them have ripped out and the mainsail became sloppy and very nearly intractable. Turning on the engine, sliding the gear forward, and turning the wheel to windward, I ordered the mainsail hauled down.

I do not know what happened, in the all but total absence of stress—we had used the engine only to get out of Lucaya—to the beautiful new key; to the set screws; to the stainless-steel pin, but I was accosted by the distinctive purr of an engine in neutral. We were still three or four miles from the bight, but with less than an hour of daylight, and we needed to make way. I gave instructions to fasten on the storm trysail. As we wrestled with it, Peter Starr, having peered forward, rushed back quickly to the wheel. I have known him since he was a boy, and have sailed with him 100,000 miles. His voice had the imperative ring to which one pays very special attention. We are, he said quietly, about 300 yards from a reef, breaking in the sea and stretching right out along our course.

I looked up from the trysail operation. There it is, clear as pitch. A mile south of the shoreline, as far as the eye can see, exactly where the chart indicated a passage. To starboard of us was upwind. To port, land. We rushed forward, made ready the sixty-pound Danforth, lowered the headsails, payed out 150 feet of chain, and held our breath. The waves and wind pounded against us, and our twelve-foot bowsprit rose and plunged like a bronco. But the anchor held. On the whaler, Danny took out a second anchor, the plow, attached to one-inch nylon, about the same distance, forty or fifty feet to the right of the Danforth. Frank Warren dove below to alert the Bahaman Air Sea Rescue station at Freeport, forty miles west, and to report that thus far we were not dragging, that we were a mile from the beach, that the mainsail was inoperative.

Freeport replied that inasmuch as we were not in any apparent physical danger, they would not send out their rescue vessel, which in any event was busy right now with other emergency duty. I dispatched Danny and Warren in the whaler into the womb of Deep Water Cay to request a fishing boat to come to us to take the ladies—my wife and sister-in-law—to the club, there to take refuge from what I knew would be a tossy, emetic, nerve-bruising night.

The boys returned, three hours later, tatterdemalion, announcing that the alleged channel through which we proposed to pass had, even at high tide, scratched the whaler's eighteen-inch propeller shaft a half dozen times. That the club was inoperative. That there were no boats anywhere in the vicinity. That they had hitchhiked twenty miles to the nearest telephone, whence they had called Freeport once again giving more exact details on our position. This much we had known. We were guarding 2182 and Freeport had called in to report that the boys were safe, and would spend the night ashore. Instead, they elected to make their way back to *Cyrano*, where they now huddled, wet and exhausted. We sprawled about the huge cockpit, covered by canvas, looking past six squat candles smug in their colored chimneys, gazing through the large windshields at the wind and the sea and the rain.

During the long night our position didn't change. The anchor watch reported not a detectable foot of drag. The boat's motion made sleep difficult. The gusts, though specially strident in our fixed circumstances, probably didn't reach more than thirty knots. We were not shipping water, and the reserve anchor, to judge from the tests we put it through on the forward winch, was itself nicely kedged. If it had happened that both our anchors had slipped, *Cyrano* would have floated toward the shore, on the safe side of the vicious reef, there either to be battered or, if we were lucky to get there at high tide, which would come just after midnight, and not again until noon the next day, to be lumpily beached, in whatever chaotic way (she is thirty-five tons). We could briefly hold the boat away from the beach by pulling it with the whaler (and its 40 hp outboard); but in this sea, this would not have worked for more than long enough to try one time or perhaps two to re-situate the anchor. We had on board two six-man emergency life rafts, which would have drifted our crew and passengers, a total of eight people, safely to the beach. We had repaired the mainsail by pulling the runners out of the trysail and stitching them in. The halyards were poised ready to lift all sails. We needed a wind shift, though not much of one: forty-five degrees west and we could sail away from the reef on a starboard tack; twenty-five degrees east, and we could sail back toward Freeport at a safe distance from the shore, but schooners are not designed to tack out of an acute angle.

But the wind held. Then, unaccountably, just after dawn as I was listening gloomily to a weather forecast that gave no indication of a prospective change in wind or weather, a Coast Guard cutter approached us over the horizon, slowly, sniffily. Through the wind I could hear the bagpipes! But it was so much unexpected, I found myself waving my cap, lest the cutter should ignore us or continue east.

Within a few minutes we could see the Coast Guard cutter *Cape Shoal-water*, which soon came within hailing distance. Moments later two men in a powered rubber life raft approached us, Chief Green, an engineer, and Seaman First Class Mike Harvey. They required, first, to inspect our documentation and our safety equipment. We passed triumphantly. It transpired that at about 22:00, Freeport, without our knowledge, had called over to Fort Lauderdale to request assistance in our behalf. Within one hour, *Shoalwater* had collected its standby crew of twelve men, under the charge of Lieutenant Bowersox, and started out on the 120-mile journey. Pretty damned good show.

Chief Green inspected our drive shaft, and in an incredible forty-five minutes had it reconnected—a dazzling feat of virtuosity, which had required him single-handedly to slide the entire shaft forward with only the tools at hand. (Alas, it slipped out again twenty minutes later.) Captain Warren, outside my earshot, had meanwhile asked, wistfully I assume, if the cutter might tow us all the way to Miami, instead of merely to Freeport, since in any case the cutter was bound eventually to Fort Lauderdale. Within minutes, the portable telephone relayed the request to the cutter, the cutter relayed it to Fort Lauderdale, and the request was approved. A very long hawser was slipped out over the *Shoalwater*'s stern, bound to our samson post forward, and we were off on a sixteen-hour trip to Miami, with Mike Harvey aboard to relay necessary signals on his radio. Sixteen hours later, averaging just under ten knots (we do ten and one-half maximum under sail) we reached Government Cut at Miami, and there a small tender took us over.

As the tender pulled us through the cut, we heard from behind a strangled cry from Danny, who at my instruction had leaped into the whaler as was our mode coming into port. We could not see in the dark what had happened to him; we attempted to get the tender to go back and fetch him, but were told that would come later—first came the job of depositing *Cyrano* a mile down the line at the marina.

As we drew into the dock, Danny was getting out of a car, right in front of us. The huge outboard, the fastenings loosed by the long haul, had jumped up over the transom of the whaler and purred away underwater for a minute or so, gurgling finally into silence. Danny, who is as resourceful as Robinson Crusoe and as buoyant as Styrofoam, used the water skis to paddle to one side of the cut, and bounded up to flag a passing car. The driver instantly obliged. It developed that he was working on his twentieth can of beer, and asked Danny where he lived. Danny replied Stamford, CT, whereupon the driver looked blearily at his map for the most direct route to Stamford. "No, no," Danny said. "Miamarina, Fifth and Biscayne, would do just fine... and that was only twenty blocks away.

At the dock there were reporters and a couple of cameras. Evidently Dick Cavett had heard the news and observed brightly on his program that he hoped I had not run my yacht off the edge of the world. I was too tired to riposte that if the edge of the world had happened to be located in the Bahamas, the detail would have escaped the attention of the man who drew chart 26320. The *Miami Herald* was already out with a report taken from Freeport radio, which was quoted as observing: "They either had no sail aboard or no one who knows how to sail." Peter Starr and I could not work up the strength to be indignant. Somehow, I mused, it would never occur to a newspaper to write: "Apparently no one in the Caribbean area knows how to connect a drive shaft." We settled for professing our gratitude to the Coast Guard. That gratitude is keen. How best to express it? By passing along the word.

The Searches Go On
February 27, 1973

GSTAAD, Switzerland—In the past few weeks, the search of airline passengers and their handbags has become institutionalized. It is now quite general and, one gathers, quite well accepted, like the queues in wartime London. I think this a pity.

A correspondent, Mr. John Brown of Berkeley Heights, NJ, writes to insist that the searches are unconstitutional. I think that highly unlikely. Anyone desiring to visit the offices of the Supreme Court of the United States, lawyers included, is required to submit to a search, including a search of his briefcase. Presumably if it were clearly unconstitutional to do this, someone would have taken the easy access to the justices of the Supreme Court who make the rules governing the use of their own building, to make the point. I think the justices would say that the real point is you don't have to visit the Supreme Court Building, if not-being-searched is your principal objective.

And we all know that on returning from a trip abroad, a search of one's luggage is routine and, so far as one knows, has not been questioned as constitutionally unreasonable. Once again, one needn't travel abroad, as one need not board an airplane.

But Mr. Brown's extra-constitutional objections strike one as sound. Is the search *plausible*?

During the last year, domestic airlines boarded 170 million passengers. It isn't known with precision how many hijackings there were—a couple of dozen. But in order to avoid contest, let us assume there were several times that many. For mathematical convenience, let us put the figure at 170 skyjackings. That is, one per million boardings.

"Eastern Airlines," writes Mr. Brown, "Just to pick an example, schedules approximately 1,000 seats from Washington to Newark every day. If every seat is filled, that's 300,000 boarding passengers a year. At one skyjacker per million boarders, guards would have to search every passenger at that gate for three years before they could expect to see one skyjacker. That's if they were efficient, which they are not 100 percent. If they are, say, efficient, they will have to search every 10 percent passenger for thirty years to encounter one skyjacker!" (The logic here is slightly deficient, because of course the hijacker might be discovered on the very first flight).

And even those figures are not reassuring, says Mr. Brown. "Ten percent is a generous estimate. I have been through approximately a score of search lines in the past year, including the 'tough' ones in Newark, Chicago, and Washington. They have often been intrusive and annoying, but not one of them has been good enough to have detected a weapon if had been carrying one."

Concerning the latter point, we simply do not know—perhaps the airline companies have detection machines more sophisticated than Mr. Brown supposes. But it is true, as he says, that one needn't carry guns in order to skyjack. "According to newspaper reports, skyjacking has been done with no more weapon than a Coca-Cola bottle full of colored water, and once with nothing more than a briefcase full of books and with a string hanging out."

The factor of human inconvenience and humiliation, combined with the statistics, would appear thoroughly to discredit the personal search. Possibly an exception would be the highly nubile routes, which carry a heavy incidence of terrorist-attracted people. Flights in and out of the Middle East would be an example. But flights from Washington to Newark are surely altogether susceptible to Mr. Brown's analysis, and the danger is precisely that the bureaucratic mind should fall into the habit of personal search without a sensible justification for it.

This does not imply that other means of deterring skyjackers should not be pursued. Mr. Brown's suggestions sound at first blush a little wild, but they are worth meditating. "We might start by putting the monkey on the miscreant instead of on the unoffending passenger. Put those guards on the planes, not concealed but in full uniform and armed to the teeth. That's what they do in bank lobbies; they don't search the customers. Better still, arm the stewardesses. An outlaw might try to face down a professional guard, but even the nuttiest skyjacker would surely hesitate at the thought of challenging five armed women."

And, of course, there are the fringe benefits—armed stewardesses could dispose of other problems. Surely it would be worth an experiment. The airlines could, to begin with, reduce their categorical approach to mere spot-checking; as we keep our eyes on the figures. A little resentment by passengers is clearly overdue.

Midsummer Notes
August 2, 1973

LOS ANGELES—The plane was late taking off from Mexico City, so the latest edition of the paper was on board. The headline stretching across eight columns read: "LOS ANGELES BOUND JET CRASHES, ALL KILLED." It occurred to me on reading it that I was at that moment on a Los Angeles-bound jet and thus far un-killed, though I suffered from a Mexican stomach (Lomotil, two immediately, then one every four hours).

The crash, it transpired, was off Tahiti, and when a few hours later the captain intoned over the loudspeaker that there would be no delay in landing in Los Angeles, my son, mimicking the voice from the cockpit, added "because of diminished traffic coming in from Tahiti." I reminded him that the tragedies aside, plane travel still gets safer and safer every year, and he said yeah, so do the moon shots.

It had been a long day, beginning with the stomach seizure at 3:00 a.m. at Guadalajara, whose Autonomous University is a great venture in nonradical education, where they occasionally mount guards with machine guns at the gates to discourage marauding bands from the neighborhood university and, while they are at it, to regulate the length of the students' hair, which is Regulation 1950s. The occasion was a convention of journalists and educators to ruminate on the theme of "educative journalism."

I began my lecture with a jocular reference to my father's having been exiled from Mexico in the early Twenties for having "involved" himself in Mexican affairs. Accordingly, I had been raised in the tradition of noninvolvement. But I said, ho ho, noninvolvement can be overdone. For instance, there was the professor in Czechoslovakia last summer who said that Czechoslovakia is the most noninvolved country in the world: "We don't even involve ourselves in Czechoslovakian affairs." I broke up. Unfortunately, nobody else did. The rumor went about that I was sicker than I really looked. I asked my son how did I sound on the simultaneous translation earphones they were mostly wearing. "Like Donald Duck," he said. I comforted myself by recalling that someone said that Walt Disney has been the best instrument of inter-American understanding in this century.

We rushed to catch the plane, Guadalajara to Mexico City, so as to catch the plane from Mexico City to Los Angeles. At the airport I focused on the geography, and realized that it was like rushing to catch a plane from Washington to Boston so as to catch the plane from Boston to Miami. Nobody had told me you could fly from Guadalajara to Los Angeles.

The plane was late. Why—why?—don't they give you the reason? More and more the American airlines do. But I do not think it has ever occurred to Aereo Mexicana to do so—though it would be more appropriate in their case to apologize for punctuality, than for lateness. I was in one of those moods, so I actually asked the ticket clerk why was the plane late?

I know now the expression on the Beadle's face when Oliver Twist approached him and asked for more. Stupefaction, graduating to hostility, graduating to a resolve to seek revenge. I tried giving him a helpful hint, a sort of verbal multiple-choice, check one. Had they run out of gas? Was the plane hijacked? Had the pilot forgotten to put his watch on Daylight Saving Time? The clerk retaliated by painstakingly scrutinizing my ticket, as though it might somehow betray my imposture, or contain in the fine print something about the plane's being late.

Mexico is flourishing. It is a melancholy commentary that this seems to be the case wherever there is political stability. Melancholy because wherever there is political stability in Latin America there is usually a one-party state. Mexico is wonderfully skilled at giving the illusion of democracy. The cynics call it "*la democracia dirigida*," a programmed democracy. But every five years they conduct elections as though they were the real thing, and the opposition is permitted not the handful of votes they go in for behind the Iron Curtain, but ten or eleven percent, and the press makes it sound like a hair-breadth-victory. It is a fascinating country, and I shall continue to visit it often, and I promise never to involve myself in its domestic affairs.

Getting About in Italy
September 6, 1973

PORTO ERCOLE, Italy—It is generally accepted as an act of divine intervention that planetary order should have come out of the universal chaos. It is no less a miracle that one can travel in a mere seven hours the 200 miles from the Isle of Capri to Porto Ercole. With changes in Naples and Rome. But the odyssey is eventful, instructive, and expensive, and one concludes not only that in Italy every other laborer is a baggage porter, but that the porters are the bedrock of the capitalist class.

There were three of us, with eight bags, and it cost us $60 in tips. At that we were left feeling misanthropic, the genius of the Italian porter who sets out to rob you. You ask him how much for toting eight bags in his cart from one train to another leaving an hour and a half later. "Seven dollars is the tariff…" he will tell you, the final word pitched high, the Italians having learned the art of aposiopesis from the Greeks 2,000 years ago. It is rather as if, cracking open the safe in the bank, you turn to the manacled, gagged manager and say to him reproachfully, "Do you realize that after all the trouble I have taken, you have here only a lousy one hundred thousand in cash?"

My friend coaxed the taxi driver at Naples up to the quay where the hydrofoil disgorged the passengers after the forty-five-minute run from Capri. For some reason, the native population separated from us as if we had the plague. Quite. As we drove off, the driver explained in an ebullient English—he had spent a month in "Yonkers-New-York" as a drummer with a jazz band—that when he had been asked to come shipside to pick us up because the lady had a *gamba mala*, which was the nearest we could come in Italian to describing my wife's twisted knee, he inflected *mala* in such a way as to suggest to the milling crowd that he was proceeding to pick up a lady with a diseased leg; and since the disease *du jour* in Naples is cholera, we found ourselves with the leper's right-of-way.

The driver rejoiced over his gentle duplicity, talking all the way, braking to frenzied stops every few blocks to wave at fellow drivers and friends, giving us a running narrative about the Germans during the war, when he was a boy of fourteen, and, arriving at the station, all but embracing us goodbye.

Unfortunately, it was the wrong station. Back went the bags, after tipping prodigiously the three porters who took the bags off the taxi only to put them back onto the taxi after telling us the train left from the *other* station. The driver was enchanted at the prospect of another few minutes with us and promised he would make the connection.

There followed a ten-minute drive that will remain in memory. When I say it was a drive that paralyzed my wife into silence, I mean such drives are truly paralyzing. My wife will complain of recklessness at the wheel at twenty-five miles per hour, but would be stoical perched on top of Saturn II during the countdown. The driver reenacted the chase in *The French Connection*, hurtling through Naples around trucks and buses and applecarts, ricocheting through tunnels, and singing lustily the songs he learned at

Yonkers-New-York, especially favoring "I Luff Noo Yohk Eeen Choon" and we arrived with ten minutes to spare.

Four porters grabbed two bags each and forced us to run as best we could keeping pace with one diseased leg, and we made it to the baggage car. The four porters desired 2,000 lire each, or $3.50 for the two-minute run. Our traveling companion, whose day it was to act as purser, resisted. Whereupon two other parties joined us, listened gravely to the contending parties, and rendered their judicious verdict that the porters were correct in the price they requested.

At this point, the train about to pull away, we capitulated, and just then the taxi driver rematerialized. He had forgotten to give us his card. "You feela free to write me *any* time!" he said exultantly, and we said, thanks, we certainly would, as the door closed on us and we could see the porters cheerfully chatting until, the train beginning to move, they saw that we were looking at them, whereupon their expressions changed, as if Arturo Toscanini himself had trained them, into a harmonized despondency over the human condition which our miserliness had jolted them into reconsidering.

Overweight?
September 17, 1973

Pursuant to my resolution occasionally to write about airline travel, hoping to make it ever safer, and more agreeable, I contribute a recent experience and a few observations.

It was Rome, a week or two ago, and I was checking into a TWA flight to New York, with five bags. The passenger agent verified my ticket, told me the flight would be two hours late, looked down at the scale and said I had some overweight. Then, speaking in Italian *sotto voce*, he whispered to the supervisor, whose grunt instantly communicated to me that TWA's decision was to get full ransom for my excess baggage. "You will have to pay us for overweight," the agent said. "How much do you pay me for being two hours late?" I asked playfully, handing over my credit card.

A moment later he gave me the voucher to sign and I saw that it was proposed to charge me $220. Two hundred and twenty dollars! I told him never mind, just cancel my reservation. I got a porter, collected my luggage, and walked across to Pan American. There the lady whispered to me as she wrote out the boarding pass that they would need to charge me because TWA's supervisor had shot down the word that I was overweight, and a sense of corporate solidarity required PAA to be as unforgiving as TWA. I whispered back that I understood her plight completely, that for the moment I cared not about paying the overweight, nor even about the unnecessary stopover in Paris, that my cup was spilling over with satisfaction at having denied the predator over at TWA not merely the $220 for the baggage, but the $500 for the canceled airplane seat. I was rather sorry to do this to TWA, because they are lovely people, except for that avaricious creature in Rome.

But I began to muse on the question, and have done a little arithmetic on the great overweight swindle, and I invite Ralph Nader, the Legion of Decency, and the World Council of Churches to look at the figures.

The overweight charge, Rome–New York, is $2.50 per pound. Now, the airline will fly you Rome–New York in the off-season for as little as $155 each way. Let us say you weigh 155 pounds. They are therefore charging you $1 per pound to fly you to Rome, but they are charging your luggage $2.50 per pound. Since they give you two meals, wine, a movie, (some) leg room, lavatories, and even a little lounge, the question is raised. In a rational society, why do the airlines charge more for luggage than for passengers? In such a situation, you are better off getting a piece of luggage made in the shape of a (comely) human being, buying an extra ticket, strapping your luggage into the seat next to you, and consuming all of its free champagne.

Now these who believe that the tax is by design punitive rather than revenue-raising are quite simply wrong. The modern jet airplanes, unlike the little planes of yesteryear, have tremendous holds which are seldom filled by passenger baggage. There was a day, again in another aeronautical age, when the cost of fuel per pound carried was an important economic item—no longer. The cost of kerosene, compared to the cost of high-octane gasoline, is minimal, and the extra cost of fuel in a jumbo as a result of passenger overweight is simply exiguous.

No one should resent paying overweight. It is the paying of overweight at the current preposterous scale that boils the blood of free men, and I for one pledge not to patronize any airline that is literal-minded about over-weight. They will tell you that they have no alternative, the rates are pressed on them—by IATA or the CAB, or whomever.

But where is the airline lobby pressing for reform? The full-page ad by TWA deploring the overweight tariff? Perhaps they are all content to suppose that the seigneurial instincts of their agents will cause them to overlook overweight. But this they cannot count on, cannot count even on their agents disdaining from tippy-toeing over to Pan American to report the haughty American loose in the building with thirty kilos of overweight.

There are a lot of airline associations around that are mostly useless. One of them ought to pass around a rating geared to those lines that are sensible about overweight and those that are not. The word would spread very quickly.

Travel Notes at Christmas
December 27, 1973

It being the season to be jolly, one forces one's thoughts away from the world of getting and spending and plea-bargaining. And this means, as usual, traveling, concerning which a few recent notes.

There is a gentleman attached to the Metroliner train who if his name were known, would fill any cars he services, booked years in advance. He was on duty this morning, on the train from Washington to New York, stops at Baltimore, Wilmington, Philadelphia Thirtieth Street Station—"the only stop we make in Philadelphia, ladies and gentlemen, so take advantage of it—I mean, if you want to go to Philadelphia"—Newark, and New York.

On the whole, one wants to watch out for the ho-ho-hearty types, for instance the occasional airline captain who is a frustrated geologist and will not take you from Los Angeles to New York without instructing you on the glacial ages, and their impact on the geography of America. But the Metro-liner conductor, who is W.C. Fields, aged about forty-five, is irresistible. "Please leave the car from the rear, if that is convenient." *If that is convenient!* To hear such words from someone connected with the railroads is, as the kids used to say during the late unpleasantness, mind-blowing.

When he takes your ticket, he thanks you heartily, and wonders whether your seat is tilted back at a satisfactory angle? "Here, try it at this angle—it's my favorite and maybe it will appeal to you." He appeals to me, and who knows, maybe he is that way because he read about the new bill in Congress that would pump in at least four billion dollars into the railroads. But I suspect he was born happy, and non-bureaucratic-minded, and I would put him in charge of a great big school, wherein the dramatic story would unfold over the course of the semester about good nature triumphing over technology and the bureaucracy.

The bureaucracy. I have had, surely, the ultimate encounter with it. So, I am flying to New Orleans and am offered at lunch a wine which must be from the same vineyard Professor Hugh Kenner drank from during his honeymoon. His description of it is graven in my memory. "It was a New York State Rosé, which tasted as if a few drops of Coca-Cola had been mixed with old battery acid."

But that night the manager of the hotel was so thoughtful as to provide me and my wife with a plateful of cheese and crackers and a half bottle of sound-looking St. Emilion. This we did not consume, and I thought to put it into my briefcase. And sure enough, returning to New York, the smiling stewardess offered us another draught of Professor Kenner's potion. Triumphantly, I produced my half bottle of St. Emilion and asked her please would she let me have the use of her corkscrew. She paused, then, sadly, shook her head. "We can only let you drink, according to the regulations, our own beverages." "Very well," I said brightly, "I will present Delta with this bottle, so it will be yours." She was puzzled. "I'm sorry, sir, but we are not allowed to accept gratuities."

I thought to tell her about Abraham Lincoln, but I was discouraged. It was a receiving line, in the White House, and a bumptious lady plunked a huge bundle of flowers in the President's hands, causing instant social paralysis. "Are these really mine?" he smiled ingenuously at her. "Yes!" she whinnied. "In that case," he said grandly, "I can think of nothing I'd rather do than present them to you."

Ah well, the stewardess was very charming, and in the Watergate age, one doesn't want to break the rules. What would the Special Prosecutor say, if she had accepted the bottle for the purpose of opening it and serving it to me? She would not have been living up to the Spirit of the Laws.

And this morning at 8:00 a.m., before my encounter with the euphoric conductor, the telephone rang. "This is Allegheny Airlines. The flight you were going to take to New York at 9:10 has been cancelled because of a problem with the equipment. We have you on a flight at 12:30 if that's not too late." I thanked her. Much more perfunctorily than I was disposed to do. I was disposed to tell her that I and the whole American public loved her for her thoughtfulness, and consideration, and that I would never criticize Allegheny ever, for anything. And then, of course, it was on account of her, that I met Santa Claus on Amtrak.

Travel Notes
April 16, 1974

The chief purser of the *SS France* put it this way. "When the Arabs quadrupled the price of oil, they wrote an end to *The France* as easily as if they had aimed a torpedo at her side. Do you know how much fuel we will burn on this round-the-world cruise?"

If I had known I would not have answered, would not have deprived him of the pleasure of administering the shock. "Five hundred thousand tons." That is a lot of fuel. I figured it at thirty tons per hour. "They talk about handling our deficit with little economies. Do away with caviar at night! But why do people come on *The France* in the first place? The point is we're *not* the Holiday Inn. Then they say: Do away with the free table wine. Do you know how much that costs us?" The shock this time was not how much, but how little. "About twelve cents per bottle. We buy whole harvests."

There was a little frenzied optimism as the huge steamer left Capetown for St. Helena, that Gaullist Pride might save this exquisite ship. Perhaps Charles de Gaulle would have put up the estimated $25 million annual subsidy. The present government would not, and President Pompidou himself would go, and with him much of what is left of Gaullist pride, before *The France* completed the cruise.

We got the bad news just as we pulled out of St. Helena, but the crew of

1,200 took it as stoically as their Emperor had taken that "damnable rock," as he referred to the little island 1,200 miles from Africa, 1,800 miles from South America. The only happy man in St. Helena that night was the gentleman who picked my wallet.

I did not bother to cable the Diner's Club. The next boat to St. Helena wasn't due for four or five months. The only time there was ever heavy traffic there was when Napoleon was in residence, and two British frigates circled the eighteen-mile coastline, one clockwise, the other counterclockwise, day after day for two years, lest the most explosive human force of the nineteenth century should slither out and bring tumult yet again to Europe. Instead, become listless, he lay much of the time in his bathtub at Longwood, the dreary house the British built for him, dictating to his dwindling staff. When he died, Longwood was used to shear sheep, and finally the French bought it from Queen Victoria, and it survives scruffily. How will visitors get there, now that the passenger ships are disappearing?

Places of exile should, one supposes, look like St. Helena, and smell that way. If it comes up tails for Nixon, San Clemente would look and smell like Longwood in a matter of weeks. Meanwhile, the sun, as it set, penetrated the clouds and put a halo on St. Helena for just a few minutes as *The France* pulled away heading for Dakar. The French Line thinks of everything.

Contrasts, always. St. Helena and Versailles, Dakar and New York. One wonders whether the sidereal fever or whatever it is that rages in your system in protest against going to sleep in Dakar and waking up in New York—isn't partly a matter not only of a metabolic resistance to traveling across six time zones in six hours, but of a cultural resistance to seeing so much contrast so sharply.

At St. Helena, Napoleon, overlord of Europe, was surrounded by four courtiers and two women, and had seven servants. The 200 soldiers on the island were not at his disposal, but at that of the sadist who governed the island, his full-time warden. Tragedy was defined long ago as the fall from a great height. At St. Helena you feel the full horror of it, and it is best approached at 30 miles per hour, aboard a boat, than at jet speed. Easier to come, easier to go. But the accent, now, is uniformly on speed and the French will spend another quarter billion dollars to develop a supersonic jet while *The France* slips into dry-dock. They call that the wave of the future. "So," I said to the purser, "in that case *La France* will go down?" He corrected me. "Non, Monsieur." "*Le* France, pas *La* France." He may be right.

Airline Talk
August 6, 1974

I have not lately remarked on the airlines, for complicated reasons. For one, most of the people one runs into—at the terminals, for example, are the nicest in the world, and one does not like to criticize. This extends even to most of those who search your briefcases for hand grenades. I say most, because I have in mind the lady in Los Angeles who plucked out a package of Preparation H and demanded to know from me in loud tones whether it works.

And, for another, the airlines have been going through a very rough period. Indeed, they were losing money at a frightful rate after the Arab states thought it would be amusing to quadruple the cost of oil. But the response of the airlines was faintly optimistic, and one had the impression that they cancelled a lot of flights less because they needed to conserve fuel, than because they wanted an excuse to retrench their services. Of course, one can hardly blame a company losing money for pulling back its services; still, when in doubt try candor, I say; and a little more of this would be helpful.

There are, besides, the little opportunisms. Two months during the winter I work in Europe, and of course am required by the light of my life to take along our three small dogs. Shipping them back, this last time, in two small kennels, the bill came to $435. I wrote to TWA asking whether the billing machine might have slipped a decimal point to the east. In reply I received a letter telling me that excess baggage is calculated at a rate that takes into account weight and cubic volume. The fact of the matter is that the airlines have got themselves a rate that makes it about as expensive to send a dog by steerage, as a human being first-class, even as the differences between the two modes of travel continue to diminish.

TWA is developing some irksome habits. Boarding the other day at San Francisco at noon, it was after 1:00 p.m. before they got around to serving you what they call "an alcoholic beverage." Why should it take an hour? If they tell you it's because they are overworked, the obvious reply is that they are understaffed. In fact, it is a matter of organization—pure and simple; as witness that some of the airlines manage in a matter of minutes to accomplish what takes others hours.

And then I have bad news for Aeronaves de Mexico. It is altogether possible that Iberia is winning the contest. En route back to New York recently, Iberia served some *hors d'oeuvres* that were hard to beat. One in particular, a pale pink cheesy thing, with sodden crust, tasteless bitter center that crumbles in your fingers, sticks in your throat, and curdles in your stomach. Aeronaves has clearly taken years and years to develop the worst cuisine in the air, and obviously takes pride in its long primacy—but Iberia has over a considerable period been hard at work, and I offer it as the opinion of this amateur that the crown is theirs. There is no movie, no music, the food is inedible, the bar closes a couple of hours before you reach New York, the lounge is unoccupiable because a little moppet is sitting there, the niece of the niece of the inspector, the service is medium-sullen. But here, Aeronaves definitely has the edge, inasmuch as the service there is somewhere between sullen and mutinous. I am told by my weathered friends that people fly whole continents out of their way—going, for instance, from Venezuela to Spain via New York—in order to spare themselves the ordeal of flying Iberia.

I predict, on the matter of food and drink, that there is a future for the *really* good box lunch. It should be sold at major airports and contain maybe a little celery *remoulade*, a cold slightly breaded veal, a super chocolate pastry, a little cheese and maybe a fresh fig, plus a mini-bottle of an Alsatian white wine that you can drink even after the temperature rises, and a mini-bottle of good Bordeaux. Then ring for your coffee, and inquire after the dogs.

The Pan Am Crisis
August 29, 1974

Concerning the imminent bankruptcy of Pan American Airways, a few observations:

1) A direct subsidy, by the government, is, or ought to be, excluded. It is

always the easiest thing to do—to bail out an enterprise in economic trouble. It is usually the wrong thing to do. There are exceptions, mostly to do with the national defense. If the only company in the United States engaged in the manufacture of intercontinental missiles is faced with bankruptcy, obviously you bail it out. But the normal way to do this is to pay enough more for the missiles to keep the company afloat.

Pan Am is not entirely unconnected with the national defense. A country the size of ours needs a strong back-up civil air force. And the facilities of Pan Am are extraordinary, perhaps even unique.

2) Pan Am argues that it cannot effectively compete for two reasons primarily. The first of these is that the airlines against which Pan Am does compete are for the most part subsidized by foreign governments. How— she asks—is it possible, let us say, to compete against Air France, when Air France receives a government subsidy greatly in excess of the subsidy Pan Am receives for carrying the mail?

It is true that foreign air carriers are for the most part government subsidized. And this permits them to continue to fly passengers at rates that disguise the real cost. However, it is also true that the International Air Transport Association sets uniform rates. So that Air France flying passengers from Paris to New York must charge the same fare as Pan Am charges.

The suspicion is that having knocked off the private airlines, the public airlines would revise their fares upwards, to minimize the drain on the sponsoring governments. If Pan Am and TWA were knocked out of the skies, Air France would have a jolly time getting all American business to Paris from New York. For so long as it costs Air France more money than an American passenger pays out to make the trip, then in effect the French government would be making a gift of the difference to American passengers. But in fact, either the price would eventually go up; or, having knocked out the competition, the seats on Air France's planes would be so full that the line would become profitable.

3) Pan Am's second complaint is against the institution of cabotage. She is not permitted to pick up a passenger inside the United States except to land that passenger in another country. She has, in a word, no feeder airline. Clearly, before asking the United States government for $10 million

per month, Pan Am should be permitted either to merge with a US feeder line (the first step); or to merge with our other principal world airline, TWA. There can be no plausible excuse for standing in the way of such a merger under these circumstances.

We are reminded, once again, of the awful distortions caused by the increase in the price of oil. Pan American has been losing money for about seven years. But things were beginning to look up when we were zapped by the oil cartel. In the twelve-month period after the quadrupling of the price of oil, Pan Am would need to spend an extra $200 million for its fuel.

That sum, almost double the amount of the requested subsidy, reminds us of the great distortions that continue to be caused by the oligopolistic advantages of the oil exporting countries. And reminds us that we really have not developed a national strategy to protect ourselves against the ravages of that economic act of aggression. It is all very well to smile our way about the Middle East with the leaders of these governments. But meanwhile they are impoverishing the world, and bringing insecurity to great industrial institutions—like Pan Am.

We are talking here not economics, but politics. Oil is selling not at the price that would result from a free-market bargaining situation; but at a price controlled by politicians. It is simply overdue for the United States government to devise a formula for self-protection.

CHAPTER THREE

1975–1979

A Day in Israel

May 17, 1975

TEL AVIV, Israel—Leaving Israel is a revealing experience. It is hard to begrudge an air terminal that has suffered what Lod has suffered the right to impose any indignity on transiting passengers. So, when the lady asked me what was my profession, I answered good-naturedly, "I am a journalist."

"Show me your journalist card."

"What do you mean my 'journalist card'?" I answered. "In America, we don't have 'journalist cards.'"

Well then, she said, how could I prove I was who I said I was?

When you come to think of it, proving you are who you are, when your interrogator declines to accept your passport or your American Express card as proof, isn't the most obviously easy thing in the world to do. But that was when my inspiration took me. In my briefcase I was carrying a copy of one of my recent books, promised to my host at Athens. I reached for it triumphantly, because on the back of it is a large photograph of seven scruffy looking people of whom I am one, and the central figure is most indisputably Dr. Henry Kissinger, secretary of state of the United States, whose signature appears on all our passports beseeching foreign officials to permit us to pass without let or hindrance. The occasion of the photograph was the swearing in of the United States delegation to the twenty-eighth General Assembly of the United Nations.

On seeing the face of Dr. Kissinger I regret to report, the lady instantly left and came back with a man dressed in khaki, about thirty years old, sinewy, tough.

"How long have you been in Israel?"

"One day," I said.

"What did you do?"

The Lord, I thought, had delivered him into my hands.

"Well as a matter of fact, I spent an hour in a television studio with Prime Minister Rabin."

With this, the gentleman became forthrightly hostile and suspicious as, one supposes, he'd have done if I had said I was Napoleon.

"Where are you going from here?"—he answered his own question by examining my airplane ticket which showed I would spend two days in Athens, and an evening in London, before going on to Washington.

"Why are you going to London?"

I thought it best not to yield to the temptation of saying, "I can't go any longer without listening to Big Ben."

"Because you cannot get to the United States if you leave Athens after 2:00 p.m.," I said, "and my business in Athens does not end until 2:00 p.m., so I am hitching a ride to London where I shall spend the night visiting with my goddaughter's parents in Wiltshire, catching the early flight the next morning to Washington."

"That isn't true. You can get to Washington or New York directly from Athens."

"Look," I said, "what business is it of yours where I go after I leave Israel? What if I wanted to go to Iceland?"

"I am the chief security officer," he said.

We had, really, reached an impasse; and so he decided, grudgingly, not to detain me. Instead, the two of them inspected my baggage with lascivious care, even unto squirting my Right-Guard, thus further diminishing the ozone barrier outside. Before boarding the airplane, each passenger had to stand by his checked luggage while it was examined.

"They are really uptight over there," a journalist in Athens commented, on hearing the story. He used a word which, mercifully, has very nearly gone out of fashion. But he used it truly, and there is every reason for Israel to be in a high state of jitters.

Yet having remarked this, I found in conversations with Mr. Rabin and with a newspaper editor, an academician, and an author, that there is a mood of subjective, fatalistic optimism in Israel. They figure that the price of bringing Israel down is a price the world, really, isn't prepared to pay. Don't ask me how I found out, and thank God Ninotchka didn't know I was leaving the country with this piece of knowledge, but the Israeli high command figures it could stand six weeks of war before finding themselves in the logistical jam they were in after six days of the Yom Kippur War.

The feeling is that the Arabs simply do not want another war, and that the claims of the Palestinians will not drive the Arabs to another war. It is obvious that the Israelis are genuinely ready for some horse trading, and through it all, they are sustained by a great spirit, which tells them that if Apocalypse is ahead for them, they must accept the fact—fatalistically. But the feeling is that Israel will survive. Returning home, one finds, in America, true gloom.

Please Don't Eat the Daisies
October 14, 1975

They have made a pretty good effort in recent months to adjust to the problem of the anti-smoker, so that now when we board an airplane we are politely asked, "Smoking or non-smoking, sir?" I have been giving routinely the answer, "I don't smoke, but I don't mind it if others do"—the only answer I could plausibly give, unless my wife and I occupied separate dining rooms.

Of course, such an answer is the horrible equivalent of saying at a cocktail party, when asked, "What can I bring you from the bar?"—"Anything. Anything at all." People who say that mean to be accommodating. Actually, they merely confuse and exasperate. I'd rather a guest asked me for a Brandy Alexander than for "anything at all." To be sure, I would have to learn to make a Brandy Alexander.

But there remain uncrystallized civil accommodations, notably the typewriter. Now I am, for reasons unknown and irrelevant, the most instinctively undisruptive of men. I even hesitate to hang on the doorknob outside my hotel room the sign that says DO NOT DISTURB without first attempting to write in, "Please." It horrifies me as much as the English that we decorate our national parks with such barbed-wire phrases as "KEEP OFF THE GRASS." I'd have made a very good Jap. All the above on the understanding, of course, that when the bugles sound, I am ready and dressed to defend Pearl Harbor.

Like other journalists, I am saddled with the problem of The Typewriter. Wherever I go, I must use it. No, I don't mean at restaurants or at public receptions at the White House, or at funeral processions. But other times: notably, on planes and trains.

The other day, traveling New York to Washington, I elected to go by Amtrak, thinking to have my dinner and begin typing my notes for a television program that would begin at 9:00 in the morning, followed by a second program beginning at 10:15. I chatted with a friend during the brief dinner hour, then went to work. I had no sooner begun to type than I was accosted by a tall, middle-aged man with the bearing of an ex-colonel, who approached me and said in tones loud enough to sound over the hundred mph noise of a train whistling through the night on tracks laid down during the Grant administration: "I want you to know," he said without any introductory civility, "that I think you are the rudest man I have ever seen. My wife and I paid over $60 to travel on this train and to have a little peace and quiet, and all we get is the sound of your typewriter." He marched away, and all eyes were on me. Did I want to move? the porter asked me. Move where? I replied—the car was full.

I resumed typing but, actually, I found that I was not concentrating on my work. Suddenly every stroke of a key sounded like an acetylene torch triggered under a honeymooner's bed. It is a psychological cliché: the ticking of a clock that is entirely unnoticed can be made—in a movie, say—to sound like the rumbling of a juggernaut merely by having somebody say casually, "When that clock reaches midnight, London will be destroyed."

Every note I tapped sounded louder than the others. Every pause between strokes sounded like a provocative attempt at cacophony. People around me who had been dozing or reading, utterly unaware of the sound of the typewriter, were suddenly looking at me malevolently. This I'd have understood easily enough if they knew what I was writing. But for all they knew, I was copying out "Twinkle Twinkle Little Star…"

I don't like rules, but they can be liberating. If the sign says, "Smoking Permitted Aft of These Seats," then it is only a matter of ascertaining which way is aft before lighting up; and nobody has a legitimate case against you. You guessed it. I think they should get around to signs that say "Typing Permitted Aft of These Seats." Aft of *those* seats could put you with one foot in the baggage compartment, but at least you would have your own turf.

Some will say that, really, we are asked to make too many concessions: that people should try to curb their sensibilities. There is a case for this too. I don't like magenta. Should I have said to the gentleman on the train: "I'll make a deal, pal. I'll stop typing if you will tell your wife to go to the ladies' room and come back dressed in another color—any other color." "Magenta Permitted Aft of These Seats." To be sure, we are left without a solution for the man aboard an airplane who can't stand wings.

Sunday in Leningrad
December 30, 1975

LENINGRAD, USSR—Forget Gulag for a moment. In Russia it is also the little things. You are much better off traveling here in groups, because the Soviet state thinks macrocosmically. Twenty, thirty, a hundred people are palpable. One is a nuisance. But the trouble now was a subgroup. Twelve of us wanted to go to church on Sunday. This is not, by the way, a Provocative Act for a foreigner in Russia—he is free to attend church, and leave the country peacefully.

We are at the newest, largest hotel in Leningrad, a city of four million people. You would suppose that the lobby is bustling at 8:30 in the morning. It is not. You look outside the door, into the Arctic dark, and there is no taxi line. You go to the desk where the sign tells you they will call you a taxi for thirty kopeks, but there is no one there. You go to one end of the main desk, and the lady hears you out; and then points to another woman, at the other end of the desk—*she* is the one who speaks English. You go through it again. She tells you you must go to Information on B Floor. You go to Information on B Floor. There is nobody there. You return to the main desk. She tells you to talk to the lady on your own floor who keeps the room keys. You complain that she does not speak English. You are told she will understand you. You go back to Floor 5 and explain that you desire f-o-u-r taxis, counting the fingers on your hand as in This Little Piggy Went to Market, to take t-w-e-l-v-e people to church. She nods, and picks up her telephone. But it does not work. She says something in Russian which has got to be earthy. FLASH! She reaches for a key, obviously to an unoccupied guest room, half-way down the hall. In two minutes she is back, and scribbles the number of a cab which will come to the door of the hotel in a matter of minutes. What about the other three cabs? Go down, she says, and advise four members of your party to occupy the cab with number 76-30. "Then come back here, and I will tell you the number of the next cab."

You go to the elevators, but four of them are out of order, and three are not enough to handle rush hour traffic, which has now begun. So, you run down 4, 3, 2, 1, PAST THE MYSTERY FLOOR—nobody knows what's there; perhaps Howard Hughes has hedged his bets—B, A, bark your orders to four communicants, and bound back up the six flights. She is at her desk. As you reach her, she hears the telephone ring, bounds down the hall, returns with the number of the second cab, and instructs you to rush down and Fire Two. You ask if you might not simply wait downstairs as all the taxis arrive, and she says No! Under no circumstances! How would you know what the number is of the cab that is dispatched for your use? You do not argue in Russia. I expect you would not argue even if you knew how to argue in Russian. The logical gears are non-reciprocating. On the other hand, the management of the largest hotel in the most cosmopolitan center of Russia finds nothing abnormal in organizing something like Houston Control to round up four taxis at nine in the morning on Sunday. On the other hand, you have the feeling that if you had appeared at the main desk and asked for six B-52s, you would not have been required to make any extra exertions.

We got there. There were perhaps 200 parishioners. The priest was venerable, and he spoke to a congregation that must have been born, every one of them, before the revolution. The priest read extensively in Russian—

from the Scriptures, one supposes. You take fugitive delight in calculating that there probably isn't enough religion left in Russia to attract the attention of the new liturgists.

So, the old priest spoke the Mass in Latin, in the old rite, and the old women, and a few men, bowed their heads. Behind the altar is a huge florid painting of the romantic school, the cross figuring large with the legend, IN HOC SIGNO VINCES: *by this sign, ye shall conquer.* You sigh under the weight of all that is undone, in Russia, and outside Russia, before the Church can be called triumphant; but then you ponder the fact that it—the little tatterdemalion church—is still there; and ponder even the demisemiquaver of a miracle—that all twelve American tourists got there. And anyway, after a half-century's experience with Communism in Russia, impatience with chiliastic Christianity is childlike. Someday, when the statues of Lenin are as windblown as his thoughts, the major shrine in Leningrad will probably be that little Christian church, that went on and on, Sunday after Sunday, as if nothing had happened.

Restoration in Russia
January 1, 1976

LENINGRAD, USSR—In his brilliant forthcoming book (*The Russians*), Hedrick Smith of the *New York Times* confirms the worst we have suspected, namely that the exhilarating movement of the dissidents in the Soviet Union has been skillfully choked back by the Communist nobility, to ghostly proportions. It is reduced to three superstars, on whom brilliant but episodic lights continue to shine as they sweatily perform their death-defying trapeze acts in a progressively sequestered ring of the huge auditorium, once filled with an elated constituency of artists, intellectuals, poets, and pilgrims; who for the most part are absent now when, with increasing frequency, the act goes on. The crowds are back in their crowded quarters, queueing up for a fresh orange, reading—or not reading—the Soviet press; dolefully appeasing the ugly demands of their ugly society, even though this requires them to join in ritual denunciations of the three great dissenters among them, Solzhenitsyn, Sakharov, and Medvedev.

They take you, in Leningrad, to Peter and Paul Fortress, built in the beginning of the eighteenth century when Peter the Great decided to westernize Russia through a resplendent new capital. The prison cells at P&P bear the pictures and biographies of the latest occupants before the revolution, the most celebrated of whom are the older brother of Lenin, and the poet Maxim Gorky. The guide will tell you in catch-throated sentences about the horrors of prison life under the czars. He then tells you that the prisoners were seldom incarcerated for more than six months, dying thereupon on the gallows, or of tuberculosis; or, subsequently, of overexposure in Siberia. It is true that Lenin's brother died on the gallows. His infraction was that he contributed his scientific knowledge to the production of a bomb designed to explode the czar. The bomb, however, misfired. "Upon his death," the guide tells you, "we lost a young genius, already at twenty-one recognized as the leading young light of Soviet science." Those who have followed the vicissitudes of Soviet science will understand that its provenance was a misfired bomb.

But that observation apart, it is hard to get worked up about executing somebody who tried to blow up his emperor eighty years ago. We will deal with Squeaky with condign severity. The other prison cells record matter-of-factly the death dates of their former occupants—in the Thirties, and Forties of this century, for the most part—comfortably escaping execution, TB, and terminal experiences with Siberia.

The craze in Leningrad, so greatly devastated by the German siege of 1941-1944, is for *restoration*. The exquisite palaces of the czars and czarinas of the past 200 years are re-created with brilliant eye and numinous hand, and there is nowhere in the world such repristinated splendor of decorative detail, achieved by a society that will hang a sign: DO NOT TOUCH! on a hard marble staircase, which sign it would not hang over the genitalia of dissenters from the system dragged into the torture cells for interrogation, unavailable for inspection by American tourists.

There is something about the past of Russia that Modern Soviet Russia cannot let alone. The exception is intriguing. It is the desolate palace of Nicholas and Alexandra, the last czars. They will drive you right by it to Catherine's Palace, only 300 yards down the road. You need to make a major scene to slow the bus down to let you look at the one unreconstructed palace in the great complex around St. Petersburg. When, finally, the guide sulkily consenting, the photographs are taken, she divulges "our resentment" that "so many Americans" should be "interested" in the habitation of the last czar. "For us," she says—I would guess she was born twenty-five years after the czar and his family were murdered—"the Czar Nicholas is not history, he is still evil, he did much to hurt Russia. ... How would you like it," she asks, "if I went to New York and took a picture of, of—the Bowery?"

Her audience was greatly amused, and one of them suggested she would probably get a prize from the National Endowment on the Humanities, provided the picture were gruesome enough.

Why, one wonders, do they fear so much the memory of that pallid, awkward, maladroit monarch, drawing curtains over his relatively modest palace, while restoring busily every gilded filigree in every antechamber of his ancestors? Is it a psychic fear of illegitimacy? Anastasia-in-the-closet? The felt need to immure the link between the fastidiously restored past, and the gruesome present? Lest Restoration should become more than a craftsmen's passion.

Okay on the Concorde?
January 27, 1976

On February 4, we are expected to hear from the secretary of transportation whether the British and French may schedule six flights per day across the Atlantic, including two to JFK, two to Dulles. There are other authorities floating around with substantial powers to delay, appeal, and even override Mr. Coleman's decision, but it will be heavily significant symbolically. On the one side you have: the diplomats, the science-minded, and the go-go internationalists; on the other, the environmentalists, the residents who live near the two airports, the Luddites, and—very subtly—America's airline industry.

The environmental arguments have been widely discussed. On the basis of a quick reading, and an intuitive feel of the matter, I would tend to score the ozone worriers as hysterical, the fuel conservation people as irrelevant, the noise abatement lobby as serious but not conclusive; and indeed each of these could be written about separately.

What has not been publicly pondered in any detail, that I know of, are the implications of highly subsidized competition. To escape the emotions of the Supersonic Transport for a moment, let us suppose that the Common Market powers agreed to subsidize all automobiles exported to the United States to the tune of, let us say, 75 percent. This would mean you could pick up a new Volkswagen for a thousand dollars, a Renault for about the same, a Jag for $2,500, and so on.

The classical economic texts, pursuing most honorably and most correctly their presumptive opposition to a tariff, will tell you: Why should we object if, in effect, the taxpayers of Western Europe desire to make a gift to American automobile buyers? But we will be forced to reply that this is one gift horse we'd be wise to look deeply in the mouth of. The objective of the Common Market powers would less likely be to take pity on the underprivileged American class of car buyers, than to drive Detroit out of business; and, having done so, advance toward a cartel in the automobile world.

Now the Concorde's promoters began by selling their governments on the vision of 400 airplanes. Thirteen years and three billion dollars later there are orders for sixteen airplanes. But hear this. Deep study of available routes, on the assumption that every major nation votes to receive the Concorde, establishes that the Anglo-French combine can only hope to sell, maximum, forty-five airplanes. And—still more—on the manufacture of these airplanes each of the two countries stands to lose $30 million per plane.

Now once the airplane is airborne, the extent of the operating loss—the capital cost is irretrievable—will be determined by the size of the surcharge and, of course, the occupancy rate. The planes are very expensive to operate (two to four times as much fuel per passenger mile) and have a very small payload (max. 144 passengers).

The French have reluctantly agreed to a 20 percent premium over first-class fares on the run from Paris to Rio. The English haven't yet decided but are temporarily asking only for 15 percent more. If the International Air Transport Association (IATA) continues to set rates with some reference to economic costs, it may decree a premium as high as 30 percent.

Even so, the Concordes, though they would be losing money per plane sold, and per trip taken, would minimize their losses substantially depending on the extent of American patronage. American businessmen as a single class of people might, in substantial numbers, pay the huge premium for the luxury of cutting travel time in half. And they would be willing to do so—you guessed it—because their travel costs are for the most part tax-deductible.

And so, we have an ironic situation. The United States government would be subsidizing two foreign airlines to drain from American carriers, passengers whose patronage is (in some cases) marginally critical. That doesn't make sense, even for us free-traders. And perhaps one of the questions that should be thrown into the hopper for discussion is: for so long as the governments of France and Great Britain subsidize the Concorde, should IRS disallow deductions for American travelers electing this form of indulgence?

Unsung Victory
March 25, 1976

I have not met Mr. Donald L. Pevsner, attorney at Miami, FL, but I have in my briefcase for him two boxes each of Villars Larme de Cognac, and Larmes de Kirsche, a brand of Swiss chocolates, a propensity for which, in the years we have corresponded, is the only fleshly weakness he has ever betrayed. If, as a people, we were punctilious in expressing our gratitude to genuine public servants, no American traveling through Switzerland would cross the frontier without first getting some Villars chocolates for Mr. Pevsner, who has just finished saving them hundreds, and in the course of a lifetime, thousands of dollars. He has singlehandedly gotten the Civil Aeronautics Board to reduce the biggest rip-off in government-regulated industry: the overweight baggage charge.

Several years ago, I pointed out in this space that a well-built man, weighing 220 pounds, could buy a first-class ticket from New York to Rome for exactly the same amount of money he would need to pay for 220 pounds of excess luggage sent in the hold. Mr. Pevsner, an attorney who does his best to spot injustice in the regulatory agencies, appealed to the CAB, which turned the matter over to its Administrative Law Judge.

This gentleman—would you believe it?—"discovered" that forty-four pounds of luggage for an American traveling overseas was really quite enough, that there were no complaints, indeed that most people weighed in with less than forty-four pounds. He might as well have discovered that there are no complaints in the Sahara Desert when the weather reaches 140 degrees and it fails to snow. No one has ever contended that you cannot travel to Europe with less than forty-four pounds of luggage. The contention is that you need more than that in thousands upon thousands of cases—the student, off for a year's study; the writer carrying necessary research; the couple planning a trip to cold and hot climates. The sub-contention was never that the airlines should carry excess weight for nothing, but that the schedule of cost—one percent of the first-class fare—was at a scale of usury which in the Middle Ages would have brought excommunication. All these points, and many others, Mr. Pevsner, who had no clients, argued systematically, painstakingly, before the CAB, which last week gave him his smashing victory.

Ninety days from today, charges for each kilo of excess baggage over the first twenty kilos (forty-four pounds) will be reduced by roughly two-thirds: from one percent of the one-way first-class fare, to seven-tenths of one percent of the one-way economy class fare. It is important to note that the probability is that the end of the rip-off will quickly reduce the incentive of the international air lines to weigh luggage. Instead, they will do what is done for internal flights: merely designate the acceptable size of your luggage, permit two suitcases, and leave it to you what you want to stuff in them.

Within one year from today, the carriers will be required to change to a system based on space rather than weight.

Mr. Pevsner worked out a concrete example of the change as it will affect, for instance, someone traveling from Miami to London.

Present charge per kilo: $6.28 ($2.85 per pound).

Anticipated charge (based on low-season economy fare) $2.39 per kilo ($1.09 per pound).

Savings: 62 percent.

"Well," comments Mr. Pevsner, "it appears that this is the first time an individual has taken on the entire world airline cartel and beaten them, to the tune of several hundred million dollars per year potential savings. The effort cost me three round-trip excursion-rate tickets to Washington, on each of which I combined additional business or pleasure with CAB hearings, plus about $100 in copying and postage, for an estimated total of no more than $550. It is a gratifying comparison." It is more than that—the biggest bang for a buck in recent legal history.

The airlines have their troubles—do not forget that. The question is whether they should seek to solve them by utterly irrational charges. Donald Pevsner, an independent attorney, has said No.

Misadventures of William F. Buckley Jr.
Motor Boating & Sailing, October 1976

When I first saw *Cyrano*, I was undecided whether to let Pat aboard. Better to wait until after the renovations...? I knew that on examining it, she would pronounce it a lost cause, even as I might do on first seeing a room or a house before such transformations as she can visualize. But I did let her see the boat, and it was as I thought: *Cyrano* would *never* do. I bought it anyway. Ned Killeen, the broker in the transaction, had himself once owned a shipbuilding yard, and volunteered to take a leave of absence and serve as my agent for the purpose of effecting the alchemy; later he became the boat's captain for three years. Our initial sail was memorable.

We would begin the little cruise by sailing the boat from the yard at Ft. Lauderdale, where it had been rebuilt, down to Miami—a four-hour sail. Pat brought along her matronly, endearing, spartan, humorous, arthritic mother, Babe Taylor. Christopher and Danny were about sixteen, and my sister, Priscilla, and Reggie were there—and off we went.

To reach the harbor of Ft. Lauderdale from the boatyard one has to proceed along a canal about fifty feet wide for about one mile; then through the harbor and out to sea. Mrs. Taylor was comfortably installed in a deep deck chair in the covered cockpit section, and I was at the wheel. About a quarter of a mile down the canal, the engine suddenly stopped. I roared out to Ned, and he tore down to the engine room. Two long minutes later he came up, his Douglas Fairbanks moustache twitching, and explained that the drive shaft had been frozen by the octopus action of electric wires that had wound 'round it. Why had the wires wound 'round it? Because they were not properly tied down, said Ned, a little defensively, and the revolving motion of the drive shaft had caused one of those knobbly protuberances on the shaft to snag a wire and, like a propeller on a fishing line, others with it; the lilliputian threads finally bringing the stainless-steel shaft to a halt. How many of the other boat wires? *Every wire in the boat*, Ned finally forced himself to say, his voice now a sort of whiskey-falsetto.

We were, then, without engine, sail or electrical power; floating without steerage way down a narrow canal with traffic of every kind barreling past us. I called Danny and told him and Christopher to jump into the whaler, which is the ship's dinghy, start the outboard engine and tow *Cyrano* back to the yard. They did so eagerly, and Christopher gave a powerful yank on the starter. So powerful that the 40-hp out-board, which had not been properly secured, leaped up from the transom and dove to the bottom of the canal.

At just this moment a sight-seeing boat with about a hundred people on it trolled by. One of the tourists recognized me, and shouted my name in greeting. In the general clamor, the pilot of the boat slowed, and then reversed his engines to permit his guests to take pictures of Mr. Buckley and his friends cruising peacefully aboard his yacht. No one had any reason to suspect that Mr. Buckley and his friends and his yacht weren't going any-where at all for the simple reason that there was nobody around to push. They must have thought it genial of me to stop my boat to allow them all the leisure they wanted to take our picture. *Noblesse oblige*. Under the strain of posing unselfconsciously for a dozen cameras, it was difficult to continue with our war game. But Ned finally volunteered to row the dinghy to the far bank and then to run back to the boatyard to get the yard tender to tow us in. *Don't let that electrician go home*, I growled.

A half hour later the electrician, who moonlighted for the yard—his regular job was to install navigational gear for National Airlines—not only volunteered genially to sail with us to Miami, which would give him the necessary time to splice together the forty or fifty severed lines, but to lend us his own beloved 30-hp outboard, provided we would agree to treat it as one of the family. Pat contributed the observation that unless I agreed to treat it much better than one of the family, the engine was surely doomed. He had meanwhile pulled the wires out of the way of the drive shaft, so we were at least able to start our engine, and now, as we slid down the canal, every half hour or so an additional electrical installation would begin to work as, on his back, the electrician worked chirpily away in what proved to be dreadfully uncomfortable weather with heavy swells.

We could not get stability from our sails because the wind was from the south, and Mrs. Taylor began to vomit regularly, causing Pat, who has never quite believed that I don't secretly control a weather switch, to stride back from time to time to the wheel to accuse me of *deliberately* trying to kill her mother. Suddenly the wind swung right around, and we quickly lifted the mainsail. Ned proudly fastened a brake strap to the drive shaft, to prevent the propeller from turning unnecessarily while the engine was turned off. An hour or so later Christopher and the very young first mate began to lower the dinghy, the electrician's precious family outboard attached thereto, into the water, so that it would be readily available to us on coming into the harbor in Miami. They were unskilled at this operation, with the result that the flowing water suddenly caught the edge of the dinghy, swamped it—and the second outboard flew out into the water.

Without a second's hesitation the young mate dove overboard. "Keep your eyes on him!" I shouted to Christopher, tossing over the life ring. I then started up the motor and slipped the boat into gear. Mrs. Taylor roused herself from her comatose state to point out in a weak voice that smoke was coming up from directly under her. "Great God!" said Ned, shouting to me to put the gear back into neutral. He had forgotten to loosen the strap. He disappeared below, and in due course told me I was free to engage the gear. We hauled up into the wind, dropped the sail, and in ten minutes were abeam of the mate, who said proudly he was certain he was still swimming directly over the outboard engine.

The electrician, smoked out from his ghetto below by the drive-shaft fire, was marvelously stoical about the separated member of his family, but took careful bearings—depth of water, triangulation on points of land, etc.—and said that the next day, in daylight, he would venture out with his son and try to find the motor with a scuba outfit; and so, we resumed our way, dropping anchor in Biscayne Bay forty-five minutes later, feeling as if we had crossed the ocean. Ned hung out an oil anchor light of which he was very proud, fastening it on the headstay, and Mrs. Taylor began to revive as her daughter and friends began to joke about our maiden voyage. She did not, however, say anything until, finally, she looked at me and said, "Bill, dear, is there supposed to be a fire up there?"—pointing to the bow of the boat.

The kerosene light, for reasons unknown, had fallen into the collapsed genoa below, which was now beginning to light up like a bonfire. Ned Killeen rushed forward with a fire extinguisher. The electrician, who had finally emerged sweatily from his completed task, a Coke and a sandwich in his hand, continued eating. "You know," he said, "I've been doing marine electrical work for years, but this is the first trip I've ever taken except on my fishing dinghy. Is it always like this?"

I knew she would be the first to speak, even though I'm fast at the draw. "Yes," said Pat, calm as Ethel Barrymore. "Oh, yes. In fact, tonight was one of the more *peaceful* sails we've ever *had*."

It does not exactly classify as a misadventure of the perils-of-the-sea variety when your ship sinks and you are not in it, but it is the kind of thing that creates apprehension in people like Pat, and even in people unlike Pat.

It was only two months before our first Bermuda Race, and the office operator told me the boatyard was calling. (I have, by the way, long since discovered how, if you want to get through on the telephone to otherwise unapproachable people, you do it to yachtsmen. You simply tell the operator you are calling from the boatyard. No yachtsman in the history of the world has ever been too busy to talk to his boatyard.) It was Miss Swann. Miss Swann is imperturbable. Her voice is high, but softly pitched. But what she had to inform me of this morning simply could not be done equanimously. It would have been a violation of taste, a confession of—insouciance.

"Mr. Buckley, I'm afraid I have some bad news."

"What is it, Miss Swann?"

"*The Panic* sank."

"Sank?"

It transpired that, going down to the dock that morning, the yardmen had seen, in the space previously occupied by a forty-four-foot cutter, only fifty feet of mast rising straight, indeed, proudly, one supposes, out of the water. Everything stopped, and the whole force of the yard was mobilized to pump out the boat and bring her slowly to the surface.

The damage was unspeakable. When the seawater reached the level of the batteries, the acid drew out. Since the hull was made of steel, the entire boat was converted, so to speak, into a huge magnetic field which corrosively began to gnaw away at the wiring, reducing it in a few hours to copper filigree.

Miss Swann having prepared me, she put me on to Mr. Muzzio, the volatile, peppery, omnicompetent owner of the yard.

We would need, he said, new wiring throughout, a rebuilt engine, a new generator, all new upholstery, a new radio direction finder, a new radio-telephone. He was sure the sails had survived—they had been quickly washed in freshwater. The gas and water tanks he thought would survive. And he did not know whether all that work could be completed in time for the Bermuda Race, but he would make every effort.

"What happened?" I asked.

"I don't know," he said. "We checked all the sea cocks. They're okay." If Mr. Muzzio didn't know what happened, it was unlikely that anyone would know; but even as the work began, I found it endlessly disconcerting that the boat, sitting jauntily at dock one night, three days after it had last been sailed, should simply... sink. I have found that there is something less than an unquenchable intellectual curiosity among professional boat people. The insurance company had to pay out $10,000 to put *The Panic* right, but I found it impossible to engage the company's inspector in anything like an exhaustive discussion of what might have been the cause of it all, even though Stamford, CT, does not lie within the perimeter of the Bermuda Triangle, where one Isn't Supposed to Ask What Happened. The reason there are so many mysteries at sea is that nobody bothers to try to solve them. This particular mystery, continuously disconcerting—I was half afraid to leave *The Panic* at anchor alone for the balance of the year—was

solved, quite accidentally, under circumstances more hectic than the sedentary, regal sinking in the womb of Muzzio Brothers Boatyard.

It was over a year after my family had rechristened my boat *The Ti-panic*,
and we were racing from Annapolis to Newport. All night long we had tack-
led against a relentless southerly, fighting our way down the Chesapeake. At
10:00 in the morning I was off duty and sound asleep, with Mike Mitchell
at the wheel, when Reggie woke me. In his calm way he told me to look
down at the floorboards. They were underwater. I jumped up, tore open the
floorboards and saw a mass of water overflowing the bilges, rushing up into
the lockers with every leeward roll of the ship. Reggie and I could feel no
water coming into the boat from the engine water-cooling system or from
the stuffing box. A quick investigation of the sea cocks showed them to be
in good working order. Two crew members were mobilized to work the big
hand pump. Working steadily, they managed only just to keep pace with the
leak. I raced back to the cockpit, and Reggie, Mike, and I conferred. The
water is shallow in the Chesapeake, and in the southern section there are
stretches of mud and sand at depths of two feet. We decided the only thing
to do was to head for a sand shoal and beach *The Panic* before it sank under
us. I took the wheel and a bearing, bore off the wind and headed for shallow
water about a mile away while Mike jumped into the bilges to have his own
look. Seven or eight minutes later he ambled up, a smile on his face and a
beer in his hand. "Let's get back on course. I found the trouble."

The electric bilge pump, which Reggie had switched on even before waking me, was of course the first mechanism I checked, and it was humming
away industriously, though its capacity was insufficient to keep up with the
flow of water coming into the boat. But Mike, unsatisfied, unscrewed the
hose from the pump, thinking that perhaps the rubber impeller had burned
and, if he replaced it, we might get some relief. He found that the pump was
working fine, except that instead of drawing water from the boat into the sea,
it was drawing water from the sea into the boat. Astonished, he turned the
switch off, then on again—and suddenly the flow of water was in the right
direction. In a minute or two he could see the water level receding.

Here was the mystery, solved. An electrical pump sucks water from the
bilge and pressures it up a hose that becomes a copper pipe rising above the

water level outside the boat. The pipe elbows around, and the water falls by gravity down the pipe and out to sea through an open sea cock.

We could now easily reconstruct what had happened. A piece of mud or sponge or whatever had been sucked up from the bilge and was rising under pressure up the pipe just at the moment, sometime during the night, when the bilges were last checked, and a crew member, finding the bilges dry had turned off the pump. There the foreign matter lodged, beneath sea level, like a cork, sustaining the weight of the water above it. In due course the cork began to dissolve, and the dammed waterfall poured into the bilge, creating a suction sufficient to bring a continuous flow of water up from the sea to the elbow. And now, by the law that specifies that water will seek its own level, Chesapeake Bay was happily filling up the cavity in the hull of *The Panic*. And, of course, the more water we took in, the lower the boat sank, guaranteeing a disparity in water level until our boat's decks were level with the sea. At this point water would cease flowing into our bilges, a point of only academic comfort since the boat would now sink like a full bathtub. When Reggie turned the electric pump on, the impellers were set into motion, but the pressure of the water flowing down redirected the innocent pump's energies, which now added mechanical pressure to the gravitational pressure bringing seawater into the boat. It was instantly clear what had caused *The Panic* to sink the year before, but on that occasion it had taken two-and-a-half days for the clot in the pipe to disintegrate.

Three months after every Bermuda Race and every Annapolis-Newport Race, which run in alternate years, comes the last of the season's major ocean races, the annual Vineyard Race, in which I had made my debut the year before. This time I was the skipper. We had rounded the lightship and were headed now 130 miles almost due west, to the finish line at Stamford. Mike was at the tiller when I went below to sleep. The spinnaker was flying under a stiff northeasterly, the fog was pearly thick, and we posted a member of the crew forward to listen hard, away from the distractions of cockpit talk and grinding winches, while every few minutes we sounded our own fog-horn and occasionally looked up at the radar reflector, designed to attract maximum attention on the radar screens of the big boats.

I slept fitfully, and in due course was summoned to relieve Mike. It was nearing midnight and, always the competitor, he was very excited. *See over there!* he pointed ahead. I could make out a few lights through the fog: a stern light and masthead light, and perhaps a flashlight. "We're overhauling that poor bastard!" Mike exulted, handing me the tiller. He stepped up from the cockpit to experience from the deck the special pleasure of sliding by a competitor. Mike was right. We were getting closer and closer. I checked the compass—dead on the course I had stipulated. I eased the bow the slightest bit up to make certain we would be comfortably to wind-ward of the boat. Then came the screech, the ricocheting crunch of steel bouncing over rocks and, in a moment, motionlessness.

There is nothing to match the motionlessness of running solidly aground. It is as if concrete had suddenly hardened around you. Now that we were no longer moving downwind at eight knots, the wind on our backs was eight knots stronger. A hundred yards away was the boat we were pursuing, now plainly visible: two forlorn streetlights, one mile north of Point Judith. We were two miles off course.

I looked down at the compass in dismay. Even now it pointed us in the direction I had charted. All in due course. Meanwhile there was urgent work to be done. Already Reggie had the tide tables out. He told us in his matter-of-fact way that we were one hour and a half past low tide, that the water would be high just before 5:00 in the morning. We called Peter, who was thirteen years old and asleep in the forecastle, but there was no rousing him. We pulled up 100 yards of chain past his ear, and 200 yards of line, and he heard nothing. The boat's steel hull ground away on the rocks, and he heard nothing. We put our heaviest anchor into the dinghy, and dragged it 100 yards back, tying it to the heavy nylon line. We strung a second line from one of our heavy genoa winches, forming a bight ten yards out to sea, back to the corresponding winch at the other end of the cockpit. To the end of the bight, we tied the anchor line. Now we had a harness of sorts, allowing us to apply simultaneous pressure on both winches. Thus prepared, we began working the boat aft, using also the reverse power of the engine at full rpm. We succeeded in moving about five yards, but we came then on something like an underwater stone wall, over which, under the careening force of eight knots, *The Panic* had leaped. She was not about to leap back over even at the urging of a couple of No. 4 winches. We finally stopped and I cut the motor.

It was the moment to call the Coast Guard.

To my astonishment, the Coast Guard station at Point Judith, which, after all, was almost within hailing distance, acknowledged our distress signal immediately. After a considerable conference at the other end, we were advised that we lay in waters so pock-marked with rocky shoals that no Coast Guard vessel could approach us to bring help without endangering itself. The officer recommended that we wait until the next day and get a barge from Newport to float us out. We were not, after all, in any personal danger, the Coast Guard reminded us—all we had to do, to start out life afresh, would be to abandon ship and walk to the beach. And, to be sure, wake up Peter.

There was nothing to do except to make a massive effort at exactly high tide. To lighten the boat, we emptied our water tanks (we had 120 gallons, which at about eight pounds per gallon is a lot of weight). It was then, I think, that, noticing the spotlight was weakening, I decided to put a fresh battery into it to be ready for the big effort at four thirty, but I couldn't find flashlight batteries. Mike poked around. "Here it is," he said, opening the binnacle box. I removed the battery. "Do that again," Reggie said, "—and look at the compass." The battery removed, the compass changed its heading 11 degrees. I can't remember exactly what I said. I think it was "Shee*yit*." I had recently read *The One Hundred Dollar Misunderstanding* and was much influenced by its idiom.

We made it, but it was close. If the wind had been from the southeast, we would not have had the lee of the peninsula opposite, and the waves during the night would have battered the boat to pieces. A wooden boat would probably not have survived. As it was, the damage to the keel and rudder was extensive.

That was the episode I thought we could safely conceal from our families without any problem at all, and it was agreed all the way around. There was, theoretically, no need to conceal it from Peter, who was entirely unaware of it, waking relaxedly at about 7:00. I would simply say that we had withdrawn from the race because our spinnaker had blown out, and there was no substitute. In the early afternoon we stumbled into a marina in New London and docked. I went to the telephone and reached Pat in Vancouver, 3,000 miles away. Her first words were peremptory: "What time did you get off the rocks?" At least she said it before listening to a vivid narrative about the decomposition of the spinnaker.

I could not tease out of her the sources of her intelligence until, home from her visit to her parents, she finally broke down, with great relish. She had been at a cocktail party while her father, at home, listened on the radio to the evening news on what must have been a very slow night, because the last item was to the effect that the Coast Guard in Boston had reported that the cutter *Panic*, owned by the writer William F. Buckley Jr., was on the rocks off Point Judith, RI. My father-in-law was a heavy man of decisive mien and habit. He dispatched the chauffeur for his daughter, authorized only to instruct her that she was to return instantly to the house. There with great solemnity he gave her the news, and in due course the Canadian Admiralty in Ottawa was on the telephone to the Coast Guard in Boston, which relayed back a conversation with Coast Guard Point Judith to the effect that nothing more had been heard from *The Panic*, but that there was no reason to fear for the safety of the crew. Mike's father had heard the same broadcast, and welcomed his son home exuberantly with a new drink, "Point Judith Scotch" (on the rocks).

Airline Update
February 8, 1977

RIO DE JANEIRO, Brazil—It has been a while since I filed one of my occasional reports on air travel, but now I must caution against flying by Viasa, the Venezuelan airline, if you are among those who a) desire to read aboard an airplane; or b) prefer not to eat lunch at three in the afternoon; or c) tend to prefer the company of amiable crew. It is probably unfair to file a report based on a single experience, but it is equally unfair to fail to pass along the word after two consecutive experiences.

To be sure, waiting at the airport in Rio de Janeiro is especially trying. The other day the temperature there was 110 degrees. The airport is not air-conditioned. There is a single room there that is cooled, but access to it requires that you call twenty-four hours ahead to reserve a seat. This may strike you as unreasonable, since in the United States we are not accustomed to going to airports for the purpose of going to waiting rooms. But it makes a certain amount of sense in Rio where—just to begin with—the habit of mind is bureaucratic. At that same airport, if you want to check a bag in the baggage room, a form must be completed in quadruplicate, including your passport number.

But the main reason for waiting at the Rio airport is, presumably, because flights by Viasa don't usually land on time. Why then not wait at home, or in your air-conditioned hotel, knowing that the flight will be late? Because there is no way of ascertaining whether a particular Viasa flight will be late: You see, Viasa does not answer its telephone.

Two-and-one-half hours late, the flight to Buenos Aires finally took off, and since it had turned dusk, the handful of passengers on board turned on their reading lights. A faint glow issued, rather like wartime London protecting itself against the blitz. Questioned, the stewardess tells you blithely that no one has ever complained before: you tell her that, as of this moment, the record is broken, but she does not smile with you. FLASH! Why not go forward to the compartment with the table in the first-class lounge.

You do so, and the light is gratifying. But in a moment, in storms the Jefe de Cabina. "This lounge is reserved for the crew." Surely not, you say: It is clearly an amenity for all the first-class passengers—and nothing less than an oasis for those who have work to do, and need light to do it. Besides, there are approximately 104 empty seats on the plane, wherein provided they don't want to read, the crew could relax.

The steward retorts that the crew has been working for nine hours. You retort that you have been sitting two and one half hours in Rio and worked seven hours before that, and that it is not your responsibility that the airplane is late: whereupon—the ultimate weapon!—The Chief of Cabin, who ought to be featured in Viasa's next series of advertisements, turns off the overhead light, leaving you in the dark. Ah so. The *Jefe de Cabina* does not know that I can type in the dark.

Three months ago, boarding Viasa in Panama at 2:30 p.m. for a three-hour flight to Caracas, a Teutonic stewardess with brushed-back blonde hair, plunked assorted cold matter in front of me at 2:45, and I observed that having lunched at 1:00, I had no appetite at 2:45, but would be grateful for the sustenance at, say, 4:30. She harrumphed, as if I had made an improper proposal, that refreshments were being served now, and not again! There is of course no point in eating when you are not hungry—unless you are a bear preparing for hibernation: so, I passed. But I did observe the lady who, a good two hours before landing at Caracas, everyone having been served, reclined in her chair, there being nothing to do. Save possibly hate passengers. If her thought turned to contempt for patrons of Viasa, I must concede that she was intelligently occupied.

By and large, Venezuelans are the most hospitable people in the world. But there are some who become positively Russian in their attitude toward customers. The Russians, as readers of Mr. Hedrick Smith's wonderful book will recall, actively resent patronage of any facility by which they are employed. My own experience suggests that the Teutonic lady, and the Jefe de Cabina will be happy only when their airplanes are entirely empty of passengers. They may not have long to wait.

Keeping Cool in Cozumel
Motor Boating & Sailing, March 1977

There is something awfully alluring in sailing to a *foreign* country. But no foreign country is finally exotic if the natives speak English: thus, a trip to the Bras d'Or Lakes in Cape Breton, though there is much to be said for it, is not quite the same thing as it would be if M. Lefevre and his Parti Quebecois practiced a little irredentism and recaptured Fort Lonisbourg. One of the charms of the Leeward Islands is the need to accommodate to a different language virtually every time you throw out your anchor. Sailing to Europe meets all the tests, but is something of an enterprise. Sailing to Yucatan is less than a transatlantic labor. Indeed, Miami-Yucatan is less than Newport-Bermuda. But you achieve the feeling of having slipped away to a remote and thoroughly foreign country, and as a matter of fact you have.

When you dwell on the distance between the Dry Tortugas and Isla

Mujeres—290 miles—you need to fight the feeling that your outing has been on the order of driving from San Diego to Tijuana. It is more than that for several reasons. Not the least of these is that lying in wait for you if your attention flags, just a few miles to the south, for over one half the distance, is Fafner, guarding the forbidden treasures of Cuba. How far offshore from Cuba, I asked my friendly patron at the State Department, must I stay? They assert three guiles of territorial sovereignty, and twelve for Customs, I was told; but it does not do to tease them in the matter, as Lloyd Bucher did the North Koreans. On *no* account slip past the twelve-mile limit.

"What happens if you do?" There's the rub. *Anything* can happen. One day a little Cuban Coast Guard vessel will politely usher you back out of Gulag waters. But another day, the same vessel will take you to port, seize your boat and submit you to a large dose of the People's Hospitality, for days, maybe even weeks, depending on the temperature of international relations and the caprice of the Maximum Caudillo. The mere presence of Castro over one hundred miles or so of coastline is bracing, in the morbid way the Berlin Wall is bracing.

Although determined that on setting out from Miami aboard *Cyrano* the ship would be totally prepared and equipped for the journey, the fore-knowledge that we would be passing by Key West encouraged a kind of nonchalance inappropriate to the preceding excursion, a year earlier, when the identical crew, save one substitute, set out from Miami bound for Marbella in Spain. This time we knew, subconsciously, that any egregious act of neglect could be corrected ninety miles down the road.

I had my ritual bout with technology, which struts its imperfections with special flair aboard *Cyrano*. This year it was the single-sideband radio-telephone. This wonderful machine we had used with extravagant delight going across the Atlantic. But no sooner had the vessel returned when the telephone company announced a new rate structure. The rate had been a dollar or two per call plus the local rate, so that a casual phone call from, say, Longitude 25 to Longitude 75 was something of a bargain. No more. The item escaped our attention until, after our Christmas cruise, the telephone bill came in, which I returned to the phone company with a cheerful note suggesting they oil their computers and send us a fresh bill.

The awful news transpired by return mail. The rate is now a flat $5 per minute, and that's how much it is even if you are only just out of reach of the VHF channel, say thirty miles out of Miami. Hardly the way to encourage the diffuser graces of rhetoric. I put in a call to the vice president in charge of extortion, and was dismayed to learn that the new rate schedule had indeed been approved by the FCC upon presentation of the financial records of the operation, which documented the loss sustained by the company on its high-seas operations. Moreover, said the telephone company official, the ocean-telephone business is not a government-protected monopoly: anyone can get into the act, and, in fact, a station in New Orleans, WLO, has set up an antenna, and we were welcome to hire its facilities if we wanted to, and found them cheaper. Accordingly, I had given instructions to install a WLO crystal.

By the time we finally told the technicians (there were two) who had fussed over the installation for four hours, "Never mind, please just let's begin our trip," they had mutilated our beautiful telephone, so that a) the emergency antenna would not put out on the crystal that goes to the Coast Guard, b) five of the crystals have never worked again, and c) we never did raise WLO.

The other problem was the air conditioner. The heat, in Miami in early June, can be fearful, and was in 1976. *Cyrano*'s captain accosted the problem by the simple expedient of telling me that the air conditioner was working just fine, putting up his hand against the grill, where the milk-warm air lisped out, and then withdrawing it sharply, as if taking care to guard against frostbite.

A word on the subject: a passage to Yucatan in June is a passage into the hottest latitudes on earth, and if you are disinclined to suffer from oppressive heat, you should either not go then, or else you should equip your boat with air-conditioning—which isn't that expensive these days. The idea of an air-conditioned sailboat—I judge from published comments about a recent book—strikes some as indefensibly ostentatious or effete, raising the question: Why? Protection against the weather is the most elementary biological need, after food. It is as perplexing to me that a sailor intending to spend time in the tropics should wish to air condition his boat, as it is that he should desire his boat to be leakproof. Sure, the generator presents a problem: but so does one's preference for a boat that doesn't sink. It is one thing to say that a particular sailboat is designed in such a way as to make it impossible to adapt it to air-conditioning: that is good, plain, responsible talk, to which the good, plain, responsible reply is: Don't sail in that sailboat to Yucatan, especially not in June of 1976.

One day, at noon, diligent in my pursuit of navigational precision in order to keep a safe distance from the Cuban shore, I brandished the sextant for the noon sight, and found myself contorting my body in order to keep the sun on the horizon. I looked reproachfully in the direction of my son at the helm, expecting to see him chatting away while the boat (we were tinder power, no wind) did lazy figure eights. But he was grimly engaged in keeping his course, and I found myself examining my sextant, wondering why the sun was executing circles around the horizon mirror. That is the generic reflex, like kicking your television set when Eric Sevareid goes out of control. But my eyes suddenly focused on the altitude registered on my sextant, and it was 90 degrees! I looked at the Almanac and, indeed, the sun, at that moment, was *directly overhead*. Since there was no wind, and the humidity was not unexpectedly, high, we could lay claim, however fleetingly, to being located in the hottest spot on earth. I went below, closed the hatch, turned on the air conditioner and recorded the event.

The passage from Miami to Key West is insufficiently celebrated. It is the ideal way to prepare for an ocean voyage. What you have is about ninety miles of water protected from the ocean by a string of shoals and beaches, assuring you lakeside security from swells and waves; but a stretch of water open enough to receive the full stimulus of the wind. Since going down Hawk Channel, as they call it, the course sets off to the south, then eases off toward the west-southwest like a slow golf slice, you are nicely situated in a southeasterly, first to proceed close-hauled, then gradually to relax the sails. It is a dream sail, permitting you to stop anywhere, throw out the anchor, and declare this your own private, landlocked sanctuary.

We left Miami at 11:30, ran aground smack in Stiltsville Channel at 12:15, called the Coast Guard at 12:16, which appeared (most obligingly as always) at 12:30, in a large Whaler, the command of a bright and energetic young man who, however, was visibly embarrassed inasmuch as, after attending to our own needs, he had to call the Coast Guard himself a) on our telephone, because his didn't work; to report b) that his motor was disabled. We kept him company until a mother ship arrived.

There were no other problems, but when, two days later, we slipped out of Key West, we got no further than 100 yards when a rain squall broke over us, cutting visibility to zero. We quickly dropped anchor and waited the forty-five minutes until it passed. Then, preparing to pull away, we were arrested by an electric bullhorn from a police car onshore calling my name—was I aboard? An emergency telephone call. A dramatic political interruption. At the pay station I learned that Ronald Reagan, running hard against Gerald Ford for the Republican nomination, had in the past twenty-four hours been made to sound as if he proposed to send the Marines to Angola and Rhodesia. An expert on the Rhodesian situation, a friend who gave my name, had proffered his aid. Question: Is he an okay guy? Yes, I said to Reagan's aide, cleverly concealing that what was on my mind (it is ever so at sea) was not civil war in Rhodesia, but—would there be a succession of squalls during the night?

Negative, as it turned out. And as we slipped out of Key West, and up the northwest channel toward the departure point for Dry Tortugas, the air conditioner in perfect working order, the crew flaunting its sea legs, the sky turned Prussian blue. We threw out the anchor and cooked dinner, the stars coming out, a profusion of diamonds on a jeweler's velvet, and a fresh wind came up from the northeast. We set out for Dry Tortugas, due west sixty miles, coming in at dawn to the gloomy, isolated fort, most famous for having infamously detained the wretched Doctor Mudd to whose house, craving medical attention, the crippled, anonymous assassin hobbled haphazardly a few hours after firing a bullet into the head of Abraham Lincoln.

From Dry Tortugas to Isla Mujeres on the northeast of the Yucatan peninsula the distance is 290 miles, the course 226 degrees. But in order to pursue this route, it is required that you head directly into the Gulf Stream, which races up the Yucatan Strait and eases northeast, swirling around Cabo San Antonio at the western tip of Cuba. Accordingly, it is advisable to cut your losses and sail south, say toward Bahia Honda, 100 miles away. From there to Isla Mujeres it is about 220 miles, so that you have gone thirty miles out of your way, but to avoid (at seven knots) a set of as much as 100 miles. It is unfortunate that the winds are characteristically from the northeast, so that you can't even count on gliding home after working your way there; indeed, on the return passage *Cyrano* had miserable northeasterlies, with squalls and winds up to fifty miles an hour, heavy rains, and entirely too much togetherness with supertankers coming down in the opposite direction.

Twenty-three hours after sailing our leisurely way from Tortugas, we descried the mountaintops of the western Sierra range. During the day we groped against the current in a windless, overcast day, straining by a radar that worked only intermittently to make out the Cuban coastline. That night, still without wind, the radar suddenly elected to work, and I put *Cyrano* on autopilot, and, with my son, came forward into the huge, sybaritic cockpit and lay back on the settee that sprawls over half the area when the dining table is down, the autopilot controls in my hand.

Outside it continued to drizzle. Inside it was dry, the radar blipping the little clusters of rain squalls, and with the autopilot we did what we could to maneuver around them, like a jet pilot operating in extreme slow motion, at one hundredth of a jet's speed. Occasionally, responding to the pressure of my thumb, the boat would turn left provocatively toward Cuba, and we would watch the radials studiously, and just before hitting twelve miles, with a switch in pressure the boat would turn east, even as the jaws of Castro's radar, in our fantasy and perhaps in fact, were readying to close. A few hours of that and we slipped away from the dreary Cuban coast, and trudged in lifeless water across the Yucatan strait. Whenever gloom began to set in, I would console myself by reflecting how acutely unhappy I would have been if we had been racing, forced to wallow in the current during that long, dull, windless day.

Just after midnight Reggie came up triumphantly from his solitary confinement next to the Loran, where he had imposed on himself a sentence to serve until the Loran yielded one coherent reading. This one was quickly validated when we discerned lights—first the flashing white off Contoy, then the Cancun light, between them Isla Mujeres, where we docked at eight in the morning after one of those endless approaches to which this

sailor will never become accustomed—you see the light, and expect within
the hour to arrive at its source; which may be four hours away, given wind
and current. The delay presaged *mañana*. We were definitely in Mexico.

Mujeres is a Mexican version of one of the Greek islands. There is a
combination of bustle and indolence. We were perfectly introduced to
the bureaucracy when the Customs officer asked for a form apparently
procurable from US Customs, notifying foreign governments that a US
vessel is leaving home waters without stigma. In the absence of this form,
Customs announced we would be fined $80. This elicited a gasp of indig-
nation, which, one gathers, is a typical reaction, because the official retreat
was instantaneous. Instead of paying $80, we must type out, in *quadrupli-
cate*, the name and document number of the vessel, the names and home
addresses of everyone on board, and a flight plan of sorts—where we
intended to sail in Mexican waters. A half hour later, this was done on my
little portable, and taken to Customs by Danny, age twenty-four, who in
due course returned to say that I would need to re-execute the form, in a
specified format, *e.g.*, the surnames of the crew must appear in CAPITAL
LETTERS—that kind of thing. So, I fished back out the three sheets of car-
bon paper and began again, painstakingly. I sent Danny with the freshly
typed forms, and in twenty minutes he was back again. I would need to
type them yet again, this time omitting the names of any ports save the port
immediately after Mujeres....

A year earlier, at an aerie in Switzerland, I was introduced to the Honorable
Miguel Aleman, former president of Mexico. We conversed in Spanish, and
he asked how was it I knew the language, and I replied that among other
things I had once lived in Mexico. When? he asked. Why, while he was
president. You don't mean it! Yes, 1951. What were you doing in Mexico?
Well, I was in the CIA, and my boss was Howard Hunt...I have had *extensive* experiences in Mexico, and know that the moment comes every now
and then when you have to call a halt. So, I accompanied Dan to Customs,
and said that rather than complete their form in quadruplicate one more
time, I would simply leave Mexico, there and then, return to the United
States and perhaps write about my experiences, in place of cruising in

Yucatan. An urbane native, sitting on a chair to one side of the inspector, commented that Americans were hardly in a position to complain about Immigration and Customs formalities, given that he had once spent seven hours in detention in Miami pending the validation of *his* papers. I told him I thought that regrettable, and refrained from suggesting that there is more contraband traveling into the United States from Mexico than in the other direction; and the tension broke when the inspector said, well, he would probably be fined for his permissiveness, but I was free to go my way, he would accept my forms; but, of course, I now had to give my clearance to Immigration. Where was that? At the airport. Thither we went, the rest of the crew having gone off for lunch.

At Immigration we reported to the designated window, at one side of which hung a large government poster with the words, "*En México creemos en el valor de una sonrisa. Séamos amables con los turistas.*" (In Mexico we believe in the value of a smile. Let's be pleasant to the tourists.) The problem was that no one was there to be pleasant to us. But, in due course, someone arrived; stamped one copy of our form for us, one for himself—forms no one would ever again consult—and we went off to a prettily situated but pretentious French beach restaurant, where we ate a hugely expensive, utterly forgettable lunch, under a thatched roof on the beach, looking out over the strait of Yucatan.

The waters around Isla Mujeres are brilliantly blue. To the south, the new resort of Cancun is opening up, with its Atlantic City-sized beach. We spent most of the day trying to diagnose our generator's problems: it had blown a head gasket. We resolved, rather than expose ourselves to the vagaries of local labor, to persuade our mechanic in Miami to take the hour-and-a-half flight to Cozumel. When he arrived, he told us we were lucky indeed he was a friend of *Cyrano*'s, otherwise he would charge us what *others* would charge us for making the trip. His continence was revealed in his bill, in which he charged $18.50 per hour for three twelve-hour days. He arrived late in the afternoon of day one, and left in the morning of day three. Subsequently the generator needed overhauling. But we were hanging in there, by our fingernails, to our air conditioner.

The night before leaving for Cozumel, we pulled out of the commercial dock at Mujeres and followed the shoreline to the north, searching out the lee, to drop anchor and have dinner. This we did opposite the Zazil Ha Hotel, and I do believe I never saw, anywhere—not in the Bahamas, not in the Antilles, not in Greece—such a feast of blues. As the sun went down the sky turned white, then mother-of-pearl. Off to one side was a shipwrecked shrimp boat. It caught the sun, and the rusty hull turned golden.

We ate the fish Reggie caught late that afternoon, and then, with the cassette player beginning with Mozart and regressing to rock as the younger generation quietly asserted itself, we played poker. After our game Christopher and Danny took the dinghy into town, which at 11:00 p.m. seemed barbarous enough. But when at one thirty they returned and, instead of going to sleep, began a fresh game of cards, the captain, owner, and father of one of the delinquents announced huffily that if they were not wide awake at 8:30 a.m. we would eschew a visit to Cancún, where I knew they wanted to visit. What sanctions does one have left, attempting to govern a twenty-three-year-old boy? Deprive him of a visit to Cancún! That's it! Pass the word along.

Cancún is not easily visited by boats drawing six feet. It has the air of an island not *quite* ready to receive the hordes of pleasure-seekers. Two days later, while we were in the island of Cozumel, fifty yards to the south Henry Kissinger, decompressing from a state visit with President Echeverria, stopped over at Cozumel for the weekend, and apparently recovered quite nicely. It is a pity, after six years of Echeverria, that all of Mexico couldn't have had a weekend at Cancún.

The passage to Cozumel was downwind, and we hoisted the gollywobbler for the occasion. The younger generation groans when the seizure comes on me, and I order the gollywobbler hoisted. This is because raising that sail requires slightly more coordination than is easily accomplished by young men who suddenly find their hands unoccupied by a) a cigarette, and b) a bottle of beer: destroying their equilibrium.

In any event, the sail was splendid, and it was nice to know that we were gliding down the gold coast of the Mayans. We tacked downwind, carefree and gay and, a couple of hours after dark, approached the port of Puerto Abrigo. This is done with trepidation, because so far as I know there is no proper chart of the island of Cozumel. And so, over a period of one hour, we glided north, and then south, attempting to find the telltale harbor channel lights. Finally, we telephoned the local Coast Guard and asked for instructions. These came in in very rapid Spanish (one assumes they had heard the request before), and the distances were given in terms of hotels. "Proceed four-and-a-half hotels south, approach the shore, and you will see a green and red light." There is ambiguity as to whether a particular building is a hotel, or merely a brummagem profile of one.

So, finally, we dispatch the whaler with the younger generation, with instructions please to find the channel entrance. They are equipped with the newest of *Cyrano*'s accessories, a walkie-talkie; and, *mirabile dictu*, it works. In due course they beckon us to the dimly announced passage, which requires you to enter, and then quickly U-turn into the docking area; which, once found, is entirely satisfactory, equipped with power, water and fuel—and an impatient diesel mechanic, in from Miami, waiting to fix your generator, so that you can face the tropics with equanimity.

Cozumel would be the end of the line for most of us. I admire those who can combine cruising with sightseeing. This requires not only a flexible schedule, but skill in adapting to two kinds of living simultaneously. I am a Stakhanovite sightseer, but I do this listlessly off a sailing boat, preferring perfunctory visits in the lands and islands I visit. Twenty-four hours after landing at Marbella in Spain, following a thirty-day crossing, we were on an airplane headed for home. We did poke about in Cozumel, but the archaeology is not particularly interesting. To visit Yucatan properly, you would need to re-cross the strait, and go inland, which Christopher and the return crew went on to do.

We satisfied ourselves to cruise about the island on motor bikes. If you do this, do not fail to stop for lunch at the Faro (the lighthouse) on the southwestern tip. There is an old couple and (I guess) two or three little grandchildren. Their kitchen is inside a withered old tent, where charcoal burns and, when the mood is upon them (at first they declined our invitation to prepare us hunch), they will come up with fresh fish, and with the best tortillas and tacos I have ever had. The Faro is situated close to the Palancar reef, to which we sailed the next day, giving Danny and Christopher a couple of hours in what is reputedly as fine a living area as you can find. Unhappily, the day was sunless, so that the colors were gone, and when this happens underwater it is as if the sunset were rendered in black and white.

In Cozumel there is nightlife (C&D reported); but, truth to tell, sailing to Cozumel is more interesting than visiting in Cozumel. The passage is the thing, surely; and the passage to Yucatan is worth making; indeed it can be exhilarating. But be careful that you do not run into Cuba, or succumb to the heat. And come armed with the archaic form from Customs, USA, and listen to the old sailors describe, from their wheelchairs, the difficulty in making out the harbor entrance of Cozumel.

Flying at Yale
Flying, September 1977

I had no fear of flying when I matriculated at Yale but a very considerable fear of my father's learning that I had taken up a sport that, in 1946, he was unprepared to concede was anything other than rank technological presumption, fit only for daredevils. It turned out that several of my coconspirators had fathers with similar prejudices, so that when our little syndicate was formed, we all agreed that communications to each other on the subject of our surreptitious hobby would go forward discreetly, lest they be intercepted. During the Christmas holidays, it was my duty to send out the accrued bills from the little grass-strip airport at Bethany where we lodged *Alexander's Horse* (as we called the little Ercoupe), and I realized, envelope in hand, I could not remember whether T. Leroy Morgan, one of the six partners, was a junior. With a name like that, I felt he must surely be a junior—was there any other excuse? On the other hand, if I wrote "Jr." after this name and my friend was in fact the "III," then his father would open the letter. I assumed his father must be formidable, since who else would live at One Quincy Street, Chevy Chase, MD?

So, to play it safe, I addressed the letter to: "T. Leroy Morgan—the one who goes to Yale, One Quincy Street, Chevy Chase, MD." It happened that, at the breakfast table distributing the mail among the family, Mr. Morgan *père* displayed an imperious curiosity about the contents of a letter so manifestly intended to be seen only by his son.

I will contract the suspense and say that in no time at all, the word passed around a circle of fathers, reaching my own. Whenever my father was faced with rank transgression by any of his ten children, he replied to it in one of two ways, sometimes both. His first line of attack would be to announce that the child could not afford whatever it was my father disapproved. He tried that for an entire year in his running war against cigarettes, but the effect was ruined when we all saw *The Grapes of Wrath* and Henry Fonda, between heaves of hunger, kept smoking. His second line of attack would be to ignore the delinquency, pretending it simply did not exist. Thus, one of my brothers, who hated to practice the piano, was relieved from ever having to play it again by the simple expedient of being held up by my father in public discussions of the matter as the most exemplary pianist in the family.

I received a brisk memorandum (his reproachful communications were normally rendered in that mode) advising me that he had "learned" that I was "flying an airplane" at college, and that the distractions to my academic career quite apart, I clearly could not afford such an extravagance. One didn't argue with Father, who in any case would never return to the subject except in a vague, sarcastic way. Three years later, he would write my prospective father-in-law, "You will find it very easy to entertain Bill when he visits you. You need only provide him with a horse, a yacht, or an airplane."

And so, for the few months of our joint venture, we continued to pass around the bills, like tablets in pre-Christian Rome. They were not, by current standards, frightening. Our capital was $1,800—$300 apiece. We paid that exactly for the secondhand airplane. We decided, after getting quotations from the insurance companies, to insure ourselves, subject to a $300 deductible payable by the offending partner. Anyone using the plane would pay his own gas, oil, and instructor. All capital improvements would have to be approved unanimously. Anybody could sell his one-sixth interest to anyone at any time. Reservations to use the airplane would be filed with the secretary of the *Yale Daily News*. These, we satisfied ourselves, were surely the most informal articles of association in modern history, though I suppose it is appropriate to add that the association was one of the briefest in history.

I was off to a very bad start. My experience was akin to arriving at a casino for the first time at age twenty and winning a dozen straight passes at the crap table. When Bob Kraut, my instructor—a dour, hungry ex-army pilot, ex-mechanic, owner of the starveling little airport, who would sell you anything from a new airplane to a Milky Way took me up for an hour's instruction, I could not believe how easy it all was. I remember it to this day: check the oil, check the gas, turn your wheel and check ailerons, pull and check elevator. Run your engine at 1,500 rpm, check one magneto, then the second, then back to both. Then gun her up to 2,250. Then exercise the knob that said "carburetor heat." Then head into the wind (or as close as possible at the single-strip field), push the throttle all the way forward, roll down the strip, when you reach 60 miles per hour ease the wheel back, and after the plane lifts off, push the wheel forward to level until you reach 80 mph. Then adjust your trim tab to maintain a speed of 80 mph. Rise to 600 feet on your course, then turn left until you get to 800 feet. Then do anything you want.

Landing? Go back to approximately where you were when you hit 800 feet and proceed downwind twice the length of the field while descending to 600 feet. Then turn left descending to 400 feet. (I forgot something: you should pull out your carburetor heat when you begin your descent.) Then turn in toward the field, reducing your throttle to idling speed, coast down, glance sideways which helps perspective, don't let your speed fall under eighty miles per hour till you are over the field, then keep easing the wheel back until your tires touch down, at which point *immediately* set your nose-wheel right down; Ercoupes, you see, had no separate rudders, the wheel incorporating that function—nice advantage except that you cannot cope easily with crosswind landings.

The first lesson consumed an hour, the second a half hour, and that very night I was speaking to a forlorn junior who had been a pilot during the war and grieved greatly that he could not be the following day at dinner with his inamorata in Boston. Why could he not? Because his car wasn't working, and no train would get him up in time, since he could not leave until after lunch. I found myself saying, as though I were P. G. Wodehouse himself, "Why my dear friend, grieve no more. I shall fly you to Boston."

It was all very well for my friend, who with 2,000 hours flying, navigated us expertly to Boston, landed the airplane and waved me a happy goodbye. I was left at Boston Airport, headed back to Bethany, CT, never having soloed and having flown a total of three times.

Well, the only thing to do was to proceed. I remembered that the plane came equipped with a radio of sorts and that my friend had exchanged arcane observations and sentiments with the tower coming in, so as I sashayed to the end of the runway, I flipped the switch and found myself tuned in to an episode of *Life Can Be Beautiful*. I truly didn't know how to account for this, and I remember even thinking fleetingly that when the traffic was light, perhaps the tower entertained area traffic by wiring it in to the controller's favorite program. This bizarre thought I managed to overcome, but it was too late to stop and fiddle with a radio I hadn't been instructed in the use of, so I went through my little motions, looked about to see that I wasn't in anybody's way, and zoomed off.

I was flying not exactly contentedly that bright autumn day. I felt a little lonely, and a little apprehensive, though I did not know exactly why. I was past Providence, RI, when suddenly my heart began to ice up as I recognized that either I was quickly going blind or the sun was going down. I looked at my watch. We should have another hour and a half of light! Ah so, except that I had neglected to account for the switch overnight away from daylight saving time. I had put forward my watch dutifully at about midnight, but today I thought in terms of light until about 7:00 p.m., same as yesterday. I looked at the air chart, so awfully cluttered and concentrated by comparison with those lovely, descriptive, onomatopoeic ocean charts you can read as easily as a comic book. I discerned that the New York, New Haven, and Hartford railroad tracks passed within a few hundred yards of the airport at Groton. I descended, lower and lower, as the white began to fade, as from an overexposed negative soaking up developing solution. By the time I reached Groton, I was flying at 100 feet, and when I spotted the lights on the runway for the airfield, I was as grateful as if, coming up from the asphyxiative depths, I had reached oxygen.

I approached the field, did the ritual turns and landed without difficulty—my first, exhilarating solo landing; my first night landing; on the
whole, the culmination of my most egregious stupidity. But there we were:
plane and pilot, intact. I hitchhiked to the station, waited for a train, and by
ten o'clock was sitting at a bar in New Haven, chatting with my roommate
about this and that. I never gave a thought to Mr. Kraut.

I have been awakened by angry voices, but by none to equal Robert
Kraut's the following morning. While hauling the plane from the hangar,
an assistant at the airfield had overheard me conversing excitedly with my
friend on my impending solo flight from Boston to New York. In the inter-
nalizing tradition of New England, he had said nothing to me about my
projected violation of the law. But he spoke to his boss about it later in
the afternoon, who exploded with rage and apprehension. Kraut called the
tower at Boston, which told of an Ercoupe having landed and then taken
off at 4:07, without communication with the tower. Kraut calculated that
I would arrive in the Bethany area in total darkness and thereupon began
frantically collecting friends and passersby, who ringed the field with their
headlights, providing a workmanlike illumination of a country strip. Then
they waited. And waited. Finally, at about ten, Kraut knew I must be out
of fuel and, therefore, on the ground somewhere other than at Bethany.
Whether alive or dead, no one could say, but at least, Kraut growled into
the telephone, he had the pleasure of *hoping* I was dead. *Why hadn't I called
him?* I explained, lamely, that I did not know he even knew about my flight
let alone that he thought to provide for my safe return. He consoled himself by itemizing lasciviously all the extra charges he intended to put on my
bill for his exertions and those of his friends, which charges the executive
committee of *Alexander's Horse* associates voted unanimously and without
extensive discussion would be paid exclusively by me.

I got my clearance to solo; and, twenty flying hours later, my license to
fly other people. I am compelled to admit that I cheated a little in logging
those twenty hours, giving the odd half-hour's flight in the benefit of the
doubt, listing it at one hour, and I feel bad about this. But I did achieve
a limited proficiency, and I would often go out to the field and take up a
friend for a jaunty half hour or so in my little silver monoplane, though I

never felt confident enough to do any serious cross-country work, having no serviceable radio.

I remember two experiences before the final episode. In the early spring I invited aboard a classmate, a seasoned navy veteran pilot. We roared off the lumpy field under an overcast that the mechanic on duty assured us was 1,200 feet high. It wasn't. The Bethany airport is 700 feet above sea level, and at 1,000 feet, we were entirely enveloped in cloud. I had never experienced such a thing, and the sensation was terrifying, robbing you, in an instant, of all the relevant coordinates of normal life, including any sense of what is up and down. We would need, I calculated, to maintain altitude and fly south until we figured ourselves well over Long Island Sound. Then turn east and descend steadily, until we broke out unencumbered by New England foothills; then crawl over to the New Haven airport, which is at sea level. I willingly gave over the controls to my friend Ray, who assumed them with great competence as we began our maneuver. Then suddenly there was a hole in the clouds, and he dove for it, swooping into the Bethany strip, landing not more than three minutes after our departure. I stayed scared after that one and resolved never again to risk flying in overcast.

Then there was the bright spring day with the lazy-summer temperature. My exams, it happened, were banked during the first two days of a ten-day exam period. In between I did not sleep but did take Benzedrine. Walking out of the final exam at five the second afternoon, numb with fatigue and elation, I was wild with liberty, and I knew I must stretch my limbs in the sky. So I drove out to Bethany, pulled out *Alexander's Horse* and zoomed off by myself, heading toward downtown New Haven and climbing to 4,000 invigorating feet. There I fell asleep.

I have ever since understood what they mean when they write about the titanic intellectual-muscular energy required to keep one's eyes open when they are set on closing. What happened was that the drug had suddenly worn off, and the biological imperative was asserting itself with vindictive adamance. It was, curiously, only after I landed that I found it relatively easy to summon the adrenalin to stay awake for long enough to make it back to my bedroom. In the tortured fifteen minutes in the air, my eyes closed a dozen times between the moment I discovered myself asleep and the moment I landed. It is safer to learn these things about the human body aboard a sailboat than an airplane. Boats can be dangerous, but they don't often sink when you go to sleep at the wheel.

My final flight, like so many others, was propelled by a certain mental fog. My best friend at Yale became engaged to my favorite sister. All my siblings had met Brent, save my poor sister Maureen, cloistered at the Ethel Walker School, in Simsbury, CT. I would instantly remedy that, and I wrote my sister, age fifteen, telling her to send a map of the huge lawn that rolls out from the school (which I had many times seen while attending various graduations of older sisters). It arrived by return mail on all accounts the most nonchalant map in the history of cartography. At the east end, she had drawn vertical lines marked "trees." Running parallel from the top and bottom of that line to the west were two more lines, also marked "trees." At the extreme left end of the paper she had marked "main schoolhouse." Armed with that map and my future brother-in-law, I set out on a bright spring afternoon for Simsbury, which was about an hour's flight away.

I found the school and flew around it a couple of times with a creeping agitation. My sister, having advised her classmates of my impending arrival, the entire school was out on the lawn, and, when they spotted us, their great cheer reached us through the roar of the little engine. The trees at the east side happened to be the tallest trees this side of the California redwoods. I buzzed them a time or two. Could they really be *that* tall? I estimated them at a couple hundred feet. That meant I would have to come over them, then drop very sharply, because a normal landing approach would have had me three-quarters down the length of the lawn before touch-down. "Well," I said to my stoical friend, "what do you say?" Fortunately, he knew nothing about flying.

I was terribly proud of the way I executed it all, and I wished Mr. Kraut had been there to admire the deftness with which I managed to sink down after skimming the treetops, touching down on the lawn as though it were an eggshell. I looked triumphantly over to Brent as our speed reduced to 30 mph. The very next glimpse I had of him was, so to speak, upsidedown-side-ways. We hit a drainage ditch, unmarked by my sister, that traversed the lawn. The problem now was quite straightforward. The aircraft was nosed down absolutely vertical into the ditch, into which we had perfect visibility. We were held by our seat belts, without which our heads would be playing the role of our feet. We were there at least a full minute before the girls came. I am not sure I recall the conversation exactly, but it was on the order of:

"Are we alive?"

"I think so."

"What happened?"

"Ditch."

"Why did you run into it?"

"Very funny."

"Well, why didn't you fly over it?"

"We had landed. We were just braking down."

But the girls, with high good humor, giggles, and exertion, managed to pry us out. We dusted ourselves off outside the vertical plane, attempted languidly to assert our dignity, and were greeted most politely by the headmistress, who said she had tea ready in anticipation of our arrival. We walked sedately up the lawn to her living room, accompanied by Maureen and two roommates. The talk was of spring, Yale, summer plans, the Attlee Government and General MacArthur, but Maureen and her friends would, every now and then, emit uncontainable giggles, which we manfully ignored. It all went moderately well under the circumstances until the knock on the door. An assistant to the headmistress arrived, to ask whether her guests had any use for "this," and she held forth *Alexander's Horse's* propeller or, rather, most of the propeller. I told her thank you very much, but broken propellers were not of any particular use to anyone, and she was free to discard it.

Eventually we left, having arranged by telephone with Mr. Kraut to come and fetch the corpse at his convenience. We returned to New Haven by bus. Brent, who had a good book along, did not seem terribly surprised, even after I assured him that most of my airplane rides out of Bethany were round trips.

Oh, the sadness of the ending. The plane was barely restored when, during a lesson, one of my partners was pleased by hearing his instructor say as they approached the strip for a landing, "You're hot!" My friend figured, in the idiom of the day, that this meant he was proceeding splendidly, so he nosed the ship on down, crashing it quite completely. As he later explained, what reason did he have to know that, in the jargon of the trade, to say you were "hot" meant, "You're going too fast"? He had a point. The estimate to repair *Alexander's Horse* was an uncanny $1,800—exactly what we had paid for it. Mournfully, we decided to let her rest, selling the carcass for $100. Father was right, as usual. I couldn't afford to fly.

Better Leave Washington Alone
June 22, 1978

WASHINGTON, DC—One expects, in Washington, a certain lassitude, the expression of the bureaucratic spirit, and one comes on it quickly. Even as— the pollsters tell us—throughout the land a universal suspicion of Washington increases, it becomes increasingly difficult merely to get there, as if the transportational facilities of the nation shrugged off the responsibility for carting victims to the Aztec sacrificial atone.

Years ago, in the sleepy days of FDR when there were only a couple of million people in Washington engaged in telling us all what to do, you could board a train at New York any time after 10:00 p.m., and it would ease out of Pennsylvania Station sometime after midnight, well after you were sound asleep in your roomette, arriving comfortably at 7:00 a.m. Now there is Amtrak, and the people on Amtrak are the kindest and most attentive in the world. Indeed, the bartenders act as though they were employed by the Intensive Care Unit.

The only trouble is that Amtrak is hardly ever on time; the parlor cars suited to one's work load are regularly and arbitrarily removed, indeed full trains are regularly cancelled; the train bed must have been laid down back when Abe Lincoln was rail-splitting. And when you arrive, late at night in Washington, your chances of finding a porter are about 50 percent. That's no problem if you are lucky. If you are unlucky and have two bags, a briefcase, and a typewriter, you have bought a trip on Amtrak and an Alpine experience.

The other way to go to Washington is via Eastern's shuttle. This is to be avoided at all costs, but given the infrequency of alternative possibilities aboard American Airlines, all costs include the cost of not going to Washington when you want to go. The Eastern airplane is probably the most uncomfortable in regular service in the United States. Six passengers abreast, hip-room designed for John Travolta, no coffee, no booze, seats that don't recline. I can think, as a competitor for discomfort, of only one other run: New York to Pittsburgh via Allegheny on TWA. However, in due course you arrive, as I did last Sunday for an extensive stay of five days carrying one large suitcase, three briefcases, and one typewriter, which debouched in due course into a baggage room with no (zero) porters.

What to do? Needless, to say, there were no passenger trolleys lying about—that will only happen when the Passenger Trolley Act is passed, at which point a scarcity will develop.But I detected a porter's professional trolley, wheeled it out of hiding, explored its secrets, and went off, devoting a full fifteen minutes, with my trolley, to promenading about the bowels of (NO ADMITTANCE! EMPLOYEES ONLY!) National Airport, trying to trace the succession of ramps that led to the taxi staging area, where in due course I arrived, and was greeted by the dispatcher with no sign of surprise.

In due course, as befalls all virtuous men, my time came to leave Washington, and with great wit I outfoxed the Eastern shuttle, booking a flight on American Airlines at 3:05. I arrived to be advised that the airplane would leave at 3:55. No explanation.What was in operation was—a "Slowdown." A slowdown is the device by which disgruntled employees disrupt an operation by interpreting strictly every regulation issued.

What happened was that the people who man the control tower at Washington had been told that the next time they flew to Europe they would have to pay something for their passage instead of getting it free, poor darlings. Accordingly, they expressed their petulance by causing 25,000 or so travelers, who had contributed nothing to the decision of the offending airlines, to spend three hours traveling from New York to Washington or back (there was a further delay of one hour in the airplane). No explanation was tendered. A distinguished old gentleman, seated beside me, was greatly indignant. His plane had suffered the domino effect. Why wasn't the action of the employees a civil offense? How is it that a small group of Americans can affect the lives of a large number of other, innocent, Americans, without running any civil exposure whatever?

I attempted to console him. You must try to understand, I said. Washington is *designed* to afflict innocent people. Whence the inertial impulse of the great carriers to bring you here.

"Why are they so reluctant to take you out of here?" he asked. I was about to reply: "To punish you for having come," but I didn't feel like wisecracking.

A Touch of Sicilian Class

Saturday Review, June 24, 1978

I can name my favorite restaurant as glibly as I can name my favorite wife, country, religion, and journal of opinion. It is (I should like to say "of course," but Paone's is not widely known) Nicola Paone, its address is 207 East Thirty-Fourth Street, New York City, and I suppose I have eaten there a hundred times in the last ten years, which would certainly account for my being Paone's favorite customer, but, believe me, in this courtship, I was the suitor.

Mr. Paone, though entirely gregarious, is a somewhat mysterious figure. One gets to know right away that though born in New York, he was raised in Sicily, that by training he is a singer, a self-accompanying (guitar) balladeer, who every now and again disappears to make a tour of Latin America. His restaurant brings you the unobtrusive sounds of Mr. Paone plucking his guitar, in random, improvisatory melodies—just the right kind of music for background—but one does not hear his singing voice, ever, and that is one of the little mysteries in this two-room restaurant that seats about forty people, and is devoted to the pursuit of extramusical perfection.

Another thing one learns quickly about Mr. Paone is that although hospitality is, along with perfectly prepared food, the other cardinal virtue, it is a hospitality that requires an unaffected reciprocity. Specifically, men must wear coats and ties. Those tieless pilgrims who wander in are given most discreetly the alternative of wearing one of Mr. Paone's own ties or of being ushered, gently but firmly, to the door. I had a wonderful experience having arranged to meet there for lunch the fabled science-fiction writer Theodore Sturgeon, in from the West Coast, whom I had never before met. I was a minute or two late and was accosted outside Paone's by a man dressed up as Mephistopheles—everything save a red velvet tail. It was Sturgeon. He had entered Paone's and in no time at all was redirected to the sidewalk. He was quite miffed about it, as we headed off toward some fish restaurant, explaining that he took great pride in his resplendent costumes because they were especially designed and cut for him by his talented wife, who aspired among other things to be a dress designer. Mephistopheles and I got on to other subjects, but Mrs. Sturgeon cost him lunch at Paone's.

And then too, for over ten years Mr. Paone would not permit women wearing slacks. My other embarrassment came on making an engagement there with Barbara Long, the writer whom everyone knew except me, and who suffered from infantile paralysis in her youth. Her crutches were not discernible in the sudden dark of the anteroom just off the midday sun, so that Mr. Paone's assistant, Franco, politely advised her that she could not enter wearing slacks. Mr. Paone, for all that I cite his hospitality, does not keep extra women's skirts about; so, she trudged up the stairwell, to the street, into my embarrassed arms. After that episode, Mr. Paone changed the rules. But the kind of behavior that is sometimes associated with sloppy dress somehow never happens at Paone's. The pressures being implicit. It would hurt Mr. Paone's feelings, which one wouldn't want to do, and if one did, one has the feeling that all the Sicilian blood would suddenly rise to his temples, and he would dispatch you most neatly (he likes to tell you that, literally, one could eat off the floors of his kitchen). The thing of it is, about Paone's, is that its owner desires a perfect experience for his guests, from the moment they enter until the moment they are (escorted) out. He will carry his share of the burden—the service, and the food. Necessarily, the guests must carry their share (no rowdiness). To interrupt the decorum is worse merely than to create noise or distraction; it is to rent the veil of the temple. An act of profanation, the awful equal of, say, an overcooked fillet of fish. I have never seen it happen and cannot imagine it happening. And yet the atmosphere is in no sense repressive. It isn't like when you were a little boy sitting at the captain's table on the *Normandie*. It is a part of that total sense of security you feel on ordering the brook trout and knowing it will be—perfect.

At Paone's, service is given the same priority as food, and if what you want is a glass of wine or a Bloody Mary or a (ugh) Coca-Cola, it will be there before your eyes have become accustomed to the dim light, the rather routine decor, the fifteen tables with ample passageway between them (a few years ago, Mr. Paone enlarged the restaurant without adding a single seat). And, eventually—at uncannily the right moment—you are brought a large wooden board on which is written the menu. Not only is it in Italian, it is in some cases in *ad hoc* Italian, since Mr. Paone is given to naming the dishes he invents (half of what he serves he has, so to speak, composed). What I find myself saying to my guests is: "Everything here is superb. Pasta, veal, chicken, beef, fish." A few years ago, dining there, I left behind some lecture notes, the disappearance of which I discovered disconsolately on returning home at midnight. I was leaving on an eight o'clock flight and thought perhaps I'd be lucky enough to find the janitor at Paone's at six in the morning to let me retrieve my notes. Who let me in was Mr. Paone (who lives in Scarsdale). Already he had been to the markets to buy the fish, and the meat. I think he would be physically ill if made to eat a fish that hadn't been swimming twenty-four hours earlier.

But I always make Mr. Paone, or Franco, perform because their descriptions—always the same—are inimitable, and I have secretly transcribed one or two of them. There has never been such zucchini as Paone will serve as an appetizer, and I ask him to describe it…"We boil them"—he speaks with the pronounced enunciations of an actor, and he manages to bring an almost libidinous excitement as he proceeds with his description: "—*al dente*, firm, a few drops of oil, a sprinkle of *parmigiano* cheese…pepper, if you wish, and…*pronto*, ready to enjoy them." It does sound silly, but I am always transfixed. The only thing I know how to cook is fudge, which I learned to do as a boy, but for the life of me, I cannot transpose my recipe into Paonese.

I fancy there his fish *Malandrino*, and ask for an explanation: "Fish *Malandrino* is a simple and light dish. We debone a fillet of sole, prepare little (note the missing indefinite article, which is a part of the flavor) rice with a subtle flavor of onion, put it in between the two pieces of sole, sandwiched sort of, and then bake with a touch of dry white wine, few drops of oil...and serve it with its own gravy."

The fettuccine is of course made in the house; and prepared in the kitchen. It is hardly possible, Mr. Paone explodes, to get proper help to carry dishes. "Imagine if we also gave them the responsibility for cooking the fettuccine!" It is incomparable, but if you are malleable, Mr. Paone will persuade you instead to order *Serenata*, "one of our modest creations." It— or, rather, "they"—is noodles "mixed with cream and cheese: ricotta in the center covered with more noodles...cream on top...first baked...then under the broiler until it acquires that blondish color...ground black pepper is *magnifico* with it."

Since as a child I swore I would never willingly eat livers again, I must mention the *Primavera*. "We prepare chicken livers in an unusual way. Then sliced prosciutto, the livers placed in the center, wrap the prosciutto around it, baked...and served with a special white wine sauce."

The wines are, by the way, available for inspection in the second of the two rooms, the wine room in the rear just before the kitchen. The supply is inexhaustible, and I have made few efforts to remember their names leaving it to Mr. Paone or to Franco to suggest a wine according to the mood. The house white wine is a California Chablis, of unknown and undiscoverable label—a house secret. The wine glasses hold exactly one quarter of a wine bottle, and are filled to the brim, never mind French protocol. I end my meals at Paone's with espresso and a cigar, and for this I am widely pitied, because the restaurant is famous for its homemade (all by Mr. Paone himself) desserts.

At Paone's, if you are told on a particular day that you must have the broccoli, or the asparagus, or the melon—order it, unless you have a mortal allergy. If I were commanded to order a simple meal for someone at Paone's for a single experience, I think I'd put in for the zucchini to begin, followed by the pompano and a small side order of fettuccine. But nobody, I think, has only one meal at Paone's.

Yes, as I feared, someone would ask about the price. It is expensive. Even so, I would judge from Midtown experiences that there is a rebate on the order of 20 percent for the indignity of having to travel all the way down to Thirty-Fourth Street. Console yourself that if Paone's were located in the East Fifties, it would be even more expensive, but the food and service wouldn't be any better, because that isn't possible.

Bumming Around Fiji

Motor Boating & Sailing, March 1979

Saturday

But yesterday was Thursday, the international dateline having been traversed, and by the ache in our bones and spirits, yesterday seemed a week ago, a thousand hours having been spent in the cramp of the economy section of a jumbo-jet-filled SRO. For my wife Pat and me the ordeal, if not exactly speaking intolerable—as a historical fact we survived it—was only just short of that. We cannot imagine having survived what our companions went through—Barbara, Bindy, Vane, and Drue are the stuff of which the Battle of Britain was won. They had flown from London nonstop to Los Angeles where we, after spending a leisurely day there, met them at the international airport.

One hour after they landed, we were all off on the 747 to Hawaii, seated cheek by jowl. I longed for the arrival there on the assumption that the great plane would immediately empty, leaving us room to stretch out on the next leg. Surely not everybody flies on to Fiji, I thought smugly; to which the reply is: Nowadays practically everybody *does* fly on to Fiji, notwithstanding that Fiji is as far (southwest) from Hawaii as London is from New York. Exactly as far south of the equator as Hawaii is north of it.

If you leave the main island of Fiji (there are about 300 islands in the 250,000 square-mile Fiji group) and head straight south, you will eventually hit Auckland. For those who care about these matters fastidiously, a nice way to remember where Fiji is is as follows: What meridian lies exactly opposite Greenwich, England? 180 degrees west longitude, obviously. What is one tenth of 180 degrees? Eighteen degrees. And—indeed—that is the southern latitude that runs through Fiji, which gives you the coordinates. I thought it would be amusing to feed into my HP97 computer the question: How far is it from Fiji to London? And: What course would one give to the navigator starting out?

I tapped the data into my little machine, only to have it—after struggling fitfully in a paroxysm of flashing, hiccoughing figures—stop dead with the word, in red-light tracery, ERROR. I could not understand this, and so tried again, only to be accosted once again with ERROR. That is a pretty abrupt way to talk back, it struck me, to a purchaser, in a competitive market, of a machine that costs $750—a machine, moreover, that is designed and sold by terribly polite people.

I reflected on it, and then programmed the query again, but this time using 179 degrees west longitude instead of 180 degrees as the starting point, and the answer, after orderly gyrations, calmly popped out (8,789 miles at 001 degrees). The problem was that the machine had been asked to settle the question whether in going from Fiji to London you should head northwest or northeast, the distances being exactly equal. Hewlett and Packard are simply not going to decide such matters for you. I mean, certain decisions are for you alone to make.

Before trying out the 179 degrees alternative, I thought to consult with Vane—we were all seated about a table in the hot noon sun, by the swimming pool, ordering sandwiches and drinks, having slept for three or four air-conditioned hours in the luxury of the Regent Hotel at Nadi, where the planes fly in. I had had no experience of Vane (pronounced VĀH-NEE) at this point, other than sleeping on each other's laps during the cattle run from Los Angeles, and clearly he thought to apprise me once and for all of a difficulty that has plagued him over the six decades of his hyperactive life.

Although a stout Croatian nationalist who deems himself a Yugoslav patriot first, last and always, and would gladly hang Tito on a sour apple tree to prove it, Vane is British to his fingertips—to the elocutionary demisemiquaver, having been schooled in the UK right through Oxford and lived there much of the time, though his homes are in Monte Carlo and Mallorca. His manner—kind, courteous, witty, unobtrusively emphatic—goes naturally with his well-set aquiline features, his graying, disciplined hair; a man accustomed to coping authoritatively with every sort of difficulty, from double agents to Fiji waiters.

Vane's problem is that his air of competence inspires everyone, on the least acquaintance, to take their problems to him. Why did a computer decline to give a civil answer? How does one insert a film into a recalcitrant camera chamber? Why did the outboard engine suddenly refuse to start? As a miserable matter of record, Vane explained to me, he is totally incompetent in all mechanical matters. He is quite certain—he is excited now, as he spins out his complaint while sipping his Puntamés—given the relative progress of the forces of evil over the forces of good, that before his exquisitely toned body (he jogs morning and night) finally collapses from natural decrepitude, he will be had up by some Bolshevik firing squad, the leader of which, looking quizzically at the newly issued rifles, will approach Vane while tied to the stake and say, "I wonder, sir, would you mind telling us just exactly how these rifles work?"

Ah, but in one discipline, arguably mechanical, Vane knows all. He is certainly the equal of the best scuba diver in the world, and unquestionably the finest teacher of the art/science. So I had been told by the organizer of this whole enterprise, Jack, common friend of everyone present, who had been detained by the death of a friend. I myself having prepared for this sailing-scuba diving expedition in the Fijis by spending one hour in a swimming pool in Puerto Rico with a fine instructor who was eloquent on the disadvantages of drowning while under water, I made a note not to irritate Vane with any further questions that presumed any technical knowledge on his part, indeed probably I carried my attentiveness to sycophantic lengths when Bindy, having asked Vane to pass over a spoon, I pointed to the spoon, lest Vane, in his helplessness, not know to distinguish it from a fork.

It occurred to me, after the hamburger and beer, to look about and see what it is about Fiji that hits you right away. Answer: Nothing. The Regent Hotel could be a super-luxury hotel in any tropical area anywhere in the world. The air is about what you would expect for spring in the Tropics. We would learn something extremely important, which is that although most of the books tell you that the rains and the clouds come to Fiji only after the first week or two in November, those books may be statistically correct but are by no means to be counted on. Nadi is at the west end of the big island

(Viti Levu); Suva—which is the center of all boating activity, and where you start from when you head out to sea on a charter boat—is about 100 miles away, to the southwest.

There it rains 140 inches per year. And most of that rain is during the three or four summer months, beginning in November. During the ten October days we were with the party, we had spotty sun for only two or three days. I read a lot about Fiji, to be sure a lot of it in travel bureau prose ("Stretches of Uncrowded White-Sand Beaches…Palm Trees…Inviting Lagoon…The Fijian Format for Rediscovering Yourself. You are fifteen miles due west of Nadi International Airport. You have just moved onto an idyllic South Sea island with picture-postcard, white-sand beaches and bending palm trees. You strip off your city clothes and dive into the sea…and here you are. Suspended in the silk-warm water…motionless.") But nothing to suggest you might find yourself motionless because if you move without moving the umbrella along with you *pari passu*, you will be deep in silk-warm water even while standing at a street corner one mile from the beach.

But our spirits were very high. We would take the little island-hopper (a Viscount turbo-prop, if memory serves) for the trip to Suva, put up at the Tradewinds Hotel overlooking the yacht basin, and set out the next day, after Jack joined us. From our hotel rooms we had the first glimpse of the great *Tau*, sitting in her slip, crowded with the usual chaos of children, electricians, plumbers, banana-vendors, and other umbilical cords that surround any large boat at the outset of a charter. She is a great yawl, designed by her architect-owner Captain Philip, who also built the Tradewinds Hotel. The dimensions (ninety feet over all; mainmast of 110 feet) are noble. But, viewed through the drizzle, one must be frank: the boat's topsides are painted in two shades of brown, what must have been the finals in a worldwide contest to select the most emetic brown pigment imaginable. I do not know which was the winner, which the runner-up.

And then, in the rear, commencing at about amidship, a strange structure which we ended up referring to as "the spare garage." It was wonderfully useful for laying out all our scuba gear, and would have been useful for storing, say, five thousand cans of tuna fish. It was not useful for much more, having only church-pew benches in it, suitable for convoying prisoners to penal colonies.

There were of course many other factors to be considered in judging *Tau*, but to these we were not to be introduced until the next day when, formally, the charter began; in a drizzle; with Jack; but without Jack's bags, which had been lost by Pan American, which had lost them undoubtedly because Pan Am was preoccupied with looking for the lost bags of Jack's wife Drue, which had been lost on our trip from Los Angeles. But we set out, to the mouth of the harbor, and we were happy in the spirit of those who come together to begin an enterprise in the distinctive unity only a boat imposes.

Monday

Jack's bags arrived, along with a few delicacies carried aboard by a half dozen native porters, and we were ready to go. One should know, in sailing the Fiji Islands, that the distances between islands are not inconsiderable. More like the Antilles, say, than the Virgins, or the Bahamas. The winds are as one would expect, ranging from northeast to southeast—I had consulted a weather chart, in a think-session with Jack, at which during the summer we made a major mistake. I shall try to remember to tell my grandchildren that just as, in order to fall, one must first rise; so, in order to travel down-wind, one must first travel upwind. We are now all agreed that it would have made sense to ask the skipper to deadhead *Tau* east—perhaps as far as Tonga (500 miles); certainly as far as Mbalavu (150 miles). Because what lay ahead was a lot of very uncomfortable sailing, concerning which a few generic remarks.

During the initial trip to the island of Ovalau, sailing on the wind, the *Tau* ripped its mainsail, depriving us of practically all lateral stability. No effort was made to mend it while underway, and it transpired that the captain, a man of great resourcefulness and, even at age seventy-two, resolution, had never heard of such American commonplaces as sail tape. We departed without battens, without adequate stitching paraphernalia, so that when, the following day and thereafter, we hoisted the mainsail, it was reefed, the tear having ripped the bottom one-third of the sail. The battens were never replaced, so that the noise of the flapping leech was almost always with us during the windward passages.

Having chartered a dozen boats, and chartered out one of my own, I take leave to express a rule of thumb. Boats longer than about fifty feet are thought by owners or captains to be—in fact—motor sailers. Experience teaches them that 90 percent of the time, the engine will be on. Sometimes the engine is required merely to move: I have traveled on boats the profile of which would appear to qualify them to race out of Cowes or Newport, but when the sails are (usually with some reluctance) hoisted: suddenly nothing very much happens. A decade's accretion of big propellers, huge water and fuel tanks, and myriad heavy, comfortable, junk, have all but immobilized them as sailboats that will cruise at eight or ten knots. At that point the captain waits patiently for *ennui* to set in among the charterers. In my case this happens quickly, and, thereafter, the sails are used primarily for the purpose of steadying the boat. In the case of the *Tau*, with its huge mast, one would have expected a moderately zippy performance under sail. Nothing of the sort on the wind. The genoa was cut like a bikini, and if we had relied on canvas to get us anywhere, these words would have been written at the other end of the international dateline.

Probably the principal fault is the charterer's. He tends to ask for mutually exclusive amenities. He wants both spacious state-rooms *and* sportscar performance, wind-wise. He wants scuba diving equipment for six people (our situation) and twelve-meter performance under sail. The postwar designers have done a great deal to achieve livability in small (forty-foot) racing sailboats. But the difficulties increase exponentially, and those who charter a sailing boat of ninety feet expecting both to sail and to luxuriate are going to do one or the other, almost inevitably the latter, since that turns out to be the preference, given the alternatives, of those who charter huge sailing boats. However, the captain or owner is not absolved from responsibility. He should frankly acknowledge the limitations of his vessel, if only to tamp down the revolution of rising expectations. And, of course, there is no organic reason for failure to carry extra battens, or sail tape, or stitching gear.

An appropriate moment, as I think back on that first day's sail—in the drizzle, and against the seas to Levuka Harbor—to define a rule I have finally decocted, and wonder that it has not been formulated before.

The sea, if you leave aside for a moment the factor of vicissitudes, which obviously overrule even the most elaborate fine-tuning, is an invitation to a number of things, one of which is tranquility. I lay it down as an unchallengeable, uncontradictable proposition that there is an irreconcilable incompatibility between very loud noise and tranquility. One can, of course, get used to anything. In the play *My Sister Eileen*, where the two principals lived in a basement apartment next to the Third Avenue El in New York City, which, before it was torn down used to roar by every seven minutes with a noise the designers of the Concorde would have pronounced intolerable, the author-director managed a marvelous manipulation of the players and the audience by causing the actors, every seven minutes for about ten seconds, to raise their voices to screaming pitch as though nothing unusual had happened. After a while the audience almost failed to notice the difference, much as one gets accustomed to old record noise, training the ear to listen only to Caruso.

But on the other hand, noise is noise, even as ugliness is ugliness. There are instruments that measure with scientific exactitude decibels of sound. Since this is the season for constitutional amendments, I propose one that would require every charter spec sheet to give out the decibel level, at engine cruising speed, 1) in each stateroom; 2) at the cockpit; 3) at the dog house; 4) in the main saloon. The prospect of a five-hour run from one Fijian island to another under power in hostile sea conditions varies in the intensity of discomfort to a significant degree with the intensity of the engine noise.

I know one or two people whose conversational patter has made me long for the relief of the robust noise of passing subways; but there were none such aboard the *Tau*, and when the engine operated, which was most of the time during the eastward passages, communication was virtually excluded in the principal areas of social congregation, and inflected conversation could only have taken place in the crow's nest. I found that most of my companions sought out narcotics, either in escapist literature, spirits, or sleep: not infrequently all three, a useful progressive curve... Why is it, on cruises, that one tends to nap in the afternoon? An odious bourgeois indulgence. We tell ourselves it is the wind and the salt and the exuberance of corporal health. I say it is probably nature's reaction to an unnatural licentiousness at lunch, a guard against the possibility of boredom during a long day; and—I say this with utter gravity—a means of attempting to solace oneself against a grinding, encephalophonic engine noise which, however we adjust to it in the manner of our sister Eileen, insinuates its insidious vibrations into our nervous system leaving us, at the end of a day's experience, with the ocean's equivalent of jet lag. A kind of noise lag.

Tuesday

A great day. Unforgettable. Where oh where have I been? Why did nobody tell me? (Everybody did, for years, but I did not listen.) The divers were convening for the first plunge. But to begin with, Vane would check me out—to see what I could handle after my hour in the swimming pool. I proudly displayed the gear I had bought on leaving New York. To wit: 1) a knife; 2) a snorkel tube; 3) a face mask; 4) an inflatable life vest; 5) flippers; 6) boots for the flippers; 7) an underwater watch; 8) gloves; 9) defogging liquid; and 10) an illustrated textbook called *Safe Scuba*. Vane cast an eye on it all and told me he thought the flippers exaggeratedly big, made to go with the boots, which were unnecessary: he would lend me some appropriate flippers. The vest was okay, though he didn't believe in them. The face mask leaked and the purge mechanism, through which one blows out water that gets into the mask, didn't function. The gloves were adjudged too coarse for the requisite flexibility. I didn't need the watch, but I did need a depthometer, which Vane provided, and a speargun, ditto. My knife was fine, and it turned out that the book, when Bindy finally opened it one evening, was good for hours of entertainment.

Vane took me down, in stages, to seventeen feet, after first lecturing me sternly on the point that there is no such thing as a macho diver, there are only stupid divers, defined as those who continue to go deeper even after feeling pain in their ears. You "clear" your ears (there are technical ways of saying all this) by applying pressure, over the rubber of the mask, to close your nostrils and then attempting to blow through your nose. Either you do, or you do not, experience instant relief. If you do, proceed on down. After another ten or fifteen feet, the pain will resume. Clear away. And proceed.

DON'T GO DOWN FURTHER THAN 120 FEET. Because below that depth odd things happen to the nitrogen content in your blood, to dissipate which your rise to the surface has to be achieved more gradually than your tank's capacity makes possible. When you do rise, do so gradually. It is a good idea, while ascending, to breathe out. When there is no breath left, pause, inhale—and then resume the ascent while exhaling. At the surface a dinghy that has been carefully following you by tracing the wake of your bubbles will be waiting. Its pilot will lift the tank off your back, collect the other paraphernalia and, perhaps a little chilly—but certainly greatly exhilarated—you will reboard the master vessel, maybe with a fish or two in Vane's pouch.

Except that my mask leaked a bit, I found it as easy to habituate myself to underwater life as I would to get used to a freshly discovered Mozart symphony. The pleasure of the weightlessness...of three-dimensional movement...the disappearance of gravity...the lights in greater, more playful variety than ever seen before...the underwater life which, observed behind the glass of aquariums seems menacing and slimy, now, suddenly friendly, frisky, endearing, though Vane pointed at a crevice in a shoal shaking his fingers and forming an M with the two thumbs and index fingers—all of which was later explained to me as the means of warning against a Moray eel he had spotted. We descended to 120 feet, and I never felt more carefree, even while looking, more frequently than my experienced companions, at the gauge that indicated how many of the precious thirty minutes of air were left to me.

The Fiji Islands are famous for the opportunities they give you to dive. I wish I could successfully transcribe the formulae by which Vane led us, day after day, to the wonder spots, but one could as easily explicate the dowser's art. He did require, I remember, that the water be deep, preferably over one hundred feet. The tide should recently have come up against the reef structure, which is something like an underwater gothic cathedral. That is where the fish collect, individually and in little and great schools: it was nothing to see ten thousand fish of one hundred distinct species and sizes during a single dive.

The whole thing has only the one disconcerting impediment, that it is impossible to smile. If you smile, alas, you drown; so that nothing is permitted to be wrenchingly funny, or wry. But the impulse to smile, as one would at a spectacular sunset, or burst of wildlife, or during an aria splendidly struck, requires concentration to overcome, particularly when there are comic encounters, as when your rump backs into something and you wheel about convinced you have backed into a shark. Nothing is less shark-like than Bindy, whose rump it was, though probably she is bigger than any shark, like Kirsten Flagstad. She is the original earth mother, with a whimsical rolling laugh that chokes off the words that are constantly amusing her, and, through her, you.

On Sunday she accompanied me to mass at Suva because, she said, although not a Catholic she thought it would be good to pray for the new pope, designated as such the previous day. I told her that was a very nice thing to do, that I had to confess the unlikelihood that I would go to mass specially to pray for the new Archbishop of Canterbury, and she said I most certainly should, since the poor man has mostly lesbians praying for him these sad, schismatic days.

The beautiful Bindy requires the coordination of two men to hoist on board the dinghy, but whole armies would disengage for the pleasure of serving Bindy, who only yesterday could have posed for the most convincing statue of Brunhilde ever struck. She saw that I was cold and, after the first day, gave me her spare wetsuit, greatly increasing my pleasure; and, as soon as we got back on board, she would make up for all the laughter we missed during the two one-half hour dives Vane permitted us every day (more than one hour out of twenty-four in the deep does something, once again, to the nitrogen content of your blood, which needs rebuilding).

It was Bindy who said to me innocently, a book on her lap during the cocktail hour, "What is an irresponsible flake?"

"A *what*, Bindy?"

"An '*irresponsible flake.*' That's what it says here." She showed me page 146 of *Safe Scuba*, under the heading, "Selecting a Buddy." I was introduced to what is certainly the most hilariously periphrastic English in print. The co-authors must, between them, have attended at least five Teachers Colleges to achieve their prose style. "Most often, we have little choice with regard to the selection of a buddy," you read on, "in many cases we may be married to our buddy, or involved in a similar relationship to marriage, or we may be assigned a buddy by a divemaster on a boat, if possible, regardless of how our buddies are selected, it is an extremely good idea to know the person with whom you are going to dive. You should know your buddy's character patterns and diving skills. If your buddy is an irresponsible flake on the surface, the chances are excellent that the same idiotic behavior patterns will continue underwater."

I told Bindy that, honest injun, most people in America don't talk that way, and took the book from her. There are acres and acres of the same kind of thing. The authors' intention, clearly, is to persuade anyone who wants to scuba dive that he (as they would put it: "He or she, as the case may be") should spend dozens of hours and thousands of dollars in instructions. My very favorite passage deals with the rather simple question: Can you swim? "Failure of a swimming test may not demonstrate the student to be in poor physical condition, but only that the student lacks effective swimming skills. The swimming does not necessarily demonstrate that the diver will function well in the sub-aquatic environment. Mental conditioning, cognitive and affective, and proper habit patterns may be far more relevant to learning diving skills and surviving in the open water than physical conditioning as the prime criteria in dive student selection." All that and one mashed potato will get you two mashed potatoes. But I had already resolved never ever to do anything, in the sub-aquatic environment or in the super-aquatic environment, to permit Bindy to think of me as an irresponsible flake.

Wednesday

The captain and crew got up early and powered the *Tau* northeast sixty miles to the island of Taveuni, which is the third largest island in Fiji, and said by some to harbor the most spectacular diving and snorkeling reef in the whole area. It is the Somosomo Channel, and of course Vane led us unerringly to a spot that could not have been more enchanting. In the late morning we dinghied out on the *Tau*'s inflatable, into which the sea-skittish Drue was coaxed on the solemn promise, reiterated by all hands, that it had the distinctive feature of being absolutely unsinkable, a proposition Drue finally came to believe until, a few days later, the inflatable sank in front of her eyes, disappearing into the vasty deep without so much as a gurgle of resistance, leaving Captain Philip in great distress.

We went ashore in part to ogle at Fijian life, little of which we had observed. We found it to be exactly as described by the *National Geographic* magazine. Men and women of all shapes and colors, pleasant, a little lethargic, that admixture of Polynesian, Micronesian, Melanesian and, finally, Indian (the Indians immigrated half way through the nineteenth century as indentured agricultural laborers, the tending of agriculture being unappealing to the native population).

They are now a peaceable race of people, which requires an exercise of the imagination to recall that on his famous voyage from *The Bounty* to Timor in 1778, 3,600 miles on an open longboat, Captain Bligh did not dare to pause in these islands, so notoriously were the natives given to killing, and then eating, uninvited guests.

The natives are cheerful, apparently unexcitable, notwithstanding the sweat they work up in their nightclub acts when imitating the frenzied manners of their forefathers. They have been self-governing since 1970, after ninety-six years of colonial rule by the British who had the uncommon good sense to leave 82 percent of the land in native hands. I am not qualified to say whether the 600,000 Fijians are competently governed, but whatever evidence there is of commercial sloth, justice is certainly swift. On the Tuesday we read in the local paper that three men had been convicted the day before of raping a young woman of eighteen, receiving sentences of from two to four years of hard labor. The rape had occurred the preceding Saturday. Earl Warren never sojourned in Fiji.

Through the town of Waiyevo, on the western shore of the island, the 180th meridian runs, and the spot on the roadside where this happens is of course properly designated, with wooden signs tapering in opposite directions, one of them marked "Today," the other, "Yesterday." We did a great deal of picture-taking, in every conceivable pose, one foot firmly planted on Tuesday, the second on Wednesday—that sort of thing. It reminded me of an experience a half dozen years earlier at the exact geographic south pole when an escorting colonel, in the fifty-degrees-below-zero cold, asked whether I would like to have my picture taken while standing on my head, making possible a postcard depicting me as carrying the world on my shoulders. That being a characteristic personal burden, I readily assented, and was lifted by my boots by an aide.

At exactly which moment my brother, then serving as the junior senator from the State of New York, in a fit of chauvinism fired off a firecracker which was programmed to waft to earth in the form of the New York State flag, which he would photograph and send out to his constituents. Unhappily the firecracker went instead directly to my nose, so that there exists only a picture of me standing on my head and being bloodied by the flag of New York State. No such infelicity marred our picture taking this time around, though I was later advised by an obstinately literal historian of the area that the official boundary marking the international dateline was, in answer to a local provocation, made to jag eastward, then south, then west, and back to the 180 degrees mark so that the whole of Fiji might repose, unconfused, in the eastern hemisphere. All that bureaucratic geographical commotion was in retaliation against an ingenious Indian vendor whose shop straddled the dateline and who got around the sabbath laws by selling from the eastern end of his shop on the western Sunday, and from the western end of the shop on the eastern Sunday. That is the kind of problem the UN was born to solve.

We returned to the *Tau* undecided whether to stop by at the neighboring islands of Nggamea and Lauthala, which are owned respectively by the American tycoon Malcolm Forbes, and the Canadian actor, Raymond Burr. Everyone knows Malcolm Forbes, whose hospitality is in any case widely advertised. The closest tie any of us had to Raymond Burr is that I had patronized his hotel in the Azores during a transatlantic crossing. I deemed this an attenuated relationship, whereupon we all decided that in any event we really did not want to visit anybody at all, so we read, and had our wines, and chatted, and listened to beautiful music from the cassette deck I had so thoughtfully provided, and went to bed in high excitement, because the very next day we would visit the fabled Weillangilala.

Thursday

Weillangilala even Captain Philip had never visited. What it is is a perfect coral crescent. More accurately, a mile-wide coral necklace, with three beads missing at the top, through which you enter. The inside is ringed with white sand and palm trees on the eastern end. It has a voluptuarian appeal for anyone who cares at all about, or for, the sea. Its stark loneliness in the South Pacific is itself striking. The perfect protection it gives from wind or, rather, from the seas—the height of the coral is insufficient to block the wind—might have been specified by a civil defense engineer.

The water is every shade of Bahamian blue; the diving and snorkeling could consume days. There was only a single other vessel there, a forty-five-foot ketch owned by an oil rigger who works six months of the year in the North Sea, accumulating enough money to sustain him the other six months of the year in Fiji, where he cruises with his wife and child, endlessly, island to island, disdaining, except in extreme circumstances, the use of his engine, thus doing little to consume the mineral he is paid so handsomely to make available to others.

At dinner that night we resolve that now that we have reached the easternmost part of our itinerary, we shall insist on using only the sails as we proceed south to the Lau group. We retired with that vinous determination to be firm with the captain which tends to silt away overnight, but we dove before breakfast and this meant, by Jack's hallowed tradition, a glass of red wine with breakfast (Vane does not permit us to eat before diving). And so, refortified in our resolve, we stipulate that only the sails will be used for our passage south to Mbalavu—from which Pat and I shall have to leave the party, to meet engagements in Australia more closely related to taking oil out of the North Sea, than to cruising the Fijis.

Saturday

It was a fine sail, and I suggested to the first mate that we board the Zodiac and take photographs of the *Tau* under sail. The first part of the operation was accomplished, but at full power in the Zodiac in a choppy sea we found we could not keep up with the *Tau*, so bracing was the wind that morning and so lively the *Tau*'s performance, unleashed on a broad reach, even with the mainsail reefed. It was an awful exercise in frustration, attempting to communicate to the people on the boat that they must slow down in order that we might photograph them. All boats should have walkie-talkies, perfect for contact between dinghy and the mother vessel. Pat has mastered the exploitation of these, and reaches me at remote grocery stores in native villages with such importunities as *"Don't forget the guava jelly. OVER!"*

That night, having consummated another fine dive, a sadness overtook the departing members, and the thought of going anywhere without Vane to guide me, or Bindy to console me; of leaving Jack, and Drue, and Barbara, was a cruel capitulation to the world of getting and spending. The lot of them boarded an ancient open bus to see us off at what is called the airport.

Our fourteen pieces of luggage were segregated, and weighed, outside a thatched hut where lukewarm orange soda was available. The terminal's scales were brought out. They were what you get from Sears and Roebuck for the guest bathroom, and one by one the bags were weighed, and a careful calculation made of the overweight, which was lugged into the belly of one of those airplanes Clark Gable used to fly over the hump in; and we headed downwind, because into the wind meant taking off uphill, and were, miraculously, airborne. Suddenly it was sunny, and all the blue, and the coral reefs that have decimated the merchant marines of the world, spread out before us, carpeting us 150 miles to Suva, where the maw of convention was waiting, impatiently, to swallow us up.

CHAPTER FOUR

1980–1984

The Folks at Western
January 17, 1980

How does it go with the airlines these days? Well, that depends to a considerable extent on how far you can manage to stay away from Western Airlines, or in any case, from whoever it is that manages their operations out of Salt Lake City.

Are you ready? The 737 was chock-full. A chock-full airplane, in these days of straitened configurations owing to high-cost fuel and deregulations, is defined as an aircraft into which you could not insinuate a healthy sardine. We are headed for Los Angeles and, at 5:35 p.m., are already thirty-five minutes late. The strangest announcement I have heard in a lifetime's flying thereupon ensued from a palpably agitated lady. She cleared her throat. "Ladies and gentlemen, this aircraft is overloaded. Now, we need thirty-three volunteers to leave this flight. We will give you a nice dinner. And we hope to get you on the next flight leaving at 7:10—but we can't guarantee it. And by the way, all the luggage that has been put on board has been removed, in order to lighten the cargo. It will be placed on a future flight for Los Angeles. Thank you very much."

The reaction of the passengers was, not unexpectedly, mesmerized. The inducements to leave the flight can only be compared to a typical ultimatum by President Carter to Iran to release the hostages. Three or four people got up and left, but could only be assumed to have been motivated by claustrophobia.

Western Airlines escalated. "Now ladies and gentlemen, we need twenty-nine more volunteers. This aircraft will just sit here until the twenty-nine volunteers leave!"

One or two passengers rose to confer with the lady and her male assistant, and in a few minutes her confusion and resentment were audible.

Western Airlines escalated again: "As a result of weather," said the lady, "we will not be landing in Los Angeles anyway. We'll land in Ontario." "Where is Ontario?" the gentlemen on my left asked. I said I had a brother-in-law who lives in Ontario, one hundred miles north of Niagara Falls. We agreed that even Western Airlines would not punish its conscripts by taking them to Canada en route to Los Angeles. There had to be another Ontario.

One passenger left his seat and addressed the lady. "Look: you simply haven't offered enough inducements to get thirty-three volunteers. Why don't you offer them a free flight to Los Angeles if they volunteer?" She replied that she did not have the authority to engage in mass bribery. To the suggestion that she address the request to her supervisor, she reacted with dumb amazement. Perhaps Western Airlines cannot afford supervisors. A half hour had gone by.

At which point a young woman—obviously the kind born to organize— went forward, and there was a summit conference. Within ten minutes she had ushered out what turned out to be her ski group, thirty or so passengers, but the rest of us were not made privy to the inducement, the ski guide having whispered to her group that it was secret. There was some rumor to the effect that a special bus would take them from Ontario to Los Angeles, which is the kind of inducement young skiers, bless them, will settle for.

Five minutes later we were airborne, and only then did we discover the reason for the muddle. What happened, the captain told the remaining passengers in jovial accents, is that the folks who fueled up the airplane, by mistake put in too much gas. You can't land a plane that's too heavy. "That's why we had to lighten it."

But the good news was that our luggage was back in the hold, so we could expect it on landing in—ho ho, Los Angeles. The Ontario bit, it turned out, was what B.F. Skinner would call a "negative reinforcement."

On arriving in Los Angeles, one passenger waiting along with several dozen others, saw the baggage-spigot begin to dribble, and then stop. A dozen people were left without their baggage. Curiously, the last thirty or forty articles that had come down the baggage pipeline were skis. So that the folks at Western, to reduce the weight, or save space, had removed bags with things like toothbrushes, underwear, shirts, and medicine kits: in order to give priority to the skis. Now this might be understandable if one were flying from Los Angeles to Salt Lake City to ski, but since there hasn't been any snow in Los Angeles since the retreat of the last Ice Age, about a million years ago, the logic behind that feat of ratiocination by the folks of Western Airlines was unclear to the dismayed passengers. One of them approached an official in the baggage department who said he would intervene to make things right. At 10:05 that night he announced triumphantly over the telephone that the bags had come in on the next plane, been located and dispatched to the hotel in Los Angeles where they would arrive by 11:30. They arrived at 7:30 the following morning.

So, the officials at Western had merely lied about the cause of the problem, lied about the luggage, lied about the weather at Los Angeles. Ah, but we can blame it all on the sheiks! How so? I figure that the folks at Western have concluded that gas is more valuable than people. Because, of course, the excess gas could have been dribbled out across the Rockies, a routine operation for overloaded aircraft. As a matter of fact, it could have been pumped out on the tarmac. But even as fuel becomes more highly valued, people become less so, as anyone occupying the shrinking cubic space for which higher and higher prices are charged will agree. On the other hand, the passengers were grateful that the lady didn't demand in mid-flight that thirty-three passengers jump out over the Rockies, which would have been an economically feasible solution. But the supervisor hadn't authorized the suggestion, and at Western we go by the rules.

See You Later
June 12, 1980

ST. THOMAS, Virgin Islands—Syndicated columnists are given two weeks off every year. And this, I note in passing, is by no means a venerable convention (in my case, the vacation came only after my fifth year in the trade). Moreover, there have been columnists who as a matter of principle never took a vacation, lest their public discover that life was possible, even keener, and more joyous, without the columnist's lucubrations.

The late George Sokolsky wrote six columns a week for King Features, and then a seventh for the local Sunday paper. When he learned that he had to have his appendix out, he carefully composed columns ahead based on all the variables in the arts of prognosis: two columns in the event everything went smoothly; four columns in the event of complications; six columns in the event of major complications. I asked him, on hearing the story, whether he wrote a seventh column in the event of terminal complications, but he replied that his interest in his worldly constituency was only coextensive with his life on earth.

Mine isn't: when I go, I intend to hector the Almighty even as, episodically, I do from here, to look after my friends and (most of) my enemies. But I confess to being uncomfortable at taking my two weeks together, instead of separating them as is my practice (one week in the winter, one in the summer). But I am setting sail on a splendid racing vessel, from here, to Bermuda, to the Azores, and to Spain. The second leg of my journey will keep me incommunicado (at sea) for eleven days, in the unusual posture of being only on the receiving end of the world's events. During that period President Carter, senator Kennedy, the airlines, the people who spend their days profaning the English of King James, may misbehave safely in the knowledge that there will be no reproach from me. It is horrifying to meditate what enormity the White House will execute, I having advertised my isolation. On the other hand, if President Carter is determined to make me a boat people, I am splendidly well ahead of the game: I need only to sail on.

But sail on to where? Ah, there's the rub, as the poet intuited 400 years ago. Where can we go if distress should come to America? There is only Switzerland: but nature so arranged it so that you cannot sail to Switzerland, and this would not be the season to rely on US naval helicopters to pick up my boat and ferry it into Lake Geneva. Accordingly, I adjure my Lords, secular and spiritual, not to be too licentious while I am gone.

What shall I concern myself with? Well, the exact time of day. I really must know—no kidding—exactly what the time is. I wear a chronometer which for several years lost exactly one second per week. Even folk as disorganized as I can cope with such retrogressions, and I happily set it right every Christmas, and every Fourth of July: and I always knew what time it was. But in an idiotic fit of hubris, I returned it to the clockmaker reminding him that my watch was guaranteed not to gain or lose more than twelve seconds per year. It has never been quite right since. So—well, I have a computer I navigate with, and it has an inbuilt chronometer. It keeps—excellent time. But, you see, excellent time will not do—you need the exact time. So, I also have a little radio ($36 at Radio Shack) which is supposed to bring in WWV from Fort Collins, CO, which vouchsafes to all the ships at sea: the exact time. Mostly the little radio brings in that signal. Every now and then it does not. In which case I ask Danny for the time, and his watch is pretty reliable. Dick's cheap little Casio keeps disgustingly good time. And I can tell from Reggie's sly smile that—he believes, in a pinch, he can come up with the time.

I need sun. Not to darken my skin, because in fact the doctor says that sun is the enemy of fair skin and I must now use something called Total Eclipse No. 15. I need the sun, and the time, to discover which way to point in order to effect a rendezvous at the Azores. If in this matter I should fail, the reader may deduce, two weeks hence, that I am absent without leave. The moon is getting lean right now, but will flower again; and when it is half-bright, it gives you a horizon, and on some magical moments you can combine that horizon with the North Star, and before you know it, you have your latitude, even as Columbus had that, and only that, having little idea of the time, and yet managed to discover our wonderful country.

The chances, then, are overwhelming that, like MacArthur, I shall return. In the meantime, the Republic is on probation.

William F. Buckley Jr. Braves the High Seas in High Fashion, with Champagne and Scarlatti

People, July 28, 1980

"Well, how was it?"

The radio-telephone hadn't worked, so I hadn't spoken to my wife since leaving Bermuda. The floor of the customs shed at Marbella, just around the corner and up thirty miles from Gibraltar, was rocking, just like the boat deck. It took concentration to keep the champagne in my glass from spilling, though Danny, Christopher, Tony, or Reggie would have filled the glass immediately even though they were all busily talking at the same time and writing out telephone numbers in various parts of America to hand over to the lone, sleepy operator. She hadn't had so much to do at midnight at Puerto Banus Marina since the night the narcs came and busted an innocent-looking, gleaming. white pleasure yawl—so much like our own seventy-one-foot *Sealestial*—and walked away with a hundred million pesetas worth of Moroccan gold and a half-dozen extremely unhappy young smugglers.

"Oh, fine. Everything fine. Rough sailing the last thousand miles. Very tough stuff. Then there was a whale...Whale. W-h-a-l-e. Dead. Circled around it: it was being eaten by sharks. And there was the survivor...No, *not* one of ours. A Belgian. He fired his last flare and our friends from Woods Hole spotted him from their ship and lugged him out of the water. What was he doing in the water? Well listen, ducky, he wasn't out swimming...I'm *not* being sarcastic. He was sailing singlehanded, three hundred miles out of Bermuda, and suddenly the bottom of his boat was swept away, but he had his life raft. It was either a whale that hit him or a sub. A *submarine*. I'll tell you about it. But not now. Everybody's waiting to use the phone. I'll call you tomorrow from the airport in Madrid. Thanks, darling. Me too."

I pass the phone to Danny, and he pours me some more champagne, but he misses the glass by about a half inch. I thrust my glass in the right direction, exhibiting that flawless sense of timing, that capacity for decisiveness under stress, that I share with Captain Hornblower. I cocked my cap on my head and, glass in hand, said to my fellow sailors: "I'm going back to the boat." They cheered. They'd have cheered if I had said: "I'm not going back to the boat." Or if I had said: "What makes you think you have the right to get drunk just because you've sailed 4,500 miles across the ocean?" What I couldn't have said, not even in jest, was that crossing the ocean in your own boat (chartered, to be sure) is routine stuff. Especially, I couldn't have said that their company was routine company, because when you decide to do it—spend thirty days in an elongated canoe however fancy—you must choose the company carefully. Oh, so carefully.

I made it the fifty yards down the quay to the boat, lit by the full moon that had paved our way from Gibraltar. Up until then the winds had been fierce, right on the nose—the notorious levanter. The next time you find yourself on the western approach to the Strait of Gibraltar make it a point to have on board an almanac that indicates the hour of high tide at Gibraltar. Because, you see, after high tide there is a half hour of stillness. Then, for six hours, the water rushes in from the Atlantic to the Mediterranean, at very nearly five knots. Then for six hours after *that*, the water turns around and flows back into the Atlantic, though at a reduced speed. So there we were, tacking against an easterly, and I decided to go on over to Africa, and maybe snuggle along the same coastline the pirates used to love, to snatch a little protection from the wind. If only I knew whether, by tacking across twelve miles to Gibraltar, the current would carry me toward Italy (good) or New York (bad).

But we had no tide book, so I said brightly: "We will use the radio-telephone!" "*C'est le bateau de voile Sealestial, je veux parler avec Radio Tangiers.*" Silence. We tried Gibraltar. Silence. We tried the emergency channel on the radio-telephone. Silence. At this point I thought to cut through ship-telephone protocol ("This is Whiskey Oscar Nine One Eight Seven, calling Gibraltar Harbor Radio. Whiskey Oscar Nine One Eight Seven, calling Gibraltar Harbor Radio, do you read, do you read?"—a half day of that kind of thing and you find yourself telling the cook you want your steak medium well medium well). "*This is a sailing vessel desiring from anyone at sea the time of high water in Gibraltar, please give it to me.*" Tried it in French, tried it in Spanish. My voice became more peremptory, combative—like Jimmy Durante launching hostilities against a refractory piano. But the fact of it is if no transmission is going out, nobody is ever going to answer you, never mind that with naked eye you can see five, six freighters, oil tankers, destroyers, all of them with radios turned on to the relevant channels.

So I figured: What the hell? We have a 50 percent chance the current will be with us, and will waft us east. At worst, we'll be blown and carried back; and spend the night in southern Spain, maybe at Cape Trafalgar, where we can pay our respects to the statue of Lord Nelson. But we gambled and we won, and when the current carried us round Gibraltar, the sea, as if directly instructed by Neptune, turned to glass, as if to say: "You've had enough. You win. Now we'll roll out the carpet for you." The sun drifted down, and there was the medley of greens and blues and pinks, laced with silver which, albescent, slowly displaced all else as the sun receded and the moon's intensity rose. We sat in the cockpit, our ninetieth and last meal together, and the sensation slowly gets to you, the sensation that animates every sustained energetic enterprise. It is so—I suppose—on finally reaching the top of a mountain. It is not so different from what happens when you write the last pages of a book. I suppose winning a political victory after long and hard endeavor is a cognate sensation. It is very special, and what it brings is the peace of fleeting self-satisfaction.

You need to go back to the logbook, or to a journal (if you kept one) to equip you to distinguish one day from another. Many different things happen, and the distractions and variations are, on board, intensely interesting. But the story line is simple. Here's what we had: a forty-one-ton (unloaded) sailing ketch, a racing boat designed for luxury cruising. It has 3,400 square feet of sail when everything is up. Then there is a motor, 108 horsepower, that consumes two gallons per hour at seven knots, which means about three and a half miles per gallon. You have 600 gallons of fuel and 500 of water. You have a radio-telephone (that doesn't work), a machine that dispenses a barometric weather chart (that doesn't work). You have a short-wave radio, and radar, and one thousand and fifteen gadgets of various kinds of which only three are absolutely central: a sextant, a chronometer, and a compass. The first two, adroitly exploited in combination, will tell you where the third should be pointed in order to reach first Bermuda, then the Azores, then Gibraltar.

Mediating between the sextant reading and the compass is a small library of almanacs and tables. You plod your clerkish way through these— *or*, you bring along a little, palm-sized machine, courtesy of Hewlett-Packard, which my protean friend the English professor has programmed. It is not surprising, under the circumstances, that it actually speaks to you in

English, eliciting, in unambiguous language, exactly those data it wants. For instance: "YEAR?" Could any misanthrope, any Luddite, facing that soft-spoken, alphanumeric display board, deny the machine the satisfaction of punching out: one-nine-eight-zero? Score one more for the memory chip, which knows where the sun, moon, stars, and planets are located every second of every day of every year, from now until the year 2049.

Do you worry, crossing the Atlantic? In a way. If, when the sea is exercised, someone should fall overboard, the chances are fearfully high that you have seen the last of him. Moral? Don't fall overboard. If there is a fire at sea you are in bad shape. Again, the moral is obvious. A standard cruising book, a part of the ship's library, reads, "Force 11—Winds 64-72 mph. Chances of yacht's survival in such conditions very low." Ah, but I have sailed in winds exceeding 72 mph! The price of survival and progress toward your destination is Extreme Discomfort. For several consecutive days, on one leg, we could not drink an entire cup of coffee without spilling some of it. What we had to worry about in particular on this trip was Christopher Little, because he opted not to permit any part of the boat to go unphotographed from any angle, and so on a typical watch we would 1) take the log reading, 2) record the barometer, wind speed, and direction, 3) adjust the sails, and 4) haul Christopher to a spreader, a masthead, or a spinnaker boom, with his laundry bag full of equipment.

Tedium? If you are off watch, you can read: read gluttonously. I even started (though did not finish) a certain novel by Henry James. You can devote yourself *endlessly* to navigation, if the subject interests you: you lie in wait (heh! heh!) for the relevant stars and planets, presetting your sextant to the anticipated arc, and then, Bang!—down goes Vega at one o'clock. Bang! You've got Spica at three o'clock. Bang! Jupiter bites the dust at five o'clock. Fifteen minutes later you have a tiny penciled triangle on your plotting sheet, for which the sailors have a naughty expression— and your boat is right in the middle of it. You rise from the navigation table and climb up to the cockpit, with studied nonchalance, and say something like, "Hmm. We've had a little northerly set. Change course from zero nine two to zero niner four." Walter Mitty never experienced a more exhilarating moment.

And, then, sometimes there is no wind at all, and you stop in the middle of the ocean, strap in the mainsail, and go swimming. Everyone tends to behave like Huck Finn or Tom Sawyer in the swimming hole. Reggie does an imitation of a World War I German submarine. Danny is on deck with the .222 magnum, in case a shark should surface, mistaking us for dead whales. Tony, for the first few days of the trip, notwithstanding that though he is only three years out of Harvard he is very nearly a professional sailor, *looks* like a dead whale, until his stomach finally settles. Van, at dinner, pouring one of the wines we selected at St. Thomas from fourteen nominees, is fussing with a new game they are playing in London, in which success is defined by artful replies to oddball questions, e.g., "What's the name of the surviving Japanese kamikaze pilot?" (An acceptable answer: "Chicken sukiyaki.") Tom feels awful, and is stretched out on the cockpit during a midnight roller coaster, up fast, and d-d-down slow, right, left, steady back on course, flecks of moon darting through the clouds, waves chasing after you, higher, sometimes, than you could touch on tiptoes, arm upstretched—but Tom listens. In a plastic bag, to protect it from the salt spray, is the battery cassette player, Fernando Valenti playing Scarlatti on the harpsichord. Tom's misery is leavened by occasional gasps of pleasure. Reggie likes to play Ghost during the long hours at the wheel, and the dictionary (an *American Heritage* is on board) is constantly being trotted out to serve as arbitrator. When, during a dead calm, that dictionary ruled in Reggie's favor in a duel with me, I annealed my companions in antipathy by announcing that I could see to it that the *next* edition of the *Heritage* should alter the word to conform with my spelling of it. "You will note," I said, looking vaguely at the horizon, as if distracted by the responsibility of transcribing the cloud formations into a meteorological forecast, "that I am listed in the Foreword of that dictionary as a consultant." Oh well, I had planned to go swimming anyway.

I stepped gingerly over the lifeline, grasping the shroud with my left hand: the other hand was not available, as there was still the champagne glass. The boat, mothballed in moonlight, was dead: everyone was ashore, telephoning, reveling, roistering. There was no breeze, no sound. I walked aft to the stern cockpit, and maneuvered down the stillness of the companionway to the master cabin, flicked on the reading light, dropped my pants, shoes, and socks with a single downward motion, and slid between the sheets. For the first time in seven days, no need to fasten the canvas leeboards that had kept me, during those screeching moments of heel, from being tossed onto the floorboards. I picked up my journal, and began to write. The dozen words I managed I cannot, at this moment, decipher. They are illegible. But I know what they say. Know what they express: gratitude.

Pan Am and Your Overweight
March 19, 1981

I forget who appointed me or when, but somewhere along the line I emerged as unofficial journalistic protector of the traveling public in the Matter of Overweight. My commission is not disinterested, since I regularly travel with excess luggage, required as I am to carry the burdens of the world with me wherever I go. The unofficial legal protector of the traveling public is a young attorney in Miami, Donald Pevsner, who warns now of the imminence of the greatest imposition on the air-traveling public in the history of aviation.

Mr. Pevsner has filed a complaint before the Civil Aeronautics Board protesting the planned changes by Pan American Airlines. Unless the CAB forbids these changes, effective on the first day of April, here's what will happen to you if you decide to travel on Pan Am:

1) If you are a discount-fare passenger, which means if you are among the 66 percent majority who fly on Pan Am, you will be allowed only one suitcase for your fare. If you have two, the second will cost you whatever the tariff is for an excess bag. If you have three or more, the extra luggage must be checked as freight. In many airports this involves a mere matter of going to a different terminal, hunting down the freight official, and turning over your bags. Now Pan Am will endeavor to see that this baggage travels with you on the same flight, but will decline to give it any priority. If it doesn't arrive with you in, oh, Nairobi, you can sit in the airport and wait for the next flight. It may be a couple of days later.

2) If you are a full-fare economy passenger, you will continue to get two bags free. But the third will be treated as above.

3) If you are a first-class passenger, existing rules will continue to apply. However, no matter in which class you travel, any bag that weighs more than fifty pounds (the present limit is seventy) will be counted as an excess bag, even if it is the only one you have.

Now Mr. Pevsner, for whom I have great respect, believes that the CAB is justly armed with the authority simply to deny Pan Am the right to make its own policies in the matter. I disagree. Inasmuch as regulations have been suspended granting monopolies on certain routes, my judgment is that if Pan Am decided to permit passengers no bags at all, Pan Am should be permitted to do so. Mr. Pevsner warns that if Pan Am is authorized to proceed, the other airlines will immediately imitate Pan Am, causing the greatest passenger dislocations and inconveniences in recorded memory. My analysis is different.

The World's Most Experienced Airline has in recent times suffered from highly inexperienced management. A month ago, routed on a succession of three Pan Am flights, I found one of them canceled, the other two late. A voyage scheduled for fourteen hours took twenty-two. Now any airline that loses as much money as Pan Am has been losing is obviously desperate for revenue. The question is whether revenue is going to result from doing the single most outrageous thing that can be done to a traveler, namely to tell him at the counter that his bags may or may not arrive at Auckland on the same flight with him.

The economic model in the free-enterprise system is supposed to work other than in the way Mr. Pevsner predicts. There are, over most routes—though by no means all—other carriers the passenger can patronize. No experienced traveler, given a choice in the matter, will mount any airplane that is vague about when his baggage is going to arrive.

We cannot predict how the CAB will respond. But it is extraordinary that an airline so closely associated with the history of aviation should even contemplate so egregious an affront to its patrons. In a year in which General Motors lost money, one must be sympathetic with the General Motors of the airlines losing money. But their decision on how to make more money is the equivalent of General Motors advising you that if you want a roof on your car, you have to pay extra.

We will see.

Buckley Rides the Orient Express
New York Times, November 22, 1981

There it stood, on Track 13. The first vision of the Nostalgic Orient Express, to give it its full title, was everything one might ask for. The impresario has a high sense of style. Outside every one of the sleeping cars was the official who would take the bags that we had sweatily delivered on trolleys into the bedrooms. And parading up and down, dressed in top hat and tails, with waxed mustache extending beyond the sides of his face, was someone who was to be, as it turned out, everywhere visible during the journey, and never visibly employed doing anything at all, except being civil. I doubt that he'd have lit Marlene Dietrich's cigarette—but he'd have smiled, and made her feel better for being without a light.

The Nostalgic Orient Express is of recent, and somewhat mysterious, origin. Its historical predecessor, the old Orient Express, had been legend, but had fallen a victim to the airlines: Why devote two-and-a-half days to going from Switzerland to Istanbul, when you can make the trip by air in two-and-a-half hours? A Swiss presence, rumored to be allied to an American presence, turned up at Sotheby's one day a year or so back to bid for some of the original equipment, the sleeping cars built in 1926 and redesigned in 1929 for the then-consummately luxurious run from one end of Europe to the other—and thus the Nostalgic Orient Express.

It is, of course the persistence of the question: *Why?* that argues the stubborn, evasive, yet strangely persistent answer: Because. There is no more reason to take the Orient Express than there is…to take a sailboat to Bermuda. The only reason to do the latter is that you like to sail. The reason for doing the former is that you are bitten by the same bug that pursues Paul Theroux, the Flying Dutchman of the rails.

Anyway: the decision had been made to go. The invitation was from Jack Heinz, who will not depart this earth if there is on it anywhere a stone he has not looked under. Our trip was to begin in Zurich at 9:00 a.m. on Tuesday, October 6, and to end in Istanbul at 7:00 p.m. on Thursday, October 8. Our route would follow that of the old Orient Express: approximately 1,200 miles east from Zurich to the eastern border of Austria, then southeast through Yugoslavia and Bulgaria, then east-southeast into Istanbul, at the end of the peninsula that juts into the Black Sea, the Sea of Marmara on the south leading to the Dardanelles. (It is worth noting that the Nostalgic Orient Express literature refers to this city as "Constantinople." This is surprising on two counts: "Istanbul" is more mysterious sounding than "Constantinople," and mystery is intrinsic to the entire experience; moreover, if you're going to put on the historical dog, why not go all the way and call it "Byzantium," which is what it was before the Emperor Constantine declared it the center of the world—which, half the city lying in Europe and the second half in Asia, with the Bosporus running in between, it still considers itself, in a way, to be.)

And so, in the bright morning, we arrived in Zurich, the two Heinzes and the two Buckleys, with the normal baggage for four busy and self-indulgent types who were, after all, on notice that dinner, both nights of the scheduled trip, was black tie. Sixteen pieces of luggage. Arriving at the railroad station in Zurich one is very quickly reminded of one of J.K. Galbraith's laws, namely that there are certain things indigenous members of affluent societies simply won't do. It is all right, in Zurich, to drive a cab. That, somehow, has cachet, so that outside the railroad station in Zurich you see, oh, forty cabs. And no porters. In Geneva you will, though with difficulty, find porters; but that is because Geneva is so very close to France, with its itinerant population of folk who really need work.

The evolution of the tolerable pursuits of the leisure classes to one side, it is not easy to imagine how, let us say, four old ladies would have managed, if they had desired to load themselves and their luggage onto the Nostalgic Orient Express. Anyone who wishes to make considerable money—certainly more than a Zurich cabdriver—should go to Zurich, get a cart, and haul baggage for grateful travelers, asking, per bag, whatever the traffic will bear (which would be considerable).

Our car was "*2ème*," so that to eat, we had to pass through "*1ère*," after which we reached the bar car. There, right and left, are red velvet lounge chairs, exactly as of yore, one is told; and, two-thirds of the way up toward the open bar, an upright piano, situated athwart the cabin, so that you make your way past the piano player, and smile, which you do most genuinely because he is inexhaustibly happy to be playing the songs of the Twenties and Thirties, or at any rate seems to be. (The circular tells you that the bar car will remain open until everyone has elected to go to bed.)

The next car is the dining car, which is called that to distinguish it from the two succeeding cars, which are "Pullman diners." The first is more silent than the second two, though the appointments are similar, heavy on drapery, velvet—the antimacassar feel, which is a wonderful relief over the TV-dinner feel of a modern train. The guests are assigned tables, and rotated. It happened that on the first day we had the private compartment in the dining car, and the four of us sank down into the billowy velvet, facing a table groaning with wine glasses and heavy cutlery and fine porcelain and linen napkins. It is right that one should be so comfortable in the dining quarters of the Orient Express, because one spends five hours a day there, and this does not count breakfast.

The six-course lunches and dinners consume two-and-a-half hours each, but it isn't easy to imagine two-and-a-half hours more agreeably spent than in looking out at Austrian forests, pastures, streams and farmhouses; or, at night, in seeing the twinkling lights of a progressively eastern Europe, with every now and then a pause at a station, but none that interrupts the leisurely rhythms of the sommelier, or the waiters.

The idea is charming, because the essence of the Nostalgic Orient Express is—well, a kind of luxurious privacy, with a certain solipsistic indifference to what goes on outside the window. To be sure, one doesn't ride through Switzerland feeling like White Russian noblemen driving through steppes of dead souls. But, on the other hand, I can't offhand think where else one can, dressed in black tie, be served dinner in candlelight while riding through Bulgaria. The sensation is perhaps sinful but, in the end, no different philosophically from getting into a jet airplane and catapulting toward freedom, from the jetport in Moscow, high over the Gulag, drinking Bloody Marys.

The train's individual compartments have a long sofa that converts into a bed and, at one corner, a washstand, with a revolving wooden door to hide it. At the opposite end by the entrance door is a small closet; and above, going around, baggage racks. The door to the adjoining compartment opens, so that you and your wife can commune. There are one or two over-and-under bunk compartments, but these somehow don't seem to be quite in the spirit of the Orient Express, where after all if you are going to be murdered, you should be alone, right?

It is a part of the ritual of the Orient Express that, every now and again, you pause in order to stretch your legs. You do this, after leaving Zurich, at Innsbruck, the nearest thing one can imagine to a Tyrolean metropolis. Rather pretentiously, the timetable informs you that you will arrive there at "2:07," which is on the order of your wife telling you she will be ready to leave for the dinner party at "8:13." But you are there sometime after two, for about an hour and a half, which was time enough for Heinz to buy himself one of those green loden jackets, and hike back one-and-one-half blocks to the train.

You are welcomed back to the train with fresh coffee and croissants, or a "welcome drink." The consumption of these is encouraged, by the way, and they are cash-and-carry, and there is no nonsense about special rates. A gin-and-tonic is $4, a liqueur $6. There are no other extra expenses; certainly nothing is spent on communications. Poor Mr. Sadat was killed on Tuesday at 1:00 p.m., news of which infamy reached the Orient Express as a rumor early on Thursday afternoon. The suspicion, however fleeting, was here and there entertained that this was a part of the scenario of the entrepreneurs, who having ruled out murder on the Orient Express itself, felt the obligation to promote the whisper of it elsewhere.

There are two complaints about the service as it is presently administered, however. Waking gradually, and at your own initiative, in a rolling train, the blind opened just enough to give you a glimpse of the countryside going by, is one of train-travel's notorious pleasures. There were two mornings on the Nostalgic Orient Express. On Wednesday, we were required to have risen and breakfasted by 7:20 a.m. if we desired to take the tour of Belgrade. And why? Surely folk who treat the railroad as their own toy, as do the entrepreneurs of this adventure, could schedule a later arrival?

The tour, by the way, is for the most part a walk about the great public park, where the old forts are, like palimpsests, visible, a series of growth rings becoming larger in circumference with the expansion of the city. The guide, competent and thorough, informs you that what is now Belgrade, capital of what is now Yugoslavia, has been overrun sixty-four times in twenty-three centuries, and there are those who hope for the sixty-fifth. But only one hour and thirty-two minutes are allocated for seeing Belgrade, and one is off again before 10:00, and just a little sleepy.

The second morning is worse. At exactly 6:45 there is a loud knock on the door. It is Yugoslav immigration, demanding to see your passport—or, more precisely, warning you that any minute now, your passport must be ready for inspection. You think back on the first night, at dinner, when the Austrian official asked for your passport, and you said smiling that you didn't have it in the pocket of your dinner jacket, but that you were the husband of that lady opposite, whose passport was handy. The immigration officer had smiled back.

So, in the very early morning, leaving Yugoslavia, you forage about for your passport, and lie back in bed, waiting for its inspection, and this time it is checked, ten minutes later. You sink back to sleep. Another ten minutes later, a knock. You are handed an entry form to fill out for Turkish authorities. The form could have been composed by Mr. Parkinson. There is hardly room for your name, nor is it clear where it should be set down. The requirement that you give your father's name is rendered in so many languages that no white space at all is left over for that vital piece of information. Having struggled with the form for some time, you lie awaiting its recovery. This happens in about twenty minutes more. You have thus devoted between 6:45 and 7:45, a grand hour for sleeping if you are on vacation, to administration.

There is, of course, no reason why the escorts of the Nostalgic Orient Express can't collect all the passports, as they do on shipboard, and cope with passengers' comings and goings in absentia. Forms could be given to you at dinner, to be collated in the passports by the staff. So, then, I'd recommend a later arrival on the first day in Belgrade, and no interruptions on the second day, for the benefit of those wishing to sleep later than 6:45.

Wednesday night was ours to visit Sofia. The train is in the station for four hours. Dinner, as usual, is served on board, but we chose to take a taxi to the Vodenicharski Mehani Folk Restaurant, which *Fodor's Guide to Europe* describes as incorporating three old mills, at the foot of Mount Vitosha above Dragalevtsi city district, and categorizes as "E" (expensive). (We did not discover the meaning of "E," failing to find the code.) The twenty-five-minute drive there gave us a panoramic view of the city at night.

Along with Albania, Bulgaria long had the reputation as the most impenetrable of the Iron Curtain countries. Now there is a studied policy to encourage tourism. The restaurant, when we reached it, was jumping, with native dancers, rows upon rows of young men and women whose left foot reaches up to the right knee, while the arm engages the waist—that kind of dancing, with music in which you begin to hear the oriental harmonies. The food was "E" for execrable.

Sitting directly behind us were six men so distinctly *apparatchiks* of the Bulgarian Communist Party they could not have passed for anything else. Age, about forty. Weight, about 200 pounds. Hair, close cut. Suits, double-breasted and just slightly ill-fitting, blue. Neck-fat forcing off-white shirt-collars, with colorless ties. Lots of vodka bottles, and noodles and moussaka and Bulgarian grapes, and hilarity over the dancers. One of the six, the concertmaster—no doubt about which one. They would leave the restaurant in due course, and resume their duties, which would be telling someone what to do.

No cabs, so a waiter volunteered to drive us back to the train. He managed a little French, and pointed out the new hotels going up, and finally brought us back to the huge, fluorescent-lit station, and thence to the bar car for piano music and a drink, and to bed and to read on into David Niven's novel. For the fun of it, I set my wrist alarm clock at 1:24, the designated time of departure, with an unadmirable smile of condescension for those who felt obliged to list early-hour departure times so exactly. But perhaps the *apparatchiks* had said that at no other minute could the Orient Express leave the Sofia station. (It left at about 1:45.)

Thursday morning brought, in addition to the annoying paperwork, a two-hour tour of the ancient town of Edirne, with its two striking mosques.

Here, in Turkey, was the consummation of the feeling, which had grown ever since we left the border of Austria, that we were entering into an alien culture, windswept by history. As we left Edirne and headed now finally for Istanbul, the landscape, at first raw and parched, became greener, finally almost lush. An hour or two out of Istanbul, we took on a steam engine— until then, one gathers, not permitted, by order of the Bulgarian Sierra Club. It was a time for picture-taking and, of course, for packing.

The reconstituted Orient Express may end up in Disney World, chugging its way around Orlando, but I hope not. It is good to travel to the ancient capital of the world aboard a train built two years after Lenin died (and fifty-four years after one wishes he had died) and one year before Lindbergh flew the ocean, and know that it still works. It is also good to know that traveling through Europe by rail, in circumstances almost stagily comfortable, can still be done—up to a point. At the Bosporus, Asia begins, and many things end, among them the journey.

Which Americans Are Ill-Mannered?
December 3, 1981

A visitor recently in England who had not been there in a dozen years writes about it that something has indeed changed, namely an erosion of that civic gentility that prevailed for a century or so, giving the British an international reputation for good manners and good humor. Remember hearing of a retired British country squire visiting in France with his wife shortly after the war and receiving, at a fancy restaurant, an obviously inflated bill. His reaction to the *maitre d'hotel* is supposed to be rendered in Colonel Blimp public school accents: *"Je ne vais pas faire une scène, mais quand je retourne, je vais ecrire une lettre au Times!"*

The gentleman, mindful of British good manners, would not make a public scene over the exorbitance of the bill, but as soon as he returned to his own country, he would write a letter of protest—to the London *Times*: where all Englishmen of pedigreed manners take their complaints, as if to an ombudsman.

I have not, in hectic trips through England, had the opportunity to inquire into, let alone verify, this complaint against modern England, but I am reminded that the talented Ralph Graves of Time Inc., on taking over the reins of *Life* magazine a dozen years ago, took a trip around the United States and remarked the obstinate good humor of Americans, with the demoralizing exception of his native New York City, where incivility is something of a tourist attraction.

But incivility, in the last analysis, is a measure of what people will put up with. And what they will put up with is of course also a measure of what the alternatives are. If you are at the airplane counter of the only airline that runs the only weekly flight to Azania, you are likely to accept incivility with fatalism. If there are alternative ways to effect your trip, or your mission, there are ways to make your protest resonantly.

On the Sunday following Thanksgiving, the train station at Stamford, CT—a major commuting stop—was as full as it has ever been with weekenders and students and family, waiting to get either a) the express train to New York, or b) the succeeding train to New York and Washington. It was very cold outside, and the moment had come and gone when the first of these trains was due but no announcement had been made over the loudspeaker as to the probable length of the delay, so that young boys and old women braved the cold outside rather than keep warm within the station. The stationmaster simply did not bother to use the public address system to advise the hundreds of people waiting of the length of the projected delay.

The express to New York arrived, and the eight or ten cars were crammed with passengers and departed for New York looking like those Japanese express trains in which efficiency is measured by a passenger-per-square-inch basis. Exactly four minutes after the first train departed, there materialized a five-passenger local to New York, empty except for a dozen or so passengers. The local requires only ten minutes more time to arrive in New York. If its imminent departure had been broadcast over the loudspeaker, 500 persons who had squeezed into the express train might have had a comfortable hour's ride into the city.

Those passengers still waiting for the Washington train—whose lateness had yet to be defined—seethed with indignation as they saw the local, still empty, pull out of the station. But the point of the story is that no one (as far as is known) expressed that indignation to the insouciant station-master, who could not be bothered to relieve several hundred people when it required the exertion of speaking into a loudspeaker.

There is talk that President Reagan may decide on lenity for those air controllers who were less aggressive than their leaders in the illegal strike. It would be nice to make one of them the stationmaster at Stamford, CT.

There are the marvelous exceptions. The telephone company people have no competition; but they are all but uniformly pleasant. There is a culture at AT&T (as in Japan), and it works. The nice people at Amtrak, who run such seductive copy in the newspapers, are burdened primarily by their agents in the field.

One Thousand Dollars a Day
New York Times Sophisticated Traveler, October 9, 1983

When, for the first time, our son would not be with us for Christmas we lost interest in spending it at home, and ever since then have gone to the Caribbean, though not to stay on islands. Our attachment to the Caribbean is to a way of visiting it; and for us this means by cruising sailboat.

Accordingly, although I have cruised the Caribbean more thoroughly than Christopher Columbus, I do not write this piece with any presumption of communicating the "magic of the Caribbean," as they call it in the coffee table books when other words seem apologetic. But I am here to say that it is hard to have a happier time than cruising there.

In your own boat. Though, having said that, I confess I have not been aboard a commercial cruising boat during the conventional one or two weeks in the Caribbean. Probably there is much to be said for this way of seeing the islands, in preference to hotel life. But your very own boat is really the way to go, and one might as well quickly confront the proposition. "Isn't this out of the question for the average pocketbook?" The answer is: Yes. But so is a week aboard any of the more luxurious liners or a week at any of the fancier hotels. In round figures—if you include meals, drinks, tips, taxis—you are talking about something over $400 per couple a day, times seven comes to —well, close to $3,000 a week. Last Christmas, we chartered a boat that cost $1,000 a day, including food, but not drinks, tips, or taxis. Throw these in even profusely, and you are still short of $9,000 a week. But there are three couples sharing the boat, so that the cost, for each couple—less than $3,000—is comparable to the hotels.

Until 1978, we vacationed in my own boat, a sixty-foot schooner for which, when last I chartered it out, the price was $3,000 a week. In the six years since losing her, we experimented with several boats, discovering in due course a seventy-one-foot ketch (it is a class called Ocean 71), my enthusiasm for which led me one spring to charter her from St. Thomas to the Mediterranean, whither she was in any case bound. I find it the (almost) perfect cruising boat (it is not air-conditioned). And in a piece that seeks to be persuasive about cruising in the Caribbean, it is worth telling you exactly what you get with a boat like *Sealestial*.

First the tangibles. There is a crew of four. A skipper (though I serve as my own), a first mate, a stewardess, and a cook. There are three cabins, in descending order of luxury the owner's cabin, which has a dressing table, a huge stuffed chair for reading and working, a private bath including shower; a smaller but commodious cabin with hanging lockers and two bunks, sharing a shower and separate toilet with the third cabin—slightly smaller, but entirely comfortable.

The principal saloon, as sailors call it, is circular and would hold, comfortably seated, sixteen people. Eight can be seated around the coffee table that lifts and becomes the dinner table, opposite the bar, music quarry, and screen for movies. The main cockpit you may choose to eat in, as you like; and the after cockpit fits snugly six people, if you wish to eat there, usually when under way. On deck there is more room than can be consumed by a dozen people who wish to lie and read, or to sun, whether or not the vessel is under sail. The rubber dinghy holds eight people, and there is diving equipment on board for four, with tanks that recharge in about half an hour. There is a radio that works, giving you almost instant contact with whomever you need to reach.

And the intangibles? You can rise in the morning, take stock of the wind and decide which island next to visit. You can decide when to set sail, after breakfast or after a tour of the island. You can, sailing along offshore by, say, a quarter of a mile (after you leave the Bahamas, the islands are nicely sheer), spot a beach and decide impulsively that you would like to swim off it. It happens to appeal so you go no farther. There is no fixed itinerary, no deadlines. When there is such a thing—perhaps a couple of friends are flying in for a few days—you can make contingent arrangements. It is easy to book a little airplane to meet your boat at a convenient island.

It is most important to turn your watches to Buckley Watch Time. There are those who call this Daylight Time. But the two do not always correspond, because in certain circumstances Buckley Watch Time advances the conventional time by two hours. The practical meaning of it all, as I have elsewhere written, is that you can start the cocktail hour as the sun is setting, and eat dinner one hour later, at eight o'clock. Otherwise, you can find yourself drinking at 6:00 and eating dinner at 7:00. The former offends the Calvinist streak in a Yankee; the latter, the Mediterranean streak in a yacht owner. Dinner is protracted and leisurely, and after dinner, according to the inclinations of our companions, we gamble, or we watch a movie, or we read; and, before retiring, we swim, and stare a little at the stars, and the moon, and listen to the little waves, from whose busty sisters we are, on the leeward side of the island, protected.

Last year, a week or two before the trip was to begin, I had a phone call from the yacht broker. A most unhappy development! Poor *Sealestial*! What outrageous people one finds in the world! And a brand-new motor at that! Unraveled, it gradually transpired that coming down after a summer in the Mediterranean, the yacht's brand new engine gave trouble—somewhere off Casablanca, I think it was. The captain accepted a friendly offer of a few miles tow, upon the completion of which the Good Samaritan put in a bill for the entire value of the boat, something on the order of three quarters of a million dollars. They settled for less than that, but the negotiations would keep the boat from arriving in time for Christmas.

The resourceful broker was, however, armed for the contingency. She proposed that we accept one of *Sealestial*'s sister ships for one week, and that for the balance of our ten-day trip we ride, without extra charge, on a new vessel built by the owner of the *Sealestial*, a monstrous big sloop, yclept the *Concorde*, eighty-eight feet, with room for twelve passengers, and a crew of six.

Boats that size move, for me, just on the other side of manageability; but the idea was seductive, and in any event, there were no practical alternatives. The only nuisance lay in packing and repacking, the freedom from which is one of the splendid perquisites you inherit if you elect not to island-hop from hotel to hotel.

And so we flew to St. Martin (a practical hint: endeavor to begin your cruise from an island to which you can fly without changing planes—and baggage).

The very first night out on a boat, away from a cold city, is an experience very difficult to compare with others, unless you get into the business of the day the gates opened and you left prison a free man. I suspect that many people cultivate, during the days and weeks before a vacation, a specially strenuous schedule, so that the contrary sensation of stepping into a boat and leaving forthwith for the privacy of a lagoon off somewhere becomes something like what the dope-afflicted call a rush.

St. Martin has two harbors, neither of them memorable, but both pleasant. We set sail for St. Barts, which is east, with its harbor so picturesque, always full of conventionally sleek but also idiosyncratic boats—the loners, who after transatlantic passages usually make land in Antigua, and almost all seem to have an appetite to see St. Barts, seventy-five miles northwest.

But we had a secret destination. A few years ago we discovered a little cove on the west side of Anguilla, which is, I think, the only piece of property that has ever inclined me to imperialism—I would like to conquer Anguilla and reward myself with that little cove.

I don't really know what all goes on in Anguilla, and it is this ignorance about Caribbean life I do not pretend to conceal. All I know is that the word *anguila* in Spanish means "eel," and that little island, about eighteen miles long, slithers its way southwest to northeast rather as an eel, that a little bit south of our little anchorage and a couple of miles offshore is the quintessential little island, the kind you see drawn by cartoonists for the convenience of the caption makers. You know—a sand-oval not much bigger than a giant turtle, with one palm tree jutting up from the middle of it. It is visible from our little anchorage, a most awful tease, as though the man who does Macy's windows had sneaked in the night before to make fun of our perfection. Never mind, I say: Never mind, Pat says; Never mind, Dick and Shirley say, and Schuyler and Betty, and we raise our glasses to our perfect little anchorage, and pity the rest of the whole wide world.

I intended an overnight sail to the Virgins. I like one of these even when one cruises hedonistically. It has a way of reminding you that somebody has to grow the peaches, and whip the cream. It is really quite uncomfortable to wake at midnight and stand watch for four hours, but the idea was not more than a velleity, so that when the captain of the substitute boat, unaccustomed to my imperious ways, said he would rather sail during the day, I suffered him to do so, arriving just before dark at Read Town in Tortola, with its orderly, rounded quay, the yachts lined up European style, stern first, the museum reminding us of the bloody history of the Caribbean where for so many centuries the idea was that everyone should kill everyone else, while all the flag makers were kept busy changing prevailing standards, from Dutch, to French, Spanish, English, Danish.

But we had come to Tortola primarily to pick up two passengers, one of them our son, and we set out with great happiness the next morning, running over to Virgin Gorda for a dive, and then a long downwind sail to St. John and Caneel Bay, where we would yield our vessel and board the *Concorde*.

We spent Christmas night at a bay just north of Caneel, and that was wonderfully happy, with Pat's lights and trees and a great volume of gifts exchanged, some of them in the form of IOUs bearing pictures of gifts that lay in waiting for us back home but were too bulky to carry. (I was not about to bring to my son the collected works of the Beatles on disks to a vessel that does not have a disk player.) The music was splendid. Boats enjoy the advantage cars enjoy. Their shape makes for a natural baffle, so that indifferent cassette players give off a very full sound, and we had aboard not only the conventional Handel but some arrangements absolutely perfect of the Christmas carols (the Bach Choir, David Willcocks conducting) done with a special originality, designed to please those whose cup is very full.

Oh yes, the *Concorde*. It began to blow quite hard from the north, so that the question was where to go with it, and we ended by taking it on two or three twenty-mile triangular courses, as if racing. It is a most exquisitely designed boat, and the cuisine below cannot be matched in the best hotel in the Caribbean. But it is a little disheartening to see two girls wrestling with each of two coffee grinders needed to winch up and then swing in the tremendous sails. To sail it for an hour or two, returning to your point of origin, is on the order of what Virgil Thomson wrote about a composition by—was it Vaughan Williams?—that it was like boarding the *Queen Mary* in Manhattan in order to travel to Brooklyn.

But there is great pleasure to be got, if that is the kind of thing that appeals to you, in studying this boat at sea, driven by the hugest single sail I have ever seen. The silky-smooth-light-suntan-oil Caribbean we think of, and indeed often experience, can work its way up into quite a lather. When these things happen at sea, bound to far off destinations, they can bring protracted discomfort. But when you cruise, the pain is going to go away sometime before sundown; and you are suddenly floating again, quite still, save for the little motion that reminds you you are on a vessel, quite alone if that is your mood, or socializing with good friends, if that is your mood; and that nothing is pressing, and tomorrow we will see what the wind is like and acknowledge that the Caribbean's weather, like its people, can be distinctive, different, pleasant, hospitable, alluring and also all those other things.

I despair of ever persuading great lots of people who spend the same money at hotels to try cruising. I experimented with every conventional inducement when I owned a vessel for hire. I don't really know the reason for the general resistance, though, of course, seasickness figures in some cases. In others I suspect it is a slight fear. Of what? I don't really know, but again I suspect it is a fear that, on a boat, it is too easy to—act wrong. Well, it's true. It's easy to make a serious mistake if you're crewing for the America's Cup. But on the Caribbean, in a good boat, with competent crew, there isn't really anything you can do to disgrace yourself—I mean, that you couldn't as well do at the Paradise Beach Hotel. Do give it a try,

but not on the *Sealestial* at Christmas time, because that's reserved until
they lower me down.

Riding an Atlantic High
Signature, February 1984

Gazpar chatted as we drove up, up across the high hills of little Faial, climbing from the southern to the northern coast. "When I was drafted in the
Portuguese army, I arrived in Lisbon. And do you know what? Zay ask me,
why are you not a Negro? And then when I tell them that I am a Portuguese
from the Azores, they do not know even that the Azores are Portuguese:
that's hard to imagine but then a recent survey revealed that an American
college freshman thought Shirley Temple was the author of *Uncle Tom's
Cabin*. But even if Gazpar had hit a singularly ignorant group of Portuguese
fellow recruits, his complaint is distressingly plausible. I know, because I
have tried explaining the islands to people—and, after a while, just gave up.

The first time was after I sailed by the Azores, crossing the Atlantic
in my schooner in 1975. I came back vibrating with the experience. "*Let
me tell you about the Azores*," I would begin. I wanted to tell people about
more flowers than in the whole rest of the whole world put together, about
volcanoes, some of which erupted with astonishing frequency, about jew-
eled lakes surrounded by a hundred different varieties of trees and shrubs,
about hydrangeas so thick they served as fences to keep the Swiss white-
brown cows in their undulating, irregular pastures, about great cliffs overlooking volcanic beaches, about a gentlefolk so proud and gracious.... But
always I found I needed to start at the very beginning. It was as if Pavarotti,
embarked on "Celeste Aida," was always being stopped after the first few
bars... "Wait a minute, Mr. Pavarotti. Just who is Aida?"

I was breathless on the subject of the Azores, because I deem them the
most beautiful islands in the world. Or, necessarily to modify that claim,
the most beautiful islands I have ever been to in this world (and you tell
me where there are more beautiful islands, because I am going there tomorrow). And so, I would begin again, patiently.

The Azores, I explained, are islands that sit approximately two-thirds of the way between us and Portugal, which is the country that owns them. There are nine of them, stretching out across 400 miles of the Atlantic, about 150 miles north to south. They take up, all told, 924 square miles. Distances between them vary from five miles to 150 miles. One of the islands, Terceira, has a huge American-Portuguese air base responsible for reconnaissance over the entire central Atlantic. They were discovered nobody exactly knows when (the islands first appeared, if somewhat astray, on Catalonian maps in the 1350s), but the Portuguese got there some seventy years before Columbus discovered America. And get this: Do you know why we are missing the name of the captain who formally—i.e., in the name of the Portuguese king—claimed them in 1427? Because in 1836 George Sand, the French author (who was a she), spilled ink over the single chart that bore the fellow's name (typical of she-authors who call themselves "George"), forever obliterating, in those pre-Xerox days, the identity of that dauntless historic figure.

On and on I would rattle, but after a while, *pari passu* with my listeners' wandering attention, I would wear out. The whole subject was, somehow, fanciful; too remote. My enthusiasm somehow surrealistic. So that it was on the order of enlisting an expedition to verify that I had indeed laid eyes on a hanging garden of Babylon that I conscripted my wife and sister, and Betsy Little, to join me and Christopher Little, who had been with me on the sailing trip, to go over to see what we had seen.

It begins to sound as though you can get to the Azores only on a sailboat. Well, that's one way, and no longer all that unusual—559 sailboats had stopped in São Miguel this year by the time we got there. There was a time, up until a dozen years ago, when you could get there by steamship. Directly after the war, most westbound transatlantic airliners stopped in the Azores for refueling. A generation earlier the islands were regularly visited by several steamship companies. And a generation before that we were in the great days of the clipper ships. There is a photograph of the harbor of São Miguel, and you can count twenty sturdy sailing vessels at anchor, and, everywhere, the appurtenances of a whaling industry. The last whale taken in the Azores was just over a year ago. The yearly catch had reduced to just over one hundred (compare the Japanese catch of 36,000); the whale oil had become only marginally profitable—so the Azores government just killed off the industry. At that point in the industry's desuetude, probably fewer than fifty men were thrust into unemployment.

But getting to the Azores now is different. You must fly. Direct from New York two nights a week during the summer, only on Wednesday night the rest of the time. We were not free to leave on a Wednesday, so we needed to go all the way to Lisbon, on TAP, the Portuguese national airline, wait three hours and fly back to Terceira, 2,000 extra miles, all told. From Lisbon there is also a daily flight to Ponta Delgada, on the island of São Miguel, which is the island that paradise gnashes its teeth in jealousy of. And, in two or three years, the runway there will be stretched out to make possible direct flights from New York, should the traffic suddenly (unexpectedly) warrant such flights. Connecting flights from island to island, notwithstanding that there are substantial differences in distance, uniformly take one half-hour, ask not why.

The point is simply that it is not easy to get to the Azores, and the reason for this is that not many people wish to go, and the reason for that is that not as many people as should know about the Azores know about the Azores. There were just over 7,000 visitors to Faial this past year, and 65 percent of these were Azorean-Americans, who outnumber Azoreans by a factor of about four to one, there being only about 250,000 residents of the Azores, about as many as people the Bahamas. The official count is a little higher than that, but there is a little doodling there because the more Azoreans there are, the bigger the slice of the economic pie from Lisbon. The Azorean population comes to about two-and-a-half percent of the total Portuguese population worldwide; and during this century every census, decade after decade, shows the Azorean population dwindling, though not so markedly this last time around since emigration to the United States and Canada had eased up a little. This is so in part because the islands were given significant autonomy after the revolution in Lisbon in 1974 that overthrew what was left of the Salazar dynasty.

Most Portuguese-Americans visiting their relatives make their way to a single island and stay there. The tourists want to get about, and although there is one inter-island steamship, which improvises its routes between the

islands with reference to wind and seas and, one supposes, volcanic eruptions, it deems vulgar any question having to do with estimated times of
arrival anywhere. It is the airline that is the common inter-island carrier.
(Nobody can give you a rational reason why the Azoreans do not like the
sea, the great Portuguese-explorer-navigator tradition notwithstanding.
The steamship is sometimes so sparsely patronized that the company finds
itself giving airplane tickets to the passengers, patting them on the back
and, with great relief, canceling that scheduled voyage.)

On every island there is a place for visitors to stay, which is how best
to describe one or two of the local caravanseries, for instance on Pico.
In Angra, the imposing little-Rio of Terceira (capital of the northeast
group of islands), or in Horta on Faial (capital of the western group), or
on São Miguel (capital of the southwestern group), there are solid hotels
from which, in rented or chauffeured car, one drives about these volcanic
greenhouses. It takes 300 to 500 years after an eruption before the ground
becomes fertile, which is why—they tell you on Faial, as they point up at the
great volcano of Cabouco that erupted in 1672—it is not yet quite green
up there. But whatever it is that slows up the fertility of volcanic ash, there
is a tidal wave of lushness when the period of maidenhood finally arrives. It
is not easy for an amateur to figure out what it is that would *not* take root
in the Azorean islands. Perhaps cactus and watermelon, but surely nothing
between. No snakes, by the way.

We were on the subject of logistics. Yes, there is another way to get
about, and we elected that extravagant alternative. If you can swing it, this is
worth doing. It is to see and travel among the islands on your own chartered
sailboat. There is a difficulty, however. Incredibly, in all the Azores there is
not a single sailing yacht based there that is suitable for six passengers and
regularly available for charter. So, if you wish to sail about the Azores, you
need to hitchhike aboard one of the vessels putting into the islands during
their twice-yearly diagonal trek across the Atlantic, either from the Caribbean to the Mediterranean (May-June) or from Mediterranean to Caribbean (September-October). During these months about fifty comfortable
sailing yachts are hungry for charterers to ferry about the islands. It's 1,000
miles out of the way to sail to Antigua from Gibraltar by way of the Azores,

but yacht owners are relatively indifferent to distances. What is another 1,000 miles in a voyage 4,000 miles long?

If you plan ahead and consult a yacht charter broker, you can tour the enchanted islands on a boat, enjoying yourself at sea as well as on land. But be careful about the dates. If you want to see the islands in full bloom, you should not arrive in the Azores much after the fourth week of September, though even then the traces of the great flower harvest are everywhere. At the other end, you should plan to arrive sometime after the first of June. For four months the islands are bathed in flowers. One tourist, deft at recording such detail, saw in a single day geranium, fuchsia rose, carnation, orange, lemon, lime, guava, grape, magnolia, palm, sugar cane, banana, tobacco, India rubber, camellia, apricot, oleander—and then, one assumes, stopped counting.

Why aren't there more tourists? A very interesting question. The promotion of the Azores is on the lackadaisical side. The Azoreans are ambivalent on the subject of tourists. Yes, they would like more people to feast on their beautiful islands. No, they do not want to transform the Azores into another Bermuda. (*We have nothing against Bermuda!* they will add, hastily, with habitual courtesy.) There are no white sand beaches—though one gets used to the darkness of basalt beaches. (Who knows, if we were well accustomed to dark sand, it might be advertised as guaranteed not to turn white in the sun.) The salt water is cool, not languid-warm. No nightclubs (they could easily be started), no roulette wheels (again, easy). There are superb little eateries—run not for tourists but for natives. The Cabalho Blanco on São Miguel would rate three stars in New York if they gussied up the serving plates and decor—you wouldn't need to do a thing to the food.

What else is there to do?

Well, that depends on whether quite awesome beauty pleases you sufficiently to frustrate boredom. Look, there is on São Miguel the phenomenon of Sete Cidades. You drive up to 6,000 feet, and suddenly you are staring down at a crater two miles in diameter. Within it are two smaller craters, lakes now, eye-to-eye. Where the nose would be is a gleaming white village with the characteristic mourning-look architecture—the austere Portuguese colonial white with dark brown trim—way down there, distant, 3,000 feet below you. The nearer lake, you suddenly notice, is emerald green. The adjacent lake, cerulean blue. Why? Well you see, the horrible King Sete discovered that his young princess had fallen in love with the humble shepherd, and so he tore them asunder. Their separation—by a ten-foot-wide land bridge—caused great sadness, such that they continue to weep copiously, his green tears filling the one lake, her blue tears the adjacent lake, lakes that touch each other, even as the boughs of Baucis and Philemon nestle together in the legend.

What kind of people inhabit the Azores? Such as you would expect if you came upon islands inhabited primarily by people concerned with survival. The first preoccupation of any people is food, and it is only after food is available that the appetite wanders, eventually concerning itself with the amenities. On the islands of Terceira and São Miguel there is a little light industry, but not so very much of it. Even so, as is true in almost any poor country, there are the niches in which people express themselves, the individuation of the species.

Consider Otto. His real name is Othon Silveira. Although middle-aged, he just got married, and did so on his twelfth trip to the United States. How does a poor Azorean manage to travel twelve times to the United States? One does not know; and one does not inquire. Especially not of Otto, because the possibilities are too wild. If he had been invited to the United States by the governors of the Cruising Club of America, that would not have surprised us in the least.

If you are lost in Horta, you will find Pete's Bar. It is a room in which twenty-four people, at the most, can be uncomfortably seated, but it is also the center of sailing life. It is at Pete's that you leave messages, for instance. For other sailors? For anybody. And it is Pete who will change your money, or tell you where to go to find a gasket for your engine. A hundred yards from Pete's Bar, up on horses, there is all that remains of a thirty-six-foot steel-hulled yacht, discovered a few weeks earlier by a fishing boat. Its eighty-year-old owner-captain, a Dutchman, was ever-so-dead. The bones were actually protruding. He had died from starvation, and the reconstruction of his last days, done by examining the boat and its accouterments, advised us that he had attempted to flag one or two passing vessels in order to advertise his having run out of food, failed; and just passed away, at the wheel. It was to Pete, of course, that the information was given, since it was more or less assumed that he would get the word to somebody in Holland, and perhaps someday someone will come and claim the hull. It is still seaworthy.

Pete is said to be quite wealthy now, and he plans to open a little museum alongside his bar, dedicated to his father, who founded the bar, which will in due course be tended by his son, Jorgé, already active.

Otto is likely to show up when you are at a native restaurant attempting to decipher the menu. Suddenly Otto will be there, speaking his excellent English, and telling you what you should order, what you should avoid. Thank you very much, Otto, and what do you do? I am a scrimshander, he says, with some pride. And so, you arrange to visit his quarters.

They are in the cellar of a little house, to which you have access through a trap door. He sits on a stool in the crowded little room, about the size of a jail cell. With his left hand he is holding a whale tooth, with his right, the little steel device, like a dentist's pick, with which he etches his designs on the blackened object which, when burnished with a rotary tool of the kind that polishes your shoes, leaves on the tooth only the scrimshander's etchwork.

But Otto is only one-half occupied with his scrimshaw. Half his time is spent twirling the knobs of his ham radio, where he is the center of a very large universe. He is relaying messages to ships at sea, to Azoreans newly arrived in New Bedford, no doubt translating menus for Americans at sea in Lisbon restaurants. Behind him in a crowded bookshelf are scrapbooks crammed with pictures and filled with messages of abject devotion. You will find on one page a picture of a huge sailing yacht. And opposite, such inscriptions as: "To my dear Othon, without whose help I would never have succeeded in a passage so dear to my heart. Dear Otto, what can I ever do to repay you? Doris Duke."

There is a great will to assist people. The Azores is the kind of place where if you ask where the post office is, the person is most likely to lead you there. Pete and Otto are in their own way unique, but they do not misrepresent the Azorean temper, which seems to desire to be as agreeable to visitors as nature is agreeable to them.

There are, they like to say, as many as four seasons in a given day in the Azores, so changeable is the weather. But it is never very cold or very hot (the temperature is never lower than forty-three degrees Fahrenheit, or higher than seventy-eight). And there is every kind of topography save dry desert—though the most recent of the titanic eruptions, in Faial, would look like desert if the ash were yellow instead of brown. But there is everything else. Moors and pasture, cliffs and ponds, mountains and valleys, spas and geysers.

The impact of these islands makes poets of people quite commonplace, for instance, a great-granddaughter of John Bass, sometime US consul in Horta. Of Faial she wrote that the "name is freighted with magic charm; it recalls an ideal home life; it suggests hedges of camellia trees, or fragrant pittsosporum, tangles of roses and fields of sky-blue flax; it brings to mind all manner of picturesque island scenes; and truly there are times when we feel God's presence, as, with the mind's eye, we behold the mountain of Pico standing like a heavenly beacon, only a few miles away from our own beloved Island." You can't say that kind of thing about just any place, now can you? Promise yourself to visit the Azores before you die, or before a definitive eruption causes that haunting archipelago to sink into the vasty deep, rejoining the continent of Atlantis to which legend has it belonging, adding to the luster of underwater life.

Ah, Solitude

Frequent Flyer, December 1984

The editor has asked that I supply a list of "survival tactics" for frequent flyers. Now, there is an element of risk in undertaking such a thing because in some situations that which causes John to survive causes James not to survive, for instance if both desire the identical seat, or the one remaining salmon steak. But often, most passengers can effect survival on the very same flight, and so I essay a brief list.

There is the matter of how you desire to spend your time while traveling. I write here for those who very much desire either to work, or to read: not to converse. David Niven was a frequent flyer, and divulged to me a contrivance by which, without giving offense, he avoided conversational lockholds. But sometimes the Niven Method brought on difficulties. Once, landed in Albuquerque en route to some place and sitting in the window seat comfortably, the adjacent seat empty, he spotted someone approaching the gangway along with the other boarding passengers from that city. Niven was a fatalist. "I knew—I just knew—that he would hold the seat number next to me. He was about six feet four, was wearing a huge cowboy hat, an open, colored sports shirt that disclosed, on a T-shirt underneath, COME HOME TO ME, BABY. And, of course—it *was* inevitable—he sat down beside me."

But David Niven, schooled in survival, was ready for him, and when the new arrival said, "Wahl ahll be gawdamned, it's David Niven!" stretching out his hand, David took it, but with his other hand clutched at his throat and let his eyes pop out expressing great turmoil, followed by a painfully extruded grunt, an index finger pointed at his throat—Charlie Chaplin could not have done better the sequences of a man indicating his incapacitation by laryngitis or a throat ailment.

"What then happened," Niven went on, "was that my companion said to me, 'Oh, don' you open yoh mouth, Mr. Niven, don' you say a word. I'll do the talkin' for both of us.'" Niven groaned inwardly.

"But one-half hour later, I knew that I had been listening to one of the most interesting men I had ever come upon. He was an atomic physicist, stationed in New Mexico, and among other friendly things was telling me state secrets, utterly safe with me since, however engrossing, I could never have re-created them." Niven, after this half hour, gave a performance no one returning from the waters of Lourdes could have bettered—his throat ailment suddenly, magically, disappearing. On the other hand, unless you have won an Oscar, I would advise against the Niven Method.

My own method is to surround myself with papers. It isn't good enough merely to be reading a magazine or a book, not even if your very life depends on your mastery of the reading material by the time you arrive in Dallas. But most passengers are sufficiently driven by what is left of the work ethic to leave you alone if they think you are *really* busy, which means lots of paperwork. I grant that sometimes I get carried away. The *Christian Science Monitor* recently reported on "Today's High-Flying Businessman:

Have Typewriter, Will Travel." "According to a longtime TWA flight attendant I know, no business traveler is quite so capable of wrapping himself in a six-mile-high cocoon as William F. Buckley Jr. 'I had Mr. Buckley on a transatlantic flight,' she said, 'and he had what looked like a month's worth of work beside him, piled all the way up to his lap. I noticed he didn't speak to the man beside him, he was so totally engrossed. When he got up to stretch his legs, the other man called me over. He said he couldn't find his shoes under the pile of Mr. Buckley's discarded papers. We finally found one and then another, but it wasn't his shoe. Sure enough, when Mr. Buckley came back he was wearing the other man's shoe on one of his feet.'" The surviving passenger mustn't in short, get carried away.

This may sound affected, but then different people are affected by different things, and—remember—this is a *personal* guide to survival, and one man's survival is not necessarily of general interest. Jody Powell, recently on a television panel to discuss this and that, was asked what he thought of CAB's temporary ruling (the board had reversed itself within an hour) that no one could smoke cigarettes on an airplane whose flight time lasted two hours or less. He replied that, as a smoker, he would greatly resent any such imposition. He smiled: "Some people get on an airplane with dirty socks. Is CAB going to rule they can't get on flights that last more than one hour?"

Nice point. Some people are more allergic to cigarette smoke than others, and us nonsmokers who happen to be married to smokestacks, a) question the prevailing assumption that the smokestack industries in the United States are in high desuetude; and b) either get used to the proximity of cigarette smoking, or else fly to Reno and begin all over again.

So it is that a wine lover who wants to survive the average bottle of white wine served on our common carriers would do well to bring along—a bottle. Of nice wine. Not expensive wine, it doesn't have to be. But a wine different from the boilerplate California white that affects some people the way dirty socks affect Jody Powell. A four-dollar bottle of wine, carefully chosen, can greatly lighten the flying mood.

I contest the frequently asserted complaint that baggage is regularly lost on airplane trips, my own record hovering at maybe over 95 percent successful reunion with my baggage. But—and this is *very* important: when your ticket stubs are written out, and you note that your bags are designated to fly to ARGO, ask, sweetly, either the porter outside, or the agent inside, what ARGO stands for. If he/she says, "Why, Little Rock, of course," then, if appropriate, say, sweetly, "But I am not going to Little Rock, Arkansas, I am going to Fairbanks, Alaska." "Ah," he/she will say, looking at your ticket, "Of course! You are going to ROAG! Excuse me!" No problem, you say. You might even add, to leaven the whole incident, "You must be a mind reader, because it's been years since I have been to ARGO, and I plan to go back there one of these days."

There is an intuitive etiquette in the matter of seating. If indeed you have work to do, and cherish the possibility of an empty seat next to you, frequently it happens that, notwithstanding that there are a dozen empty seats scattered about the cabin, the boarding passenger will deposit himself, and his own paraphernalia, next to you, requiring you to move your mass of papers. You must feel free, after you are airborne, to remove yourself to one of the seats next to which there is an empty one. A pleasant way to do this is to excuse yourself—you need to go to the men's room. Go. And, on your return, smile and say that since you have so much messy gear about you, you will move to where you will create less bother. There is seldom, if it is handled in this way, any residual offense given.

You are seared more or less amidship, working, and the cabin attendant asks that you close your window shade, if you are a passenger seated next to the window, so that your fellow passengers can see the screen with greater clarity. This you must do, even if all your life you had looked forward to looking out and seeing the Grand Canyon slip by, seven miles below you. The crunch comes on the matter of the overhead light, which distracts some viewers sitting behind you.

Now on this matter it is relevant, I think, to dwell on eschatalogical divisions. Here is where you mutter to yourself such things as, "Give me liberty or give me death!" Or, "We shall fight on the beaches, we shall fight in the fields and in the streets, but we shall *never* surrender." Or even, "What does it matter if you gain all the world, but lose your immortal soul?"

If you wish to read, or work; or read and work—you keep your light on! Having come forward with this hair-on-the-chest machismo I must confess that for many years I felt the same way about my Right to Type. This right no longer exists: passengers will not tolerate so aggressive a noise in the cabin. I suspect that traveling working writers were creepingly overwhelmed by the noiseless revolution of the lap-computers, which you *can* operate without disturbing your neighbor. I mourn the loss of those upstairs cabins with cables and simulated desks, where one was expected to work.

One time, flying nonstop from New York to Tokyo, commissioned by the *New York Times* to do a long piece on Hubert Humphrey and phone it in on landing in Tokyo, I repaired to the upper chamber, wrote half the piece, went down for my lunch leaving my papers and typewriter spread out on the table, and returned to find, neatly typed at exactly where I had left off on the subject of Senator Humphrey's longwindednese, "Mr. Buckley, I can only wish your typewriter weren't as long-winded as Senator Humphrey." That cooled the spirit.

But on the matter of your absolute, constitutional right to read while some may choose to view, I say only this, that the survival of your pride requires absolute, unmitigated maintenance of individual rights.

A hint, here: if you begin to sense that groaning miasmic feeling that manages to communicate your neighbors' impatience, put on the headset, as though you were listening to a music channel. As in the United Nations, where delegates are told always to have on their headsets—never mind whether they are actually listening to the speech from the prime minister of the Central African Republic complaining about human rights in Israel— you don't even need to turn the sound on. But you give the impression of an impenetrable fortress. And, soon, the resentment dies down, and you have done your homework, while they have seen how it is that James Bond, himself a frequent flyer, can survive anything.

CHAPTER FIVE

1985–1989

See You Later
June 11, 1985

Five years ago, setting out from Bermuda to the Azores on a sailboat, I advised friends and critics of this space that for the first time I would take two weeks' holiday at one time, instead of the customary one week at Christmas, the second in midsummer. The experience apparently entered my bloodstream because, however unremarked, there were building within me seeds great and strong in effrontery, blossoming one month ago in outright contumacy. What happened one month ago ranks with the day that Oliver Twist held out his porridge plate to the Beadle and asked for "more."

I asked my editor for one month's leave.

It isn't exactly sloth. It is that a month ago I addressed myself to the question of how to transmit my wisdom from where I would be to Kansas City, home of Universal Press Syndicate. I will be on a sailboat wending my way through Micronesia, propelled by the trade winds. I shall be pausing only four times in a five-thousand mile journey, in exotic atolls where telephones function irregularly. One of these atolls is unfriendly to visiting yachtsmen, allowing them to disembark only if wearing gas masks, because the island in question is one of the places where the arsenal of democracy, as we used to call what now goes by the name of the military industrial complex, stores its toxic gases, manufactured back at Bitburg time in case the Axis powers decided to use poison gas against American troops. Evidently there are leaks from time to time from those old rusty tanks, so one goes about in gas masks. The prospect of telephoning in my instructions through a gas mask proved the conclusive argument, my spies tell me, in this unusual act of indulgence by my friendly editors, one of whom is said to have remarked, "He's hard enough to understand speaking through plain ether; I wouldn't want to listen to him through a gas mask."

And so it is that this is the final column. Final, that is, for four weeks, after which, if the Pacific is pacific, they will resume. And the Pacific Ocean, from north latitude twenty degrees in Honolulu to south latitude five degrees in New Guinea, tends to dawdle pretty gently during the summer months, and if we have wind of a typhoon we shall show it great respect. I do not believe in accosting natural irruptions under the rubric of mutual assured destruction.

To get out of the way of a storm whose location you have established requires of course that you know where you are. Well, I will have on board two secret instruments, one conceived by me, a second by a conglomerate of geniuses. This last permits the measurement of one millionth of a second, and this translates, or will by the year 1989, into a little box that tells you where you are so exactly that you can double-park by following its instructions. The other is computer software that permits the navigator—which is me, a sometime columnist—to inform the computer where I think I am, within thirty miles, in which direction that star I just shot is, within thirty degrees, what second, minute, hour, and day it is in Greenwich, England, exactly how high up from the horizon it was—and lo! the heavens vouchsafe you the star's identity. The computer will say, "By Jove, that was Arcturus!" And you will know where you are.

Our preoccupations during this period will be with the nitty-gritty. Heat, for instance. We shall be hovering over the equator, propelled by winds that come astern, as we travel at seven or eight knots. If the wind behind you is sixteen miles per hour and you are moving forward eight miles per hour, the net impact of the wind on your back is a mere eight miles per hour. I have never measured the velocity of the wind from a house fan perched at the corner of your desk, as it used to be before God gave us air-conditioning, but I would guess the wind comes out at twenty or thirty miles per hour, which is why the skin stays tolerably cool. It will be otherwise when the sun is more or less directly above you, the temperature is hour after hour in the high eighties, and your ocean fan dribbles out only one quarter of the air you get from an electric fan. As though the motor had a speed marked Extra Special Slow. In such moments, sailors dream less of wine, women, and song than of Frigidaire.

Do such concerns get wished away, under the category of Problems of the Idle Rich? Well, the case can be made: nobody is forcing me to sail from the United States to the East Indies. But it is the human way to exert oneself every now and again in eccentric enterprises. Last week I listened to a classmate describe his ascent of Everest and wondered how it is that anyone should engage in such madcappery; but then Dick Bass was taking risks I do not contemplate in my irenic passage with my son, and my friends, and books, and music, across the great Pacific Ocean.

Sailing East of Eden
Signature, July 1985

"I'd really love to, but I can't. I'll be out of town." "Where?" "Tahiti, as a matter of fact."

That exchange took place maybe a dozen times last winter. It doesn't surprise you that it was generally followed by something like a whistle, or a smile of romantic envy, or a whaddayouknow, you-really-get-around kind of look. I say it doesn't surprise you because you tipped your hand that you expected that kind of thing when you added, after Tahiti, "as a matter of fact." "As a matter of fact" is the idiomatic tipoff to an announcement the theatricality of which you desire to attenuate ("As a matter of fact, I'm getting married that day").

The mere mention of Tahiti tends to do that, and it is here and there spoken of as the most glamorous island in the world. By which it isn't meant that it is the most beautiful or the most remote or the most anything other than just that: the most glamorous. Thought to be vaguely inaccessible, incurably romantic—the nineteenth-century analogue of King Edward VIII's seduction: he gave up his throne for Wally; Gauguin, his life and family for Tahiti.

It was, of course, to Tahiti that the great French Post-Impressionist went, renouncing the bourgeois world of Paris, so that he could dedicate himself to his muse. In his memory there is, at the far end of the island, twenty-five miles from Papeete, a nicely organized museum on the site where Gauguin lived and worked. It is scattered with memorabilia, none of them, unless it happens to be there temporarily on loan, a painting by Gauguin because—a nice irony—the Gauguin Museum can't afford a Gauguin painting, and it is even documented, in one of the display cases, what the last dozen public sales of Gauguin paintings have brought in. If he had had half the proceeds from the posthumous sale of just one of those paintings, he could have lived the whole of his life in relative luxury.

I thought the whole thing an interesting symbol of modern Tahiti. You can view a reproduction of a Gauguin painting for very little, but it costs a whole lot to buy a Gauguin. You can read about Tahiti, and it is, of course, a whole lot less expensive than going there. But people who take the trouble hardly regret it—the publisher of *National Review* has been eight times; his attorney, seven times. They are under the irreversible impression that heaven will be heaven only to the degree that it approaches the beauty, the leisure, the repose of the soul that they have both found in the area, both especially favoring the island of Bora Bora.

Sure, there are things to watch out for, and indeed it happened that we ran into them. Principal among these is the time of year. Beware. Just as you would not choose the month of December to travel the fjords of Norway, so you ought not to choose the month of December to visit Tahiti. But then you might strike it lucky. "Lucky" here is defined as that characteristically bright, balmy, sunny day, with the wind cooling you and bringing you the fragrance of the island. Remember that December is midsummer below the equator. Give it a wide berth if you want to be safe. But don't strike it from your list. There may be things to watch out for, but the joy of the island—a masterstroke of nature—makes it all worthwhile.

Well then, what are the mechanical considerations? What about price? Accessibility?

A travel agent in New York, when asked whether we might postpone our trip by a couple of days, answered with accented impatience that didn't

Mr. Buckley understand that "Tahiti is the Caribbean of California?" By this she meant to convey that just as loads of people from the east coast of America travel to places like Nassau and the Virgin Islands and St. Martin and Antigua and Grenada over the holidays, so in the west, during the holidays, they all go to Tahiti.

Comment: balderdash. It would be wonderful if they all did, because the Society Islands are hauntingly beautiful, explosively lush, tropical and unforgettably romantic, alluring. But then there are fine compensations in not running into as many people as one runs into here and there in the cosmopolitan centers of the Caribbean.

But there is also a wonderfully mysterious background story, teeming with national and corporate intrigue. It is one version of why so few people visit this enchanting group of islands.

First, some round figures.

About 100,000 people per year visit French Polynesia (Tahiti is the principal island of a huge area, the size of Europe, that includes three sets of islands). By contrast, 400,000 per year visit Fiji ("which by comparison," a hotel owner in Papeete told us, "has no charm"). And Fiji is farther than Tahiti by a couple of thousand miles. To get a more general perspective on tourism, Hawaii gets five million visitors per year (and Spain, 40 million!).

So why, Tahiti being so red-hot, do so few people go there? The proposition that it is the Caribbean of California is silly. There are forty planes leaving New York City alone, every day, headed for some place in the Caribbean. There are nine planes per week—most of them belonging to UTA French Airlines—headed for Tahiti and they leave from a single spot, Los Angeles.

There are two reasons for the relative isolation of French Polynesia. The first, stressed by more than one local hotel manager in Tahiti, is a matter of international intrigue. That thesis is as follows: the continuing colonization of French Polynesia by France is important not only for the obvious strategic reasons but in a very particular way. You see, 800 miles south of Papeete is the island where the French conduct their atomic tests. Atomic testing is not a popular ecological event these days and it requires a firm dominion over the surrounding area to get on with this activity. The thesis holds that it is in the best interests of France to keep French Polynesia on a short leash.

France sends $45 million a year to sustain the area, in which only 160,000 people live. The need for $45 million per year—about a million per week—could end quickly if the tourist rate were, oh, doubled, let alone tripled, let alone increased by a multiple of ten.

This, as the thesis explains, is prevented by the high cost of an airplane ticket. "Look," one native complained, "Los Angeles to Hawaii is five hours. Los Angeles to Tahiti is seven and a half hours. But you can go round trip to Hawaii for 400 bucks. It costs 900 bucks to go round trip to Tahiti." True. And probably true, as reported, that Pan American gave up its rights to fly to Tahiti because Paris wouldn't let Pan Am charge a true economy rate; it didn't want either the competition or the higher volume of visitors.

Moreover, once you land in Tahiti you are not by any means through spending money. In Bora Bora, at the principal hotel, the overnight charge is $300. One hot, hot noon in Raiatea, at the Kia Oro Hotel, the four of us ordered rum punches. Everything about the rum punch was delicious except the price: $5 each. Moorea has some nice boutiques. One of them sold scrimshaw. I noticed one priced at $2,350. It was designated "exquisite" on the same label that gave the price. Presumably if they had asked $3,350 for it they'd have described it as "extremely exquisite." (You can find as pretty a scrimshaw for one-third the price in Maui or Nantucket.) On the other hand, it takes the temperament of an accountant on full-time duty to remember the high price of anything on such an island as Moorea. You circle it in an open car, and for a few miles you ricochet from one boutique to another, each redolent with wares that somehow blend with the ambience. And as you get away from them, you are left with the little road winding through palm trees and flowers of every description, to your right the endless sandy beaches, to the left the semitropical grass, and the glades ascending sharply to the mountain peaks. You are made to feel isolated in a natural abundance: you notice the prices only because in Eden everything was free.

So then, arranging to go to Tahiti is not to be compared with the ease of flying to the Caribbean. Flying there is expensive, and staying there is expensive. And another concern, already mentioned, is very much related to the time of year.

The great itch to get away from America's icy season, combined with the inclination to festive self-indulgence, means a lot of travel around Christmas time.

Well, you take a chance with the weather if you travel to French Polynesia in the month of December; to play it very safe, you wait until late April or May.

Safe from what? A lot of rain. We had it ten of the eleven days we spent there, and that eleventh day's sun was as flirtatious as an ecdysiast, appearing with studied reluctance only every couple of hours, after the customers had bought enough drinks.

There is the rain, and there is the heat. If the wind is active, the heat is bearable. But sometimes the wind is dormant, or else you are shielded from it, and the temperature then becomes close to intolerable for those carefree Americans who are used to walking about under an air-conditioned parasol. There is air-conditioning in the finer hotels, for instance the Tahara'a in Papeete, but a lot of the fancy hotels that shoot out on stilts over the alluring beaches are without air-conditioning.

There was no air-conditioning on the sailing vessel we cruised on in the Society Islands—as Captain Cook designated that cluster of the French Polynesian islands, because they lie so close to each other as to represent, by the long-legged standards of Captain Cook, the equivalent of municipal congestion. Captain Cook and his crew finally reached Tahiti in 1769, after eight months at sea. One can appreciate, under the circumstances, that the sail from Tahiti to the island of Bora Bora, a mere 416 miles, was for Captain Cook the equivalent of a trip from the East River to the Hudson. For the modern, afternoon sailor, the distances between the islands are on the hefty side. Rather like the Antilles contrasted with the Virgins. A typical day's sail in the Society Islands is six to eight hours—but an engrossing day at sea, with just that vague, stimulating sense of danger that maintains the keenness of the experience. There are great stalagmites under those waters, many of which reach teasingly up to just inches and feet under the surface, so that at one moment your fathometer will show you with one hundred feet of clearance and the next moment you will be sitting on top of a coral reef. Never, says the good book wisely, go close to shore when the sun is below twenty-five degrees above the horizon. Do as you are told.

On the matter of the heat, one can hardly blame on the Society Islands the impositions of their geographical location. They are situated, as a matter of fact, slightly east of Hawaii, not west as is popularly supposed. But they are way, way south, almost exactly as far south of the equator as Hawaii is north of the equator. And it happens that, at about Christmas time, at latitude twenty degrees south, the sun is, so to speak, overhead. And unlike, say, the Galápagos, which squat flat on the equator, the area hasn't the benefit of quirky air currents that bring in coolness.

It is just plain hot. And, of course, when our hot and sticky season comes along—summertime—it is perfect in French Polynesia: wintertime, at a climate the equivalent of the Dominican Republic's in December. But most of the summer itch among US travelers is for refuge from summer heat, which is why American tourists begin to think in terms of Europe, or Canada, or for that matter the abnormal heights of Mexico City. A pity, because French Polynesia is, really—wiping away the enumerated disadvantages—a most beautiful place to visit; and, for sailors, a special joy.

One acknowledges the mischievous temptation to resist conventional myths. But this is not possible in Tahiti for so simple a reason as that the legend of this tropical paradise is based on substantial reality. The islands are, on anyone's measure, spectacular visual creations. Why (ever?) compete with Herman Melville in such matters? He put it about Tahiti:

> Seen from the sea, the prospect is magnificent. It is one mass of shaded tints of green, from beach to mountaintop; endlessly diversified with valleys, ridges, glens and cascades. The loftiest peaks cast their shadows over the ridges and down into the valleys. At the head, these waterfalls glitter in the sunlight as if pouring through vertical bowers of verdure. Such an enchanted air breathes over the whole that it seems a fairyland, fresh and pure from the hand of the Creator. The picture becomes no less attractive upon nearer approach. It is no exaggeration to say that a European of any sensibility who wanders into the valleys for the first time, away from the haunts of the natives, sees every object

as if in a dream, owing to the ineffable repose and beauty of its landscape; for a while, he almost refuses to believe that scenes like these
should have a commonplace existence.

There now, it has got to be worth it to verify whether a place so described
has that effect on you. What will Bora Bora or Tahaa or Raiatea or Huahine
or Moorea or Rangiroa or Tahiti do to you? Will you be tempted by going
there to do as Rupert Brooke did? "Tonight we will put scarlet flowers in
our hair and sing strange, slumbrous South Sea songs to the concertina, and
drink red French wine, and dance, and bathe in a soft lagoon by moonlight,
and eat great squelchy tropical fruits."

You can do all of that in those islands, and wonder at their beauty. And
it is not fair to dwell nostalgically on the memory of what they must have
seemed like as recently as a generation ago, when a visit to Tahiti was something other than a simple jet ride. With the new postwar age, there are new
conveniences, including the air-conditioning and all the restaurants and
the lovely hotels with the little individual cottages that cozy up to what
becomes your private beach.

We were glad we went. Principally, our problem was that we went to
the Louvre wearing dark glasses, to the Metropolitan Opera House wearing earmuffs, to Tahiti in the rain. Do not make that mistake. But do not,
either, make the mistake of failing to see and to explore the Society Islands.
Order your life so that next May, June, July, August, September, or October
you can answer the question "Where are you going on your next vacation?"
with, "Well, as a matter of fact, I'm going to Tahiti."

Sailing Free: A Companionable Journey Across the Pacific
Life, November 1985

Five months earlier I had said in a memo to all concerned: At 16:00, June 2,
we'll set out. From Honolulu to Asia.

Where exactly in Asia I wasn't yet certain. I leaned to Auckland…
though three months later I decided instead to go to New Guinea. It takes
that kind of time to plan *this* kind of trip. It was twenty-four months

before setting out that the crew was selected, a year before that the vessel was finally lined up. So that when—at, yes, 16:00, give or take a few minutes—eleven of us pushed away from the yacht club at Honolulu, waving to a few friends, one wife and sister-in-law, en route to the other end of the Pacific Ocean we felt on the one hand the kind of assembly-line fatalism the astronauts must feel with their two-year countdowns. On the other hand, the sensation of—yes—the explorer, because even though the oceans are now charted, and you know where the rocks and shoals and the islands and the continents lie, you do not know what else you are going to find or not to find.

I need to confess right up front that this wasn't designed as a Spartan experience. Some years ago a major magazine ran a piece about a seventeen-year-old boy who set out to sail across the Pacific singlehanded on a small boat—a thirty-two footer, as I remember. His capital consisted of the boat and its gear, drinking water and canned goods for couple of months at sea, and $50 his father had endowed him with. A haunting and exotic story, I thought: but my curiosity focused finally on a picture of a boy taking a shower aboard his boat halfway between Tahiti, oh, and Fiji. The picture depicted the showering subject, the entire sailboat and stretches of endless sea all about them. Question: How was the picture taken? Did the magazine send out a passenger pigeon trained to take pictures at sea? Did NASA contribute the use of a Peeping Tom satellite, you know, the kind that, magnifying its negatives, can read the classifieds in *Pravda* from 11,000 miles above Moscow? A strolling submarine taking advantage of a photo opportunity?

A grain of skepticism entered the system that day and guides me now to Full Disclosure. That commitment to disclosure doesn't compel me to say that crossing the Pacific on a sailboat can be made effortless. Or even that it is always fun. Or that there is no discomfort. Or even that there is no danger. But it does compel me to say that there are ways of crossing the Pacific on a sailboat that hugely lessen the exertions, physical and mental, of the experience: the loneliness, boredom, and tedium.

So that when we set out on the seventy-one-foot *Sealestial*, bound for Papua, New Guinea, 4,600 statute miles away, we were about as well insulated from the vicissitudes of life at sea as one could reasonably hope to be.

To begin, we had Liz, maybe the finest sea-cook afloat. Before we disembarked, thirty days later, she would serve up 1,000 meals. We had Noddy as first mate, who notwithstanding his truculent Rastafarian hairstyle, is a gentle and ingenious young man from Barbados. Maureen was there to serve meals and make beds and, primarily, to teach us all how to always be more cheerful. Allan Jouning, the finest skipper of my acquaintance, to help wherever help was most crucially needed.

And six carefully selected companions: our job was to sail *Sealestial*, to ascertain where we were to hold the course, to cope with squalls, to forecast the weather, to write our journals, to endure isolation in a relatively small craft, and carefully to steer our way without human abrasion through a thirty-day retreat from cosmopolitan lives of hectic texture far removed from the rusticity of life at sea.

Christopher (my thirty-two-year-old son) was among other things in charge of R&R, and every morning he would post the day's extra-navigational doings in the saloon. A typical notice: *Tonight: Bonnie and Clyde! The melodramatic adventures of the century's most sizzling bank robbers! At Sealestial Odeon, 8 p.m.!* We trolled two fishing lines and twice had exciting catches, one a fifty-five-pound mahi mahi, that, once landed onto the after-cockpit, Allan Jouning dispatched by the novel contrivance of pouring a jiggerful of vodka into his gills bringing on, to our astonishment, instant death: death rapid and ostentatious enough to satisfy the most apocalyptic evangelist for the WCTU. We had a .410 shotgun aboard and did a little skeet shooting, and a .223 Ruger rifle with which to discourage sharks while we swam during the periodic lulls and also to beat up on beer cans tossed overboard as targets.

Occasionally Christopher would screw together a miniature Ping-Pong table. The tournament was scheduled below in the saloon if it was too rocky on deck. But when the seas were especially calm, the contest was played on the foredeck, under the sunny sun. Oh yes, speaking of vodka, we had fifty cases of wine, and a little of this and that of the other stuff. One hundred audiocassettes with (very) heavy emphasis on baroque. Christopher and Danny Merritt had Walkman headsets so that, on the midnight watch (post-movie to 1:00 a.m.), they could listen to Bob Dylan or The Screetches or whomever. Jars full of cookies and candies to keep the postmidnight watch (1:00 a.m. to 5:00 a.m.) from undernourishment in the dead hours. Thermosfuls of coffee and soup for prebreakfast revival on the early morning watch (5:00 to 9:00). Four computers (two Kaypro 2000s, two Epson PX-8s) for the scriveners on the late morning (9:00 a.m. to 1:00 p.m.) and early afternoon (1:00 to 5:00) watches (one of us was revising memoirs of three years as ambassador to France; another was surveying the first 25,000 words of an ambitious book on the press and public controversy; a third was readying to proofread a political comedy, a novel that will be called *The White House Mess;* another had just done a spy novel and was collecting ideas from his companions, who read the manuscript in turn, for a final revision, due a couple of weeks after the end of the cruise). And, during twenty minutes of the late afternoon watch (5:00 to 7:00) we listened to a recorded episode from the two autobiographies of David Niven, *The Moon's a Balloon* and *Bring on the Empty Horses*, over drinks and *hors d'oeuvres*.

That was followed by star-taking time, and I had in my Epson an originally conceived program, executed by Professor Hugh Kenner, called Whatstar. The idea is: you feed the computer the time of our sight, the sextant angle of the observed body, your assumed position at sea and whrrrr!—the computer reveals that you were just now looking at Arcturus! That you are therefore somewhere on a line of position that stretches east to west, seventeen miles north of where your assumed position is. The succeeding shot tells you that *that* body was Spica, and you are somewhere on the north-south line, eight miles west of your assumed position. You post these data on your plotting sheet and rise nonchalantly to the cockpit, to announce casually to your companions that we are 1,236 miles from Majuro (our destination in the Marshall Islands on the second leg), that our course should be corrected three degrees east to 232; and that, this being Monday, we should get there maybe on Tuesday week, if the winds stay about where they are. We go down to a splendid dinner, watch the movie, and resume the watch duty that is ours twenty-two hours per day, Allan's and Noddy's during the period of the *Sealestial*-Odeon tracks the most sizzling bank robbers of the century.

Cool stuff.

But there is the downside.

Twenty minutes after leaving Honolulu I was at the wheel, while Noddy and Van Galbraith and Reggie Stoops were hoisting the spinnaker. A gust of wind caught the great sail, whose sheet had been prematurely secured so that it billowed out, causing a sudden pull of maybe two, three thousand pounds on the halyard. Struggling to take an extra loop on the winch, Noddy let two of his fingers get caught between line and winch. In the five seconds before Van, tailing the line, could let go on the halyard— the alternative being to sever two or more of Noddy's fingers, the great sail was in the water, Noddy's hand mangled, and 200 feet of line destroyed (sliced in pieces by the sheave at the masthead).

So, we limped back to Honolulu. Emergency hospital ward for Noddy; 200 feet of line purchased from another boat. Three hours later, chastened in spirit, we set out again. We had been lucky we were close to land when it happened. Lucky that Noddy's fingers were not broken. Lucky that the doctor authorized him, his hand bandaged, to resume the journey. Lucky we could find a replacement for our halyard on a Sunday afternoon.

The first leg was 850 miles, the next 1,450, the third 975, the fourth 740, the fifth and last 350 miles. During that period, we did not see a single boat, sail or steam, except in port. Our main genoa, a sailboat's workhorse, fell to pieces after two days... it was old and tired. The mainsail twice split half its seams, under the downwind pressure of sail against shrouds (Danny was hoisted almost to the masthead to insulate the spreaders). The spinnaker boom we were using to keep the Yankee to windward (we were sailing wing-and-wing) showed deterioration: corrosion. We had to make do with a substitute rig. The clew of the Yankee ripped out, making it inoperative. During the last two legs we had maybe fifty squalls, with gusts reaching up to fifty-five miles per hour, and great stretches of the time, we were drenched. If anyone had fallen overboard during one of those squalls he'd have had, in effect, a burial at sea.

Now, when you set out on a long cruise you are not acclimated to weeks and months at sea. You are happy at any opportunity for a port of call. Stare at the map, letting your eyes wander west-southwest from Honolulu, in the direction of New Guinea, and you will find nothing: with a single exception. It is called Johnston Island. Accordingly, you look at the guidebooks; but you find mysteriously little about Johnston Island, and of course this whets your appetite. Eventually you find out why the little aggregation of sand and coral is so self-effacing. It is where the US government stores (speculation), tests (speculation), and maybe experiments with (speculation) noxious gases of the kind that kill people in great, ugly wars.

I write about the subject tentatively, not entirely as a matter of sloth. The probabilities are high that if I had set out to discover more or less exactly what it is that's going on in Johnston Island, I'd have found the contacts to tell me. But having found out, I'd also have the conservative's disposition not to publish my findings. This is not to suppose for one minute that the Soviet Union isn't exactly aware of what is going on in Johnston Island. But we all abide by the protocols, which are that even though it may be certain that the Soviet Union knows what the top speed of the Los Angeles Class Attack Submarine is, as does also the editor of *Jane's Fighting Ships* who publishes that speed, still, no naval architect with patriot's blood running in his veins will tell you; and if he did, you would need to promise not to tell anyone else.

So, it was one thing to agree not to reveal any of the mysteries of Johnston Island, another to restrain ourselves to the point of merely passing it by in mid-Pacific—waving, and going on another 1,800 miles before hitting Majuro. There had to be a middle way, and Evan Galbraith, United States ambassador to the Republic of France, said, simply, "Leave Johnston Island to me."

We were quite prepared to do this, reasoning that any further pull, exercisable by other members of the crew, would be redundant. And indeed, way back last January, Ambassador Galbraith called into his office whatever admiral serves the ambassador of France. And in his friendly, inimitable way, Galbraith announced that it would be unfeeling for both parties—for Johnston Island as well as for *Sealestial*—not to nestle with one another, however briefly, during our great transpacific sail.

A few days later the naval attaché came back and delivered the equivalent of a wink. A wink is all that Van Galbraith needs. He gave me a soritical transatlantic wink over the telephone, relieving me of the necessity to call the Secretary of the Navy, a gentleman who is a friend and who is realistic enough to know that no subversive mission designed to damage to Johnston Island or US security is likely to sail out under *my* command, with that company. So, we would go with Galbraith's *laissez passer*. But, oh yes, one thing (sorry about that) but an unwaivable formality: we would need to board Johnston Island wearing gas masks.

Wearing gas masks?

I had worn gas masks in poison gas exercises when I was in the infantry. And before that, as a child landing in Southampton on the eve of the Czechoslovak crisis in 1938, when we were all (my sisters and I) handed gas masks. But gas masks in 1985?

Well, the supply-side imperative rode again, and my office discovered a wasting couple of dozen in a decrepit army-navy store in Manhattan, for sale at three dollars apiece. So that when on that fifth windy day we approached the little 640-acre atoll, which before WWII had been a mere sixty acres, we were ready for a luxurious, peaceful, dry overnight on a slip—after a long hot shower, perhaps a meal in the mess hall, a chance to stretch our limbs ashore, a telephone call home…

I steered the boat through the channel, and it was indicated where we were to tie up. We had our masks at the standby, but I was reluctant to order the crew actually to don them, for fear that the resident military might have forgotten what they looked like and taken us for visiting pirates intent on stealing the whole Western supply of poison gas. It did not seem to matter, because none of the seventy or eighty odd souls we came across, in the succeeding two hours, wore masks. I think they'd have been as surprised to see us with a mask on as if one of us had dived off the boat for a quick swim wearing a one-piece bathing suit from shoulders to below the knee.

We tightened the lines—bow, stern, and spring lines—and leapt bouncily to the slip to greet Lt. Col. Larry Predovich, commander of the island. We shook hands, and I asked whether this same slip was agreeable for our overnight stay. To which he replied that we would not be staying overnight, indeed that if it had not been for the brisk fifteen-mile wind out in the ocean, he would not have admitted us into the harbor; it had been his intention to send out a provisioning ship to give us the extra fuel we had said we would probably want and the few blocks of ice.

Ambassador Galbraith, overhearing this, startled in wonderment at the colonel *(Surely someone forgot to tell him!)*, but before he could say anything, Galbraith was interrupted by Reggie, who had just come in from using the overseas phone and had taken an urgent message for Ambassador Galbraith, namely, might he arrange to arrive back in Paris one day soon to entertain Vice President George Bush, who was arriving as Galbraith's houseguest one day earlier than expected?

Dorothy Parker couldn't have written the screenplay more spicily, because just as I began to react to the commander's draconian security measures, I was interrupted by Dick Clurman, fresh from the phone. He told me that my wife had left an urgent message with his wife to relay, to wit, she had delayed her scheduled departure for Turkey because Nancy Reagan, due in to New York, could not stay at the Waldorf-Astoria because of the employees strike and would be staying at our place, requiring my wife to make certain provisions. We wanted to reassure her she could come without a gas mask, I found myself saying to the commandant, whose smile was now at half-mast but whose edict was inflexible, namely that within two hours we would need to set sail again, lest we violate US security regulations.

Well, during those two hours we did a lot of showering and telephoning. We got our fuel and paid for it, and our ice, 200 pounds. And then the commandant gave us some fresh fruit (delicious) and some sweet rolls (ditto). We had several times invited him aboard for a drink, but he had steadfastly declined. It suddenly occurred to me to offer him a Diet Pepsi, and to this he had happily acquiesced, ducking down under the boom and boarding the *Sealestial* for the first time. I felt the temptation in my partners to tease him a little about just what it was he was afraid we were going to do in a matter of his secret gas: I had no spirit for this, though I did wonder whether the bureaucratic mind fretted in turn about the comparatively casual social arrangements of the vice president and the first lady.

As it worked out, having pined so long for a night ashore, by the time we were all back on the *Sealestial,* one of those magic things that happen at sea had happened: we were not only quite ready to go out to sea, we were raring to go to sea. We retraced our way slowly through the channel, engaged the stiff nor'easterly just past the leeward point: the ship jumped to attention and broke out instantly into a sprint, pulled by a full-bellowed Yankee and mainsail. Drinks were passed about, and we found ourselves chatting disconsolately as we contemplated the arid circumstances of the poor people who, having so zealously to guard over our poison gas, could so infrequently sally out into the brisk air, bound so resolutely for the southwest and all the adventures of Polynesia.

You need to be careful about fire (after boredom, the single greatest hazard), and there were four smokers aboard, names not to be revealed (one of them had taken a public and publicized pledge to swear off). We had wind most of the time, and on the (cumulative) three or four days we didn't have it, the engine worked just fine, except when a trailing wrapped itself around the propeller, requiring underwater disentanglement by Allan. Celestial navigation brought us in, which was providential, since the satnav (satellite navigation system) didn't work. Lucky, too, that the days of overcast came when we were hundreds of miles away from land or shoals, not when we needed urgently to know where we were. At such points we needed to fine-tune our way to our destinations, most taxingly nearing the end, having sailed 4,000 miles to the tiny atoll of Kapingamarangi, the size of a grain of sand on the great Pacific beach.

There in Kapingamarangi on the second day, Christopher and Danny with scuba gear went after and found an American fighter plane shot down during the last days of the war. I cannot imagine in what engagement that fighter pilot lost his life, because one hasn't the imagination to think of "Kapinga," as we came to call it, as bristling with anything but good humor, bananas, and large-eyed children, let alone pillboxes of hell and brimstone. But there the fighter plane was, oddly intact, after forty years, and one hundred yards from it the children gathered in one of those ocean rivers that run calmly between the sandy islands, beaches connecting attenuatedly the above-sea level coagulations of coral, sand, and earth. There the kids swim and eat lunch. Off to one side we had a picnic lunch, most of it quickly shared with the children, not because they were hungry, but because they hungered for variety, as most of us do, even if it is also true that most people like to eat the same thing pretty much all the time (the Chinese and their rice, the Americans and their hamburgers). Then everyone did what I suppose one does under more formal auspices in the Human Potential centers of California: free float about, touching fingers in casual friendship, the children becoming less shy, the skipper, or should I say admiral, a little more apprehensive about getting our show under weigh before we all became full-time Arcadians, as we could never hope to leave that atoll, even with native guidance, except under full light.

There is something residually defiant—I often reflect on this—about flying in an airplane. It is studied effrontery—isn't it?—to soar at 600 miles per hour within an aluminum carapace, smiling, condescending, at an altimeter that keeps telling you just how many thousand feet gravity would drop you if it had its solemn, natural way, which sometimes it does. It is the same feeling some of us get at sea when in a vessel that weighs a small fraction of what some of those waves weigh that come thundering by when the ocean is exercised. Just to begin with, everything depends on the integrity of your hull. And on the lines that maintain your sail at propitious angles, which sails are attached to a mast, the combination rescuing you from squatting down—immobile, helpless—1,000 watery miles from land. You rely on a fiberglass or wooden rudder that you must constantly keep turning—a centimeter's net deviation can mean one hundred miles off course after a few lazy, negligent days. And the compass, on which sailors have relied for a thousand years ever since they discovered, or rather intuited, the existence of the great emancipating deposit up there near the true north of a mountain of magnetic material that directs the compass needle toward it. The great contingencies of sailing across an ocean, a distance the equivalent of Maine to Dakar, of Cape Town to Suez, from the westernmost state of America to the easternmost state of America to the easternmost of the Asian islands just north of Australia.

And then too there is something about cruising that makes everything contingent: it isn't merely the wind, sea and stars. We had a Force-11 taste of this in the matter of Johnston Island.

You can't, then, ever know for sure what will happen, and so you rely on the odds. These are tidily reassuring ($200 will buy you $1 million of life insurance). And anyway, you don't neglect to stock your cellar or your library just because you might be struck by lightning, do you? If the odds were conclusively intimidating—why, they would intimidate! A college classmate of mine (1950) recently ascended Mount Everest, and in doing so exposed himself to danger and hardship I probably would not survive and would most certainly not court. You can fetch up all the cushions in the world, but if you step recklessly out of the airplane, you will still have a rough landing. ("What I admire about the astronauts," Phil Harris once said, "is that they do it without safety nets.") Even as, at sea, one can always be overpowered, and the unfortunate sailor is regularly overpowered; but then so is the unfortunate urban pedestrian overpowered. There has to be a reason for it all. It took us thirty active days, six watches per day, four hours per watch, to get there; and we got back to where we had started from after a mere eleven sedentary hours of flying. So, what it is?

Have you ever experienced the cockpit of a sailing ship, sails set propelling you at eight knots, the water parting, poutful but, at the margin, submissive, as you charge along all but noiselessly and there is only the sound of water, hissing to get out of your way? The moon is out, and you see shafts of silver lighting up a third of all the globe you can see, all the globe that matters. Or else the moon isn't up. It is black black, but the tiny, dim red light in your compass confirms when you look down at it that you are on a steady course. You are steering by the star over there—there—just to the right of the upper shroud, the star that beckons you along: ceding gracefully, as the celestial tapestry slides by, to its successor, down by the spreader, which, in turn yields, after fifteen or twenty minutes, to the succeeding star—this one just up by the masthead, and though you need constantly to manipulate the wheel, you are making a fairly steady course along the calculated way. It is warm, and you remove your light sweater and feel the tender air. Or it is chilling up, and you slip a foul-weather jacket over your sweater and feel the warmth of your own body, added now to your inventory of protections against the eccentric impositions of nature.

But always on reflection you are awed by the greatest insubordination of all, which is that *you* are making *headway* by manipulating craftily the carefree endowments of nature. The wind is propelling you: 100,000 pounds of hull, equipment, human beings, and Goo Goo candy bars; and not withstanding where the wind is coming from, you are making headway toward the destination of your own choosing. We could in as many hours have doused our sails finally at Yokohama in Japan; at the canal in Panama; at Anchorage in Alaska; same ocean, same winds, just set your sails accordingly and steer the course you want, and ask the sun and stars to guide you.

It adds up to a whole lot in a world that specializes even in the freer societies, in straitening rules and regulations. It is all by itself a sensation of singular order to know that everything you will need for thirty days, everything from bread to medicine to music to literature to navigational almanacs lies, at the furthest point, seventy feet away from you. That you can take all of this, and yourself, and your companions, and move without permission from the FCC, the SEC, the FDA, or the *New York Times,* from one hemisphere to another. Look in on the atoll you casually fingered, surveying the charts one night last winter in Switzerland—it hasn't seen another sailboat in three years, it transpires. There at Kapingamarangi you were greeted warmly and guilelessly by a cigar-smoking prime minister and by bare-breasted young mothers, by children of wide-eyes and Polynesian warmth and inquisitive smiles looking at that exotic white vessel that brought these strangers to their necklace of little palm-lined islands. It is an experience, above all else, in living: at such very close quarters with the same people. You test the bonds of companionship, stretch them sometimes until tight, but they don't snap, and it reassures to know how wonderfully strong fraternity can be. Always you are aware that it doesn't necessarily work. There can be tragedy, for which nature or dereliction can be responsible. And there can be what amounts to tragedy, for which human nature is responsible. But neither happened to us.

And when after thirty days we arrived at Kavieng harbor and tied down, for the last time, we knew intuitively that it had worked. Late that night, strolling along the tropical shore seven degrees south of the equator and twenty-five degrees into the eastern hemisphere, a few of us experienced the smells and scents of land, the dislocating stability of settled ground. I picked up a hefty little branch lying by the faintly luminous road along the solemn deadwood trees and used it as a walking stick. It helped to steady legs unaccustomed to the equilibrium of level earth. At sea your legs are always working to compensate for the sea's undeviating motions. The muscular adaptations had become instinctive, automatic. Back on land you are suddenly relieved of the need for them. It is the sea's momentum that puts you off balance. And gradually you become aware of all those other synchronizations you will need quickly to make, from which for thirty days we were suspended, making our long, slow, steady, isolated way across the vast ocean, savoring the heady experience of the explorer.

Alta

Signature, January 1986

"Alta" isn't a word you hear often in fashionable conversations in skiing circles. Sun Valley, yes; Aspen, yes; even Stowe and Squaw Valley; and, of course, there is the European Gstaad-St. Moritz-Klosters constellation. You can live out a casual lifetime, as a casual skier, and not know about Alta, and the odd thing is that this really suits the Alta people just fine. There is absolutely nothing about Alta that suggests commercial jingoism. Sometimes you even have the impression that the natives and the operators rather wish fewer people would go there, not more. The only thing inconsistent about this attitude is that it contradicts the hospitality of the people of Alta, and that is a phenomenon at least as remarkable as that crazy snow trap that makes the mountain there one of the skiing phenomena of the world. Would you believe 800 inches of snow in a heavy year?

Alta life is something that almost imposes informality. Everyone seems to relate skiing at Alta to personal experiences—with the mountain, yes, obviously; but also with where you stayed and with whom, from which you develop your perspectives. I stay at the Alta Lodge, the central caravansary in the Alta area, where there are fewer than a half dozen, primarily because a hostelry in Alta is, really, an unnecessary convenience. You are only one-half hour from Salt Lake City. It is hard to think where else on earth you have such an option. You can leave your office, high in a Salt Lake skyscraper, dressed in a three-piece suit, amble down to the garage in the basement, and, forty-five minutes later, a photographer can catch you whizzing down a slope 10,000 feet high. This would require some speed in changing clothes, but then Mormon energy is at least up to that kind of speed, and if it is true that Liza Minnelli can change costumes seventeen times during her two-hour show, the Salt Lake City skier will certainly undertake the challenge of slipping into ski boots, corduroy pants, parka, and gloves while managing that thirty-minute drive.

One needs to understand something about the special energy of the Mormons, because although Alta is a cosmopolitan center for the in-skier, Alta is distinctively a Mormon site, and its habits are charmingly Mormon and uncharmingly Mormon. The latter one thinks of on Sundays, when the Alta Lodge Store is closed for the sale of liquor. The former comes to mind when one buys the liquor on weekdays and finds oneself paying about what one would at a duty-free counter in Hong Kong (liquor being, in Mormonland, a vice, no one except the state of Utah is permitted to profit from its sale, which means that the consumer gets it at close to wholesale). Mormon energy is here and there illustrated by a vague inattention to labor-saving devices. This they impose only obliquely on their guests but most ponderously on themselves: one thinks especially of the Alta Lodge, built in the late Thirties as a kind of dormitory for skiers unwilling to trek back to the city for the night. After the war it grew, as most skiing facilities did; today it is a fifty-six-room hotel, each room with its private bath. But to get to the lobby-saloon from the road requires an incredible descent of sixty-three steps and three landings. Much more incredible is the ascent back up to the road, to return to one's car, or to get a taxi to the airport or a bus to nearby Snowbird, or to make the hour's trip to Deer Valley, because sixty-three steps at 8,600 feet of altitude is a strain. What does it do to the people who are carrying your equipment—your three bags plus your skis, the lot weighing 200 pounds?

It does absolutely nothing to the people of the Alta Lodge except make them more cheerful, if that is possible. I should pause to confess that over protracted encounters I have become terribly pro-Mormon. This is in part because the breed seems to me to manage a kind of cheerful courtesy absolutely uncontaminated by sycophancy. You could arrive at the Alta Lodge with a trunk carrying the entire inventory of the Bureau of Weights and Measures, and a smiling young man (the staff is mostly young men and women, mostly students taking a year of work plus ski) will lug it off the taxi and head down those sixty-three steps and three landings as if the pleasure of their descent were second only to a slide down that great High Rustler Run, which drops 2,000 feet from the top to the bottom lift.

It was more than twenty years ago that my wife and I went to Alta, soon after I had discovered that skiing was a halfway station between earth and heaven. In that beautiful corner room we were given, with great panes of glass looking out toward the grand skiing hills to the south and up-valley to the north, I absorbed something of the ambient Mormon energy, and I remember resolving that I would earn the $60 a day I was being charged by writing a freelance article, which I did. Alta and its lodge have a way of getting to you, and though we were there only four or five nights, a dozen years later I went back, searching out the same beautiful room, though without success: the lodge had grown, and now I had only one set of windows, to the south. Otherwise, it had not changed.

The manager, Mimi Muray, more or less goes with Alta Lodge, even as Aunt Jemima goes with pancakes. In due course the pretty and trim Mimi (surnames are forbidden in Alta) married the mayor of the tiny town, who is known as Bill (Levitt), who is also the owner of the Alta Lodge, and the thriving little enterprise is full of grateful guests, most of them "repeaters" during the skiing season. In the summer the lodge caters to conventioneers who go to Alta to participate in seminars during the morning and to hike in the afternoon, returning to Salt Lake (some of them) at night or staying over at the lodge.

What you get for about $100 ($153 for a large room, single occupancy; $85 apiece for double occupancy in the slightly smaller rooms) is a comfortable room scrubbed hospital-clean every morning; access, until eleven at night, to two ten-man jacuzzis, one slightly hotter than the other; two living rooms; a basement where you get a locker for your skis, right next to the store; a dining room oozing with friendliness and nourishment ("Our specials this morning are eggs Benedict, pancakes and sausages, French toast, spiced ham and eggs"). You can get as much of that as you wish, this after you have taken juice and your choice of a half-dozen cereals. The Mormons eat well. And then you get, for the price of your room, dinner as well. *Pas mal*, for eighty-five bucks? No tipping (they add 15 percent to your bill); and, of course, there is the ticket for the lifts, which is $13 for the day.

What is the skiing like?

Just fine; here and there quite tough enough for the expert experts, most of it easily manageable for the intermediates, and the easiest less than entirely hospitable for beginners, though there are slopes they too can handle. One has the impression, viewing the skiers at Alta, that there never were any beginners, that Mormon baptisms confer on infants intermediate skill in skiing, which grows to expert at about age eight. The skiing trails are clearly marked, and if you are only an intermediate and end up facing an expert trail, the fault is manifestly yours, because the markers up top are unambiguous on the matter. The skiing lines tend to move rapidly because of the ingenious configuration of lifts, and because few formalities are observed in placing you into the chairs—no impedimenta such as bars to hold you in, that kind of thing. At Alta you are deemed too sensible to wish to fall out of your ski chair. Fifteen minutes from the Alta Lodge, via two, even three lifts, you face a downhill run of about three-and-a-half miles, and you can do that again and again and again (you can manage about four runs before lunch); and then the whole thing all over again in the afternoon.

Or, of course, you can elect to stay on the top series of lifts, or you can wander east, or west, in search of the narrow trails or the broad slopes. Alta is famous for its powder (though I confess I have frequently been there without running into powder), but above all it is famous for having snow. Just after Christmas one year, a guide explained that we were at midseason. "We've had 400 inches of snow since November."

I have what the English call a chum, Lawry Chickering, a sometime editorial colleague, now a youngish foundation executive, with whom I rejoice in time spent together because we have a lot to laugh about. It happens that we are separately friends of economist Milton Friedman, and six years ago we instituted an institution, namely Alta on the Third Weekend of January, the three of us together.

During those fleeting three days (we meet Wednesday evening, disperse on Sunday), we experience the kind of thing distinctively associated with Alta. No distractions. Comfortable quarters. Privacy (though about this, an amusing qualification later). And intense social intimacy.

It is on that third weekend in January, I tell my friends, that I go to Alta to receive large transfusions of monetarism from the most famous living economist. Friday mornings, by tradition, we go to Snowbird to take a lesson from Junior Bounous. He is a senior instructor who taught Lawry Chickering when he was a boy. Without hesitation, Junior began to instruct "Milton" on that first day we skied together, provoking in Milton a smile of self-satisfaction, as he beamed at the progress he had made in the course of an hour's lesson, that—I told Junior—certainly surpassed the smile he gave off when the king of Sweden dangled the Nobel Prize around his neck. "Why did they give Milton a Nobel Prize?" Junior wanted to know, I told him that Milton Friedman was a very famous economist. Junior's reaction was that anyone who learned as quickly as Milton did how to turn without turning his downhill shoulder downhill instead of uphill qualified for any prize Junior could think of.

The first time Lawry, Milton, and I entered the dining room at the Alta Lodge (actually the second night), there was no table for four unoccupied, so that we had no choice save to sit at what they call, in the men's clubs, the "round tables." We had traveled to Alta from remote parts of the country (they had come from San Francisco, I from New York), intending animated private political-economic-philosophic-hedonistic discussions (Milton Friedman is a passionate conversationalist, and it doesn't matter whether he is talking about the Federal Reserve Board or about his Mickey Mouse watch with the calculator game on it, which keeps him occupied on long ski lines or during Democratic speeches). But there is no way, sitting at a table with a dozen others alongside, to encyst your conversation as though insulated by the Berlin Wall. And anyway, Milton is too polite, and too gregarious, to husband his thoughts, free-trader that he is.

We felt especially pressed because we had missed our first scheduled dinner. The reason was dramatic stuff, and it happens not regularly at Alta, but not irregularly either. I had arrived, but Milton and Lawry could not make the drive to Alta because an avalanche had closed the road. At three in the morning the telephone rang and a no-nonsense voice on the phone instructed me instantly to repair to the basement. I asked sleepily whether I was being given orders or merely suggestions; the answer was emphatic, and five minutes later I began four hours in the ski room, with a hundred other guests of the Alta Lodge, waiting to see what the threatened avalanche would do.

And so, finally united, we took to going across the road for dinner at The Shallow Shaft, a splendid place with splendid food, including steaks and salmon and live lobsters and modest prices. There we talked about skiing at Alta, the price of gold, the weaknesses of politicians and the invincible ignorance of everyone with the exception of Milton and Junior Bounous. Then, laden down with steak and wine, we each took one ski pole and walked a mile in the zero and even subzero cold, up the road and back again. And then we went back to my room (by right of seniority, I have first call on the larger room) and Milton and Lawry read, and we listened to music on my cassette player, and I wrote the next day's column on the theme of sound mind and body. At 11:00 we separated, to meet for break-fast (always) at 8:15, preparatory to meeting in the ski room (always) at 10:15 to begin the morning's ski. At least once in the course of the three days, we complimented ourselves on having found Alta, and the Alta Lodge and, to be frank, ourselves, which is how friendship works.

Worst Suggestion of the Year
July 29, 1986

The most dangerous, as well as the most pestiferous, proposal of the week comes from the *New York Times* editorial page and is entitled, "Hold Down Airline Carry-Ons." It is written as you and I might write an editorial on an amenable configuration of a space vessel: i.e., one gets the impression that the gentleperson who wrote the editorial has never traveled in an airplane, certainly not on a business trip.

The piece begins by insisting that there is a problem. "Flight atten-dants tell of passengers carrying aboard automobile drive shafts and slot machines, and tricycles with children. As a result, the Federal Aviation Administration is considering a new regulation."

Now we need, just to begin with, to distinguish between those who fly with only the intention of arriving at their destination and are satisfied to bring on board with them oh, lipstick, a handkerchief, maybe a magazine or book: all of which can easily be carried in a single ditty bag and stored, as is the convention, "under the seat." But there are others, and for them the airplane is their place of business. If you fly (as some of us do) as much as four or five hours every day, then you do not have the leisure to fritter away flight time on movie-watching or snoozing, pleasant though such activity can be.

There are lots of travelers who need with them on board the entire paraphernalia of their professional life. I (for instance) carry a briefcase. In it are the usual things (passport-type stuff, research material, speech portfolios); but also, a toilet bag, customized to individual requirements. Mine, for instance, includes Actifed, Afrin, and Ayr, without which I contract head colds. An altimeter, to check on the pressurization of the airplane, and a compass. I forget why I insist on carrying a compass, but I do, and would know sooner than anyone else if a hijacker had got hold of the controls and was heading toward Cuba while the passengers thought ourselves heading serenely toward Minneapolis.

Then, of course, there is the laptop computer. These come in different sizes. I have traveled with a Kaypro (about the size of a standard Royal typewriter), an Epson Geneva (about the size of a compact-disk player), and a Toshiba (about twice the size of the Epson). But more often than not you absolutely need such an instrument if you are, say, writing the speech you will deliver a few minutes after your arrival at Minneapolis.

Then, of course, there is the third bag, which is roughly designated as one's paperwork. Two hundred unanswered letters, manuscripts to read, copy to edit. For this one needs a clipboard and, of course, a dictating machine. I weigh 185 pounds, clothed. When I step onto an airplane, I weigh about 235 pounds.

Now the *New York Times* likes to find problems even where there aren't really any, or at least not where they are looking for them. It has come up with a new victimized class, flight attendants: "Hard-pressed flight attendants fight ceaselessly to enforce the rules for proper stowage of bulky carry-ons." Oh? I haven't seen these primal struggles on-board airplanes. Sometimes a bag tends to be a little too big to fit easily into the overhead bin. So, what else is new? One pummels the bag until it fits, no different from sitting on your suitcase until you can snap the lock. And the *Times* finds yet another victim: "Passengers ride in fear that they'll be conked on the head by a boom-box radio or backpack. "Oh? Do you travel in fear of being conked on the head by a boom-box radio or backpack? If so, you should be visiting your psychiatrist, instead of flying around in an airplane. I have never seen a boom-box fall on anyone in any trip, and the latches in airplanes are altogether secure. If they were insecure, why then the challenge would be, surely, to develop safer locks, not to incapacitate the passenger by denying him the tools of his trade.

Those looking for something to complain about in air travel don't have to go into the airplane proper. Consider, rather, the absence of trolleys when a passenger weighing, with his carry-ons, a total of 235 pounds exits the airplane and finds he has a mile and a half to walk to the baggage delivery room, or else to his connecting flight, and finds nothing in the area on which to offload his burden so that he might walk along toward his destination, whistling an ode to the man who invented the wheel and carrying only 185 pounds of weight. It is an inexplicable failure of the airlines to make the trolleys available everywhere. Surely the cost of them could be sustained by providing for advertising placards on the trolleys? For instance? For instance, "READ THE *NEW YORK TIMES*."

Weed Rights
August 14, 1986

Comes now the National Academy of Sciences with a report that reminds us that every now and then scientists tend to forget that human beings aren't squeaky wheels or guinea pigs. What the learned academy recommends is that cigarette smoking be forbidden in airplanes.

I wish that everyone in the whole world (my wife included) would stop smoking. Perhaps someday they will, however unlikely this is. But in the meantime, we need to remind ourselves of what smoking is, and what smoking does for, as well as to, some people. There are an estimated thirty-seven million ex-cigarette smokers in America, but, strange to say, many of them appear not to remember how it was in the good-bad old days.

I kicked the habit at age twenty-six, but even so I remember what smoking did to me. In the army, five seconds after reveille, a cigarette was in my mouth. At college during Lent, I gave up smoking until sundown. I would find myself, notwithstanding an overbearing academic and extracurricular schedule, two or three times a week at a movie house at about 4:00 p.m. Why? Because my generation had been trained not to smoke at movies: it was illegal to do so, and long years of habit quieted the itch in the lung while Greta Garbo or Humphrey Bogart distracted us from our pain. But when the movie was over—the sun was down (!) and I could resume smoking.

The purpose of this autobiographical exercise is to remind our scientists, so many of them removed from the traffic of human experience, that one of the reasons we so much deplore cigarette smoking is that it is an addiction. The doctors tell us that if smokers could be persuaded to limit themselves to ten cigarettes per day, the human system could absorb the poison. Unhappily, even knowing this to be the case, the overwhelming majority of our smokers exceed this limit by a factor of 100, 200, 300, 400—500 percent, and more. It is one thing to deplore that they should do so, quite another calmly to inform them that effective the first day of next month they are to give up smoking on a seven-hour flight from New York to Anchorage. You simply cannot do that to people who are smokers, not without turning airplane travel into torture.

When the news was given out that the academy was going to make that recommendation, there were interviews taken on the streets, and many rejoiced. One woman said on television, "It's about time." But that is to express a distaste for smoking, which is perfectly legitimate. One harbors a distaste for many things—some people don't like dogs, cats, obesity, bad grammar, film violence, film non-violence. But the American protocol is to let people do what they want to do—which is to cast bread upon the waters, given that the same protocol permits us to be our potty little selves.

On what reasoning do the scientists rely? Well, they tell you, air circulation inside an airplane isn't sufficient to contain the smoke within the narrow area of the smoker, and therefore some of it drifts out to annoy passengers, and to damage, potentially, flight personnel. The first problem is rather easily coped with: those with high allergy to smoke can recommend seats far removed from the smokers' section. As for the flight attendants, the study by the academy is not likely to document a noxious impact on the health of passengers by passing through an area in which people are smoking fifteen days per month, for three or four hours. It is likely that the same people expose themselves to the same concentration of smoke at restaurants, playing bridge or poker with their friends, or indeed inhaling their spouses smoke or, for that matter, smoking themselves.

It is when the third reason for forbidding smoking is cited that skepticism gives way to cynicism. That reason is to diminish the danger of fire on board an airplane. The statistics are not handy, but if the honorable scientists can come up with a single fatality caused by someone having set a tobacco fire to a commercial airliner, I hope they will feature this in their report.

Me, I would rather once in a lifetime (in a far advanced lifetime—of perpetual flying, I have yet to see a fire aboard a plane) be aboard a plane during a little shoot-out with a cigarette-caused fire in the corner of a cushion than be on every flight with fifty or one hundred haunted souls choking for a snort of the weed and taking out their ill humor on friendly folk like thee and me.

How I Spent My Aerobic Vacation
New York Times Good Health Magazine, September 28, 1986

Respecting physical fitness, I am plagued by two concerns. The first is universally experienced: the fear or (and aesthetic distaste for) biological atrophy. About that there isn't, really, much to be said: everyone knows that the human body needs limbering. The second concern is less widely shared. It comes to me at two levels. The first of these has to do with the dislike I feel for physical exertion. It is one thing to play tennis, ride a horse, ski, sail a boat; quite another to jog, on and on, or to push weights (up and down), or, for that matter, to dig a hole in the ground or to climb steep mountains. The key to acceptable physical fitness programs, as far as we are concerned, is brevity. There are those who get highs from prolonged exercise. You cannot take jogging away from those who "cross the thirty-to-thirty-five-minute level," writes Jack H. Wilmore, professor of physical and health education at the University of Texas. Well, bless them. But most of us have no intention of devoting 10 percent or our day to physical exercise, so the search for economy in exercise-time is a concern. I would experience a most awful frustration, on my deathbed, if it were revealed that I had done one push-up more, during my lifetime, than was necessary to keep me fit.

And speaking of dying, I venture the other level of my concern: a strategic question about ultra-fitness. The medical profession is mightily engaged in prolonging life. A good thing, but it can be done to excess. Those of us who oppose euthanasia can't really solve the problem of overextended life. There are, then, ways to die, and less agreeable ways to die. One of my favorite metaphors issued from an excited seven-year-old niece who told me breathless, when I arrived at my sister's house, that that very morning, "Aunt Amy woke up dead!" Aunt Amy, age seventy-eight, was visiting (a wedding in the family). She went home to her hotel after the evening's festivities and, to use again the fleeted phrase, woke up dead.

That is the way to die. I don't have the statistics in front of me, but no one, I think, would resist the generality that the older we get, the heavier will be the incidence of senility and the multifarious incapacities we associate with extreme old age. To establish this, I would suppose, as easy as documenting that more people, per capita, in their seventies get strokes that in their fifties. So that the effecting of a body in such fine shape as greatly to expand the life span presents a problem. There is no known cure for senility, and those of us who would rather die before senility sets in are concerned to keep our bodies in shape, but not in superb shape.

Okay?

I become now professorial and repeat some of what I learned at my fifth annual visit to Rancho La Puerta, which is a Shangri-La for fitness-seekers, one hour's drive south from San Diego, in Tecate, Mexico. I was tipped off to this stretch of paradise by a friend who goes there twice a year. Why? If you are fit, why do you need to go to a fitness center? Answer: to be reminded of what it is you are neglecting, to rekindle your determination to stay fit, and to get the psychic relaxation that goes with the isolation, the diet, and the total concern for physical well-being. My mentor there is Dean Dallman, a studious, articulate, genial taskmaster, who commutes to La Puerta from the university at which he is studying for a doctorate in physical science.

There are three elements of physical fitness. The first is aerobic, the second muscular, the third agile. (The language here is my own, and Dean and La Puerta must not be blamed if my taxonomy is unofficial.)

And—as the Bible would put it—The First of These is Aerobic. About this I take it there is a consensus: if you want to be fit you must do an aerobic exercise.

You can buy whole books telling you about aerobics and what it does for you, but it can all be said in a sentence or two. The heart needs to be made to work at a level far more active than its normal level in order to cause the blood to circulate at the desired velocity. When it does this, it flushes out your entire system, causing all kinds of wonderful things to happen, including lowering cholesterol, strengthening the heart muscle, replenishing circulation, etc. But you have not reached an aerobic level unless your heartbeat attains a certain velocity (220 minus your age times 75 percent); and you have not had a successful flush unless you maintain that velocity for twenty minutes. Here there are disagreements. Some say fifteen is enough; I am searching for the instructor reputed to have said that twelve minutes is enough; but everyone is agreed that the longer you go, the better off you are. When it comes to burning calories, maintaining an aerobic level for twenty minutes is more than a third again as good for you as doing it for fifteen minutes; and doing it for forty minutes is more than twice as good as doing it for twenty minutes.

Now, the best-known way of getting your pulse going is to jog. And, at La Puerta, there is a 7:00 a.m. two-mile fast-walk that approaches the exercise of jogging. You can, in fact, walk fast enough to bring your pulse up to the aerobic level. The men's group convenes separately at 9:00, and begins the day jogging around the track (five times equals one mile) for twenty minutes. There are other ways to make the heart pump up—prolonged exertions of any kind theoretically serve (because the heart does not know what it is that is requiring it to accelerate), but the standard alternatives to jogging are bicycling, rowing, and swimming.

Here it pays to know oneself. I have friends who jog who are capable of sustained thought during the exercise. John C. Calhoun used to like to plough a field on his plantation when time came to prepare a speech. By the time he was through ploughing, he needed only to write out the speech he had conceived, framed in his mind, and composed while ploughing.

I can't while jogging, concentrate for long enough to count from one to ten, so I can't distract from the exercise. George Will is a jogger and he diverts himself by listening to books on tape, via a Walkman recorder. My chosen method is an indoor bicycle opposite a small television set. A television set close enough to you to permit you to switch channels with the merest flick of the finger. I monitor the three morning news channels three times a week, for twenty minutes, and give the shortest shrift to the most boring interviewee.

At La Puerta, Dean told us that every-other day aerobics is recommended, but he will settle for three times a week. If you think that the odd days are therefore free, along with Sunday, you are wrong, because you have forgotten about the muscular and agile components of health.

Some muscles tend to take care of themselves; for instance, those that are used when you talk. Most are not, and these are the muscles one tends to associate with those futuristic photographs of exercise machinery, of which Nautilus is one prominent manufacturer. At this slot you lift your feet under two cushioned weights up and down for a minute. You move then to the next slot, kneel down, and bring an overhanging bar down on your shoulder, up and down, for a minute; on to the next slot where you suspend your body and lift your knees, up and down, for a minute, etc.—there are a dozen-odd slots, etc.

But though they have the equipment at La Puerta and use it, Dean tells you you really don't need all that fancy stuff. You can exercise the identical muscles by the adroit use of a couple of weights, five pounds and ten pounds, and a barbell. But to memorize the exercises needed to develop all the relevant muscles requires either a very good memory, or buying a book, of which I am sure there are dozens. But the objective is plain: keep your muscles in shape. Keep them "toned," as they put it. If you overdo this component, your arms begin to look like Arnold Schwarzenegger's, or Sylvester Stallone's, but this is not likely, unless you develop an irresistible appetite for lifting weights, up and down.

Now, what we associate with the general creakiness of aging comes from our neglect of the third component of physical fitness, which is agility. Agility is accomplished by stretching. Suppose that you were asked to assume every position a ballet dancer assumed. Answer: you couldn't. Because the ballet dancer above all spends his/her exercise-time stretching. We develop little things like cricks in the neck, or pains in the back because…we don't stretch enough. If you lift your leg and point your toes toward your head you will feel a strain in the muscles under your leg. You are stretching. If you did this every day for five minutes, after a month you would feel less and less of a strain, and your toes would point closer and closer to you. You should point your toes to the right, hard, and to the left, hard. You should do the same thing to your neck. And to your arms. And after a while, you are in fine tone: agile as a child is agile. Otherwise, decrepitude sets in, and that mortal net that one day will totally overcome us begins its crafty little incursions, narrowing the arc at which you can swing your legs or your arms, or turn your neck.

At Rancho La Puerta you begin at seven in the morning (unless you want to take the three-mile mountain hike, which begins at 6:30). And except for the hour at lunch, you can go from one exercise class to another, each hour different from the others, until 5:00 p.m. It is a vast spread, 150 exquisitely gardened acres, with accommodations that border on luxurious (e.g, a private villa, two bedrooms, large living room, kitchen, fireplace, veranda, thirty paces from a heated swimming pool, thirty-five from a sauna, forty from a Jacuzzi, 150 from a tennis court, 200 from a massage parlor, movie house, and recreation center that includes a piano). There are herbal baths. You can eat meals with the other guests (there are total accommodations for 150 people, and the seven-day cycle begins afresh on Saturdays). At the dining room you can eat what you want, but the caloric level of everything spread out in front of you is clearly labelled, and the going protocol is 1,000 calories per day). You don't ever get meat, and fish only twice a week. You eat fruits and vegetables and grains. And although in 1981, my first year at La Puerta, we were all weighed, coming and going, a prize awarded to those who had to lost the most pounds proportionately, now they do not weigh you, because La Puerta says that you are there to learn fitness, and you can learn this without reference to weight loss. Still, I lost eleven pounds during my most recent cycle, my wife seven; and were had two glasses of wine, one white, one red, with dinner at night, after which we watched a VHS movie, making a small dent on all those movies we have missed seeing over the years.

Well now, have I missed anything? Missed, but not forgotten. The question now is: How did you feel at the end of the week?

I have friends (I am thinking of one in particular, who introduced me to that wonderful health ranch) who emerge from La Puerta and feel like climbing mountains, sky diving, and swimming across the English Channel preferably all at one time. This does not happen to me. The sensation, rather, is of a kind of meiotic well-being. The muscles seem to be more happily in place, the breathing is apparently more rhythmic, the belt is slightly looser, and it girds tighter flesh.

Feeling better after a week at La Puerta is one reason why I go there. It's also why I try to continue to exercise after I return: the blessed bell rings on the bicycle, and (important!) you slow down your bike speed (if you stop suddenly, there is the possibility that the heart decelerating—but at its own rate—meanwhile is pumping your blood up vessels suddenly inert, all of which can cause hazardous internal confusion)…and you get into your shower or plunge into your pool, and find, on your way to work, that the step is somehow springier than usual, and you feel you're glad you went through that wretched twenty minutes. Tomorrow you will do your four "abs," as they call them at La Puerta, where abdomen are contracted not only biologically, but philologically. You can do the four abs (upper abdomen, bottom abdomen, central abdomen, and diagonal abdomen) in about seven minutes lying on the floor, watching TV. I have been neglecting my stretches, but next time I am a La Puerta, I'll ask Dean to tell me one more time which he would do, if he were limited to ten minutes, say, every Sunday.

So? Between trips to Rancho La Puerta, it's the bike on Mondays, Wednesdays, Fridays, the abs on Tuesdays and Thursdays; a little, stretching on Sundays, the day of the Lord who invented the whole idea of the mortification of the flesh. Which turns out to be a blessing.

Airline Talk
November 4, 1986

Professor Alfred Kahn, who presided over the liquidation of the old ways by introducing deregulation of the airlines, proudly holds up as testimonial to his good work that the consumer is paying substantially less (20 percent is the figure commonly used) than he was paying under regulation, and that, as they say in the trade, is the bottom line. In a market society the consumer is, and ought to be, king. However, the question is legitimately asked: to what extent have those airline travelers been riding on credit?

Whose credit? Why, the credit of the capitalist, the investor. If a consortium of investors brings together $100 million to start an airline service between Atlanta and Chicago and sells tickets for $10 a ride, the statistician can gleefully note down the savings of Atlanta-Chicago passengers, but before very long, the Mad Man Muntz Airline is going to go out of business, and statistics on a very different ledger are going to show that $100 million of risk capital unhappily disappeared.

Last week I flew the hour's flight from Los Angeles to San Francisco, first class, and noted with a start that my ticket had cost $180. Last summer, I flew tourist class from New York to San Francisco and back for $194. That was ten hours of flying, making the contrast dramatic. United was charging ten times as much per hour in the air in the one case as compared to the other. Granted, one was first class, but it is not seriously suggested that first class should be ten times tourist class. What it is is the wide scramble for opportunistic fares. Philanthropy today, extortion tomorrow.

All of this will shake down, but when it does, expect that the surviving airlines are going to demand solvency, and many of the apparently eternal advantages of deregulation are going to fly away into the horizon. So, deregulation, yes; free travel, no.

On another front, airlines have, in their service, become slaves to the movies. Plying San Francisco to New York on TWA, departure time was

9:15 a.m. At 10:15 a.m., the passengers were offered a sumptuous breakfast. Now, anyone who has a flight at 9:15 will have eaten breakfast, so that being served at ten is the equivalent of being served lunch at ten. Why not wait until noon? To do so gets in the way of the movie. Swissair leaves Geneva for New York at 2:30 p.m., and, I kid you not, serves you a Lucullan meal at 4:00 p.m., which is milk-and-cracker time for English kiddies.

But it all pales up against the latest social amenity experienced at the hands of Pan Am. The stewardess was taking drink orders for serving after the passengers were airborne, and had on her clipboard the names of the passengers, alongside which she would scribble in their choices. She came to me and said, "Mr. Buckley. Now, what do you wish to be called?"

This had never happened to me before, and I was struck quite dumb. I recalled the secret name I was assigned during my months in the CIA. The two aerial numbers I had while in the infantry flashed through my mind. I faintly recalled being told by my mother that I had been baptized not William Frank, as requested, but William Francis, because the priest had said huffily that there was no "St. Frank," only a "St. Francis." I was able only to gurgle, "Mr. Buckley," which provoked a cheerful, "Very well," with just a trace of if-you-want-to-be-stuffy-it's-OK-by-Pan Am, and she was off, accosting the gentleman behind me, with the same questions. He opted for a Bloody Mary and to be called Phil.

And what do you, madam, sir, wish to be called? Lillykins? Butch? It would be fun to try it out on the pope traveling incognito. Ah, Mr. Wojtyla, what would you like to be called? "Just call me Bishop of Rome, Vicar of Jesus Christ, successor of St. Peter, the Prince of the Apostles, supreme Pontiff, Patriarch of the West, Primate of Italy, Archbishop and Metropolitan of the Roman province, and Sovereign of the State of Vatican City. Evelyn Waugh was right. Intimacy, yea; formality, yea; informality, no.

Down to the Great Ship
New York Times Magazine, October 18, 1987

There comes a time when the nature of one's interest in a tragedy becomes historical, to use the word loosely; not human, to use that word loosely.

When I was thirteen, I was taken to Pompeii and the guide spoke about the phenomenon and dealt only macrocosmically with the human tragedy. The people who died because Vesuvius belched up its firestorm of molten lava were entirely anonymous "victims," like the victims of Napoleon's march on Russia, the men slaughtered day after festive day in the Roman Colosseum, or the cavalrymen who charged in the Light Brigade.

That doesn't mean any of these events is wrenched forever from the creative attentions of the artist whose design is to reconstruct the human story and therefore to reevoke sympathy: for the suffering at Pompeii, for the artist who declares eternal war against the routinization of death that followed in the wake of Napoleon's retreat, for the writer who strives to capture the majestic nobility of the naked Christian, praying as he is prepared for the Lion, for the historian who with mordant scorn portrays the bureaucratically homicidal idiocy of General Cardigan, who ordered his men to charge into suicide.

But the time comes when one's interest is taken by other aspects of the phenomenon. Such times must come, else we'd be drowned—every one of us—by preoccupation with our personal sorrows and by our knowledge of the suffering we know to have been endured in so many historical events. Zero Mastel could not have given us his version of *Fiddler on the Roof* if the audience had been permitted to ponder only the pogroms in Russia, and the ultimate solution they would lead to in Nazi Germany. If I went tomorrow to the mausoleum at Verona, I would probably find myself asking the guide whether there actually existed such a drug as Juliet took, brilliantly to feign death while all that was really happening was a moribund sleep, pending her reanimation by Romeo. I would not, by asking that question, deaden myself to the poetry of one of the great romances in literature.

If you want one item (there are thousands to choose from) that will recall the awful poignancy of the death of the *Titanic*, I offer you this. A day before the *Carpathia* reached New York, on April 18, 1912, with the 705 survivors it had picked up from the lifeboats a few hours after the *Titanic* had gone down, the *Mackay-Bennett*, a cable ship, set out from Halifax in search of corpses: men, and women, and children floating on the Atlantic in life preservers dead from exposure (this is how most of the *Titanic's* victims died). Several hundred were retrieved. Some, because of decomposition, were thereupon buried at sea, but efforts were made to identify them and, when successful, to advise relatives of their fate and to itemize any special effects that had been retrieved with the corpse. Notification went to one couple concerning their young son. This is the text of the letter received back by the authorities in Halifax:

> I have been informed by Mr. F Blake Superintendent Engineer of the White Star Line Trafalgar Chambers on the 10th that the Body of my Beloved Son Herbert Jupe which was Electrical Engineer No. 3 on the Ill-Fatted Titanic has been recovered and Burried at Sea by the Cable Steamer "Mackey-Bennett" and that his Silver Watch and Handkerchief marked H.J. is in your Possession. He bought him half a doz of the same when he was at Belfast with the RMS Olympic to have a new blade put to one of her Perpellors we are extremely oblidged for all your Kindness to my Precious Boy. He was not married and was the Love of our Hearts and he loved his Home But God gave and God has taken Him Blessed be the Name of the Lord. He has Left an Aceing Void in our Home which cannot be filled.
>
> Please Send along the Watch and Handkerchief marked H.J.
>
> Yours Truly C. Jupe
His Mother is 72 Last April 4th
His Father is 68 Last Feb 9th

Reading that letter, in the summer of 1912 (if indeed the letter was read other than by the recipients—it is unearthed in Michael Davie's *Titanic: The Death and Life of a Legend*, outstandingly, along with Walter Lord's, the best book afloat on the *Titanic*), one could be expected to feel sheer civic rage against the executioners of Herbert Jupe; and moral historians are ever free to cry out that justice was never really done after the great ship went down.

True, the White Star Line had to pay out $2.5 million, which is a lot more than it sounds, if you close your eyes for perspective: Captain Edward

J. Smith of the *Titanic* was the highest-paid seaman in the world, receiving £1,250 per year.

Oh yes, Captain Smith. He paid a stiff price for ignoring four Marconigrams (as they then called wireless messages) warning of circumambient ice. After all, he went down with his ship. But, in fact, that was incomplete consolation to the relatives of the other 1,500 who went down.

Captain Stanley Lord of the nearby *California* chose to ignore eight distress flares on the extraordinary grounds (a judgment he reached from his cabin, half asleep) that the color of the sighted flares probably meant that they had been touched off as a sort of celebratory handshake in midocean, a merchant vessel spotting another from the same line somewhere in the distance. Captain Lord turned over and went back to sleep in his immobilized liner (he had ordered the engines stopped because of ice conditions). Captain Lord, who might have saved 1,500 people from drowning, walked into historical obloquy, though his professional career was unobstructed, and indeed there rose to defend him what appropriately were called "Lordites," who stressed inconsistencies here and there to justify Captain Lord's insouciance.

Who else was punished? Not Harland & Wolff, which had built the largest moving object ever created: the great Belfast shipyard had complied with the nautical specifications of the British Board of Trade, and no one at H&W had ever said the *Titanic* was "unsinkable." That unsinkable business was nothing more than the creeping vainglory of a jingoistic age in which the leading sea power in the world was trying to make a public demonstration of her infinite resources in order to assert her clear dominance over the brash competitor on the other side of the Atlantic, and to impress the Kaiser. It was not advertised that the British champion was financed, and in effect owned by, American bankers.

What about the Board of Trade itself? Why were there lifeboats for only 1,200 people, given that there were 2,227 on board? Well, you see, the Board of Trade reasoned that any ship that had watertight bulkheads that could be raised to sequester an accidental inflow of water didn't need the traditional ten cubic feet of lifeboat space per passenger. The contingency simply hadn't been considered that raising the bulkheads wasn't enough if the bulkheads weren't designed to rise to the ceiling of the topmost deck.

As it was, what happened in the *Titanic* was that water under pressure flowed merrily uphill, even as water flows from one cube in a tilted ice tray into the next, and so on.

What was one to do to the Board of Trade?

You could give it a little rhetorical hell, and certainly Senator William Alden Smith and his investigating committee did so. If Senator Smith was a moral slouch, then so was Cotton Mather. He subpoenaed all the surviving officers of the *Titanic* and twenty-nine members of the crew. When he learned that five other crew members, ducking the subpoena, had sailed furtively out of New York aboard the *Lapland*, Smith responded by sending a vessel to bring them back. (Senator Smith simply asked President Taft for a naval ship: request granted; *Lapland* stopped.) The tenacity with which he challenged the behavior of British officers, British architects, and British administrators was undiminished by Senator Smith's ingenuous ignorance of the sea or of shipboard terminology (he did not know that a ship's "bow" was different from a ship's "head"). The investigation so provoked (and titillated) the popular press in Britain that a derisory invitation was issued to the senator to come to London to lecture at the Hippodrome on "any maritime subject."

And, of course, the British had their own investigation, conducted by Lord Mersey. It is fair to generalize that the Mersey board concluded in effect that although the North Atlantic route taken by the *Titanic* on its fateful passage ought not to have been taken, in fact it was the workaday steamer route; that binoculars should have been available to the lookouts, though binoculars are not necessarily aids to spotting objects at a distance; that more lifeboats should have been available, though it was not justified to indict the Board of Trade for failure to foresee that which was unforeseeable; that the behavior of the officers and crew would have been more orderly if clearer instructions had been given, but that under the circumstances they performed well, indeed in some cases heroically.

Leaving the parents of Herbert Jupe with what? Concretely, with £100, the per-seaman settlement from the civil lawsuit concluded in 1916. Civic rage had to satisfy itself by other means, and to that rough end an entire literature sprang up, each book, or article, with a slightly redistributed gravamen.

There came, early on, the philosophizing of it all. By conceiving a vessel of such arrant luxury and size, we Lilliputians had stirred the attention of the gods, who stretched out an admonitory finger, casually but sternly to remind us that we are mortals, and ought not to engage in extra-human conceits.

The Great War came, and gradually the memory of the *Titanic* receded, though always there were the full-time practitioners, however sparse at times they seemed (the first issue of the journal issued by the Titanic Historical Society got only forty-five subscribers). But the legend was rekindled by Walter Lord's stirring *A Night to Remember*, and by the movies and the television reenactments of that night to remember. The Philadelphia Maritime Museum became the formal showcase of Titaniana.

And then, in 1985, the great bell rang. First, a French research vessel, and then the little, pilotless submariner *Argo*, under the direction of the naval exploratory vessel *Knorr* from Woods Hole, MA, were "mowing the lawn" over an area 150 square miles in the neighborhood of where it was calculated the ship had actually gone down. The anxious operation was conducted under the direction of a French and an American scientist. The process had been going on tediously, day and night, ever since July 11. In mid-August, the fancy little sub, with its congeries of surrealistic technological devices designed to sound and permit to be seen objects on the ocean floor, began its slow sweep. At 1:40 a.m. on September 1, the excited French scientist found himself staring at a ship's boiler. The *Titanic* had been found.

Two years later, at eleven in the morning on the identical site, 963 miles northeast of New York City, 453 miles south of Newfoundland, after being asked one final time whether I suffered from claustrophobia, I was directed to the shoulder-wide opening of the little submarine, leading to vertical iron railing steps descending into the tubular control center of the *Nautile*.

It is the $20 million diadem of IFERMER, a scientific offshoot of the French government—an underwater exploratory vessel built with titanium, six feet in diameter at its widest point and weighing only eighteen tons. It can descend to depths of 20,000 feet. The chief pilot occupies the berth on the port side. Behind him, sitting on an abbreviated chair, is the copilot. The starboard berth is for the "observer," in this case me. Each of us has a porthole built of one-foot-thick plastic. The copilot, in addition, has two sets of eight-inch television screens. The first set looks ahead via remote video, one camera video trained to look dead ahead, the other to pivot. The second set of videos portrays at close range and at longer range the exact operation of the mechanical arms operating from the side of the *Nautile*, designed to pick up objects from the sea bed. With aid of the video, the operator can exactly instruct the arms.

The overhead hatch is now tightly sealed and as you look about you, you close your eyes slowly, hoping this will not be the moment you contract claustrophobia. Once lifted and positioned by crane and halyard, the *Nautile* is dragged by cable to the launching end of the *Nadir*, the mother ship, dropped into the ocean, and towed by the *Nadir* and by frogmen on a rubber Zodiac a short distance through the water. The descent begins.

At about 2:20 a.m., losing finally its fight to stay afloat, two hours and forty minutes after it glanced the iceberg, the *Titanic's* stern rose up so high that the huge ship was almost vertical over the water. It paused there, appeared, in the description of some witnesses in their lifeboats, to shudder, and then eased back to an angle of about forty-five degrees, as if cocking itself to spring ahead on its long descent. Seconds later it catapulted into its plunge, with its live company of some 1,500 people, including the eight-piece band, which had been performing for the condemned right up until it was no longer possible to stand up. Like everyone else, they were wearing life preservers. It is calculated that it took the *Titanic* approximately ten minutes to reach bottom and that it was traveling, when it hit the ocean floor, at a speed of twenty miles per hour.

To descend the same distance, two and a half miles to the ocean floor, the *Nautile* takes ninety minutes, which means a descent at just less than 1.66 miles per hour. You try to sit up, which requires you to raise your knees six inches or so—there is no room to stretch them out. You have been advised not to eat breakfast, and dutifully you have not.

It is 11:30 a.m., thirty minutes after our descent began, lunch time aboard the *Nautile*. The copilot, Pierre Yves, brings out the two little packages wrapped in aluminum foil. The first course is a hard-boiled egg. Do I wish any salt? "*S'il vous plaît, oui.*" Then there is cold roast beef and French bread. Followed by cheese and a plum or a peach.

"Do you have anything to drink?" I ask abstractly. Answer: yes; they have water. But it is not thereupon proffered, though you are left believing that a direct request would produce the plastic bottle. It isn't any lack of French hospitality, it is just that it would be such an awful *dérangement* if the observer along the way experienced an undeniable call of nature. Just the physical gyrations necessary to accomplish this bring to mind a Marx Brothers three-in-a-bed sequence. You pass.

What to do, as the pilot and copilot exchange rapid, technical French? I had arrived on the *Nautile* with two bulging plastic bags, causing the chief pilot, Georges, to frown and ask, Did I really need all that—*équipage*? Embarrassed, I had pulled out the larger of my three flashlights, and three of my six cassette tapes. But that did leave me with 1) two small flashlights; 2) a book (a thriller to distract me, during the long descent and the long ascent); 3) a little dictating machine (I might want to make notes, and there is hardly room for even the smallest laptop), which dictating machine serves also as a Walkman, for which, 4) I was left with three cassettes. The second parcel carried 5) a thick white sweater to augment protection from the thirty-eight-degree cold at ocean-floor level already provided by long winter underwear, regular sweater, and the fire-resistant coveralls provided by the French; 6) a little can of Right Guard, in case the chill exercised less than all its usual functions; and then 7) a set of kneepads furnished by Ralph White, my new best friend, an American professional jack-of-all-trades, a genial member of the entrepreneur's team who knew more about diving, history, mechanics, ships, airplanes, and the sea than anyone I had ever met.

Why kneepads, for heaven's sake? You will see, Ralph said; and, indeed, I would see. When you are lying with your nose against the porthole you need to put your left knee somewhere, since there is no room to stretch out. So, it ends up on the narrow knurled ice-cold titanium bottom strip between you and Georges. Try then bringing up your knee when it is protected only by underwear, pants, and fire suit for a half hour against the cold grid; and then give thanks to the Lord for Ralph. The kneepads plus gloves for hands that would become cold and, 8) perhaps most important, an inflatable rubber pillow, this to lay over the little metal bar that runs either under your chest while you are lying down, or else under your back when reclining during the vertical passages. There are moments when you wonder whether an extra million dollars might not have been dredged up to cushion that bisecting rod.

But the great moment is coming. We will reach bottom at 3,784 meters, and Georges will turn on the outside beams when we reach 3,550 meters. We are in place, standing guard by our portholes. The lights flash on. Nothing to see, though the water is startlingly clear, diaphanous to the extent of our light's beam, an apparent twenty-five to thirty feet ahead, never mind that it is pitch dark out there.

Then, gradually, it happens: we descend slowly to what looks like a yellow-white sandy beach, sprinkled with black rocklike objects. These, it transpires, are pieces of coal. There must be 100,000 of them in the area we survey, between the bow of the ship and the stern, a half mile back. On my left is a man's outdoor shoe. Left shoe. Made, I would say, of suede of some sort. I cannot quite tell whether it is laced up. And then, just off to the right a few feet, a snow-white teacup. Just sitting there, thank you, on the sand. I liken the sheer neatness of the tableau to a display that might have been prepared for a painting by Salvador Dali. Will we, I ask Georges anxiously, pause to scoop up the shoe?

No. The expedition does not pick up articles of personal clothing.

What about the teacup?

Only if it is embroidered in blue. The distinction, I learn, is that the blue-bordered china is rarer than the plain white, which was used by the 712 steerage passengers. The 337 first-class passengers had the fancier, blue-bordered china. Enough of the former has been picked up in the twenty-six previous dives. Time is limited, and we will not use it up on redundancies.

On and on we float, our bottom resting sometimes six inches from the ocean floor, sometimes a meter or two. We are looking for targets of opportunity, which is why I am expected to keep looking hard to starboard, but also specifically for a piece of the command mechanism from the bridge (the signal handles brought back sharply by First Officer William Murdoch when he reversed engines, moments after the iceberg was sighted dead ahead). The control mechanism has been photographed lying on the ocean floor in the area we are now covering, and instructions are being radioed from above ("130 degrees, proceed for sixty meters") to direct us to our quarries. And then a portion of a leaded window, missing from a reconstruction of an ornamental *vitrine* window that had been a part of the luxuriant decorations in first Class. And a man's leather satchel, contents unknown.

We were below, searching and scooping, for six and one-half cold hours. Ralph said I would find it surprising how quickly the time passed. That was not exactly what I felt after two or three hours. But the sensation, in micro-cosm, was vivid, exhilarating, and uncomplicated by any philosophical mis-givings about our mission. I did not feel any kinship to the voyeur; no more than when, a year earlier, I ogled the tombs in the Nile or, a dozen years ago, the catacombs in Lima beneath the great cathedral where the bones of thousands of Incas lie.

I was a passive part of an archaeological venture that was also an adven-ture—only about 150 men and women in the world have dived as deep in the water as I have now done. The excavation is singular because it is being conducted in a part of the planet heretofore thought totally inaccessible, let alone accessible to people who have in mind actually collecting an inven-tory of items that, for seventy-five years, have lain on the ocean floor, objects last seen by men and women two-thirds of whom died a quite awful death, victims of the hubris of an assortment of thoughtless naval architects, cocky seamen, and mindless money-men.

Finally, the moment came to terminate our sortie, to begin our slow ascent. After a few minutes, permission was requested over the radio (per-mission granted) to jettison one of our two lead weight ballasts, permitting a sharp increase in our rate of ascent.

I tried to sit up, just to find something different to do with my bones. But I had to lean just slightly forward. Otherwise, I might lean just slightly back, in which case I might brush up against one of those hundred tog-gle switches behind me and, who knows, flip the one that would toss me out between the shoe and the teacup—the pressure out there was 6,000 pounds per square inch.

Time to use the Walkman? But to recover the satchel, dig out the relevant parts, and wire in my ears represented a series of exertions on the order of stopping to change one's socks while climbing to the top of Mount Everest.

So, I half-froze, half-continued trying to read my stubbornly unprepossessing thriller with my flashlight between my teeth, my hands behind me supporting my arched back, and exchanged every now and then a drollery, in my kitchen French, with the pilots.

I looked for the one-hundredth time at the fast-changing depth meter. This time it joyfully told me that we had just about reached the surface. I knew we were within fifty meters when the little sub began to roll, reflecting surface turbulence. It seemed an age before the frogmen were there to secure us to the halyard coming down from the ship's crane. But eventually we were airborne into the mother ship's womb. The hatch was turned and I climbed out, a Superman grin on my face, I have to admit.

What began all this for me was that day in August when I saw that Senator Lowell P. Weicker of Connecticut had introduced a bill that would prohibit the import of any artifacts from the *Titanic* for commercial gain in the United States. To do any such thing, the senator inveighed, was to profane what ought to be an international maritime monument. Etc., etc. I dug out the Congressional Record thinking that maybe I'd find there a rationale for this legislation, and there I saw that Weicker, who is my senator, had said that "it is only a matter of time before the world is going to have to turn to these oceans for food and fuel." So? Isn't that a reason for encouraging the ocean's exploration?

And, "When the Earth does turn to the oceans for its food and its fuel, do not forget it has to be a resource that lasts millions of years rather than just a decade or two to satisfy our most immediate desires." Which served only to remind me that my most immediate desire is another senator.

I ruminated, and wrote a column making two points, the first of them that you hardly consecrate the artifacts that went down on the *Titanic* by leaving them on the ocean floor. The second is a libertarian point. I do not understand where Congress got the idea that it has any business telling an adult American what he can and what he cannot purchase from a willing seller, if you're not talking drugs or machine guns. I mean, who told Congress it could come between me and the *Titanic*, which lies in international waters and is no one's property?

A couple of days later, a phone call—an invitation, of all things, to join the expedition and to dive down to the *Titanic*.

Well, why not?

I would do a little exploring of my own. We flew to St. Pierre, the little French island off Newfoundland where the *Abeille Supporter*, the French support ship on which I would spend the next ten nights, lay waiting to take us the thirty-six-hour ride out to the site where the diving was going on. We were a varied group, the central two members being John Joslyn of Los Angeles and Robert Chappaz of Paris. They brought with them a half-dozen friends, relatives, and investors (in some cases all three at the same time).

During the long and very stormy ride out to the site, I spent a little time trying to taxonomize this here operation, which for convenience I call Titanic-87. I swear, you would need Woodward, Bernstein, and Deep Throat to figure it out. This much I can report authoritatively, that involved in Titanic-87 are 1) the French government (it directly subsidized the development of the *Nautile*, and indirectly subsidizes its rental); 2) the American government (it pays most of the bills at Woods Hole and owns the exploratory vessel *Knorr*, the command vessel at the time the *Titanic* was discovered; 3) a French company which undertook to guarantee to the French government that all the artifacts retrieved from the *Titanic* would be presented to museums (thus making the Weicker bill supererogatory anyway); 4) a semipublic French company that actually operates the *Nautile* and the *Nadir*; 5) an entirely private French company that operates the *Abeille Supporter*; 6) a California entertainment company (Westgate) that owns rights to the television show that will air October 28 on the doings of Titanic-87, and 7) individual investors whose return, if any, will come from ancillary activities that grow out of Titanic-87 (books, exhibits, T-shirts, for all I know).

The people I associated with during the ten days are, in my judgment, above all adventurers, pioneer types. Jennifer Carter, the amiable, attractive assistant producer, at once an academic dean, a diver, and a solicitous den mother, married to an Oscar-winning musician: she wanted above all to be the first American woman to have dived to that depth; she is. Al Briggs, Atlanta computer software, brother-in-law of George Tulloch, Greenwich BMW distributor and enthusiast, who fondles a theory about what it was that finally pushed the *Titanic* overboard that could revolutionize the *Titanic* story. Larry D'Addario, a young manager of a huge cement plant inherited when his father was killed in an airplane accident last year.

John Joslyn, perhaps uniquely experienced as a producer, had to come up, along with Tulloch's investor group, with the daily bill. Just the rental of the two French ships comes to $50,000 per day, as best I can figure it out, asking discreetly here and there: after all, the two ships require fifty-three people in crew, among them highly experienced scientists.

What is coming from it all? "Don't you understand?" a reader wrote me just before I left. "Senator Weicker and all those people just don't understand archaeology." It was this that set me to contemplating the question: when does the focus change? When do you put down the glasses that see only tales of distress and suffering and pick up the other set, which focuses on science and history, on surviving artifacts—the sort of things that bring us to museums for whatever reason? Because they are beautiful, or because they are unique; or because they are intimately associated with a great historic event.

What happened that night in April was certainly that. No one will deny it. Titanic-87 has been accused of "exploiting" the event. To say that is on the order of saying that Gauguin exploited Tahiti. Or, if you strain at that, that Quaker Oats exploits Iowa. The Titanic-87 people have refreshed a legend are making possible scientific and historic discoveries, and have among other things consumed ten days of my time, willingly given, abundantly rewarded.

How to Make Planes Run on Time
June 5, 1987

A dozen times in the past month I have left New York between 5:00 and 7:00 p.m., and a dozen times in the past month I have departed New York late and, by the ineluctable laws of physics, arrived late at my destination.

This can be a mild inconvenience if your destination is simply at the other end of where the aircraft is flying. If your destination involves a connection and it is missed, you spend the evening at Chaos House, and by the time you are in bed, your misanthropic glands are in high gear.

And, so, we read that the National Transportation Safety Board recommended that flights landing and departing from twenty-two cities be reduced by 20 percent during the rush hours. The Federal Aviation Administration said: No, that is ridiculous—passengers are perfectly safe as it stands, and if ever the situation should move so as to make them unsafe, we have contingency planning ready to go.

But none of this, of course, has to do with the question of punctuality, so the airlines on their own initiative are making an effort to solve that problem. But corporations are not supposed to conspire together about such things as price and (where relevant to production and marketing) scheduling. There are anti-monopoly laws that presuppose that such meetings between competitive businesses result in action taken in restraint of trade. So, a ruling from the Justice Department is needed granting them immunity from prosecution if they meet with the exclusive purpose in mind of figuring out how to unclutter the rush hours in the late afternoon and the early morning. That is how matters stand. What is not settled is the question: How will the finite and popular hours (e.g., 5:00 to 7:00 p.m.) be allocated? By lot? By rotation?

There is the obvious way to do this when a larger demand accosts a finite supply. It is by invoking what the economists call the price system.

Let us, to use round figures, suppose that LaGuardia Airport can accommodate 500 landings and takeoffs per hour, or 1,000 between the rush hours 5:00 to 7:00 p.m. And (again, to use round figures) let us suppose that the average takeoff and landing fee for a commercial airline is $400. The classic way to ration the use of desired time is to charge for it. Moreover, the elasticity of price lends itself perfectly to fine-tuning.

Suppose that LaGuardia were to experiment during the month of June, charging not $400 but $800 for a landing between 5:00 and 7:00 p.m. The airline would specify to the ticket buyer departing (or landing) at that time that he was paying a surcharge of $4 in return for accommodating his demand for landing during a desired hour. Let us suppose that the extra $4 does not sufficiently slow down the demand. Very well then, in July make that $8. And so on, until passengers varied their schedules in order to avoid the high cost.

A version of this is already done by the cheap night flights. Not many people want to leave at eleven o'clock at night to arrive in Miami at two in the morning—so the airlines make it worth their while. The businessman or lawyer earning $100 per hour can afford to pay the surcharge in order to accommodate the schedule of a high-earner. By contrast, the vacationer who is not under pressure of economic deadlines can leave after ten o'clock in the morning, and arrive before 5:00 p.m., or after 7:00 p.m.

A dozen years ago a professor at the University of Arizona wondered out loud why the price system was not being used to regulate pollution. As he put it, there is a large self-emptying wastebasket in the sky that will handle X cubic meters of pollution per day. We suffer not when the basket is full, but when it is overflowing. Let the factory or the car owner that disgorges contaminants pay a license fee according to the quantity of his emission. And let the price of that license fee rise or fall accordingly as the basket fills or does not fill. It would be stupid to charge a landing fee at LaGuardia so high as to leave the runways from 5:00 to 7:00 p.m. empty save for an occasional sheik from Araby coming in on his private 737.

The wonderful pliability of price works for us except where the demand is inflexible. When inflexible demands rise beyond the capacity of the producer to satisfy, then—and only then—is it necessary to expand production. That is when you get more airports built. Meanwhile, if you leave LaGuardia at 6:00 p.m., and expect to arrive in Chicago at 7:00 p.m., be advised: you won't.

Pitcairn Lives
November 12, 1987

PITCAIRN ISLAND—In 1800, John Adams was preparing to step down from the presidency of the United States, having survived a mutiny against King George III. In 1800, another John Adams ascended to the unstructured presidency of Pitcairn Island, the last living survivor of a mutiny against William Bligh, captain of the *Bounty*, faithful, heroic, sadistic servant of George III.

Pitcairn is regularly referred to as the remotest island in the world of insular notoriety. St. Helena, where Napoleon was sent off to rusticate, is a mere 1,200 miles from mainland Africa. Pitcairn is 3,000 miles from Latin America to the east, 3,000 miles from New Zealand to the west. South of Pitcairn is nothing until you hit the Antarctic. John Adams arrived here in 1790, eight months after the mutiny headed by Fletcher Christian. They came from Tahiti: nine mutineers, six Haitian men, twelve Haitian women.

In those days, the king pursued insubordinate servants more vigorously than we pursue our traitors. Adams & Co. came to Pitcairn because practically no one knew of its existence, because it was remote (twenty-five degrees south latitude, 130 west longitude); deserted (no Polynesian was left); equable in temperature (think of Northern Virginia); fertile (bananas, mangoes, pineapples); small (two square miles); and highly inaccessible except to friendly visitors (mounting an invasion of Bounty Bay might be compared to an amphibious operation up Niagara Falls).

They came here and burned the *Bounty* to eliminate it from preying British eyes. Meanwhile, those of their companions who declined to leave Tahiti to go to Pitcairn were being brought back in irons for trial in London. Three were hanged, a half-dozen (including Franchot Tone), granted clemency because of ambiguous prosecutorial evidence. The point of those who went to Pitcairn was to get safely away until it all blew over.

Twenty-five years after the mutiny it did blow over, and the little colony at Pitcairn was told more or less officially that all was forgiven. At that point, after all, only John Adams was alive, his fellow mutineers having been, for the most part, murdered, during one of Pitcairn's unruly spells. But *Mutiny-on-the-Bounty* watchers were astonished at that point, even as everyone was astonished on two subsequent occasions, when Pitcairners simply declined to evaporate.

In 1831, the whole colony moved to Tahiti, thinking this a reasonable thing to do; but lo, in a matter of months, suffering from homesickness, they mostly returned. And then again in 1856, resolving that 158 islanders threatened a population explosion that would overwhelm the resources of the little mountainous island, the entire colony packed off to Norfolk Island, north of New Zealand; but the same thing happened. After a couple of years, one-quarter of the islanders returned to Pitcairn. Their descendants populate the island today.

Whereas, during the heavy whaling days, boats stopped by every week or so at that southerly latitude, visitors are infrequent now. Supply boats come every three months or so; a half-dozen times a year, random passenger boats stop by.

Barnaby Conrad, the writer and artist, wanted all his life to visit Pitcairn, but managed to coordinate passage only a year or two ago, spending a rapt couple of days here. On bidding an islander who had befriended him goodbye, he said, "Maybe I'll see you next year."

"No," the islander replied, sadly but fatefully. "People only come to Pitcairn once. Goodbye."

In the past few years, the primitive-lifers at Pitcairn have got themselves a dozen mountain-climbing motor scooters, greatly relieving the exchequer, because up until then there was only the single tax on firearms, and these are practically gone. And they have a generator that operates about six hours a day, and allows the islanders to see the thirty-odd movies in the inventory stashed in the church (it is said that children know all the lines by heart). There are refrigerators and washing machines, along with the same old outhouses. The average income of the inhabitants in estimated at $70 per month, money got mostly from trading with passing boats, to which curios are sold. (I own a VICIOUS-looking wooden shark, which cost $7.)

The islanders are Seventh-Day Adventists, which means among other things that none of them will take a drink, except the ones to whom you offer a drink. The pastor, on two-year duty from New Zealand, says that attendance at religious services tends to diminish these days—"But isn't it so everywhere?" He is resigned today—Saturday, Pitcairn's Sabbath. Services are delayed because too many of the islanders, exercising a little self-indulgence, are plying their modest wares, so modestly priced, aboard the visiting *Sea Cloud*, before returning to the island for church services.

At high-tea time they are all on board, four generations of islanders. They spend three happy hours, communicating their cheer. And, after sunset, they board their longboat—80 percent of Pitcairn's population and sing out their happy-melancholy farewell songs.

"In the sweet bye and bye / In the beautiful land beyond the sky.../ We shall part, nevermore, when we meet / On the Be-yoo-tee-fool shore...."

Gilt Trip
Power & Motor Yacht, November 1987

There is a captivating line in *One Hundred Dollar Misunderstanding*, a novel that, thirty years ago, was the season's rage. The author's formula: alternating diary entries by (a) a smug twenty-year-old Ivy League college senior, and (b) an eighteen-year-old black whore with whom (a) was spending a one-hundred-dollar weekend. The book's sheer joy lies in her hour-by-hour outwitting the young *pomposo*, resulting in a frustrated entry in his journal on Sunday morning: "Sometimes I wonder just how all this could happen to a bright, white, Protestant college senior like I." How beautiful, that!

I found myself wondering something of the sort as I and my sister Priscilla and a friend Schuyler Chapin neared our destination on the Delta flight to Fort Lauderdale. We would spend a week on a ninety-three-foot Broward, heading out from Fort Lauderdale all the way to New York's Twenty-Third Street Marina, pausing to pick up three friends at Charleston, SC.

Most Sea People who grow up on sailboats are instinctively suspicious about powerboating. The provenance of my trip was a blend of curiosity and opportunism. I was curious to have the experience of life onboard a powerboat like this one. And the venture was opportunistic inasmuch as the ride wasn't costing me anything: the Broward had in any case to travel north, where its owner uses it during the summer months. The ingenious and thoughtful broker, a friend of long-standing, thought to advertise the Broward's availability as a charter boat in my magazine, accumulating credit points for trade-off.

It is probably the moment to talk a little turkey, so to dive joyously into a mixed metaphor, here are the nuts and bolts of the arrangement.

To charter this Broward, you have to pay $24,000 per week. But the rate, if you desire to use it not to cruise the Bahamas but to ride up to New

York at the time it suits the owner to bring up the vessel, is one-half that fig-ure. Twelve thousand dollars will buy you four pages of ads in my magazine (*National Review*). Which is how come a sixty-one-year-old white college graduate Catholic like I found myself, in mid-May at nine in the evening, ushered into the most opulent ninety-three-foot boat I had ever stepped into.

Now I have been in a lot of powerboats, one of them almost a thou-sand feet long, the forlorn *United States* we would, on Day Five, pass by in Norfolk, rusty, sad after twenty years' desuetude—I sailed in her in her prime. And—en route to a ninety-three-footer—I have disported, in the Aegean, on a 230-foot grandee. And, as a matter of fact, my father owned a 100-footer, but it was a staid vessel, built in the early Thirties to cruise the Chesapeake. It looked like a bath-tub model of the *United States*, whereas a Broward is renowned as one of the glitziest postwar ships-at-sea, architec-turally unrelated to the staid vessel of my father's Palladian time.

To give you just a synecdoche of the kind of thing you can expect from a Broward, the master stateroom on ours has a his-and-hers jacuzzi. The exterior styling of the Broward in question was done by Jon Sonnenberg, who also did Malcom Forbes' new *Highlander*—another way of saying that you cannot buy higher-priced advice.

To be sure, that is not necessarily the same thing as saying that Bonnen-bergiana are for all people the optimal utilization of a ship's cubic poten-tial. I last took a jacuzzi (as it happens) an hour or so before writing these words—had a hot bath right here where I live—which proves that I am a practitioner, acquainted with joy. It doesn't follow that I would devote one-fiftieth of the area on a boat to that particular diversion. For instance, I'd rather have on electric organ: but I am here to write about another Bro-ward than the one I would have, if one were designed to accommodate my own eccentric pleasures.

Does the Captain Sleep?

We were greeted, that balmy May night, by a crew that turned out to be exemplary cicerones and providers. The captain was born in Britain (where he look his captain's license), but he has been here for twenty-six years and has even lost his accent. Much about Stewart Moyes is remarkable—his general navigational knowledge, his equilibrium, a speaking voice the serenity of which would be envied by the acousticians of Forest Lawn (using the ship's radio, he instantly subdues the other party, whatever his/her temperament, into putty).

But most singular of all his attributes is his ability to stay endlessly awake. The following day, anxious to arrive in Charleston in time to meet our friends, he rose early, and in due course we set out on our 580-mile course, accomplishing the voyage in twenty-eight hours during which he slept a total of two hours, without any abrasion of temper.

Second in command is a Danish engineer, Rene Simonsen, also calm, solid, savvy; 180 pounds of Scandinavian stamina. The three young, attractive, enterprising ladies cook the meals, serve them, along with refreshments, all day long, make the beds, clean the cabins—and wash and press your laundry. You can do with your hands on a Broward 93, but you are better off with five, the captain says from experience.

In the huge, mirrored, silk-upholstered lounge we had a late supper. Forward of the sofa area is a huge television set, especially gargantuan for the sake of the owners' kids, as also a hi-fi, etc. Aft of the sitting area is a large, round, enameled dining table, suitable for ten, perhaps twelve. On the starboard side a large, sinewy bar with an icemaker. And, sliding open the gloss paneled doors aft of that, a small *lanai* outdoors with several deck chairs, in case you want to sit there to read and take the sun. If you want the sun and wish to sit elsewhere, you have all of the top deck waiting for you.

We went finally to sleep, woke, and departed a little later than expected. We were up to see the boat snake its way out of Fort Lauderdale, with its bustling ship life, the proliferating condos, and the sense I always have there of only fragile protection from the juggernaut outside, where the Gulf Stream catches you up in its somnolent but tenacious way, enduringly anxious to tailgate you along, and deposit you a few hundred miles northeast, along the shores of Georgia.

I had so calmed Schuyler the night before with talk about how a Broward has—*stabilizers*! that Schuyler quite forgot to affix his scopolamine onto his neck, and now, declining so much as a cup of coffee, he struggled, white-faced, to the top deck of our vessel. I, remarkably steady athwartwise, but pitched fore and aft into a hardy northerly, causing Schuyler (and one of the ladies) a few hours' discomfort; but, verily, only until the numinous agents of whatever drugs hide behind that circular bondage entered his pallid bloodstream, restoring color to his face, and balm to his spirit.

The next morning, at breakfast, I heard him say to Monico in his modest voice, "I'll just…have, oh, coffee, and a little juice, and…some cereal, and er…one fried egg and…a little bacon." From that point on, I would occasionally ask Schuyler to pass me "just" the salt.

A Sailor Learns about Fuel

So then, my first day on a big private luxurious powerboat steaming ahead. What struck me most forcibly?

Well, the noise, actually. Now that is not entirely just, because of course when you sail without power you hear no noise, except those sounds you associate with the elements. On the Broward we heard the engines. But then the captain was at full cruising speed, anxious not to jeopardize our engagement in Charleston. He was doing about 2,000 rpm, using both of his twin Caterpillar 3412 diesels, with their 3:1 reduction transmission. That and also the generators: twin Cat 55-kw 3304 diesels.

I communed with the captain on the top deck, where he preferred to operate. It gives him fore and aft views of everything from markers to little fishing boats. With some help from the Gulf Stream, we were making about fifteen knots. How much fuel, I asked, was he consuming?

About 65 gph.

I gasped, but later calculations confirmed what the captain said: it takes about five gallons of fuel to drive the Broward one mile.

How much fuel did he carry?

Six thousand gallons. I withdrew to make calculations, and then asked how was it possible to advertise this as a boat capable of crossing the Atlantic?

The answer is that it is perfectly capable of crossing the Atlantic, but that when you do this you operate the ship differently. You use only a single engine—"for maybe a week." Then you turn on the other engine, shutting off the first. What does that cost you in speed? Oh, about one and one-half knots. How much less fuel is consumed?

Well, said the captain, we use about sixty-five gallons with both motors and generators on, about thirty-five gallons with just the one engine.

I did not pursue the question why the extra 1.5 knots (thirty-six miles per day) was worth burning 500 gallons of extra fuel. I asked whether it was quieter with just the single engine going? No, he said: As a matter of fact, it is a little *noisier*... More vibration. I went below to read.

Do Powerboatmen Have More Fun?

An interesting point here. Aboard a sailboat, even fully crewed, there is more often than not something that prevents you from total repose. You are perhaps heeled over, and suddenly you are dumped from your seal or bunk. Or else someone comes smilingly to dislodge you—the grapefruit juice in the locker, just under where you are sitting. Or there is a squall and you need to get out of the way to permit the ports to close after which you suffocate.

By contrast, at sea in a modern powerboat—provided the fore-and-oft pitching is not too distracting—you are free to immerse yourself totally in your reading, your writing, your card playing, or your desk work. That may be among the reasons why the Broward has such varied electronic gear as a telex machine and, yes, a satcom.

I have often envied the boat that permits you to pick up a telephone wherever you are at sea and simply dial away, just as in the television ads; as though every day were Mother's Day, and every editor you write for is a mother. It transpires that the wonderful satcom, indeed a miracle, comes with certain economic depressants. Like ten dollars per minute's use; so that the single call we ventured on it—to relay to Schuyler's wife, Betty, the estimated time of our arrival at Charleston—evolved as the most peremptory call Schuyler *ever* made to a wife of forty years' standing. This time, when he announced that he had just one thing to say, he had just one thing to say (cost: $12). The satcom, by the way, if you feed it $35 a day, will give you a daily news bulletin seven paper-feet long, which reaches right to the extremity of the day's news, like how many Contras can dance on one Boland Amendment.

On Day Two, five hours ahead of schedule, we made our determined way into the great harbor at Charleston, passing by Fort Sumter where the great war began, 126 years earlier; and soon we idled down, cruising into the harbor at decorous speed. Over the ship's radio, the Ashley Morino operator instructed Captain Moyes to dock starboard-side to just ahead of the 110-foot *Victoriana*, along the wharf. It was hard for me to imagine, when I heard that transmission, that there actually existed a boat bigger than ours.

Day Three: Life on a Plumb Bob

There was much jollity when one hour or so before midnight Schuyler's wife Betty Chapin and the two Olivers joined us; Don (who is Chairman of the FTC and on ongoing delight), and Louise, bright and vivacious mother of six. They were all served a late, light dinner, and I outlined the alternatives I had discussed with the captain. Most experienced sea captains have mastered the technique of laying out seagoing alternatives, having already decided which of them they have privately settled on, but it is always nice to shuffle the democratic deck with just enough skill to give out the plebiscitary feel.

Actually, my plan made incontrovertible sense. At the terminal end of our journey, we absolutely needed to be in Manhattan by noon on Friday. If we waited until morning and set out inside, in the waterway, Charleston to Beaufort, that passage would consume two days (Monday, Tuesday—you cannot readily travel along the waterway at night). Another two days (Wednesday, Thursday) to Norfolk—and then we would face the need to travel from Norfolk to Manhattan in a single day and night.

Too far, too chancy; and besides, doing it that way would deprive us of the few hours I had planned for Atlantic City. None of us had experienced the glitzy casinos since the great reconstitution of Atlantic City, which I had last seen as I slipped away from it on my forty-foot sloop in 1964, headed home after a hectic four days covering for my syndicate that anointment of Lyndon B. Johnson and experiencing the horrible premonition that he would win the forthcoming election even though, in our hearts, we knew that Barry Goldwater was right. That Atlantic City was like today's Coney Island, and I was anxious to have a two-three-hour look at Las Vegas East.

Accordingly, we decided to travel, nonstop, beginning immediately—at midnight—on the ocean, right to Beaufort. Captain Moyes was delighted at the prospect of another sleepless night. We pulled serenely away from Charleston, all of us observing, from the top deck, the receding lights, the crystallizing channel markers: experiencing the everlasting romance of the seagoing vessel slipping out from the sanctuary of harbor into the dark, and whatever the dark holds out for you.

By midnight we were asleep, my sister now occupying the "den cabin" on the main deck, the Olivers and the Chapins the two guest cabins, I the master cabin, alone, without my wife, who was still on crutches after her hip operation, forbidden by her Philistine doctor from joining us even though I *tried* to tell him (!!!) that life at sea on a Broward was like *life on a surveyor's plumb bob*, I mean, nothing for a post-surgery hip patient to worry about!

The rumble of the engines, curiously, disengages from consciousness. A psychic phenomenon. It is so, I have found, of record noise: my Caruso singing *Vesti la Giubba* sounds to me as though it had been recorded yesterday, so accommodating is the ear when undistracted by human conversation. We slept as though in the quietness of tents in a desert.

Beaufort is a charming little southern town, directly opposite the more commercial Morehead City, on the entrance to the waterway that provides passage on the inland side of dreaded Cape Hatteras. We were in Beaufort in mid-afternoon, in good time to walk about and to explore the brief commercial street. Returning to our boat we resumed our reading and writing and research, ate a leisurely dinner, and then watched *Goldfinger* on the ship's VCR, unquestionably the most boring thing we had done during the day (we had all seen it before, and James Bond is okay once, disastrous the second time). We looked forward the following day to a stretch in the light waterway, to perusing, under way, the passing profiles of the canal, as we wended our way, at reduced speed, up toward Albemarle Sound.

Day Four: Naval Architects and Windows

Now here is a complaint I have against almost every ship at sea. I speak of the exasperating habit of naval architects to situate the bunks, and the chairs, and the couches at levels that permit the eye's reach, even of six-foot-tall men, to fall short by an exasperating few inches of the horizon. Every seat on our Broward shares the same problem with the *Queen Elizabeth*, the *France*, the *Ile de France*, the *United States*, the *Europa*, the *Andre del Sarto*: in order to view the horizon, you need to rise about five inches from where you repose, as if practicing a ski jump.

In my schooner, *Cyrano*, I forced the architect at gunpoint to situate the nose ports level with the mattresses on which we slept, to permit staring out into the sea, above the horizon and, when heeled, below the horizon, as one lies there, an experience neither forgettable nor available in any other situation, unless you have a private submarine and control your own periscope.

So that in order to be able to look at the shoreline passing by, here jungle-like with large gnarled vines, there spooky with Spanish moss, occasionally just pastoral-neat, we needed to perch in the afterdeck, or on the top deck—seated in the lounge, so nicely air-conditioned, we could see only the top half of the trees gliding by.

Still, it was a lovely, effortless, noiseless ride, those eighty miles to Belhaven. Beyond that we could not go on Tuesday, as there is no resting place suitable for the Broward until Norfolk, an impressive 130 miles beyond Belhaven, with its dramatic antebellum mansion situated just behind the little marina, the inn where they serve (we are told) sumptuous dinners.

On a boat, one wishes to eat on board; so, we rejected the kind invitations to take the Belhaven special. How distinctive, one notices, the social manners of the southerner. The young merino attendant (eighteen years old?) introduced himself to us, wished us a happy stay in Belhaven, and invited us to use (free of charge) the marina's three golf carts that would convey us the six blocks into town. There, the liquor store operator questioned—after I meditated the huge posters warning against age-imposture—on whether he had a lot of trouble with teenagers pretending to be twenty-one, replied, "Not really. You see, I recognize just about everybody who comes in here, and I know when they get to be twenty-one."

One more night of relaxation—but interrupted by a sudden squall, and on-the-spot excitement when a thirty-six-foot sloop ran aground on a sand shoal only a few yards from the ventral belly-button of our beautiful Broward's hull, causing consternation in as much as the thirty-knot wind was bending the little sloop directly your way...What if, suddenly, it floated free of the sandbar...?

It did; and our Danish engineer was prepared, maneuvering the largest fender ever manufactured over the side. But the little sailboat swung well away, abeam the wind, under power, and moments later arched back into the wind, sliding into an empty slip; all was again serene.

Another movie (awful).

Day Five: Fun, Fun, Fun

This was our most arduous day because, finally, the weather went sour. Rain, squalls, cold. At the little waterway settlement of Coinjock we stopped to pick up a staggering 2,000 gallons of fuel. It was too cold, and the waterway is too fetid, to swim; but I remembered that two days earlier, en route to Beaufort, I had asked the captain about swimming and he told me it would be difficult to haul myself back on board from the water because the hull would have risen eighteen inches from the consumption of fuel. Well, at least we were floating back on the waterline, the boat now fully reloaded, making it possible to swim the next day (Thursday), en route to Atlantic City.

But that was not to be. We arrived late in Norfolk, only a half-hour before the Rouse Center, opposite the Morino, closed up. I hadn't before heard of a Rouse Center, but of course the captain had. They are most nearly likened, I would say, having toured the one at Norfolk, to a Disneyland compressed into about three acres: shops, delis, entertainments, souvenirs, junk and not-quite junk stores, fun, fun, fun.

It is a psychologically arresting experience to travel from a half-hour at a Rouse Center back onto a quiet, sleepy, secure vessel in which you have come 850 miles over canals and ocean. There is a special smugness that attaches to your cloistered boat, tethered for the night in the dark, with only the night-lights at the boats around you, and the sparklers of the Rouse Center gradually reducing to dim night-lights.

Day Six: Annapolis by Rickshaw

The next day was bad. Outside, the radio reported the seas at ten feet, the winds thirty knots northeast—on the nose of my projected course.

That meant: no Atlantic City; no New York. The alternative, which would give us a final day aboard the Broward, was to go up to Annapolis, one hundred miles north, but under the lee, however remote, of the eastern shore of the Chesapeake.

It was one more long day on the water. We had only just completed our evening meal when we tied up, finally, at the marina at Annapolis. Earlier in the day the sun had turned suddenly bright, and the sun worshippers among us sat outside, on the stern deck and on the top deck above, with their books and suntan oil, reading avidly, taking advantage of the equilibrium of the 157-ton vessel as it roared up toward the town that, briefly, served as the capitol of the United States.

We disembarked, bent on a walking tour of the city. A seventeen-year-old boy, in shorts and a sport shirt, pedaling a rickshaw, accosted us: Would we like a scenic trip of Annapolis?

Indeed, but there were six of us...

Never mind; he reappeared a moment later with two other high-school juniors, pedaling their two-man rickshaws. They took us, with great stamina, along those amber streets, the colonial houses white red yellow, shutters crisp and tended, the little plots of flowers verdant.

After Scenic Annapolis, back to our Broward. Should we, what the hell, see the last of our rented films? Why not?

Out of Africa is quite wonderful, Meryl Streep the most dominant female figure on the screen since Bette Davis. So, alongside perfectly maintained eighteenth century Colonial America, with its pleasing and sturdy intimation of the exuberant national character, we sat in our Broward, touring plantation life in early twentieth century Africa, experiencing the melodramatic highs and lows of primitive native and exurbanite life; secure aboard our insulated pleasure dome, a hundred feet of modernity at sea, on entry in any contest featuring heady concentrations of the skills and brains of the world right up to day before yesterday.

I am not yet ready to forsake my little thirty-six-foot sloop, and I do not expect ever to command the resources to purchase a ninety-three-foot Broward, but it is good to know that such proud and seaworthy and sybaritic creatures are actually being made in America. Not, granted, at

Williamsburg; but in America, home of Rouse Centers, Cape Canaveral, Disneyland, and Horatio Alger.

Forced Landing

Cruising World, August 1988

The invitation was as welcome as it was unexpected—to bring Peter's thirty-eight-foot sloop back from Abaco in the Bahamas to this part of the world. I say "this part of the world" because the exact destination was unstipulated: the idea was to take the boat as far as possible toward Norfolk, VA, in the time we had. At Norfolk, Peter's friend, a professional pilot, would ferry *Astraea* to its destination in Stamford, CT.

Peter Flanigan, I came to know, is skilled in every aspect of sailing, but he hasn't had ocean experience and for that reason desired a skipper-navigator along. We have been friends for many years, and I have observed him using his shrewd mind and incisive tongue at home (New York, Purchase), in the Oval Office (he was an assistant to President Nixon), and at the Metropolitan Opera (Peter attends, does not sing). He was born competent and along the way developed sharp executive skills (Dillon Read).

Accordingly, I could tell, early on, that he envisaged this passage as mine and for that reason left it to me to put the crew together. "I should think four would be enough," he said over the phone in November. I countered with five. "Someone may be seasick." I have almost always found it so, e.g., in all four races I did to Bermuda, sailing my own boats with eight crew on board.

But then when racing we'd always have three men on watch. When cruising, two are enough, with a third hand on call. Peter agreed and in the ensuing period rough calculations danced about in my mind—it is always so, well in advance of an ocean cruise, vague thoughts given to the upcoming sail. But the day comes when you cannot prudently put off the fine-tuning. I was away from my charts when that moment came and, in Switzerland, had to make do with a *New York Times Atlas* and my Hewlett/Packard 41c computer. I wrote to Peter, "I don't know where in Abaco your vessel squats, so in making calculations I posited Elbow Cay, at 26-15 north, 76-40 west.

Our destination at Morehead City, NC, lies as you told me, directly north (359.6 degrees). The distance is 508 miles. On the assumption that we can average five knots (modest, but safe), the passage would take us 4.2 days. My guess is that with the Gulf Stream working with us about 25 percent of the time and with broad-reaching winds at fourteen to eighteen knots, we will more likely make the trip to North Carolina in about seventy-six to eighty-two hours. Now, if we leave at noon on Saturday, April 9, we should reach Morehead late on Tuesday. The approach there is easy at night, no sweat. So, it wouldn't matter if we got in at midnight plus."

As my own D-Day approaches, I always manage to feel a little like General Eisenhower planning D-Day. The weekend before leaving was the weekend for The List—of things to bring along, which included such conventions as sextant, *HO 249* tables, plotting sheets; and a few nonconventional aids to life-at-sea, such as three trays of tape cassettes, two Walkmans, and my laptop computer and recharging paraphernalia.

There is something to be said for maximum exertion the day preceding your first night on a cruising sailboat. The polarity between hectic cosmopolitan life and the stillness of the lagoon heightens. My radio alarm woke meat 6:15 a.m. in Los Angeles, CA. Several hours later, at the Eastern gate in Miami, FL, I met Van and Claudio, who had come down from New York. There also to meet me was the pilot who would fly us to Marsh Harbour on Great Abaco Island, an hour and a half away by Cessna.

All that Peter, who had come ahead one day, had felt he needed to tell me was that I should take a taxi from the airport to the "water taxi" at Marsh Harbour. There a launch would be waiting to ferry us to Man O' War Cay, where the *Astraea* would be waiting for us.

The instructions sufficed and we'd have gotten there earlier except that, along the way, we ran into...a party! On the clubhouse lawn, not twenty yards from our waiting launch, the Cruising Club of America was celebrating something or other and we fell into the arms of old friends and sailing companions, including former Columbia University dean Schuyler Chapin and wife Betty, and Walter Cronkite and *his* Betty. Norrie Hoyt *et ux* were there also. Norrie and I once fired shots at each other in print (that was thirty years ago and I pause to record that Norrie was unquestionably right in defending, I wrong, in my callow youth, in mocking, the exacting standards set by ocean racers). Cronkite told me he didn't know I was in the yacht-ferrying business, else he'd have engaged me to take his *Wyntje* back to the States. Much general jollity, compressed into twenty minutes. And then we were off, reaching the fine, spic-and-span *Astraea* just as the sun fell.

We rowed to the shore, heading for a restaurant for dinner, in two sittings on the rubber dinghy manned by the fifth member of the crew, Tony Leggett, at thirty-four a veteran seaman and racer who once sailed across the Atlantic with me in 1980. I reflected, on reaching land, that I had never before been in Man O' War Cay but that it was here that my *Cyrano*, a schooner I owned and sailed for ten years, had been built. "The last of the big boats," the water taxi driver had told us. *Cyrano* was—is—wood and the yard that produced that lovely creature long since ran out of commissions for bulky sixty-foot schooners.

It always surprises me how the great bulk of things one brings on board (more exactly, the great bulk of things I bring on board: others practice moderation. My rule is to bring along everything you might want, plus 25 percent) has a way of disappearing even on boats of modest size, if only one is diligent and ingenious, as Peter was. He effected, after two hours of hard labor, the deliquescence of two cumbersome seabags hoarding emergency amenities, a reservoir against contingent want. We had a glass of Peter's soothing Moselle and went to our bunks.

I picked up my night reading, and was prompted then and there to tell my companions the story I had heard from Walter Cronkite years before. He had been on his feet on television an endless number of hours in connection with the launch or Apollo 9 (I think it was). It was Christmas Eve and he was dead on his feet. He had plotted forward to a week's sailing vacation and flew off to his sailboat where, the sun beginning to descend, he sat contentedly with wife and another couple, eggnog in hand, when a trim yacht tender hove in. The mate doffed his cap and announced that he bore an invitation from the yacht *Seascape*, whose owner would be delighted if the only other cruisers in this remote lagoon would join him for a Christmas Eve drink.

"I shrugged my shoulders," Walter reminisced, "and thought what the hell, it's Christmas Eve, we'd better be fraternal. So, we all got into the launch and went over to the large motor yacht a mile across the harbor, climbed up the companionway and—my God, IT WAS ROY COHN!"

I read a couple of chapters of *Citizen Cohn*, by Nicholas von Hoffman and lazed into sleep, hoping vaguely that the predicted northwest winds would not materialize the following morning.

But they did. My experience has always been that weather reports that are not welcome, eventuate. Those that are welcome, do not. The trouble with a northwest wind, of course, was that northwest was where we planned to head in order to glide into the Gulf Stream, in order to glide into Morehead City. Nothing doing.

Two days before leaving I had a long telephone conversation with my oldest sailing companion Reggie Stoops, in the hospital for abdominal surgery and for that reason not with us on the trip. Reggie likes to take courses, however supererogatory, in anything to do with sailing or flying and had just completed, after forty years of sailing at sea, a course on safety procedures at sea.

There were the usual dos and don'ts, but two novelties, he told me. The first is different recommended procedures in the event of a man overboard.

1) Toss over a life cushion or two (time allowed: two seconds). 2) Assign a member of the crew to keep his eyes on the man overboard (time: one second). Then 3) come about, leaving the headsail harnessed exactly where it was, so that now it is aback (time: five seconds). 4) Sail on a broad reach for the few seconds required to position yourself to one side of the "victim"—as the Coast Guard refers to him. 5) Then downwind past the victim. Then 6) upwind, bringing down the sails as you coast up toward him. At this point you need either a sling, attached to your main halyard, to bring him up, or else a floating line to your fixed stern boarding ladder.

And second (said Reggie), you should test your EPIRB emergency radio transmitter. The way to do this, he explained, is to wait until the hour (any hour). Between the hour and five minutes past the hour the Coast Guard monitors ignore all distress signals, on the understood assumption that they are hearing sets being tested.

"Where do you check to see if the signal is going out all right?" I asked. "On Channel 15."

For a startled moment I thought Reggie was talking about television, but of course he was talking about the VHF radio. We went through the motions on the *Astraea* and Peter showed us how to flash on the signal. At exactly 9:00 a.m., Peter broadcast the SOS signal and Van twiddled the radio dial. Ah, but the dial went from—Channel 12—13—14—to Channel 16. No 15. I would need to ask Reggie if he wanted to take another course, after leaving the hospital, on how to find Channel 15. The stipulated exercise is akin to the reading of inscrutable instructions. Best to give up, until a tutor materializes.

We set out—and promptly ran aground, never mind that we were well within the channel. I felt very much at home, running aground in the Bahamas, as I did on *Cyrano* for a full decade. A cheerful couple in a small motor launch hauled us out and we were off on our westward passage, under lee, one hundred miles due west to Walker Cay, unless the wind changed and gave us leave to slip out into the ocean earlier on our northerly course.

Van Galbraith—to examine the schedule from the other end—had to deliver a speech at a luncheon meeting in Paris on Thursday. It was now near sunset, Sunday. Earlier that afternoon I had told him soberly, sadly, dividers and calculator in hand, that perhaps he should disembark at Walker Cay, to be absolutely protected against the possibility of a late arrival in Morehead.

I was vaguely familiar with the facilities at Walker Cay having visited there in 1970, summoned by Richard Nixon in the golden days before Watergate. The president was relaxing with two friends after the Congressional election and was pleased by the election of my brother Jim to the Senate in New York. Getting there had been a wild flurry of Air Force One, small jets and helicopters, to the insular preserve of the president, courtesy of his friend Robert Abplanalp. But the following day my wife and I relied on conventional transportation to take us from Walker Cay, to West Palm Beach, FL, and on to New York. I told Van there was commercial airline service to Florida, but then Peter aborted the suspense by saying that he did not mind if we made an emergency stopover at Charleston, SC, in the event time did run out; so, happily, Van stayed aboard.

The question now was whether to head directly for the Gulf Stream on a course of about 280 degrees, or to take the hypotenuse (due north) and meet the stream later, but saving distance traveled. I opted, by feel, for the first course and proceeded on it. Van gives earnest attention to any challenge that might shorten by ten minutes life at sea, so he went down to the chart table. A half hour later he informed me that I was correct: he had calculated we would save one hour by going directly to the stream.

Which we did, happy as the sails filled. As we sat about the cockpit before dinner, watching one of those transfixing Bahamian sunsets, I delivered my lecture (it lasts about two minutes, twenty seconds) about my Pacific epiphany: the rediscovery of wing-and-wing sailing on my voyage from Honolulu, HI, to New Guinea. At lecture's end, we went to work....

I had thought it unwise to raise the spinnaker, as night was falling and forecasts from Fort Lauderdale, FL, radio were of brisk winds during the night. Accordingly, Peter gave us the ship's protocols for lowering the spinnaker boom from the mainmast and positioning it for the genoa clew—in every boat the procedure is just a *little* different ("You *have* to get the end of the pole down first, touching the headstay," Peter demonstrated).

But having completed the maneuver, *Astraea* wobbled, denying us a steady downwind course. I then remembered, aboard *Sealestial*, that after we had lost the big genoa, on day two, we put up the Yankee and the fit was thereafter tight, secure—perfect. Ah, and the *Astraea* has a roller furling headstay. Bringing in eighteen inches of genoa gave us just that desired tightness and the good ship settled doggedly on its dead-downwind course, holding there under the gentle prodding of the little Autohelm automatic steering, while we went below for dinner and a nice burgundy Peter had got in Abaco.

The moonless night was uneventful, save for the garish luminosity of the parting seas as we barreled down at seven-and-a-half knots toward the Gulf Stream. We hit it sometime after midnight, a juncture instantly decipherable from the leap in the Loran speed. (When and if I reach St. Peter's gate, I will ask to see the man who invented Loran, so I can say, "Thanks.")

Having hit the stream, we changed course and hugged the axis of the current, loping along at a speed of nearly ten knots.

The following day was bright and sunny, but the winds were freakish. At one point we had practically none, so we stopped to swim. I contemplated the fixed boarding ladder and recalled the awful tale told me about the *Sea Cloud* last November by a man who had been called to Atlantic City, NJ, a few months before to help a friend in critical psychological shock. Four men had been sailing to New York from Cape May. Opposite Atlantic City, ten miles out, one of the two brothers was pitched overboard while tending a sail in rough weather. He was thrown a line and grabbed it. The other three then tried for a heartbreaking hour to lift him back on board: but, finally, in the swirling sea, they lost the fight. If they had had a fixed boarding ladder, they could have managed easily. If they had had a sling and a tackle, rigged to the main halyard, they'd have managed. A grisly story, the implications of which I hastily shook off, on mounting the *Astraea*'s boarding ladder.

The balance of the day was of the sort that, however apprehensively, one simply gets used to being at sea. Something is telling you that there is confusion in the elements and odd things are likely to happen. Not hurricane-odd —there is nothing on the barometer, or on the radio, that indicates any such danger. The weather report is still talking fifteen-to twenty-knot winds from the southeast. But in fact, the winds are coming and going, the sun is coming and going and the clouds are ditto, as are squall patterns off in the distance. A careful examination of navigational particulars suggested that yes, we would probably be in Morehead City by midmorning Wednesday—but there was a chance we wouldn't be and Van would need, in any case, to travel from Morehead to Charlotte, to La Guardia airport and to J.F. Kennedy airport to make his Wednesday evening flight to Paris. So, by dinnertime, we resolved to head up to Charleston, 200 miles closer. No course change was indicated until four or five in the morning. So we more or less uniformly battened down.

I came on watch at 23:00 and instantly undertook an extra reef on the mainsail. The genoa had already been furled. We were on a broad reach with southeast winds. And these were coming in in gusts which, a half-hour later, were reaching forty and even fifty knots, with shafts of driving rain in successive bursts that lasted fifteen or twenty minutes.

I spotted a light at about eleven o'clock on our course, more exactly visible through binoculars, two tiny blurs of light. Tony, though off duty, came up to the cockpit (sleep below was impossible, as we rolled and tossed). Tony suggested in his quiet way that the ship was bearing down on us and that he thought it would be appropriate to come about. I recited my philosophy in such matters: I approach oncoming ships until quite close and only then make course changes, definitive in nature. We watched the ship through the blinding rain and howling wind, making out both its running lights. It didn't change in its bearing to us, which told us we were on a collision course.

What spooked us was that the ship seemed to come no closer. I doubt it was traveling at four knots, let alone sixteen. Finally, I came about, primarily to ease the mounting psychological pressure in the cockpit, in the anarchic circumstances of eccentric and screeching winds.

An hour later Tony was on watch with me (my watch system specifies social rotation): and, suddenly, there was that same vessel again, this time coming at us from astern. Again, we watched, for fifteen, twenty minutes, wondering why it did not overtake us. Again, I came about, with the purpose primarily in mind of losing our pursuer. We had a little bit the feeling of a rudderless pursuer stalking us, this time from behind, awaiting the auspicious moment to pounce. A logical next step would have been to power on the radio and ask, "What-in-the-hell are you nice people dogging us for?" Tony allowed himself to speculate that the Spookship was out here awaiting a drug drop. If so, would it react against a thirty-six-foot sailboat out here in the wild seas that had spotted it?

The stuff of post-midnight fantasies in stormy weather. Although I cannot even now explain the behavior of the *SS Spook.*

The wind began to quiet down at 4:00 a.m. and by daybreak we were under power. A dull day, cloudy, as we headed now toward Charleston. There came, along with the altered course, the gray skies and the reduced speed as we pulled away from the stream, a detectable lesion in the ship's morale.

Nothing serious, but nonetheless palpable. After a long day, at sunset after dinner, it was time to close in on the first marker in the long (twelve-mile) channel to Charleston Harbor. One reaches, finally, the harbor opening and then zigs and zags another ten miles, past the fort where the Civil War began, before reaching, finally, the marina.

Now that inland leg proved rather an ordeal. It took five hours from the first marker to our berth. The heavy wind was back: thirty-five knots on the nose. The current (foul) was over three knots. And the weather temperature dropped, during that period, from about sixty-five to about forty degrees. We gunned up to 2,200 rpm to get an extra half-erg of energy and powered—and powered—and powered away. The range lights were not easy to line up. The eyes, after several hours facing the wind, became inordinately dry. When the marina finally materialized, I tried to berth against a beam wind of thirty knots into a narrow slip. This did not work and so we puttered anxiously about, looking for a berth with a more hospitable axis to the wind; finally found it and, sometime after midnight, tied up.

I left the wheel and went below to the head to remove my contact lenses. Only to find that I could not bring my frozen thumb and index finger together to grip them. It required a full five minutes, my hands nestled in my underarms, before the fingers would work again.

Everyone who has sailed in blue water knows two sensations, exhilaration and exhaustion. We had more of the latter, at that moment, than of the former. If we had been greeted at the berth with the news that we had come in first in the great Abaco-Charleston race, we'd have experienced the two emotions, synaesthetically. Instead, we just sat down, had a glass of wine and creeped into our bunks.

I closed my eyes and thought of Harvey Conover at the end of the 1958 Newport-Bermuda Race, addressing us in his capacity as commodore of the Cruising Club of America. "Fellow maniacs," he began. Six months later Conover was dead, drowned off his anagrammatic *Revonoc*, voyaging on Christmas Day from Key West to Miami, FL. But then it happens, even before you go off to sleep, that the mind turns to other moments in the passage, for instance Sunday night, driving wing-and-wing downhill at hull speed through the lambent water, and you are prepared to smile when they tell you you are a maniac for going to sea in a sailboat. You can't see the expression on the face of your seagoing companions, in the drowsy mists, but you know that on the face of us defendants is a smile, a patronizing smile. Pity them, not us.

Marjorie's Slow Boat to Paradise
Condé Nast Traveler, October 1988

When Marjorie Merriweather Post first laid eyes on her new boat, the *Sea Cloud* (we will skip her numerous other names), she might reasonably have concluded that a million dollars would, in 1931, get you anything. In the next twenty years or so she would spend millions just to maintain the boat, and when, finally, Marjorie traded her to General Trujillo, she got only a secondhand Viscount turboprop in return. On the other hand, who wants—can afford? is willing to pay for?—a 360-foot boat requiring a crew of about sixty?

The answer is Sea Cloud Cruises, the German syndicate that operates the most seductive commercial ship at sea.

Before boarding a boat for a trip that by its comprehensive hedonism would numb a Puritan's soul, it helps to have struggled a bit with workaday life. You would not, after all, want to start in on Scheherazade's *A Thousand and One Nights* rising from your couch, interrupting only your consumption of bonbons. For us (my wife and me), the preceding twenty-four hours solved the problem of self-abnegation.

We would meet in Los Angeles for the flight to Papeete, arriving in Tahiti with a leisurely thirty-six hours before boarding the *Sea Cloud.* During the preceding twenty-four hours, I'd preside at a two-hour televised political debate in Houston. The following morning, I'd complete two one-hour television tapings of *Firing Line.* A private airplane would get me to San Francisco in time to rehearse for a public social event that required me, among other things, to perform on the harpsichord. A second private plane would get me to Los Angeles "with over an hour to spare."

However... 1) the plane was delayed several hours en route to San Francisco, where I arrived only just in time to dash to the harpsichord, sick with nervousness, and rush through my pieces. I slaughtered Bach. Following the cocktail reception and dinner, 2) I was rushed out to the airport to learn 3) that we were fifty-fifth in line for takeoff. At Los Angeles, a car drove me furiously to Continental Airlines, and its 11:55 p.m. flight, at the other side of the airport. I sprinted to the departure gate, arriving at 11:45 in time for 4) the announcement of an hour's flight delay. Followed by a second hour's delay. Followed by the flight's cancellation. After 5) a scramble at 2:20 a.m. for Continental's emergency toothbrush kit, we went by bus to a motel. Followed 6) three hours later by a 6:00 a.m. phone call: the plane is fixed, will depart in exactly forty-five minutes. We arrived in time for 7) the announcement of an hour's delay. Followed by a second hour's delay. Followed by another cancellation. Back at the motel, as my wife stepped gratefully into her bath, we 8) got another phone call: plane fixed, immediate departure, quick, hurry up. We arrived and this time were led to our seats and given a glass of champagne (Chateau Triumpho: Here's looking at you, baby). Followed by a second glass. Followed by 9) a third, newest cancellation. We were led to the Air France waiting room, having been resignedly advised by Continental to switch allegiance. Air France flight 10) delayed two hours.

But it did finally leave, arriving in time to give us some sleep and three hours to survey Papeete. Then we had a quick lunch and went on to the *Sea Cloud*.

There was a moment when we thought our curse had traveled with us: a shipment of provisions from Australia was delayed and we might not be leaving the harbor until midnight. But an hour later, bells and things began to sound, and the *Sea Cloud* zigzagged its way from the dock, turned clumsily about, and headed out of the harbor in balmy, cloudy weather. We were setting out to visit the remotest little insular notoriety in the world, a full week ahead of us, followed by a second week's sailing to the second-most-remote island in the world.

The bags unpacked, I surveyed the most pleasant bedroom (it has a fireplace) I have ever sailed in. It was Mrs. Post's—excuse me, Marjorie's—prime guest room, less the adjoining room, once her prime guest's boudoir, now a separate cabin. (On the *Sea Cloud*, Mrs. Post is always Marjorie, even to people born after she died, as in "This is where Marjorie used to sit.") We walked out through the corridor, which looks like a high Williamsburg Colonial reproduction, to the main deck and climbed up to the Lido deck, where champagne was being distributed to the fifty-seven passengers. The moon was out, and the lights of Tahiti gave us a modest, gradually evanescing perspective. The boat's engines (sails would be set the following day) were nicely unobtrusive; the generator, practically soundless. Climbing down the stairway brought us to the main lounge, set up with four or five tables for dinner, as were another four or five tables in Marjorie's adjoining dining room: two rooms of intimate dimensions, exquisitely furnished. There was candlelight and good cuisine. After dinner we walked out to the stern, which they call the Blue Lagoon (I don't know what Marjorie called it). It is a quarter acre of blue cushions; you can sprawl out on them and see the moon and the stars and the waves go by, and you will say. or at least I did, "This ship is a wonderful idea."

Marjorie had a roaring good time aboard the *Sea Cloud*, it is generally agreed. Her then-husband was E. F. Hutton, a big, romantic Wall Streeter who loved to sail. But, it appears, E.F.H. loved not only sailing and Marjorie but also some of her friends and at least one of her servants, which led to his being jettisoned and to her wedding with Joseph Davies, a journalist-businessman-politician who was appointed Roosevelt's ambassador to Stalin's Russia. That was a very good deal for Stalin inasmuch as Joe Davies a few years later published one of the most sycophantic pro-Stalin books (*Mission to Moscow*) ever penned this side of Izvestia, Inc. It more than made up for the anachronistic arrival in the USSR of the *Sea Cloud,* which hove in for duty in Leningrad—I swear, you would have thought it was the overture to a Romanov Restoration.

But Ambassador Davies didn't particularly enjoy sailing, so the *Sea Cloud* was used primarily as a place to entertain—in Leningrad and, subsequently, in Brussels, where he also served as ambassador. Marjorie divorced him, one forgets exactly why (maybe she read his book?), and then World War II was on us and the *Sea Cloud* was turned over to the Coast Guard, which removed her masts and used her as a weather boat.

After the war there was a revival of the *Sea Cloud* as of the old days—the Duke and Duchess of Windsor deftly suggested that a cruise to Havana would be nice (they had never been to Havana, poor dears); but Marjorie's mind was on other things, and before long she offered the boat for sale, $1 million without furnishings, $1.2 million with. There were no takers. Eventually General Trujillo came along and incorporated the *Sea Cloud* into his happy entourage of cars, planes, castles, and plantations. A while later, they shot Trujillo. His son Ramfis inherited the Dominican Republic and the *Sea Cloud*, aboard which, a journalist observed, "star-studded parties became so raucous that one morning, painted on her gleaming white sides, appeared the graffito 'Zsa Zsa slept here.'" When the reformers went after Ramfis, he decamped on the *Sea Cloud* with several million dollars but got only as far as Martinique. There, Dominican authorities got the crew to return the ship soon after Ramfis stepped ashore. He later reached Paris, but without the money.

After that, the *Sea Cloud* sat about unused for years, until the German syndicate refurbished her for the luxury trade.

I don't know how much money they spent, but boats require endless sums of money. It was necessary, for example, to add more cabins, and so what amounts to a whole extra deck of cabins was piled on amidships. This hurt her original profile, and of course the diesels had to be upgraded to cope with the added weight and windage.

Now on the matter of sailing. From Tahiti to Pitcairn to Easter Island you travel for the most part into light headwinds. Whoever laid out the course reasoned that passengers would not acquiesce in two weeks aboard a sailing boat without sailing. Accordingly, we laid off the wind by day, permitting the sails to be set. Late every afternoon, the sails would be furled and we would proceed under power for the next sixteen hours.

There was an unpleasant surprise in store. It was the peculiar effect that Pacific underwater glop had on the *Sea Cloud*'s bottom: it cut her speed by as much as two knots, requiring much more time under power to make up the time lost under sail. While sailing in a light wind, we came pretty close to the sensation of no forward movement at all.

Never during the 1,400-mile journey to Easter Island did the great *Sea Cloud* sail as fast as my thirty-six-foot sloop. We ended up sailing on only five of the fourteen days, thanks to the burdened hull. Sailing at snail speed, however, was not without pleasure and excitement. There was the spectacle of eighteen deckhands (fourteen boys, four girls) performing one of the truly heroic anachronisms at sea: the setting of sails on a four-masted bark. The sight of young seamen aloft on the yards, some of them more than a hundred feet above you, lingers in the memory.

And at whatever speed you make, a boat under sail simply gives off a different sensation, whether you are making ten knots or five. Ten is more exciting, and the *Sea Cloud* is easily capable of ten knots. When her bottom is clean and the wind is accommodating, she can sail up to one-half the speed of the wind. But there is this caveat: if the ship heels more than ten degrees, sail is reduced.

More than ten degrees! God! My wife is scared by white mice, yet to the inclinometer of my first ocean sailboat she affixed a sticker reading "Patsy gets off" at thirty-five degrees! Ten degrees! A knowing smile from relief captain Richard "Red" Shannon: management knows best what elderly passengers like, what they do not like. "Make that twelve degrees," he corrected.

Everybody—*everybody*—one ran into among the professional crew was obliging, attentive, good-natured. And Captain Edward "Cas" Cassidy, a Coast Guard retiree, was everywhere, mingling with the passengers, running the ship, and telling us, in about as many words, that there was nothing we were not permitted to do except fall overboard ("It creates a great deal of paperwork").

The days at sea were heavily unplanned but had just enough way points to give them a little punctuation. At first, I wondered that there was no movie. But on day five we could see *Mutiny on the Bounty* after lunch, in the lounge; and every day after that there was a movie, mostly comfortable old-timers (*Some Like It Hot*), some more modern (*Tootsie*). Every night, a schedule of the following day's activities would appear on your bed. The day began with a half hour's calisthenics led by the pianist, Tom Hawk. If there was a lecture that day (I was a lecturer), it was scheduled at eleven. In the course of time there was a Trivial Pursuit tournament, skeet shooting, a treasure hunt. Lunches were buffets on the main deck. Depending on the weather, you would take the tray up to the Lido deck (more exactly, a steward would materialize to take the tray up for you: this required steadiness of foot, especially under sail) or dine on the main deck, outside, or in the air-conditioned lounge. After dinner Tom would play, and generally there were those who would accompany him in song. One night twelve deckhands came up to sing for us, each one of them a fit subject for a cover picture of Young America (or Sweden, or Norway, or New Zealand, or India). Their singing was indescribably awful; they were only episodically in union and never, absolutely never, in harmony. A charming, unprofessional, indeed anti-professional performance.

So it went: fifteen days of relaxation—twelve of them sunny, eight with a moon—day after day. But there were two high moments.

The first was the end of the day at Pitcairn Island. Fifty-six people live there. We had foraged about the two-mile-square island where, about the same time our John Adams left the White House, their John Adams (the only surviving mutineer of the mutiny on the *Bounty*) took charge of the minuscule colony that mysteriously survives. Forty-eight of the islanders boarded the *Sea Cloud*; four generations, some haphazardly offering this and that artifact for sale, all of them talking, laughing, listening, the children obsessed with the toilet (they have outhouses on Pitcairn—and YCRs). They are Seventh-Day Adventists who do not drink unless you offer them a drink.

The time came for the *Sea Cloud* to leave. Three-quarters of the entire population of Pitcairn went down to their longboats, but, before casting off, they sang to us. I swear they sounded as good and as full as the Mormon Tabernacle Choir.

Returning to their little island, they managed to leave our urbane company—headed out on our luxury vessel toward civilization—feeling lonely.

The second moment produced high anticipation and then nearly caught us off guard. It happened, we learned, that headed toward us was the *Eagle*, a three-masted bark manned by Coast Guard cadets, a vessel Captain Cassidy once commanded. We would effect a union at sea! A thousand miles from the nearest point of land! Very well.

At dinner came the disappointing news that the *Eagle* was hopelessly off our own course and would pass far south of us. But then, just after 11:00, we learned that she would materialize in fifteen minutes. Everyone lined up along the port side. The moon was playing tag with the clouds, so that we had its illumination only intermittently. Came the magical moment when we spotted the dull yellow blur, two or three miles ahead.

It was a half hour before the *Eagle* was opposite us, a few hundred yards off, all sails set. So it must have been, in these waters, two hundred years ago, when an approaching ship was spotted and one wondered, in those bloody days, whether she was manned by pirates or by privateers with letters of marque and reprisal from a nation at war.

But there was never, ever, a more fraternal bypass than that night's: two sailing ships, one with its sails full, the second headed into the wind under noiseless power. The cadets' cameras popped in the night, opposite our own, a ghostly simulacrum of cannon flashes exploding at each other at sea. An unplanned moment, breathlessly beautiful in the on-again, off-again moonlight, the indulgent northeast winds blowing balm over the elated participants.

The Story at Eastern Airlines
March 8, 1989

Concerning the Eastern Airlines strike, a few observations:

1) Representatives of the striking union (the International Association of Machinists and Aerospace Workers) speak repeatedly, even as their placards reiterate the point, of a "fair" wage. What it is that makes for a "just" wage has been argued through the ages. There is general moral agreement on the proposition that a wage insufficient to sustain the life of a worker is at least "unjust," and indeed, the labor theory of wages, incorporated into Marxism, diagnosed the capitalist imperative as reducing to subsistence level all wages so as to maximize profits. Theologians in the Middle Ages tended to gather in greater and greater numbers around the maxim that a fair wage was *secundum estimationem fori*; that is, a fair wage is a reflection of the working of the marketplace.

Nobody is arguing that the machinists don't have a fair wage by subsistence standards, but it is certainly true that the machinists are being paid less than machinists who work for other airlines, and at $2 an hour less than the fraternity, there is bitter and understandable resentment. What to do about it?

2) The "working of the marketplace" doesn't mean that the just wage is that offered by the managers of Eastern Airlines. It means those wages offered by Eastern that are acceptable to the machinists. Well, Eastern has said:

—How can you expect us to pay higher wages given that we are at the present level of operations losing $1 million a day? Here you are asking for a wage package that would cost Eastern $150 million per year. This would add almost 50 percent to our current monthly deficit.

—To which observation the machinists tend to slur off into animadversions on the management of Frank Lorenzo, whose personality poses no threat to Perry Como's. It isn't easy to decoct the machinists' message from the picket signs or from public pronouncements, but what they're saying is two things. That Eastern's management is seriously defective; and that Eastern is surreptitiously engaged in a fight to break the unions, even as Continental's unions were broken by the device of sliding into bankruptcy, and then out of it, with, lo!—no unions.

3) Few analysts question that Eastern made some bad decisions during the past ten years. But the question then arises: when a business makes bad decisions, who is supposed to suffer? The stockholders obviously; they are on the primary line of fire, and should be. But it is inevitable that the company's workers will also suffer, because when a business enterprise takes a bad turn, either it dies or else it struggles to stay alive, and this means it has to reduce the cost of supplying its product or its services.

4) At this point in the classic labor-management struggle, the process of collective bargaining is employed. Now the president of the machinists, William Winpisinger, is a socialist. He has a personality at least as abrasive as that of Frank Lorenzo and in that sense, they are perfectly matched. With, however, this difference: namely, that the socialist is quick to put a class struggle aspect on any labor-management division, and indeed Mr. Winpisinger lost no chance to do this. And the epigoni jumped in. Sure enough, there was Jesse Jackson, with his unerring eye for public mischief, joining the picketers and declaring that if Eastern management can't run

Eastern Airlines (Mr. Jackson means by that give in to the union demands and continue operating), then let the workers run Eastern Airlines.

Now the trouble with analysis of this nature is that it begs all the critical questions. Even if we concede that Lorenzo Inc. isn't an effective manager of Eastern, what makes us think that Winpisinger Inc. would be an effective manager? Could the machinists succeed in getting bank credit? I mean, other than from S&Ls? Barring that, would the machinists' union be willing to bankroll Eastern, beginning with $1 million per day?

And then, 5), the machinists union thinks instantly of collective bargaining as pitting all the forces of unionized work against: the management of Eastern. To this end, the Eastern pilots have already refused to cross the picket lines, and Eastern is for all intents and purposes grounded. But Winpisinger wants most (what he would love most is a national strike and then maybe nationalization of all the airlines) is to get other airlines to throttle down to minimum flight, and perhaps ground the passenger trains and why not?—the taxis and buses. President Bush has said he will not interfere with collective bargaining, but his spokesmen have also said that they will dig up and try to get passed through Congress a tough law against secondary boycotts.

What we have is the militant-union equivalent of the controllers' strike that faced Mr. Reagan in 1981.

A-Traveling We Will Go
March 31, 1989

As a freshman at college, I was taught economics by a young socialist, an enthusiast for Henry Wallace for president. He didn't call himself that—very few people did in those days, and not all that many do so today, Professor Galbraith being a notable, noble, exception. Our instructor taunted the class with the odds against the commercial success of any novel enterprise, given the heavy breathing of the monopolists and oligopolists who surround us.

It didn't matter, he said, what the novel enterprise was—service, manufacturing, invention, you name it—you come up with a good idea, and somebody will steal it from you. Suppose you invent a terrific new mousetrap—the Upjohn Mouse Trap—and try to peddle it? Forget it: some shark in a smoke-filled room in Chicago will run you out of business and get the patent for nothing.

My Upjohn Professor's strictures floated through my mind when last June a forty-four-year-old Miami lawyer told me he and a partner in the travel business in Miami had conceived the idea of a round-the-world trip on a Concorde with this special zinger: travel would all be over water. There have been round-the-world trips on Concordes before, but none without hours and hours over land, where you are not permitted to fly more than the standard jet—600 mph.

Now riding a Concorde at 600 mph, Don Pevsner explained to me over the telephone, is like driving your Oldsmobile in first gear. You go berserk thinking, Gawd, this here aircraft can fly at twice the speed of sound, faster than 1,200 miles per hour; Mach 2, the pros call it. And yet we are having to traverse, in the traditional round-the-world itineraries, the whole of India (or China, or Russia, or the United States) at 600 miles per hour. When you take the Concorde to London from New York, you aren't permitted to rev up to Mach 2 until after you have passed Nantucket, and it seems an age until this happens. The Concorde is not built like a men's club with huge leather reclining chairs and great big windows. Whatever sacrifice is made in physical comfort is compensated for by the knowledge that we are traveling as an army on a forced march travels in one day. Or, if you prefer a nautical analogy, you travel in three hours the distance Columbus traveled in seventy days.

Whee?

Well, that depends, because Don Pevsner and his partner Jack Guiteras are not entirely typical. Don gets flush with excitement when he travels on an abandoned railroad track and pines for the return of the old steam locomotive. He's the kind who, if he lived in Niagara, would every morning of his life jump up from bed, slam open the curtains, and stare with dumb amazement at the falls. Question: Would enough Americans want to shell out the kind of money necessary to subsidize such a trip? Or would the whole experience become routine, like the third landing on the moon? A question of money, just to begin with.

What kind of money? I asked. Well, he said, we paid $100,000 down to British Airways last week. And on December 7, we have to pay British Airways $1.5 million, and then there is promotion, hotels, tours, insurance, etc. I clutched the arm of the chair and whispered, "That means charging how many passengers how much money?"

"Ninety-eight passengers, $39,000 apiece."

As I reflected on it, it didn't seem to me a winner in the sense that Upjohn's Mouse Trap was a hypothetical winner in the economics class. And, therefore, the two entrepreneurs paid down the 100,000 bucks and launched their slow, problematic campaign to line up passengers for whom this trip would be worth that kind of an investment.

On December 10, the partners had seventy-six passengers lined up—two short of the number needed to raise the money. They stayed up all night wondering whether to risk it—and they decided, sweatily, to go ahead. They went to a bank and pledged personal assets so that they could pay British Airways one-and-one-half big ones. Two weeks after the deadline, they were—oversold.

A tiny capitalist venture, as ventures go—if we think in terms of starting steel companies or founding Silicon Valley or financing *Gone With the Wind*. But nice, I thought, reminding myself that though not an investor, I was a part of the deal. Yes, I would accompany the partners and their passengers as an on-again, off-again lecturer, lining up here and there an interesting local leader or commentator, filming some *Firing Line* episodes in Australia and South Africa, and—my editors having asked if the idea appealed—taking three weeks' respite from the political world of getting and spending to report on an unusual itinerary. New York, Acapulco, San Francisco, Hawaii, Tahiti, New Zealand, Sydney, Perth, Sri Lanka, Capetown, London. Track it on a map and you'll find practically no land you need to fly over—Don and Jack aren't going to let you fly at less than twice the speed of sound.

We'll meet at John F. Kennedy International Airport at noon on April 1, and whee! from that point on, for twenty-three days, we'll explore the question, among others, whether wheeing for that long at Mach 2 is something that is going to provoke the envy of that prehensile monopolist in Chicago who will want from now on to take over—as our instructor told us in Economics 10 AB—a venture that not only got off the ground, but did so at twice the speed of sound.

Concording Around the World—Acapulco
April 4, 1989

ACAPULCO, Mexico—The entrepreneurs of the round-the-world-over-water Concorde trip gave four high-school seniors who had excelled in science a little tour, a flight (only in America!) from hometown Miami to London where they spent four days, then on the first leg of the Concorde trip to New York where they would spend two days before returning to Miami. All four submitted brief biographies before accepting their Concorde diplomas. I liked best a sentence in seventeen-year-old Mark Bridges' statement about himself: "My belief that things can only improve gives people the idea that I am free of problems because I have a very composed personality; trifles never seem to disturb me."

An admirable young man, destined to matriculate to Morehouse College, where Martin Luther King came calmly to the conclusion that Jim Crow was other than a trifle, and a revolution was born. The one hundred passengers on the round-the-world trip were impressed and amused. A number of them did not think it a trifle that they were setting out to travel for twenty-three days over 39,000 miles at a cost of $40,000 apiece, yet allowed to carry only a single suitcase weighing not more than seventy pounds. "Alas," said tour director Donald Pevsner, "I can't change the laws of physics."

These laws inform us that the Concorde has only a 4 percent payload. Fully booked, and traveling to parts of the world where spare parts aren't sitting in the home hangar, the aircraft uses up many cubic feet for contingency equipment. One hundred people in one Concorde and it is bulging at the seams, but even so, as it rose up from JFK, reaching an altitude of 60,000 feet and a speed of 1,200 miles per hour in less than a half-hour, it conveyed the feel of a fleeted, magic cylinder. In just over an hour, we could see Bimini on the left, requiring a gentle but decisive turn to the west, lest we bounce over Cuba and maybe get mistaken for a peeping-Tom U-2, which occupies about the same altitudes.

In a minute we could see Key West, and then it was the Gulf of Mexico until, hitting the eastern coast of Mexico we began to slide down, with that exactitude that goes with the most finished passenger plane ever designed, touching down at Acapulco after two hours, fifty-six minutes, eighteen seconds of flight, within one minute of the estimated flight time. It was, by the way, a world record, New York-Acapulco, 2,900 miles.

I've been here maybe twenty times, first as a schoolboy when there were only three hotels (cost per night at one of them: $1.75 including breakfast). That was in 1943, and the major spectacle continues: the young divers who, waiting until exactly the right moment when the surf comes in at exactly the right speed and height into the rocky grotto one hundred feet below, spring from their little platform and, bathed in klieg lights, dive down into the seawater—the spectacle happens about three times every night, and a collection is taken from the nightclub viewers. One night, back then in 1943, the diver would be—Johnny Weismuller, playing Tarzan. All the cameras and sound equipment were there, and if I recall, also Boy and Jane somewhere down near the barrel of water you need to hit. Johnny Weismuller looked down, was given the go-ahead by the master diver—and…thought about it. It was forty minutes before the waves were just right again and, receiving the signal, again he thought about it. A double was finally recruited.

The young divers risk their lives, but at least they make a living, which is more than five million Mexican young people are able to earn, a witty and learned American journalist lectured to us in the late afternoon. Mexico, George Byram Lake told us, is an economic mess, for which we have graft and socialism to thank. "If you take a look at a 1,000-peso bank note you'll see what I mean. That note was worth eighty US dollars in 1976. Today it is worth, for the moment, forty-one US cents. It is the shame of the Latin American nations that with rich natural resources and with $350 billion in aid from the developed nations, they should slip into debt and dependency at the very time four little Pacific nations, with few resources and very little aid, were becoming rich and independent industrial powerhouses."

The hardy and affluent Concorde round-the-world passengers listened. Much of this they knew already. These are people wise in fiscal street-knowledge, undertaking this original hegira for assorted reasons. One man wanted, he said, to go to New Zealand, wanted to go to Kenya, but didn't much like the idea of endless plane rides, so why not do it all at once on the Concorde and while at it learn a little here and there? One passenger is taking a break from his total absorption in teaching American students algebra—he has written a textbook that seeks to overturn the traditional and misdirected pedagogy of the books in general use. It is not surprising that he already had met a fellow passenger who, retired from the army, has not retired from the wars, the enemy being the creeping illiteracy of American students who read with their lips because of the discredited look-see teaching methods.

Some are just enjoying themselves, and we spent three hours doing just that, lunching on a 200-foot catamaran, touring the big natural bay to which, 400 years ago, the Spanish conquistadors brought Peruvian and Colombian gold for the overland trek to Veracruz, whence Spain's Atlantic fleet would take the treasure to Madrid to fill the royal coffers. All that gold, a hundred years' passage of it, wouldn't reduce the current debt of Mexico to the West by 10 percent. The tourists who study the problem and then leave can only take satisfaction in knowing that they have left a few flakes of gold behind them.

Concording Around the World—Hawaii
April 6, 1989

MAUNA KEA, Hawaii—There's a term for it in physics—"hysteresis," if memory serves that applied here translates to: you are going to travel on the fastest commercial vehicle in the world, from Acapulco to Oakland, CA, to Honolulu, at speeds that dazzle the mind. Only you have to have your bags packed at 7:00 a.m., which is a barracks-life hour, not your super-luxury hour, which our round-the-world trip indisputably argues as Right for our Crowd.

But add the time to pick up luggage from ninety-eight passengers quartered in little bungalows (each with its private swimming pool), deliver the baggage to the airport and submit it to terrorist-age security examination, and it is 10:30 a.m. before your Concorde's delicate nose, backed by its Percheron engines, lifts you, liberated, for the 2,350-mile trip to Oakland, which consumes just over half the time it took you between when the bags left the hotel and you were, finally, seated in the plane. One thinks of standing in line an hour to spend a minute getting a passport stamped. The problems of the idle rich.

Why go to Oakland, when your destination is Honolulu? After all, the latitude of Acapulco is about seventeen degrees north, and of Honolulu, approximately twenty-two degrees north, and Oakland-San Francisco is way up there at nearly thirty-eight degrees north... Well, the Concorde has to abide by safety rules, and if one engine blanks out, you dive down from your haughty 60,000-feet, 1,200-mile-per-hour trajectory to the vulgarian world of mere jets, and in doing so you lose 25 percent of your range. If that were to happen to a Concorde flying directly to Hawaii, past the point of no return, you'd, well, land in the water, and British Airways and Lloyd's of London and entrepreneur Don Pevsner of this round-the-world extravaganza are not going to risk that!

So we land at Oakland, are served a fine Chinese meal at the airport, which comes about sixty minutes after the fine meal en route from Acapulco, and precedes by about sixty minutes the fine meal en route to Honolulu, which precedes by about three hours the fine meal served at Kona on the island of Hawaii at the Mauna Kea Hotel, to ninety passengers dizzied by jet lag; then the touchdown at Honolulu before boarding the chartered DC-9 for the thirty-minute hop to the island of Hawaii, where the bus driver on the twenty-minute drive tells you you are headed toward the "most exclusive" hotel in the world, originally the creation of Laurence Rockefeller, who on a casual flight over the island twenty-odd years ago spotted a beach around which he thought a super hotel absolutely HAD to be built, whence the Mauna Kea.

En route the bus driver passes a splotch of green where, he tells you with gravity, some really serious nature lovers, including Sylvester Stallone, have built an oasis—a true organic little paradise. "They have no telephones," he announces over the loudspeaker, "and no television. Just a little private heliport." I am reminded of Art Buchwald who, years ago after President Nixon's first nominee to the Supreme Court, Clement F. Haynsworth, was turned down because he owned stocks and bonds in companies that had been involved in litigation that came before the bench, wrote that President Nixon had nominated to the court a retired and reclusive Southern lawyer in north Georgia who was instantly surrounded by the press. "Do you own any stock, Colonel?" "No, sir." "Any bonds?" "No, sir." "Any real estate?" "No, sir. All I own is a few slaves."

The following day there is general exhaustion. Five thousand miles of travel in one day, even aboard a Concorde, is debilitating, so that when the bus showed up to take ninety-eight potential passengers on a nine-hour tour of the volcanic delights of the island of Hawaii, only nine Concorders showed up for duty. The rest rusticated: a little beach life, a little reading, a pickup of energy in the early afternoon, a helicopter trip to the volcano's roiling maw (it erupted as recently as 1984, and belches up enough gas to suggest it is gathering its strength for another molten extravaganza that could just reach Rambo, down in that little pastoral enclave, unless he makes it in time to his heliport).

And then we settle down and listen to the chief economist of the Bank of Hawaii. David Ramsour, born in Hawaii and intimidatingly learned (having studied and taught in Japan, Sweden, and Lebanon), speaks of "this lake," by which he means the Pacific Ocean, with its staggering economic potential. "One billion people waiting for contact lenses." Hawaii is quietly prosperous, with the lowest unemployment rate in the United States, but hark!—40 percent of its income comes from tourism, and if you apply, says our learned economist, a 2.04 multiplier on that, you get something on the order of 80 percent of the Hawaiian economy dependent on tourists, and that is just plain not safe. All those pineapples and macadamia nuts—the whole of the agricultural produce of Hawaii—bring in only 4 percent of its annual $20 billion income. Hawaii must hope to bring that tourist income down to not more than 30 percent, developing its other facilities.

Like what?

Well, he tells us, the economic explosion on the borders of the Pacific lake is creating a need for a mini-Geneva. The great Oriental economies—South Korea, Japan, Singapore, Taiwan—don't like litigation. They prefer to face economic problems via arbitration, and increasingly they think of Hawaii as truly cosmopolitan (25 percent Japanese population, 15 percent native Hawaiian) and also as an outpost of a superpower with established constitutional procedures. Down the line, Hawaii may become a great service center, brokering the conflicts that might otherwise bring sclerosis to an area exploding with demand and latently with supply. Hawaii, the Geneva of the—Far West? Far East? It depends on whether you are looking at Hawaii from New York or from Hong Kong.

The questions from the Concorders are shrewd, experienced. They weigh the question of Hawaii and the Pacific market with agility. Is there a risk that the next generation of commercial aircraft will travel at such speeds as to make Hawaii a mere way station, a mere refueling spot, en route to major industrial Pacific centers?

It doesn't seem conceivable, looking out on Laurence Rockefeller's yellow-white beach, the neighboring volcano sullen but not mutinous.

Concording Around the World—Tahiti
April 7, 1989

PAPEETE, Tahiti—It is the same exasperating-amusing thing yet again, a wake-up call at 6:45 for a departure from the Kona airport at 9:00, the short hop to Honolulu, whence at 10:30 departure, destination Tahiti, 2,781 miles in two hours seventeen minutes. It is in such moments that one thinks of travel by Air Force One. One has to assume that the president wakes at 8 a.m., flies off at 8:15 and somehow—his bags materialize. If not, the two-party system is getting out of hand. The flight by chartered DC-9, the stewardess announces, will take only twenty-five minutes, so that hospitality is limited. Passengers must restrict themselves to a Mai Tai, a planter's punch, a Bloody Mary, Coca-Cola, Pepsi-Cola, Perrier water, orange juice, grapefruit juice, coffee, or tea.

At Honolulu, waiting to board the Concorde, we crowd the tiny little waiting room—the sanctuary, one assumes, of the pilots of private planes, a few of whom are visibly unnerved by the arrival of ninety-eight Concorders. It is mid-morning and an appropriate time to visit the facilities. But these are limited to one toilet in the men's room, one in the ladies' room, which results in the composition of a unisex line leading to the separate doors into the washrooms, and in such situations conversation is not entirely spontaneous. Twenty minutes, from one end of the line to the head of it, I calculate, and on returning to the reception room I am asked to sign the visitors' register, and only just resist the temptation to write, "Buckley pissed here."

One pilot, who looks like Gary Cooper aged, oh, fifty-one, introduces himself as the former Air Force pilot who flew the Herc-130 that, in 1972, took a dozen of us along as guests of the secretary of the navy to visit Antarctica and the South Pole. I remembered the captain well. His voice had come in halfway from Christchurch, New Zealand, to McMurdo Station: "If anything happens from this point on, gentlemen, and we have to set down to a sea landing, reach for the nearest heavy object, tie it around your neck, and go down as quickly as possible. The water temperature is about 20 degrees and we are four hours from any possible Coast Guard help." Those pleasantries linger in the memory.

One needs to remind oneself, or at any rate I do, that Papeete, Tahiti, is actually east of Hawaii, approximately as far south of the equator (seventeen degrees) as Honolulu is north of it. The voice of the Concorde captain comes in. "We are at one degree North latitude," he says. "I will tell you when we reach the equator." That pilot, I nudge my wife, is playing into MY HANDS. I happen to know that one degree of latitude is equal to sixty miles, that we are traveling at 1,200 miles per hour, which means twenty miles in one minute. So, we will cross the equator when? Right! In three minutes, so I look at my watch and smile gloatingly when my hand accidentally knocks my wife's crab leg out of her mouth—immediately followed by the captain's announcement that we have crossed the equator.

I think simultaneously of two things. The first is that passenger John Saxon, the firebrand aboard who is trying to rescue American youth from mathematical illiteracy with his revolutionary textbooks, would be pleased even by this elementary exercise; and the second, that suddenly it has become not early spring in the Northern Hemisphere, but early fall in the Southern Hemisphere. I pray that Tahiti will have left permanently the awful rainy season that dogs December, January, and February.

We arrive in the rain and go to the Beachcomber Hotel, as many as possible to cabins that perch right over the sea, permitting you to go out to your *lanai* and descend down into the ocean water for a swim—absolutely necessary in the eighty-five-degree heat. The following day an air-conditioned bus takes us the one hundred miles around the island, past the Gauguin museum, about which it is most striking that it cannot afford to buy a single canvas painted by the melancholic who came here about one hundred years after Captain Bligh's famous mutiny.

Tahiti is perhaps the single most celebrated small island in the world, its natural raptures rapturously recorded. But there are those, and they include Herman Melville and Captain Cook, who inveighed against the wanton ways of the Tahitians of the nineteenth century.

Today, they remain a very small body of people. It is striking to remind oneself that French Polynesia has a population of only 180,000, spread over 130 islands, which occupy an area larger than continental Europe.

It is no wonder that Paris is anxious to maintain its hegemony, notwithstanding gradual steps toward self-government, most recently in 1984. The politics of Tahiti, like the politics of Puerto Rico, has to do with how close, or how far, a political party wishes to be associated with its historical godfather. There are those in Puerto Rico who would kill to become a state, others who would kill to sever all ties to the United States.

It is so here in Tahiti. The French (it is subtly and plausibly argued) don't want a flourishing Tahiti because that would feed impulses to separation. Better to continue with the annual subsidies, so that French Polynesia will continue to depend on France, to which it sends many of its seventeen-year-olds for a year's national service every year. And there is the delicate question of the island of Mururoa, 750 miles south of Papeete, where the French set off their nuclear explosions. It isn't just anywhere that a nation can conduct nuclear tests. For instance, they wouldn't like it at all in the champagne country. A great big Pacific area is not only useful here but virtually indispensable, and much of the politics of Tahiti pits the end-the-bombers against those who believe that France must continue to develop its *force de frappe*.

And so, it does not surprise that the morning's newspaper gives significant notice to preparations for the celebration of the 100th anniversary of the birth of Charles de Gaulle, whose vision comprehended the loss of French Indochina and French Algeria, but not of French Polynesia.

These questions the Concorders will reflect upon tomorrow, when we convene on the largest sail boat in the world, the computer-guided *Wind*

Song, which will take us to the island of Moorea and, unless it capsizes, back, to listen to a lecture from a gentleman born in Great Britain whose parents brought him to Tahiti when he was seven years old. We will need to dispose of Tahiti's problems before taking on those of New Zealand, which awaits us on Saturday, with predictions that a quarter-million people will gather at Christchurch—a mere 2,800 miles west of us—for their first view of a Concorde supersonic aircraft.

Concording Around the World—New Zealand
April 11, 1989

QUEENSTOWN, New Zealand—Twice I've left Tahiti with little internal grumblings about a) the heat (can you be happy, even at the best outdoor *luau* since they celebrated the mutiny against Captain Bligh, when the temperature is eighty-five degrees?); and b) expense (e.g., $12.50 for one of those airplane-sized scotches, $20 per page for a fax to New York). But that is to break a butterfly on a wheel, because beautiful, aromatic Tahiti stays in the memory, including the sail on the *Wind Song* to Moorea, which has got to be the loveliest island in the world. (I mean the second loveliest, after São Miguel in the Azores.)

But our pilgrimage, like Chaucer's, has fixed dates of departure, and one does not keep a Concorde waiting, so that by 10:48 we had outpaced the speed of sound, by 10:58 we had doubled it. Our leader, Don Pevsner, confessed over the microphone that he never really fully understood the whole business of the International Dateline, so never mind an explanation. Take your choice: either set your watch ahead by twenty-two hours when he gave the signal, or set it back by two hours. Most of us could figure out that this would amount to the same thing, though for those watches that also record the date, there is a subtle difference between the two maneuvers.

Now Captain Cook never got to Christchurch, so it may not be surprising that no Concorde had ever been seen in the third largest city in New Zealand. But we all felt like Queen Elizabeth because more than 100,000 people were out there to see their first supersonic passenger aircraft land, and to celebrate this welcome our captain did a majestic sweep over the city. I remember being told once that a royal hand wave is best practiced by pretending that you are unscrewing a light bulb. I passed the word along.

The greeting was formal and ceremonial in a most dramatic fashion. We were driven to City Hall and there were told to submit to the ritual interrogation of a Maori chief, who appeared before us with a chorus of thirty young girls in tribal costumes arrayed behind him in three tiers, silent until he gave them the word that we were Friends, not Enemies.

Now this venture in epistemology required the chief to exercise himself in frenzied gyrations, slashing his spear this way and that, the sword in his left hand thrust forward toward the throat of the spokesman for the visiting tribe. Since I was serving in that function, my eyes grew wider and wider as the chief approached me accompanying his savage motions with emunctory sounds coming from his mouth that could only be interpreted as that he thought I would make a very good meal.

My mind turned intuitively to instructions learned a few years ago from an expert on how to deal with someone approaching you intending mortal harm when, suddenly, the chief gave a cooing sound, dropping his knife on the floor. The girls behind him began an irenic chant, and the Maori princess on my right instructed me to pick up the knife and then to proceed (she pointed) to the very left of the front line and to kiss, by rubbing noses, everyone on the front row.

Having only a fortnight ago been involved in the production of my play, my theatrical juices were running and was prepared to wiggle my nose across the noses of ten young ladies, but found myself propelled first toward the ferocious chief, and then—to the mayor of Christchurch. If you wonder what that challenge felt like, imagine being propelled toward, oh, Woodrow Wilson, having been told to rub your nose against his. Well, eyes closed, I did it; and then the mayor saluted us, speaking in English; we were given food and drink, and dispatched on buses for a three-hour tour of Christchurch (established 1850, and often cited as the most English city outside England).

It is too bad, that business with Prime Minister Lange, because my third visit to New Zealand confirms my conviction after the first and the second, namely that there is nowhere a race of kindlier and gentler people than the

Kiwis. David Lange, as we know, forbade us in 1985 from bringing in a naval ship unless we first declared whether it contained any nuclear bombs, which declaration for obvious reasons it is against US policy to make. The hand grenade David Lange threw into our delicate network of treaties had the anticipated result: the Green Party of West Germany went mad with delight, the Low Countries' unilateralists suggested every other ally should take the same step, and for a tense few months the question arose: What would the United States do?

If New Zealand had to defend itself, it would rely on an army about half the size of the police force of New York City, and a naval fighting force of four aging frigates. Obviously, the idea was that Australia and New Zealand would supply the bases and the harbors, and we the technical armory in the event of an attack. Which looked, back then, to be remote, and certainly seems remote today. Even so, New Zealand was formally drummed out of ANZUS by Secretary of State George Shultz, and we all more or less promised to forget about it and now we mention it only in...a whisper, though it would be nice if Mr. Lange were replaced by an ally solider in his understanding of treaty commitments.

And, arriving in fabled Queenstown after our tour of Christchurch, the Concorders could find no one—no one at all—disposed to talk about the America's cup problem. At this point, pending to be sure judicial appeal, New Zealand possesses the America's Cup. Because it prevailed over a US sailing boat? Not quite. The spirit of New Zealand's victory was best caught last week by cartoonist Jeff MacNelly when he pictured an America's Cup sailboat racing at sea with the caption: "New Nautical Terminology." The skipper, gavel in hand, is bellowing out, "QUASH THE WRIT!!...HABEAS THE STARBOARD CORPUS!! ISPE OIXIT ABAFT THE AMICUS CURII!!" The steadfastly polite New Zealanders simply did not wish to discuss the question with visiting Americans and, having pledged our friendship to the Maori chief, we agreed to let the matter drop.

And let Queenstown distract us. It is 250 miles southwest of Christchurch, which makes it pretty cool the first week of April, heading toward winter, the wonderful fortnight when all the trees, including the spectacular poplars, are changing color. There are mountains with flecks of fresh snow there, and the lake runs fifty-two miles north and south. The temperature of the water is never inviting. In fact, Queenstown reposes at just about the equivalent latitude of the *Titanic* when, exactly seventy-seven years ago, it went down: temperature of the water was twenty-eight degrees, in Queenstown about thirty-three degrees. So, you cannot swim (for any protracted period), but you can ride a little steam train, almost Disneylike in appearance but actually a survivor of the pre–World War I, 3.5-gauge trains, with only Jesse James and his six-shooter missing.

And then you board a 168-foot steamboat, launched (another coincidence) the very day the *Titanic* went down. And put in at a sheep farm where you see a miraculous black and white collie-shaped dog minister to his owner's orders with miraculous precision, bounding away a full mile to bring in a half-dozen errant sheep. One of these is brought in to be sheared, so that we can see how the operation is done. The sheep farmer is from New Zealand Central Casting, bronzed, handsome, sardonic, amusing, fluent, witty. He subdues the sheep without any difficulty whatever as he reaches for the electric trimmer, which will slice away four kilos of wool (worth $60). I wondered out loud to my companion how is it that the sheep is so passive while being fleeced, and my friend tells me he sees no difference between New Zealand sheep and US taxpayers.

And so, we wander back in our steamboat to Queenstown, and will dine tonight as individual guests of New Zealand families, expressing hospitality in the most traditional form. We will speak about every subject in the world, except the America's Cup and ANZUS. One more day in these parts, and we zoom in on Sidney.

Concording Around the World—Sydney
April 13, 1989

SYDNEY, Australia—When you leave Queenstown in New Zealand on such a day as this, you come close to knowing what it was like when the clock struck midnight for Cinderella. Leave it at that, but put it down on your wish list: a few days in that green-white valley with the endless blue lake and the poplar trees and people to match—I mean, the telephone operator hopes you will come back soon and wishes you a happy next leg on your trip.

There is, one pauses sadly to note, no way you can have a happy leg Queenstown-Christchurch because the Hawker Siddleys that carry you are less comfortable than the pre-World War I train you gamboled about on yesterday, and when the stewardess tells you before landing to make your seat upright you grimly guffaw, because Cook Airlines has seats that were upright pre *partu*, in *partu*, and post *partum*. That is a fancy but gratifying way of saying that Mr. Cook's airplane seats were conceived upright, delivered upright, and live upright.

At Christchurch our Concorde was waiting for us, and off we wheel to Sydney—needless to say, set on breaking yet another speed record. It was not difficult, since no Concorde had ever before set out from Christchurch to Sydney.

There was tension, but the reasons for it were Top Secret. Just before takeoff, our leader Don Pevsner whispered to me that the probability was that our Concorde would not land in Sydney, but in Brisbane. This was not a so-what alternative, since three *Firing Line* episodes had been laboriously scheduled to begin one hour after landing at Sydney, one of them featuring the feisty, ingratiating prime minister of Australia, Mr. Robert Hawke. The trouble in Sydney is an air traffic controllers' teaser-strike, which during the past few days has immobilized the airport, usually in the mornings and late afternoons—but, advance intelligence informs us, will today do its calisthenics at midday. The result of landing at Brisbane instead of Sydney would do to us, given theatrical deadlines, something on the order of what landing on Saturn instead of the moon would have done to our astronauts.

And so, I stared at the Concorde's graphic public displays giving altitude, plane speed, and time-to-go to destination. We had reached maximum speed (Mach 2) when there was this, well, this little tremor…and almost instantly we heard from the captain, in the British version of accents Tom Wolfe has described in *The Right Stuff*, that there was nothing to worry about, just a little flame whichwhat. Accordingly, we worried about nothing, and those of us in the know experienced only elation that nothing had been said about a forced landing at Brisbane.

A half-hour later, after a perfect landing, there was an unusual delay in lining up the steps. And there were all those fire trucks surrounding us....

As all the world now knows, since it never happened before, ten square feet of our tail section was missing. A melodramatic gash, as if a huge tiger from outer space had reached down for a great big munch. Our pilot, swamped by the press on the apron, explained in almost, though not quite, as many words, that he was glad to establish that the Concorde could land half-arsed.

Prime Minister Bob Hawke, who was a Rhodes scholar and a trade unionist in the I-eat-capitalists-alive tradition of John L. Lewis, has been in power since 1983, and his government has since then twice been returned to power. He suffers at this point for political and personal reasons. The Australian economy is in the doldrums, though of course the spirited polemicist Hawke declines to acknowledge what the street-smart economists cannot deny: namely that high inflation, high interest rates, high tariffs, and high taxation have hurt Australia.

Two hours after he left the television studio, he announced to Parliament reforms that headed in the right direction, though not sharply enough to address the point nicely made by Alan Reynolds in the *Wall Street Journal* a little while ago: "Australia is simply going to have to look more like Hong Kong and less like Argentina. It needs to become a tax haven complete with much freer trade and a stable currency."

What you have to understand about Australia, columnist-commentator Phillip Adams had informed us in the earlier *Firing Line* program, is that "nobody calls him 'Mr. Prime Minister,' they call him 'Bob.'" I objected that no matter how republican the spirit of polemical exchange, I thought it odd to call a prime minister "Bob," and probably would have a problem doing so even if the prime minister were my son.

Now the question of how exactly to think of the prime minister these days is especially relevant because a few weeks ago he went on the air to announce, with tears in his eyes, that in days gone by he had been not only a drinker, but also an adulterer, and he wanted to apologize right here and now to his wife, Hazel. What, Phillip Adams of Australia wanted to know—he is his country's Bill Moyers-Walter Cronkite-Art Buchwald—

was what would the United States do if President George Bush were to go on the air and make similar revelations? His point was that the republican intimacy that traditionally binds Australians to one another makes for a singularly compassionate treatment of those who have fallen.

I replied that our president is chief of state, not merely chief of government, and that if Queen Elizabeth had gone on the air to say such things as Mr. Hawke had said, possibly even latitudinarian Australia would have felt a certain geological shock. As it is, I ventured, Mr. Hawke's public act of contrition distinguishes him as someone who acknowledges that adultery is wrong, even as we are commanded to forgive its occurrence seventy times seven times. But surely, I insisted, this had nothing to do with Australian informality, reminding myself that Evelyn Waugh had once written to a friend that whereas he welcomed intimacy, he despised informality.

Accordingly, when he came in, I said, "Mr. Prime Minister, have you learned from your experience as—prime minister?" I quoted to him a sentence he had spoken ten years ago on *Firing Line* when he appeared as head of the Australian Council of Trade Unions: "Anybody whose opinions don't change as the result of experience should be booted out." Had his views changed about plenipotentiary rights of labor unions—e.g., to stop air traffic? Did he approve President Reagan's action when the US air traffic controllers struck in defiance of the law?

Ah well, we would learn yet again that men in high office do not answer questions, they maneuver. The prime minister rambled about, talking about the differences between US and Australian cultural traditions. Concerning which books can be written, and indeed have been. But it's nice to think that no country is so distinctly different from any other that it cannot profit from a Bill of Rights.

On the other hand, if the air traffic controllers in Sydney had closed down the airport, who knows? Maybe our Concorde would have retained its tail. As we regrouped in the late afternoon, the Concorders were divided on several questions, one group proudly hailing the durability of an aircraft that can fly with clipped wings, another—a much smaller group—wondering if strange vibrations are emanating from the anarchic centers of unconfined power Down Under. Perhaps the wildcat strikers are saying: It's OK to fly into Sydney, but don't go and break speed records in doing so.

Concording Around the World—Sri Lanka
April 18, 1989

SRI LANKA—There is that Marquis de Sade in each one of us that shows its prurient little head on occasions, as when our Concorde got ready to lift off from Sydney after its humiliating loss of one-third of its tail, now remedied at the cost of a twenty-four-hour loss in our round-the-world schedule. Just as we pray that the matador will survive the bull and the Challenger the launch, there is even so the trace of sadism that accelerates the heartbeat when the man traversing Niagara Falls on a bicycle suddenly begins to tilt over…and…But then everybody knows that the crowds that used to go out to see Evel Knievel bound across the Grand Canyon or whatever were there in part because he might just…not make it.

The photographers and the television crews were out there in force, but our Concorde lifted resolutely into the Tasman sky with that saucy lift of its delicate mandibular nose—and the next thing we knew we were in Perth.

But only to refuel. The carefully scheduled twenty-four hours during which, among other things, we were to hear and view exciting things involving the America's Cup were forfeit to the wasted rudder. One-half of the passengers, whose principal spokesperson was my wife, wondered indignantly why the Concorde hadn't gone up for a test run before presuming to lift up all ninety-eight of us. I tried to explain that you don't need to test a new parachute, but this explanation provoked only a farrago of contempt for my diminished powers of reason; but then the other one-half felt that there was no reason to suppose that the new tail, installed the night before by British Airways engineers, was born defective. Do you worry about a new screwdriver?

From Perth we traveled on to Sri Lanka, just barely recrossing the equator, back into the Northern Hemisphere. We arrived there after ten hours of travel, if you count from the moment the alarm clock rang. Only six-and-one-half of these were spent in the air. But it astonished those of us who have traveled nonstop New York-Tokyo to be informed that we had traveled an equivalent distance.

Sri Lanka is not an ideal place to land after traveling 6,500 miles in one day. Although our constant provider Donald Pevsner had equipped us with, no less, the reconditioned private railroad car of the sometime imperial viceroy, at one time Lord Mountbatten, to conduct us the ninety minutes from the airport to the Mount Lavinia Hotel, the heat overwhelmed the viceroy's air-conditioning as conclusively as Ceylonese nationalism had overwhelmed the crown.

To travel the final hundred yards from the station depot to the hotel by bus would have been easy enough except that a huge elephant, dressed in pajamas of some sort, which had been a part of the welcoming committee as we got off the viceroy's train, waddled before us on the narrow little road at about three miles per hour, resulting in an extra fifteen minutes before we reached the hotel, never mind that we could see the oasis over the elephant's rump. We were too hot and demoralized to get out and walk to it, circumventing the elephant, with our hand luggage.

It did not help that our rooms were less than cool by US air-conditioning standards, so that when at the inevitable beach *luau*, even with the redeeming breeze coming in from the great, surf-breaking sand arc, sweetly lit in yellow light around the remote boundary of the 100-year-old colonial hotel, science-fiction laureate Arthur C. Clarke told us that he had lived here for thirty-five years because he was convinced it is the "most beautiful place on Earth," the Concorders murmured our acquiescence in tones that would not have passed a lie detector test. What we wanted at that point was sleep, before the twelve-hour excursion plotted for the next day.

Now the beginning difficulty of the beginner engaging Sri Lanka is the question whether the first word has one or two syllables. There is an unalterable division on the subject, but I shall die pronouncing it "Si-ri" Lanka rather than attempt "Sri." To do so puts me in mind of Sacheverell Sitwell's admonition that in order to learn to pronounce Portuguese idiomatically you will need to learn to pronounce "Tottenham Court Road" as a single syllable.

What used to be Ceylon is something of a historical hybrid in which the French, the Dutch, the Portuguese, the English, and the Indians have had a hand. A year ago, anticipating the elections just past, *The Economist* urged its readers to "think of Sri Lanka as a witches' cauldron. Blood and venom are added daily. Stir these vigorously into the original poison of religious-racial loathing, emanating from both the minority Tamils and the majority Sinhalese. The consequence during the past month (March 1988) has been at least one hundred more deaths, mostly of innocent bystanders; that is, people who got killed just because they were Sinhalese or, in smaller numbers, Tamils."

The struggle can be compared to that of the Catalans in Spain, whose protracted episodic terrorism, like that of the Tamils, is motivated by separatist obsession in both instances in the northeast of the nations that consider them integral. Sri Lanka, about the size of West Virginia, is a country of 16 million people, with a per capital income of $340, a gross national product of $5.3 billion, more than 6 percent of which is spent on "defense." Their deficit is, by US standards, a gratifying 12 percent of their GNP, or about four times as high as our own.

I remember (I had truly forgotten it) the first day I met Whittaker Chambers, at his farm in Maryland in 1954. Our conversation roamed over the profile of that day's news, which included an account of the ordeal of the gentleman designated by President Eisenhower as ambassador to Ceylon. He had been asked the day before by the head of the Foreign Relations Committee, "What is the name of the capital of Ceylon?" "Well, senator, to tell the truth, I can't quite remember." "Well, what is the name of the prime minister?" "Well, senator, to tell you the truth, I can't remember."

Chambers laughed heartily. "How," he asked me, "can anyone forget the name of Solomon West Ridgeway Bandaranaike?"

Concording Around the World—Kenya

April 20, 1989

KEEKOROK LODGE, Kenya—Getting here took almost two hours more than designed, because as our Concorde was about to rev up for takeoff, an official tallied his roster of bags aboard against the official roster and found an incredible discrepancy of eight pieces. Since that discrepancy was a matter hypothetically involving security, the quick worst-case assumption was that eight distinct attempts were being made to explode our Concorde.

We were asked if any of us had checked baggage previously consigned to overhead compartments but that accounted for only two pieces, with a residual discrepancy of six. And that meant emptying out the entire hold, each passenger to identify his own bags. All of them were accounted for, which meant that six pieces had been furtively checked but not acknowledged at recount time. Whose they were, we never knew; and being a genial lot, there has been no public speculation over the question.

In two and one-half hours we had flown over the Indian Ocean, passing over the Maldives Islands, and landing at Mombasa where eight disparate aircraft met us to fly us the two hours to the Keekorok Lodge, a guest enclave within a 700-square-mile national park. It is 5,200 feet above sea level and can therefore laugh at its equatorial fix. The temperature warms to a balmy warm at midday, and creeps slowly down to a balmy cool at sunset.

Talk of creeping, a most fearful number of animals do just that all about us—and that, of course, is the reason for coming to this paradise for nature and animal lovers, where the great boundless pastures of green and bushery surround us and the acacia trees dot the profiles of the ambient hills. One would think it a part of central-north Spain in October.

The schedule permitted you to survey the animals at 5:45 a.m. aboard a balloon that floats you at a comfortable distance above the lions, anywhere from fifteen to 1,000 feet. Or you can tour, in the morning or late afternoon, in a kind of jeep-mobile. Yesterday in three hours we ran into, or rather not quite into, a half-dozen elephants, a hundred topis, four jackals, six hyenas, eleven zebras, four giraffes, a hundred gazelles and as many elands, four horrible warthogs, six vultures, one water buffalo, and two baboons, the latter frolicking in the quadrangle of our little lodge, from which one is warned strictly not to wander after sunset; no, not even by fifty yards, for fear of the one truly aggressive creature among which we live, the Cape buffalo.

For that reason, we felt less than empathy with the carcass of the buffalo we saw at close quarters being devoured by three lions—they eat, each lion, seventy-five pounds of buffalo each—after which? The jackals come in to nibble at what is left. They are sitting there, two of them, only twenty yards from the lions, waiting their turn. And twenty yards behind them are two vultures; they will pick at the remaining remains. One stares at them all, and at the lovely gazelles, the graceful giraffes, the nimble and sprightly impala. But, one or two of us need to ask ourselves, for how long? I mean, the first time I saw her, I sat and stared at the Mona Lisa for only seven or eight minutes, so do I need to devote more than one hour to staring at a giraffe? But then I need to confess personal abnormalities: after four days in the Galapagos Islands, I went mad with boredom.

Modern Kenya is, incidentally, the country in the world with the highest population growth (4.1 percent), which one would never guess from the distance we needed to travel to inspect one Masai village of about one hundred people living in dung huts and bringing in their cattle to their enclosure at night to protect them against the predators. Kenya is just smaller than Texas, has twenty-one million people and is very much dominated by its president, Mr. Daniel Arap Moi. Even under the great Kenyatta, the George Washington of Kenya, Moi was around as vice president.

Fifteen years ago, visiting in Kenya, I noted a remark Mr. Moi made in which he announced that foreigners "have nothing to teach Kenyans. In fact, if anything, Kenya can teach them many lessons because contrary to what some people try to make us believe, the African way of civilization is the best. Foreigners," Mr. Moi observed, referring to the brief period during which it was fashionable to disrobe and run through a public square or whatever, "go streaking, running naked," he said scornfully in his speech in Parliament, to which one might have responded that the streakers in America were only going about in what many Africans consider their native dress.

Kenya long since jettisoned competing political parties, but last year President Moi abolished even the secret ballot. To vote in Kenya you have to "queue up" in front of a photograph of the candidate you intend to vote for, which device has a way of discouraging aberrant political behavior. Not only "queuing," as they refer to it here, came, but also an end to any independence in the judiciary: President Moi introduced and got quick approval for a constitutional amendment giving him the right to fire judges at will. Moreover, Mr. Moi is not a Kikuyu, the dominant tribe in Kenya, which, anyone would have guessed during the reign of Kenyatta, would rule the country for generations to come. He proved a super-shrewd manipulator whose specialty was discovering issues Kikuyus would quarrel with each other about, and the result is that there are no longer any issues with which any Kikuyu can quarrel with President Moi about.

Although Kenya is perhaps the most pampered Third World nation in the world (nations compete to lend it money), its per capital income is only $322, and unemployment is a sad 30 percent. Where there is unemployment, you may have noticed, there is also bureaucracy. I was under the vague impression that carbon paper no longer existed—until trying to change $100 into Kenyan currency. This transaction requires a form completed in triplicate, in which you post your name, the country you live in, the agency that arranged your passage, your passport number and the place in which it was issued. Then comes, and I quote exactly, the heading, "Foreign Currency Amount Encashed or Accepted in Payment." To answer that inquiry requires hard concentration, particularly because the operative word "encashed" is not common usage. One suspects it does not really matter what one puts down in that column, it mattering only that a finite, or preferably infinite, number of Kenyans devote their time to storing away these slips of paper, giving them something to do.

We will have spent a wonderfully restful two and one-half days here, and heard yesterday a lecture by one of our fellow Concorders on the delinquency of modern mathematical pedagogy, in which time is wasted and demoralization is invited by attempting to teach elusive concepts, when what comes naturally at that point is drilling in technique. I found myself wondering, that night after my wife and I had carefully bolted the door against any possibility of wandering warthogs or water buffalo, how Pythagoras went about not so much demonstrating as explaining to his students his theorem about the hypotenuse of a triangle, if indeed he did so, but soon I was asleep, comfortably insulated from all those wild, exotic, romantic beasts out there, protected from everything except themselves.

Concording Around the World—Cape Town
April 25, 1989

CAPE TOWN, South Africa—The 3,000-mile flight from Mombasa, Kenya, past Madagascar, rounding up to the southern tip of Africa at Cape Town, set another speed record, and in anticipation of the Concorde's arrival a considerable crowd had gathered, including one hundred journalists. But the kind of tension that grips this tormented country was prefigured by the cordon that held back the spectators—along with a half-dozen police dogs. Police dogs, to hold back people who want to see a supersonic passenger jet?

It was not until the second day that the newspaper reported that the function of the dogs wasn't to bite South Africans, whether white, Indian, Colored, or black, but to sniff out explosives. After all, we had landed in a country in which a state of emergency had been declared, way back in 1986, after several hundred deaths had resulted from riotous demonstrations fueled by apartheid, or at least ostensibly fueled by apartheid, given that there are a lot of riots and violent deaths in sub-Saharan Africa where apartheid doesn't exist.

There was barely time to settle into our hotel on the beach, two or three miles from downtown, before the taping of the one-hour special edition of *Firing Line*, featuring five prominent figures in South African politics. Of the five only one—Mr. Kent Durr, minister of budget and works—was a member of the National Party, which has ruled South Africa for forty years.

A second guest is whip for the Conservative Party, which is the political party that, to the general dismay of everyone except presumably its constituents, emerged in the last election as the second-largest party in Parliament—the official opposition. And that party thinks the dissolution of apartheid is going too damn fast, not too damn slow. Mr. Koos van der Merwe is a large, beefy man whose principal message is that the United States should mind its own business and that to engage in sanctions is to promote violence, wherefore the United States is guilty of violence.

Mrs. Helen Suzman, who is a mixture of Eleanor Roosevelt and Clare Boothe Luce, is a co-founder of the Progressive Party and began opposing apartheid about the time of the Boer War: no living white South African is more ardently identified than she with opposition to apartheid.

Mr. Oscar Dhlomo, the principal braintruster for Chief Buthelezi, the head of the KwaZulu tribe, is needless to say an opponent of apartheid: more, he and his boss decline to discuss South African policy with

President P.W. Botha until Botha releases Nelson Mandela from jail, where he has been since 1962.

And the fifth guest, Mr. James Ngcoya, is a former truck driver who organized a taxi service and a labor union that lobbies for equal rights for black entrepreneurs.

All five participants argued different modalities of the South African question, but every one of them fervently opposed economic sanctions by the United States, the consensus being that black progress within South Africa is something that is happening *pari passu* with economic progress, and that to freeze economic progress is to freeze black prospects for equality.

The hour was supplemented on the following day by three half-hour examinations with different experts, all of them opponents of the government, of the South African problem. What, I asked, about the statement by Nelson Mandela, made in 1962, that "under a Communist Party government, South Africa will become a land of milk and honey"? What about the continuing ties between the African National Congress and the governments of North Korea, the Soviet Union, and Cuba?

These are questions of manifest indifference to black South Africans, who are as unimpressed by the excesses of the ANC and its leaders as Palestinians are by the past, and prospective, excesses of the PLO. The ANC is their movement, and do not try to alter that fundamental reality.

The anti-apartheid spokesmen included a gentle-voiced black intellectual, a benign version of the late James Baldwin. Neville Alexander spent years in prison in London, alongside Nelson Mandela and teaches now at a university, styling himself a Trotskyist, which in my experience is simply a way of saying, "I am to the right of Stalin, and to the left of practically everybody else." Mr. Alexander is a gifted woodman, and what he was saying, ever but ever so delicately, is that black South Africans are orally in a condition of belligerence against the whiter government, and any violent exchange under the circumstances in properly viewed as an episode not of anarchy but of revolution. By Western tradition, the individual who revolts against the state either prevails—as Washington and Robespierre prevailed—or else imprisoned or executed; and, thereafter, depending on the vectors of history, is honored as a prophet, or dishonored as a distraction on the great dialectic by which progress is peaceably effected. The bloodless revolution of 1688 is to be preferred to the regicidal protests of Oliver Cromwell.

But, of course, the Concorders were not in South Africa to help settle political problems. The ninety-eight exuberant travelers, on the last leg before our landing in London, are as ever interested in what goes on in the lands we visit, but we are unrepentantly absorbed in the swinging experience we are having, popping from continent to continent in our privately chartered Concorde, swamping the staff of *The Guinness Book of World Records* with fresh speed records, and exploring the sights and sounds and tastes of diverse peoples right around the world.

The shoreline along Cape Town is majestic even in the prolonged drizzle that affected everything except our spirits. The wine country in the lush Stellenbosch area is as exquisite as the wine produced. And, of course, as we near the end of the trip we are bound by common experiences and progressive knowledge of one another. Yesterday there was a lecture by a gentleman who in the past twenty years has casually accumulated a collection of Americana second perhaps only to that of the Library of Congress—he can tell you what John Adams' private thoughts were on Lord North.

One lady, advanced in years, scratched her memory late on afternoon and played for me two or three sonatas by Scarlatti that she hadn't played in twenty-five years. Another lady is busy in her off-moments preparing the musical schedule for 1990's Newport Music Festival; an elderly lawyer who clerked for Chief Justice William Howard Taft back when chief justices had one, not five, clerks, is here gently to correct historical or legal solecisms.

Two passengers protested against the quarters preferred by our central hotel—it isn't easy to get seventy-five ideal rooms—and for reasons not readily apparent to their fellow travelers, thought their inconvenience worth the attention of the press, which gave it to them on the front page, otherwise devoted to sex, murder, and mayhem.

Tomorrow we will go a fearfully long distance, 7,200 miles, from about thirty-four degrees south of the equator to about fifty-five degrees north of it, with a refueling stop in Monrovia, Liberia. Where I intend to freeze in my seat, finishing Robert Hughes' wonderful book on Australia, resisting any temptation to learn in one hour the inside story of Monrovia, Liberia.

We must refuel quickly, because our cicerone Don Pevsner wants another world record, and this time we are contending against another Concorde that flew this route in years gone by.

Whether we break the record or don't, we shall arrive in London breathless, after traveling 39,000 miles in twenty-three days.

Reflections on the Concorde
April 27, 1989

Concerning the advantages of supersonic travel, there oughtn't to be any question. If you are in Cape Town, South Africa, and you want badly to be in London, the best way of accomplishing this is via Concorde, even if you have to stop at Monrovia, Liberia, where there is no air-conditioning.

It was very fashionable in the early 1970s, when the United States stalled on the question whether to develop its own supersonic jet, to take the attitude: "Aw, come on. Isn't 550 miles per hour fast enough for you? Life is too turbulent as it is. The time has come to cool it." The static from this Luddite sentimentalism resulted in protests in Queens, NY, over the noise the Concorde would generate, and court protests against granting landing rights. These came close to causing severe damage to the Franco-American alliance. But finally—eventually—the Concorde began its regular runs.

The trouble with it, universally recognized, is that it is too bloody expensive for general use. It is for the very affluent or for those whose time is enormously valuable to corporations that want Mr. Jones in New York NOW and are willing to pay the costs of the magic carpet. Yet as things now stand, there won't be any supersonic jet travel after the turn of the century.

The British have seven Concordes, the French seven. The French fleet will evaporate sometime before the British fleet does because it makes no spare parts, satisfying itself to cannibalize, which means a regular attrition on flyable aircraft. Given that the cost of developing the Concordes was absorbed by governments, and British Airways was subsequently privatized, it is not surprising that the British operation netted $24 million last year (the French operation continues as a division of the government and cost figures are accordingly difficult to calculate). But this is made possible by charging a huge 34 percent-above-first-class fare, in the knowledge that there are enough business travelers who will pay that sum.

Now Aerospace Toulouse of France and its British equivalent have said that they can develop a modern version of the Concorde using 1990 technology (the existing Concorde is based on technology almost forty years old). The prototype would cost $555 million. Subsequent planes would of course be much cheaper. Though it is not yet possible to arrive at a fixed figure, it pays to remind ourselves that the new 747s cost in excess of $100 million apiece.

The Concorde II would be larger than the existing model, accommodating 150 passengers instead of 100. Its range would be 5,000 miles, not 4,000. The efficiencies in fuel consumption and design would probably make it possible to handle transatlantic travel charging what is now charged for a business seat—about $1,300. One could reasonably expect droves of patrons willing to pay $1,300 in exchange for a three-hour ride to London or Paris.

The maddening feature of it is that no one has yet come up with a means of eliminating the sonic boom, with the result that heavy traffic lanes, for instance New York to Los Angeles, would still be prohibited. But notwithstanding the sonic boom's exclusion of overland flights, there would be heavy patchwork advantages. A flight from San Francisco to Hong Kong takes fourteen hours and forty minutes. Aboard a Concorde II, even stopping in Hawaii to refuel, the distance would be handled in eight and one-half hours.

Japan, interestingly enough, flatly refuses to allow a supersonic jet to land on its sacred territory, making the sole exception in permitting President Mitterrand to land on his Concorde in order to attend the funeral of Emperor Hirohito. But who knows, Japan would probably come around, if it meant good business to do so.

President Reagan has spoken rather airily about a future jet of a suborbital character that would take you at Mach 8 (5,000 miles per hour) to Japan in a little over an hour. That's OK to dream about, and dreams are very American. But meanwhile, it become progressively clear, especially to those of us who have rounded the world traveling 39,000 miles in thirty-nine hours of flight, that serious thought should be given to the next generation of supersonic flights, even if these were restricted to overwater passage.

Miami to London nonstop might not justify two flights per day at $1,300, but not inconceivably would I justify one such flight. The prospect of saying goodbye forever to Mach 2 seems a strange way of saying goodbye to the twentieth century.

For Sail: One Writer

Newsday Magazine, May 21, 1989

There are, in my reckoning, three cognate sports: skiing, gliding, and sailing. I suppose you could add a fourth, namely parachuting. They all depend on natural forces and on the elements to achieve the sensations they make possible. You are either tugged by gravity, or propelled by wind. In the case of gliding, by both. The knowledge that you are not depleting the physical resources of the world, when you engage in these sports, is oddly gratifying, though, God knows, in sailing there is attrition enough of another kind: frayed lines, canvas, and—especially if you race your boat—temper.

But the rewards are for some abundant, for others, like me, overwhelming. The sensation of being able to go wherever one wants is rather special, and it is yours on any scale you desire. The lake sailor can decide, within the boundaries of the lake, where he wishes to go: there is no highway to funnel him onto pre-directed courses. A day sailor on setting out on Long Island Sound from Oyster Bay can go to New York City, or to Connecticut, or to Block Island. When four years ago my hand was on the wheel of the seventy-one-foot sailing ketch heading out from Honolulu, a northerly turn of a mere fourteen degrees would have taken us, 5,000 miles later, to Tokyo Bay rather than to New Guinea.

For many years I used to race my boats, and there is a special thrill in doing this, making them go as fast in every situation as possible. The thrill has to do not only with meeting the wind's challenge and exploiting it to the point of hazard, but in (occasionally) outwitting the other vessel: it is a contest, done with sails hoisted. When I gave up racing it wasn't because

I had grown tired of it. Rather, it was fatigue with the infernal problem of lining up a crew, deserting your home on scarce weekends. Then you focus on the alternative, which is cruising. And that is what, now, we do. To cruise in a sailboat combines the exposure to the sea with the electrifying relief of finding shelter from the sea. No man who ever sailed exuberantly out to sea is less than ecstatic upon sighting land. It's the thrill of the cadence at the end of a stretch of music in which you are spellbound.

There's all of that and, always, the feel of the wind, so cupcakeable so much of the time, so furious and wanton at other times. You love and you hate it, and always you respect it. Sometimes it overwhelms you, as do airplanes which, sometimes, crash. Men die aboard sailboats, but mostly they live on them and glory in an experience that never palls.

Living and Working in Gstaad
Primary Color, September 1, 1989

GSTAAD, Switzerland—Almost every reference one hears to ski centers in Switzerland supposes that the interested party is going there in order to ski and, probably, to revel in the perquisites of after-ski life, some of them commendable, others less so.

The imaginary fortnight in Gstaad (or Klosters, or Grindelwald, or wherever) is a vision of a relaxed night flight, a rented car with skis piled alongside bags full of fanciful winterwear. In due course one pulls into the hotel or chalet as the sun is falling and the darkening skies over the Alps dye the surrounding snow lavender-blue, and the mountain ridges and glaciers, gullies and ravines exercise their muscles. Soon the procrusteanizing darkness robs them of their distinctiveness.

You know that the following morning, after a luxurious dinner and a long night's rest, you will be at the lift with your two-week pass, your companion, perhaps your ski guide, and a wallet already far diminished in amplitude. But we live only once.

There is another life here, though it is not experienced by many. It is worth examining for those Americans who cherish skiing and have independence of movement. I am one such, and though strictly speaking my first two vacations in Switzerland were in 1931 and 1932 (I was six-to-seven years old), I count the winter of 1959 as the first for these purposes. The succeeding year, for complicated and irrelevant reasons, we went to Zurs in Austria for three weeks; the year after, to Stowe in Vermont. But, these were our only infidelities. Which makes for twenty-seven straight winters in Gstaad.

I don't tire of reminding friends of a maxim of Winston Churchill that greatly appeals. It is that a vacation is defined as "doing something else." There is a sense in which the insurance salesman from Hartford, or the doctor from Key West, or the ballerina from San Francisco are doing "something else" when they go to Gstaad to ski and perhaps to party a little. But Churchill's point was that the continued, strenuous use of the mind, when it is engaged in different enterprises from those that normally engage it, is: refreshing.

In his (famous) case, he liked to paint. I have done a little of this (mostly in Switzerland) and can absolutely corroborate that no work I have ever done has required more concentration. The stability of the very world itself seems to hang on whether you correctly inflect with that pink-gray oil the soft underbelly of that cloud. In fact, the world never does right itself when I confront a canvas; but even so I leave the studio an entirely relaxed man.

Switzerland—specifically, Gstaad—offers both kinds of vacations. Everyone knows about the first variety—up at a leisurely hour, meet your guide at 10.00, up the lift, three or four runs before lunch, an appetizing and mildly vinous Swiss lunch (salad, veal, French fried potatoes, a tart, coffee, a glass or two of Valais or Dole); back up the mountain—probably a different mountain—for the afternoon, with ten or fifteen miles of skiing; then, at about 4:00, back to the chalet, a hot bath, a half hour with a book, a nap, rise at 7:00 to play cards.

The drinks start coming in at about eight. Dinner at nine-thirty, and sometime after eleven or twelve, sleep, the whole body grateful for the day's exposure to sun and snow and wind and animating nutrition. In ten days, you are, as they proclaim, a new man.

Gstaad is the name rather lazily used to cover an area about twenty-five miles square. The town itself ambles along a valley at 3,000 feet of elevation. To reach Gstaad you must leave the French canton of Vaud, and that happens at Rougemont (where my wife and I stay). You enter the Bernese Oberland at Saanen, turning right to go to Gstaad. If instead you turned left, within three kilometers you will be at Schonreid. Three kilometers farther on you arc at Saanenmoser. The towns just described compose, loosely speaking, "Gstaad." And there is not a more enchanting area of that size in the world, we who go there say and think, swear to God.

It is also the chalet capital of Switzerland. Yes, there are fine hotels, including the famous Gstaad-Palace, a great Graustarkian thing built as if Walt Disney had decided then and there to launch his fantasy world, and maintained in its high, haughty, fortress-like magnificence ever since its opening, before World War I. But in Gstaad there are more chalet-beds, as they are called, than hotel-beds. Most visitors want their own chalet. These are abundant and range greatly in price, for example a modest $500 a week for a two-bedroom chalet in the far reaches of Saanensmoser, to ten and twenty times that a week during the Christmas season in the royal enclosure of Gstaad (roughly, within 700 yards of the Palace Hotel).

Now this other life I speak of is appropriate especially, but not exclusively, to the writer, painter, or musician. Someone who arrives in Gstaad intending to ski—heaven forfend that he should not ski in that territory: one might as well visit Brussels resolved not to eat. But he/she has other things in mind. In my case it is, always, a book I need to write.

Since I also have concurrent administrative duties, the mornings must be given over to formal duties—reading manuscripts, editing, answering mail, writing a syndicated column. (I pause here to proclaim that there is no greater worldly help on Earth in such a situation as mine than computer-cum-electronic communication. I can send 1,000 words to New York for about $6.)

Then, at about 12:30, you have a date. Say at the restaurant at the top of the Eggli. You are skiing that day with Doris Brynner, a whiz-lady, bundles of talent and fun. She was married to Yul at one point and, when that fell apart, she took her beautiful daughter to Gstaad and Montreaux, establishing in each a classy boutique. You eat and are merry and begin to ski. Your schedule (you must be back to start your serious work soon after four) fits her perfectly, since she must be back at the shop, to see that the cuckoo-clocks are ringing the Angelus on the hour and that the chinchilla mittens are toasty and warm.

Oh my, how many glorious hours of skiing you can have in the Gstaad area. From where I live, I figure eight separate mountains, some with as many as six separate lifts, within ten minutes. Or I can amble down the back road a hundred yards and take the Videmanette lift up to an aerie from which you can spot most of the mountains in Switzerland. There is up there (of course) a restaurant. To reach it you ascend over a ski trail that might have been painted by Hieronymus Bosch intending to remind you of the torture of hell. That is the famous Black *Piste* of the Videma-nette, and the idea is to brave it once in your lifetime, so you can say, nonchalantly, "Oh yes, I have done the black *piste*."

(It is humiliating to learn that once a year, at their exclusive party, the ski teachers go up to that little restaurant, wine and dine, and come down that ghastly trail at *night*, their sparkling flambeaux providing exiguous illumination; and, leading the snaky line of skiers, is a great big gentleman playing an accordion. If the actuaries at Lloyds of London spotted that trail, that night, they would suspend trading rather than insure anyone's survival. But the pros laugh about it later that night, at the tavern.)

So, then you are through skiing, after an hour or two; and you are back in your study, or your atelier, writing a book, or attacking a canvas. Danger. After that good lunch and the exercise and the bright Swiss air and the exhilaration downhill followed by a hot bath there is one thing you *cannot* count on doing. That is reading a book. Why? Because you will go gently, but quite irreversibly to sleep.

If you want to read, you have only one alternative, and that is to nap for one hour. But the afternoon is getting away from us, and we are wary of losing that hour, which deposits you at your desk, after you wake up, a little drowsy. So: attack that which stimulates you. Write; or paint; or play an instrument.

My friend, Professor John Kenneth Galbraith, the most celebrated liberal economist in the world, has an apartment in Gstaad. He likes to write in the morning. There are those, friends all, of economic liberty, who wish he would spend the whole of his time skiing, neglecting altogether his writing. But no, in fact he has diminished his time on skis in recent years (doctor's orders). There is no authority, given the First Amendment, that could order him to restrict his writing.... But, one likes to think, Gstaad unsexes the most militant ideological appetites of people who experience it.

I really do believe than even J.K.G. would be sorry if the Swiss made it impossible for the Palace Hotel to operate there, or for Elizabeth Taylor and assorted kings and queens to wing in, or for the English woman who constructed a swimming pool under her large living room to give her all-caviar parties.

People who go to Gstaad year after year are quite unconscious of all that ambient high-living. Husbandry lives! J.K.G. got mad at Hertz, Avis, *et al.* years ago and punishes them by refusing to rent a car. Instead, he walks, and takes the local train: this he is especially happy to do in any event because Swiss trains are socialized, lose money, and are quite lovely. So, the socialists can point to the Swiss system and deplore others.

But Switzerland is a country of anomalies. The most militaristic country maybe in the world (a Swiss man faces more weeks of duty-on-the-field than anyone not a professional soldier; but they don't fight wars, haven't for 150 years).

The president of Switzerland is quite simply unidentifiable. You could construct on Swiss TV a *What's My Line?* show featuring the president of Switzerland, and I swear, nobody would guess who he was. That's what I call good government: invisible governors.

What do you get there, spending the winter in Gstaad, that you might not have gotten elsewhere? Well, there is no other Switzerland, is the best way of putting it. And although I have spent thirty winters there, I am not an expert even on Switzerland. Nevertheless, based on superficial acquaintances with other ski centers, I will go back always to Gstaad, with its abundant ski runs, the succulent food (a bad restaurant in Gstaad would be a tourist attraction, like a gorilla in the zoo), the relaxed atmosphere of the chalet-life.

That is a vacation that turns out to be—a productive vacation, because you are back home, after six or seven weeks, not only with forty-five afternoons of skiing but with a book under your belt; or, if such is your inclination, a toy railroad; or the biggest crossword puzzle, Guinness-size; or twelve watercolors; or the F minor Bach concerto in your fingers, finally.

Maybe J.K.G. will put a winter vacation in Gstaad on the Democratic platform at sometime. Meanwhile, let's keep it a secret.

CHAPTER SIX

1990–1994

Just Say No
Cruising World, April 1990

The impulse to sail to Bermuda rises in me every three or four years. On my thirty-six-foot Lancer, *Patito,* my hard-core sailing set and I attempt one significant cruise every summer, and we thought this year to go to the Bras d'Or Lakes, accompanying a friend on his thirty-eight-footer, something I have never done; a *gemütlich* ocean passage with continuous fraternization by radio and, who knows, when the seas are especially still as every now and again they are we'd raft together to swim and dine...But as it happened, my friend needed to give priority to a hip replacement, and so the piquancy of a joint passage gave way to alternatives. The Bras d'Or Lakes on Cape Breton Island, 125 miles northeast of Halifax, are after all a long way from Stamford, CT. I know having made the rewarding journey on my (late) schooner *Cyrano* a dozen years ago. And there is the further disadvantage that until you reach the lakes themselves you can't swim much, a hundred miles or so after leaving Nantucket, not unless you are a member of the Polar Bear Club.

Why not go to Bermuda, Danny Merritt suggested.

I could think of no reason not to cruise again to Bermuda. I've raced to Bermuda four times, and arrived there under sail a half-dozen times cruising, one of them (October 1958) through the edge of a hurricane, which endowed me permanently with the wonder of a boat's performance properly hove to, as also with the conviction that surviving the sea's extravagant dis-pleasures can be something of a theatrical exercise. The ocean likes to prac-tice terrifying its clients, pushing them to the brink of destruction...and then, grudgingly, it will pull back, sullen for a few hours, but then before you know it, it is smiling sweetly at you as if to say: there there, we didn't really mean it. Sailing to Bermuda is always an experience.

And there would be special excitement on this trip because I would have aboard the last word in electronic navigation, the Trimble GPS Nav-Graphic, which is the ocean equivalent of the postman who knows how to find 22A Maiden Lane, undistracted by 22 Maiden Lane, which is a half-dozen beguiling yards off to the right.

Off we went. I redeemed a carefree invitation made to me by the Coast Guard a year or so back, proffering me the hospitality of Governor's Island in return for a little favor I had done the spirited complement of men on that strategic little island, so critically situated for anyone passing by New York City, so scandalously short of overnight berthing space. And, so, we brought *Patito* there at sunset on the Sunday. We would take off for Ber-muda on Wednesday.

It was a grand introduction to the NavGraphic because I designed the installation so that, in clement weather, I could situate the monitor to that navigation miracle on the cockpit under the dodger. That way we could all actually see *Patito* sail, second by second, westward from Stamford, past Execution Rock, up into the East River, past Hell Gate and La Guardia Airport and Rikers Island, to Gracie Mansion and then south down the length of Manhattan. On the screen, a tiny facsimile of a sailing boat, slid-ing along an illuminated chart, identical to your sailing chart, expanding or diminishing in scale according as you push ZOOM IN or ZOOM OUT, keep-ing always in front of you the course to your destination and the distance to it, the Estimated Time of Arrival, the Course Made Good—all of those plums to which Loran has accustomed us; but now all there on a live-TV screen in front of you, so that when you get to the Brooklyn Bridge, *Patito* is shown under the Brooklyn Bridge—uncanny. Granted, it is a luxury item. The Trimble unit sells for about $12,000, but it is delivering up to you, at no supplementary cost, the fruit of about $12 billion dollars of Department of Defense technology. The DoD's GPS satellites are to the NavGraphic as the alphabet is to a keyboard.

But I would put the unit through its special paces when under way to Bermuda, with special, concerned attention to the refractory CD player that feeds the NavGraphic after you have inserted a disk (cost, $400) covering the area you are navigating in: e.g., North Atlantic, Central Atlantic, Chesapeake.

No ocean trip should, in my judgment, set out, so to speak, unlaunched. In 1958, preparing to go off to Bermuda in October we served beer and champagne and pretzels at the marina at Twenty-Third Street and my oldest brother brought as a departure gift—an eight-foot palm tree. Just the thing for a forty-two-foot cutter setting out on a 700-mile passage. We lashed it good-humoredly to the backstay and there it rested, clinging to life, like the rest of us, right through the hurricane, coming to symbolize for us Mother Earth; the staff of life. We would need an appropriate launch.

Now one pleasant way to do a send-off party is to hire the *Petrel*. It is a retired seventy-two-foot racing yawl and works out of the Battery at the tip of Manhattan as a lunch-dinner head boat. You charter *Petrel* with its crew of five and sail off in the general direction of Ambrose Light. You take your sloop and harness it to a winch on *Petrel*'s stern. You join your friends and family for a couple of convivial hours of this and that, and then at about 1:00 p.m., you and your crew bring up the trailing line and do a little *geland-esprung* onto *Patito*, haul up our own sails, and wave at *Petrel*'s landlubbers, one party going off to sea, the other back to land; one party wistful, the other exuberant, and no one ever knowing for sure which is which.

Danny and I have sailed together for twenty-five years, beginning when he was thirteen and my son's best friend. He cares for *Patito* in what spare time he has, looking after a wife, three children, and fifty advertising accounts for *Power and Motoryacht* magazine. He is the most wholesomely attractive and competent young man I have ever known, and moreover is blissfully uninterested in the world I inhabit, creepy-crawly with things like Republicans and Democrats, Communists and fascists; syndicalists, and singletaxers—Dan just smiles and works his way through life and has a good time and charms everyone and rises to the top of the mast at the least provocation, and is forever forgetting to buy an ice pick. Van Galbraith, lawyer, banker, diplomat, by contrast eats politics and descries ideological leanings in the sailboat's shrouds, when he is not laughing, or making others laugh. Patrick Ciganer, a fresh sailing companion, races his own thirty-seven-foot sloop in San Francisco and went recently to Trimble as director of the marine division. I came to know him when he expressed interest in my software program, WhatStar, designed to give you the identity of the star you just shot by computerizing, a) the time you shot it, b) its altitude, and c) your estimated position. He is a Paris-born, thoroughbred European, with Russian, French, and Spanish blood in his veins, science in his mind's eye, and the sea and everything related to it vivid in his vivid imagination.

We were off. And we exchanged reflections on the data that Van (our meteorological officer) had discreetly (he has not circulated it among our guests aboard *Petrel*) collected after three days' phone calls to the National Hurricane Center in Miami. A tropical disturbance 500 miles east of the Antilles working its way westward, and projecting a northwesterly swing... perhaps achieving hurricane force, and projected to pass five degrees east of Bermuda. But, said the gentleman on the phone you can't ever track tropical disturbance itineraries with exactitude, and what and where Hurricane Berry (as it would be designated a day later) would be doing, about the time we would be approaching Bermuda was... unknown, and for the time being unknowable. But there was sufficient apprehension, in meteorologic HQ, to dispatch an airplane to probe the disturbance. We would need to be careful.

We don't have a single side band radio aboard *Patito*, and would therefore need to rely on shortwave and inter-ship communications. Meanwhile we had set our course—147 degrees—and we headed, close-hauled on a port lack, toward Bermuda. The watch system was activated (I do 4-4-4-6-6 with social rotation, so that halfway through everyone's watch, a new crew replaces the crew that has been on duty for a full watch), and the sun gave way to a black night, followed by a refractory dawn.

We all know what it's like. The skies get grayer and grayer, the wind more and more huffy, the boat increases its heel. Twenty-four hours after waving goodbye to *Petrel* we had in the course of three hours, a) taken a single reef on the main; b) reduced the genoa by one-half its area; and c) taken a second reef on the main. Alas, the energumen that roams the seas seeking the destruction of health began to score. Patrick would not eat lunch. Van nibbled. Danny bravely cooked a three-course meal, which he then—transcended. Van had been hard at work on the Sony shortwave. But coastal America was uninterested in the huge front that was now giving us thirty-knot easterlies, rain, and a waspish sea. It was so for ten hours and at about 3:00 p.m. Van made contact with ("spoke," as they say in orthodox ocean lingo) a vessel only dimly visible on the horizon. A Dutchman fluent in English told us that the front we had penetrated was forecast to follow us down to latitude thirty-six degrees. That translated to 140 miles southeast of where we were, suggesting more of the same for, oh, thirty hours. And then, our Dutchman added, it wasn't yet known whether the tropical disturbance, which was now moving in our general direction at about twenty knots, would dissipate or accumulate to full hurricane force.

What-to-do time.

Just Say No reached my mind as plainspokenly as if Nancy Reagan had been sitting there in the cockpit, dispensing basic lessons in rudimentary morality. The memory flashed back to the Annapolis-Newport Race of 1967. We had beat bravely down the Chesapeake. Pulling out of the bay the winds increased. The #2 blew. Up went our #3; in an hour it was gone. I didn't have my second #3, made of tougher material, on board. I hoisted the storm jib and the storm trysail and we bobbed along comfortably—but the boats behind us, more appropriately rigged, began to slide by. After a few hours such boats as we would spot seemed to have been arrested by the furious wind. I decided to return to the Chesapeake and in one hour reversed the distance it had taken us a grueling six hours to climb. We felt better, the following morning at Norfolk, to learn that thirty-four boats—a whopping 24 percent of the fleet of 125—had said No.

Harder to Say No when racing than when cruising. Cruises are undertaken with greater emphasis on the marginal delights of the passage than on the delights of successful competition. We were racing against nobody. Still, to Say No is psychologically vexing (should we have persevered, never mind that no point of honor hung on our reaching the top of Mt. Everest?) and spiritually taxing—at sea one expects mortification of the flesh: were we shrinking from our Lenten duty? I reflected briefly on these questions, and decided to Say No to the temptation to go ahead.

With the wind now well abaft our beam and the genoa reduced to handkerchief size, stomachs began to restabilize, and I was able to engage Patrick in the mysteries and promises of GPS.

You should know that the Trimble unit feeds on GPS for as many hours during the day as it can do so, which is to say, for as many hours as at least three satellites are within its reach. A fresh satellite is scheduled to be launched every ninety days, so that three months from now a full complement, for two-dimensional positioning, will be circling day and night above us, three satellites within the reach of any GPS receiver, anywhere in the world. Will that mean that a year from now every boat with GPS will know exactly where it is?

Well, no. The reason for this being that the Department of Defense "degrades" the signal available to the civilian user population, and does so erratically, i.e., in such a way as to make it impossible to predict exactly what the deviation is. The existing protocol has GPS lying to us up to 100 meters, maximum. Why? Well, imagine a terrorist with a projectile that can launch a mini-bomb exactly guided by GPS to plop down the main chimney of the White House. We would want to avoid that, would we not, at least during a Republican administration? So, DoD causes GPS to oscillate by as much as 100 yards.

Now this doesn't mean, however, that in the course of ten or fifteen minutes you can't outwit GPS's ruses. Because if you are following a set course and clocking your GPS position, which is refreshed every five seconds, you will transcribe its swivel-hipping distractions and soon deduce exactly where you are. DoD of course knows that you can do this in a boat (or on a truck, or airplane) but this does not mean that a terrorist could project, via GPS, exactly where to aim its missile because missiles-in-flight can't make the interpolations required to outwit a wobbly signal.

The dream—no, the hard-boiled intention—of the GPS people is to equip not only surveyors, but also trucks and automobiles with receivers (estimated cost, a year or two down the line, $5,000; a year or two after that, $2,000) that will oblige you if you are a passive customer (a driver looking, say, for 322 Beacon Street, Boston) with instructions that flash on the screen telling you when next to turn right, when left; and if you are also an active consumer, you will be continuously transmitting to your home data bank your own location, on the basis of which the dispatcher at Headquarters can tell you to sidle off and pick up a truckload of pecans in Shreveport. The faculties have been developed at Trimble, for example, to cope with the DoD Degradation Increment, and subscribing users (surveyors, large industrial firms) have already been equipped with differential receiver stations that wipe out the discrepancy. Imagine such a system on a heavily laden supertanker navigating its way out of a tricky harbor passage. With safe navigation channels indicated on the NavGraphic, and the relative meter precision of differential GPS, a (non-drunk) ten-year-old could navigate with absolute confidence. Moreover, such technology could be consulted at the Coast Guard monitoring station for surveillance far more effective than that currently supplied by radars.

For yachtsmen? What we have most to hope for is that the Soviet Union and the DoD will agree to combine their technologies. Ours, needless to say, is far advanced over theirs. But there is this advantage, namely that if both they and we have the same satellites, their anti-satellite weapons (we have none) will presumably not be interested in destroying in space satellites owned in common, giving out surefooted signals to both parties. If that technological union should happen, tomorrow's yachtsman will know within ten yards exactly where he is, courtesy of GPS. And airplanes, when the stationary land units are set up, will have three dimensional fixes allowing them to know—again, within inches—where they are, when coming in for a blind landing.

If that pooled technology does not happen, DoD might even degrade to 200 meters, leaving GPS a poor second cousin to Loran with however this advantage, that it will be available everywhere in the world. It will be useful for every navigational purpose save entering Kennebunkport during a fog.

The front stayed right where we left it, a big, thick mother that would have given us the ugly time we experienced for yet another day and one-half. But halfway to Atlantic City we were out of it and saw the sun for the first time beginning in midmorning. We lunched heartily a mile outside the breakwater and then went into Farley's Marina, alongside Trump Castle, fatigued; but Danny left us at 3:00 p.m., while we coped with the wet but intact boat and napped. By 7:00 p.m. we decided that young Danny was fatally in the coils of Mr. Trump, mortgaging his next year's salary. We wrote him a note telling him where we would be for dinner. As we were leaving *Patito* he showed up, a shy but triumphant smile on his face, Hannibal coming down from the Alps. He opened his right hand wordlessly and counted out eighteen $100 bills, handing me to keep for him, against later temptation, fifteen of them. With a whoop, we invited him to invite us to dinner. After which we visited Caesar's Palace casino. I had last been in Atlantic City to cover the Lyndon Johnson Convention in 1964 and had opined in my column that the worst mistake Atlantic City had ever made was to advertise its existence to the 2,000 journalists who suffocated from boredom, beyond even that generated by LBJ, for five whole days. So, I hadn't seen Atlantic City-Vegas, and had difficulty in finding my sea legs in that room of oceanic dimensions. Could it be two, three, four acres big? I had two quarters, and within two minutes, they had multiplied to thirty-eight quarters, which I distributed among the senior crew. Danny had perched down at a blackjack table. One-half hour later, the senior crew were down to the two quarters—just enough to buy the *New York Times* and retreat to our little *querencia*. *Patito* was smugly dry, after six hours of sun; and we played Red Dog and I won $23. Danny showed up (I learned) at 5:00 a.m. It was difficult to revive him when at 8:00 a.m. I announced it was time to resume sailing. But we succeeded, and he opened his eyes, and managed a smile, reaching into his pocket to exhibit forty-eight $100 bills.

We'd GPS'd our way with fascination up the New Jersey coast, abandoning our plans to sail to Montauk in the teeth of a fresh northeasterly wind. I came to know, for the first time, the fishing resort of Manasquan, two-thirds of the way up to New York from Atlantic City. We had no charts for New Jersey on board, having had no intention of coming near New Jersey. So what? NavGraphic showed us exactly how to cope with Manasquan Harbor. The following day the front had moved toward us, and we went in the drizzle up to the vicinity of Ambrose, eased over to the channel leading to Manhattan, contriving to arrive there when the tide would shoot us up the East River, which it did, on schedule. It looked like a beat back to

Stamford but suddenly, at Execution Rock, the wind lifted us, northeast to east, and we could head right for Stamford.

Not another boat was visible. The wind blew at twenty knots, we had half the genoa tucked in, the full main, the autopilot silent and obedient, and so we went below for a three-course dinner—soup, charcoaled steak, onions and potato sticks, salad, chocolate mousse, cheesecake, and Moet et Chandon champagne. We were traveling at hull speed. The NavGraphic gave us all the information we needed, save for the human periscope, propped up every ten or fifteen minutes to reassure us that no one else was so besotted as to go sailing in that weather. We finished our meal, put on our weather gear, and went back to the cockpit and flew, I mean flew to the Stamford jetties. Ten minutes later we were tied up. An hour later, we were asleep, reassured that it can pay dividends, at sea, to Say No.

Moscow: Waiting for Mr. Hilton
July 24, 1990

There is a lot of good news coming out of the Soviet Union, but pilgrims who travel there to see a land transformed by *perestroika* and pluralism should be warned that although free-market principles have been accepted by the government, they are very far from having been implemented. Anyone who doubts that there is a need for reform should spend a few days at an Intourist hotel in Moscow.

The economic idea of arbitrage—the process that prompts people to buy a product where it is cheap and sell it where it is dear, until prices level out—has not even worked its wonders within the Intourist hotel in Moscow, let alone in Greater Moscow, let alone in Great Russia. On the second floor of the Intourist Hotel you can buy five ounces of caviar for $29. On the first floor, the same can of caviar costs $44. Outside, the five of you ask for a taxi and you are told that five people are too many for one taxi, so that you need two taxis, and to take you where you are going will be $5 per cab. You hesitate—and the entrepreneur visibly relents, to tell you grandly that you are not to worry. He will make an exception, and take all five of you in his cab for—$10.

In your room there are problems. There is no air-conditioning in the tiny living room, and to go to the bedroom requires that you turn on the light that illuminates the dark stairway. But having reached the bedroom, you then need to turn off the light when it is time to sleep. But you cannot do that without descending the stairway; there is only the single switch. So, you climb up in the dark.

You need to telephone a companion staying in another room. You call the operator. It rings busy. You try off and on, for one hour. It is very important, so you descend to Hotel Reception and ask the woman at the desk: Where is Mr. Peter Samara staying?

What then happens is as if you asked your grandmother to come up with the picture of her high-school graduation. The receptionist hauls up a lapful of yellow slips and begins to go over them one by one. At the end, she says: "He is not here." "Yes, he is here. He has been here for two days." "He is not here." At that moment, Peter shows up. You exchange intelligence, and ask for his room number, which is 601, so that you can dial him directly.

The next morning you wish to call 601. You follow the hotel dialing instructions. To call 601, you must dial 203-20-97. Well, you can manage that. Does that mean that to call 602 you would dial 203-20-98? No: 203-50-40.

At 3:30 p.m., on your way out, you report to the concierge that your toilet is stopped up. You come in at 11:00 p.m. and note that it is still stopped up. At 9:00 a.m. it is still stopped up. It occurs to anyone scheduled to check out of the hotel that morning that there is an obvious way to leave the mark of one's displeasure.

The airport in Moscow is an extension of hotel life. You arrive three hours before flight time, as you are told to do. The airport at Moscow does not resemble what was there before, either in shape or in patronage. It is now stockyard-cavernous in size, and all of Mongolia was there today, headed east.

You need to complete a form that reminds you of Stephen Potter's book *One-Upmanship* because you are not given, where crucial, room enough to supply the information Moscow desires, in its *glasnostian* fury, to get from you. (If you are carrying $87, you must write not merely $87, but "eighty-seven dollars" in approximately one-half inch of space, on a form that no Russian in his right mind, which includes a lot of Russians, is ever going to read.

Arrangements are studiously made to move hordes of men and women from rooms with chairs to sit on into rooms without chairs to sit on, with never less than one full hour of waiting for your flight in the area where the duty-free shop sits. It may be duty free, but for 1.73 rubles, you are given $1, and purchases of goods may be made only in dollars. On the street, you will find enterprising *perestroikans* who will offer you fifteen rubles for $1. Duty free in Moscow means only 90 percent more than you would pay in New York.

But somehow, it is not as it was in previous visits. There is the smile— not universal, granted. Gorby hasn't, in a couple of years, made Moscow into Tahiti. But there is exuberance in the air, and no wonder. It is absolutely predictable that in five years the Intourist hotel will actually know, without having to call the KGB, if Peter Samara is in residence, and if so, in which room. And—this is a prediction, and you may hold me to it—my guess is that five years from now someone will have called on the airport authorities with a sadist-detector in hand, relieving half of the personnel there of all their fun.

So, hang in there. But don't, don't go today to Moscow if you are expecting something like, oh, the Hilton hotel at Budapest. In Hungary, over a period of a decade, they let the free market come in slowly, on little cat feet, and already the land is bright.

A Place in the City
Private Clubs, September-October 1991

It is so with many New Yorkers. Your first regular job in the city and you swear you will commute daily. Better the train, even twice a day, than the expense and the dreariness of having to spend the night in New York, with your wife all alone in the country. That lasts for about, oh, three months. That is when your wife and you converge on the need for a little *pied-à-terre*, the French term almost universally used to suggest one bedroom, maybe a little working space, and a bath; yes, maybe a refrigerator; and, I suppose, an oven, just in case (inconceivable) you ever want to cook your own dinner. Ours was wonderful: one huge room on Thirty-Eighth Street, with twelve-foot-high ceilings, two handsome beds, one each on adjoining sides, then three beautiful pieces of furniture, latticed windows ten feet high looking into a grassy courtyard, noiselessly air-conditioned, and absolutely perfect—for about a year. You decide that there is a school in New York just right for your child, and this means massive expansion of the *pied-a-terre* to make room for one child, one nurse, one cook, one maid. That lasts for several years. Then one day she says that since we are spending as many as three nights a week in the city, she wants to get something "comfortable" for a home away from home. She has just finished seeing a truly comfortable *maisonette*—a ground-floor apartment attached to a condo building, with its separate entrance to the street, which (this is 1964) can be bought very reasonably. We confer with our bankers and end up occupying the same apartment in which Dag Hammarskjold lived (I was about to say before he died, but perhaps that is obvious). He was, of course, secretary general of the United Nations and needed to do a lot of entertaining, as for various reasons we'd need to do.

Fine, because (my wife having erased all previous traces from the apartment) it has one exquisite all-red study-library, in which twelve people can comfortably sit, and plot. A second living room in which fifty people can sit to listen to a musical concert, or to celebrate Christmas, or to roast that one-in-ten elections in which you are gratified by the result (my brother Jim was, so to speak, elected to the Senate in that room). And down a long hallway, into a very beautiful dining room with two round tables, each of which will seat eleven guests. There are appropriate kitchen and maids' quarters. Upstairs, one master bedroom, one tiny study, and one small bedroom. occupied by son when away from boarding school and in New York (like his parents, he preferred Stamford, CT, our home, about which he has written in *Architectural Digest*.)

My initial experience at our Ultimate Apartment was memorable. I had just run for mayor of New York, and written a book about my experiences. My brother, the future senator, had served as my campaign manager, and we were working in what would become the library when we began moving in the next day. My wife had banished us from the quarters in which she and I lived because she was packing up to move. I would spend my first night in the apartment alone, after Jim and I got through going over the manuscript.

That wasn't until 2:30 a.m. I said goodnight to him and walked wearily up the barren staircase to the bedroom, closed the door, turned on the makeshift lamp, stripped to my shorts and T-shirt—and stopped dead. There was no mistaking the sound. Footsteps. Heavy footsteps. Slowly climbing the staircase. I rushed to the door to lock it. But there was no lock. So, I trotted into the bathroom, shut that door, locked it, turned off the light, cursed myself for forgetting to turn off the light in the bedroom. and listened…I could now hear labored breathing.

What to do? I lifted my window as noiselessly as possible. There was a substantial ledge outside it allowing me to reach over one knee on the ledge, and tap lightly on my neighbor's window pane. Tapped again, harder. Still harder. No response. Below, one flight, there were cars whizzing by, an occasional truck crossing Park Avenue. I knew what I had to do. The Prisoner of Zenda was a great teacher.

My wife had equipped the bathroom with towels. and I took three of them and tied them together, making a ladder of sorts reaching down to jumping distance from the pavement. I tied the top end to the radiator and slowly let myself down. I made it, rushing to the corner where I opened the door of a cab stopped for a red light. The driver changed the color of his ethnic origin on seeing this semi-nude, youngish (thirty-nine) man enter his cab, but was relieved to hear his instructions: "Take me to the police."

That proved easy because there was a squad car only a block away. And it didn't hurt that we were only three months past an election in which I had been the candidate favored by the police because I had taken all the virtuous stands in respect to criminals. I quickly stuttered out the problem.

He was a man of action and barked into his radio phone. I told him that I absolutely required more clothing other than my shorts and T-shirt and could he please go just three blocks, and I'd snatch a raincoat from my wife. He drove me there, and I pressed on the buzzer until she appeared sleepily.

"What are you doing dressed that way?"

"Quiet! Give me a raincoat!"

"Are you quite mad?"

I managed an explanation, grabbed a coat and a key to the apartment (my own was in my pants, in the bedroom), and was back in the police car. On arriving at the apartment, I was feeling sorry for the intruder. He didn't have a chance. There were eight squad cars with searchlights, and the officers had their pistols drawn. You see, as the former home of the principal international diplomat on the world scene, our apartment carried, in police HQ, a packaged plan of action in the event there was a disturbance at that particular *maisonette*. The lieutenant asked me for the key to the heavy iron door, I handed it to him, the door was opened, and the police blared out an order to the intruder and then focused a huge searchlight into the corridor. Six armed policemen rushed in, followed by another six or eight. They fanned out with their beamy lights.

In a few minutes the entire place had been searched, including every cupboard and closet. Empty. But visible were grimy handprints at several points on the wall. There was nothing in the apartment to steal except my typewriter. And yes, it was missing. My visitor had come and gone.

The crisis was over, but six policemen felt they should keep me company in the event of a return of the invader. I said appreciatively that obviously he had got in only by reason of my brother's failure to shut the great door fully, which would not happen again. But they wanted to talk, and so I went to the refrigerator and got out some beer, and two hours later they were still talking about the awful, terrible, unspeakable record of the man who had been elected mayor, and how everything would have been different if only I had been elected, and let's drink to that, which we all did.

But it was daylight now, and they said, Well, they may as well get going, and I thanked them for the fifteenth time, and as we walked out I had a thought.

There was no way to get into the bathroom.

I had locked it. I would have to go back through the same passage I had come out from: the window. No problem, Mr. Buckley, no problem at all, whereupon three of the policemen assumed a kind of human ladder position, one man on top of the other, the third on top of him—useful in getting people in and out of windows when there is a fire. I was invited to walk up on their backs, which I did, reaching the ledge. Just before entering the window head first, the adjacent window, which had spurned me in my distress a few hours earlier, opened and a man's voice was heard, "Is this the way you always come home, Mr. Buckley?"

That was my introduction to our current New York *pied-à-terre*. It isn't home, never will be, but is something of a tribute to my wife's distinctive eye for interior pleasures. That dining room is blanketed with paintings by the renowned Robert Goodnough: very nearly a gallery, with its round marble tables and soft lights. The red room has oils and books, and a leopard skin, and a beautiful leather antique desk. The large living room is indescribable by an amateur but is arresting in its combination of style and comfort. There are beautiful oils there by Raymond de Botton of Spain, and Lorjou of France, and a grand piano that belonged to my wife's parents in Vancouver, a Bösendorfer on which great pianists have played. An interesting point here: noises from the streets afflict ground-floor apartments less than they do those on higher stories—say, the third, or fourth, or fifth floors. I guess this is because noise travels upward. I didn't do much with physics at school, but I can think of no other reason why we can listen to a harpsichord in that ground floor room without hearing any noise at all from outside.

So then, what are my conclusions? If you wish a comfortable place to spend those uncomfortable hours in which you need to live in New York City, and don't need a lot of bedrooms because you have only a single child, or your children are dispersed, buy an apartment previously owned by Dag Hammarskjöld, retain my wife as interior decorator, and be sure the door is locked when your guests leave. But just in cast, keep a little beer in the icebox.

Haute Boat
FYI, March 16, 1992

In the Tobago Cays on October 23, 1991, a stroke of lightning hit the middle of the five masts of *Club Med 1*, advertised as the "world's largest sailing ship" (and there are no dissenters). What happened?!

The hot electrical current tore down a cable and blew out four computer cards!
So?

So? Well, so several things. One of them is that the replacement cost of the cards is $12,000. Until the cards are back in (ten days later, the replacements haven't yet arrived), the officers on duty will need to attend to a little more detail than they were used to.

Is that something we need to worry about?

Well, come to think of it, no, not really. The extra work can easily be done on the bridge, using fewer fingers than you have in one hand—to depress this button and that one, which the computer would ordinarily have governed. The gentlemen on the bridge suffer only from the humiliation of it all: a windmill without wind, a vintage claret without a corkscrew. When the computer is working, any sudden increase in pressure against the ship's seven sails (they measure 8,970 square feet) is automatically weighed, and derivative instructions sent out to the ship's moving parts.

Explain, please.

A hard gust of wind generates pressure on the sails. The extent of that increase in pressure is measured, and the computer instructs the sheets, which are attached to the clews of the sails, to slacken off—spilling the incremental wind and thereby easing the tension. Simultaneously, the computer instructs the windward seawater ballast to ingest more water, while the leeward ballast chamber rushes to empty its supply of water. It is most terribly important to do all of this before the ship lists over more than two degrees, that being, on *Club Med 1*, the limit of official toleration. If the ship were to heel more than two degrees, passengers might notice that they were under sail, and that isn't really the idea, on the world's largest sailboat. So that everything described above happens within approximately three seconds. Without the control cards, the maneuvers, executed in response to finger-depressed buttons, might take as much as fifteen or even twenty seconds.

The visitor at the bridge reacts, "Miraculous! The passengers are certainly impressed by that, I can imagine!"

"The passengers," the officer replies with Gallic nonchalance, a) don't know that this is happening; b) wouldn't be interested if they were told; c) never know whether the sails are up or not; d) don't care; e) care mostly "zat zehr shood nat be no comossion."

"Why then do they bother to come to a sailing-cruising boat instead of to regular cruise liners?"

"Because ze sails arre romantique."

But there are other reasons for the sails. In the best of breezes, they will propel *Club Med 1* at nine knots, and this adds up, in the course of a year, to a reduced fuel consumption of 25 percent.

"Does the saving in fuel compensate for the cost of the sails and the rigging?"

"Not nearly."

This was the second week of the second Caribbean season of *Club Med 1*, a remarkable architectural achievement built at Le Havre at a cost of $100 million. The 617-foot megabark arrived in New York in October after a *gastronomique* crossing, Le Havre-Azores-New York. How management was able to make that trip more "gastronomic" than is routine aboard *Club Med 1* is difficult to imagine. The menu on Friday night: vegetable soup; duck liver from Périgord with a citrus fruit jelly; crispy vegetables light on vinaigrette sauce; "Meli-Melo" place, gambas, spiny lobsters, scallops; spaghetti with garlic; fillet of beef, sauce béarnaise; salad "Bagatelle": vegetables in cream sauce; cheese trolley; assortment of breads; pastry gourmet; sorbet of the day. And all of the above Four Seasons quality. The table wines, red (C+), white (B-), rosé (B), are on the house, in good French tradition. You can, of course, order special wines from the cellar—which does not rock more than two degrees.

From New York she cruises down to the Antilles to begin the winter season (October 15 to late May); at which point she returns to the western Mediterranean to do the same kind of thing, with Cannes as her home port. After dinner, every night, there is a musical spectacle, which is pretty spectacular when you consider that it is being executed by the same people who, during the day, teach you bridge, manicure your nails, lead the gym class, instruct you in sail-fishing, scuba diving, snorkeling, wait on cables, and give you massages. Thirty-two officers run the ship. Two hundred men and women serve the passengers (386, when the ship is sold out).

Utterly indulgent service, one quickly learns, is, along with the cuisine and the sporting life, the Club Med's proudest tradition. Any boat especially designed to heel not more than two degrees is obviously above all things user-friendly, and everyone from the janitors to the captain is either congenitally appealing and solicitous, or else has cultivated the habit of aiming to please, without, one hastens to note, that extreme unction that can make Oriental hospitality so cloying. And this notwithstanding that some of the young crew members are on duty eighteen hours a day. On the seventh day, all they need to do is discharge the lame duck passengers at different times of the day, depending on whether they are returning to New York (about one third), or to Paris (about one half), or to other destinations; render the entire boat spotless; take on seven days' supplies; and board the next set of passengers at 5:00 p.m.

The cabins are identical (with two larger, more expensive exceptions). They are advertised as the largest cabins on any sailing vessel, which isn't a difficult claim to make. They are 188 square feet, and include, of course, a complete bathroom (shower only). There are two large portholes only a little bit higher than eye level when you are sitting down, which, however, only one occupant can do: there is no chair for the second, who will need to stretch out on one of the beds. An ingeniously anchored television set can be turned toward the front of the room, to be seen while making up in front of the mirror, or toward the portholes, to be viewed while lying down on the bed. The regimen is interesting and not entirely satisfying. A single movie is selected every day on the English Channel, and when it finishes, it simply begins again. I had never seen *Raiders of the Lost Ark*, but now I have seen about four-tenths of it: one-tenth at breakfast time, one-tenth before the afternoon nap, one-tenth after the gym workout before dinner, one-tenth before falling to sleep. (One day I will catch the missing segments, maybe on a future trip aboard *Club Med 1*.) A second channel gives you continuous sea-scene allurements, specializing in dolphins, and water skiers, and sailing boats.

It should be noted that the hours are wonderfully latitudinarian aboard *Club Med 1*. Maybe you stayed up late, cavorting in the underground disco, or breaking the bank at the casino? Or maybe you are an early riser? Either way, breakfast is austere if you want it at 5:00 a.m.—you will need to settle for hot croissants and coffee and juice. If you manage to sleep until seven, you can have just about anything you would want to eat in the morning, and a whole lot you almost certainly won't want to eat, like exotic underwater life. If you sleep in later than 11:00, which is when the breakfast room closes, you will have to continue hunger until 12:30, when lunch begins. Or you can order a light meal in your cabin—twenty-four hours per day.

Amateur economists wonder how the company can hope to amortize its $100 million investment, let alone the $150 million investment in the sister ship scheduled for duty in Tahiti. At $1,690–$2,390 per passenger per week (depending on the deck in particular cruise), one figures the first 200 passengers' fees are going in just to pay the interest costs. It's nice to sense the worry the passengers feel for the boat, so instant is the loyalty to it: there was much more talk about Club Med's deficit than about the national deficit. It would be quite awful if the whole thing did not pan out. Unthinkable!

But the cruising business is booming, and one must suppose the *Club Med 1* will thrive. A week aboard reminds you how relaxing it can be to travel from Fort-de-Frances in Martinique—back to Fort-de-Frances in Martinique—in seven easygoing days with stops, some as long as fifteen hours, at St. Lucia, Bequia, Barbados, Tobago, Mayreau, and Sandy Island. It is profane to roll off the names of such islands, as though they were subway stops. They include beaches poor Gauguin never saw, palm trees that drive spooning apples to the altar, clear blue-green waters that mistake themselves for your portable aquarium. These are among the loveliest islands in the world. *Tout court*, as they might put it, on board.

Perfect? Not for those with demanding, perhaps eccentric tastes. For instance, those few who don't like beach life but who like total immersion other than in swimming pools. They would welcome some kind of an off-boat raft that would allow the passenger to jump into the sea from the water-level transom platform and swim over to an anchored craft, avoiding the water-skiers and scuba divers whose omnipresence now causes management to forbid M. Hulot his casual dip and the sea from the mother vessel.

But there are no other frustrations. The cornucopia continually surprises, as when on Day Four one comes upon a beach privately leased by Club Med, established there with large, thatched parasols, and the roasted lobster and white wine are brought to you by the service crew while you watch your fellow passengers skiffing about on catamarans and Sunfish, and idle snorkelers taking it all in dorsally, worrying only about *Club Med 1*'s responsibility for their swelling girths; and you are grateful that the delivery of the ship's newspaper is eccentric, so that you just might not get word right away of the latest eruption, political or natural; and then the cost of telephoning from *Club Med 1* is just high enough to discourage even the most conscientious colleagues back in the office from distracting you from the pressingly important matters at hand.

Sailing in the Wake of Christopher Columbus
Primary Color, April 1, 1992

So, what was it like for Columbus when he set sail? What makes that question so sempiternally alluring is this: we'll never know. One prominent historian shrewdly remarked that the quintessence of the heroism of Columbus wasn't the prospect of endless days and nights at sea, the struggle with mutinous sentiments aboard or with wild savages on land. It lay in his simple act of weighing anchor in Gomera on that sixth day of September 1492.

The passage (Spain to the Canaries) was not a big deal in 1492—the islands had been discovered at the turn of the century and were now being colonized. The dramatic moment came when Columbus pulled up his anchor and headed for the unknown.

It is hard to imagine that he felt about that apocalyptic event as prosaically as he wrote about it. What he set down in his journal was: "Shortly before noon I sailed from the harbor at Gomera and set my course to the west...I sailed all day and night with very little wind; by morning I find myself between Gomera and Tenerife." Those simple, declarative phrases hardly come in with the thunder and lightning one thinks of as appropriate to a launch that would discover a new world. Indeed, the New World.

What was it like?

A few friends and I who have sailed together in the past resolved to explore the point, with rigorous determination not to delude ourselves into presuming that we were undertaking anything like a re-creation of the historic crossing of the Admiral of the Ocean Sea, as Ferdinand and Isabella agreed Columbus should be titled upon completion of his mission (in the unlikely event that he did complete it).

On that November morning in 1990 setting out from Lisbon we were aboard a seventy-one-foot ketch called *Sealestial*, chartered for this occasion as twice before we had chartered it to cross the Pacific, and to cross the Atlantic (eastward). There were six of us who did the sailing and the navigating, four who did the maintenance.

By contrast, Columbus had three well-founded boats…eighty- to ninety-feet long (they were called caravels), each one carrying forty to fifty sailor-soldiers and provisions for three months at sea, with plenty of mirrors and beads for the natives. No charts, no radio, no loan, no GPS, no sextant (by modern standards), no chronometer.

Our vessel had everything on board designed to cope with every situation imaginable, except those situations we actually ran into (the sails and much of the rigging came apart, the electronics didn't work, the water all but ran out); yet, by modern standards, ours was a routine passage, about as remarkable as a scenic bus ride, San Francisco to Los Angeles.

What made it otherwise special was the sensation that came to us inescapably within minutes of setting out. It was this, that although our vessel and its facilities were very different from the *Santa María* commanded by Christopher Columbus, all else was the same. That is authentic re-creation.

Nothing has happened in five hundred years that seriously affects the winds, or the seas, or the clouds, or the stars that soothe and torment the sailor making his way across the Atlantic Ocean, following the trade winds. The speeds at which we traveled were comparable to his, except that when there were calms, we had the option to turn on a motor. Columbus could only sit. Patiently?

Don't you see, in those days the nervous metabolism was very different. If today what we see on a television channel for fifty-six seconds bores us, we flick over to another channel, and after that to a third, or fourth, or fifth. Columbus didn't know whether this afternoon's calm would last for one hour, for one day, or for four days. He and his crew sat, or paced the deck. For distraction, they ate and they chatted, and they plotted and they prayed, and they gambled.

We? We turned on the motor, activated the autopilot, and we moved along, playing chess and writing in our journals, reading books, watching movies, eating gourmet meals, and rat-tat-tatting occasional messages home with our "Comsat" units, stitching together torn sails, and listening to the BBC.

All of this so different—and yet we came away from it all with some idea of what it had been like for Columbus.

There were, for instance, the storms—we both had them. But, also, there were the prevailing westerly trade winds, on which Columbus successfully (and we, following his example) counted. He was exploring a route that would become the great superhighway of all ships heading from Europe to the Americas for the next three hundred years.

To follow the route, you needed to travel about seven hundred miles to the Canaries, and from there three thousand miles south-southwest to the easternmost islands of the Caribbean, and then another thousand miles to Florida. Between the Canaries and the Caribbean lies—nothing. We chose to put in at the closest spot of land, the island of Barbados. Columbus passed north of it, hitting one of three Bahamian islands (the question of exactly which one is hotly disputed) in the neighborhood of Salvador.

He arrived thirty-six days after leaving Gomera, and it is seriously surmised that if he had taken as much as one day more, he'd have lost his command to the mutineers. If we had been one day later, I'd have been thrown overboard, together with my sextants, my almanac, my tables, and my plotting sheets.

There isn't any sense in which by undertaking such a passage you are playacting the vanity that you are a true son of Christopher Columbus.

Contrast the men and women who a generation ago set out aboard a raft of sorts called *Kon Tiki*, attempting more or less exactly to duplicate what they imagined to be the route and the circumstances of the aboriginals who traveled from South America to the Asian islands. Theirs was an exact effort at recreating; their purpose, validate a (shaky) thesis, namely that the historical movement of human beings into Polynesia was counterclockwise [sic], from mainland Asia up to Alaska, down the North American continent to Peru or thereabouts, and then westward.

A sailing journey in a modern craft with up-to-date instruments from Europe to the Caribbean can be done without any sense of a shared adventure with the man who did it first, even as you don't have to think about Lewis and Clark to take a trailer trip from St. Louis across the Continental Divide to the Pacific Ocean.

On the other hand, if you undertake a transatlantic sail along Columbus's route you will be tempted to say to yourself from time to time—looking out over the resolute blue-green seas, up at the playful clouds, flirtatious today, menacing tomorrow; plunging through nights sometimes so dark you could bump into a new continent without any warning, sometimes ambered by the moon, like sailing over a lit-up baseball stadium—you will say to yourself, "So it was for Columbus and his men. Just like this."

In a word, you get some sense of the highs—and some of the lows—experienced by the men who did it for the first time. The good news is that, as with most human experiences, what sticks in the memory is the highs.

Here is how Columbus's biographer described the good days experienced by Columbus. Samuel Eliot Morison was a professor at Harvard, an admiral in the navy, the historian of our naval adventures in the Second World War, and a yachtsman who traced in his own vessel the voyage of Columbus shortly before the war, to write the book that would win a Pulitzer Prize, *Admiral of the Ocean Sea*. Thus, he could write:

> This leg (when he hit the trade winds) of the voyage must have been a most pure delight to the admiral and his men. The fleet sped along, making an average day's run of 183 miles. In the trades, vessels always roll a good deal, but the steady and favorable wind singing in the rigging, the sapphire white-capped sea, the rush of great waters alongside, and the endless succession of fat, puffy trade-wind clouds, lift up a seaman's spirits and make him want to shout and sing. For days on end the sheets and braces needed no attention. On moonless nights the sails stand out black against the star-studded firmament; and as the ship makes her southing, every night new stars and constellations appear. Most of his men were new to southern waters, and one can imagine them, as in Heredia's sonnet, leaning entranced over the bulwarks of the white caravel and seeing in the phosphorescent sea an augury of the gold of the Indies.

We would have all those sensations, and one has to suppose that the skies today, and the seas, are as they were then; and, of course, the stars, those fixed coordinates of a restless world. We had all that, and we had also a storm which after thirty-six hours left us limp with misery, lost, exhausted, wet, demoralized; but then, at sea, when this happens you experience also the balm that comes after, as the sun shines, the wind rights itself, the gear is repaired, the stars relocate you, and soon the pleasures on board are full-throated.

It is a fine adventure, such a crossing under sail, even if it is not to be confused with the original. You must travel with people who a) know how to sail (at least four of them); b) how to navigate (at least two); c) how to cope with emergencies (one or two); and d) how to cope with each other (everyone).

Years ago, the physicist Oppenheimer described the nuclear age, with America and the Soviet Union glaring at each other, as "two scorpions in a bottle." It is common lore in the seafaring community of ocean racers that any latent disharmony tends to fester aboard a small boat, when one person's innocent affectation can evolve as an affront at the end of the second week, an armed assault at the end of the third. Choose your companions with much attention to dispositional harmony, in good times and bad.

Bear in mind that it is more than modern man can easily do to learn to go from the rap-tempos of modern nonstop distractions, to the unsubornable tempos of the sea and the tides and winds who know not the hysterical volatilities of contemporary life and can no more be manipulated to suit your fancy than grass can be got to grow more or less quickly, to indulge madame's inclinations.

So...make an effort. Bring along a VCR—hardly an extravagance in a venture as extravagant to begin with as chartering a sailboat to take you across the Atlantic Ocean. And though you'll find that all of you are busier than ever you thought you'd be (sailboats require a lot of attention, for all that they gave the impression of autonomous passivity), subtly inquire whether your companions can also be happy reading a book.

Above all, know that you are setting out with men and women—it doesn't matter how young (well, no, I'd say sixteen is minimum) or how old (well, not too old: burials at sea are inconvenient). But no one aboard should be so jaded as to be dulled to the feel of the seas, the smell of the wind, the divine festoonery of the clouds and the stars, because for most amateurs the experience is once in a lifetime. Columbus did it four times. But you see, Columbus is what we were quietly celebrating, never presuming to imitate him.

The Skirt of Paradise

Condé Nast Traveler, May 1992

As with Mr. Nixon when asked in China what he thought of the Great Wall ("You have to conclude that this is a great wall..."), I have to conclude that these are a great group of islands. It defeats my understanding that nobody told me ten years ago about the set of islands that lies north of Venezuela. It is all the more galling to have cruised by them as I have done only now, as though they had never before entered my life when, in fact, I had been to two of them. Not, as it happens, on a sailboat; and this does, really, make a difference. On the *QE2* we stopped a few years ago for a few hours in Curaçao—long enough just to get a whiff of the place and a beautiful set of 7x50 binoculars with inbuilt compass for 200 bucks. And I had been to "Roques" (Islas Los Roques), moored offshore on a fifty-foot Chris Craft for sunbathing and snorkeling. But that was no way to explore.

This time, six of us elected to venture into the Venezuelan islands by sailboat—to be precise, a seventy-one-foot sailing ketch with two small staterooms (each had an upper and a lower bunk) and a master (or master-ish) cabin, whose distinctive feature was a deep one-man couch as comfortable as anything you have at home. On that ketch (*Sealestial,*) with a decent wind you can travel at nine-plus knots; under power, at seven knots. A comparable powerboat—that is, one that can comfortably accommodate six people—would cruise at twelve or thirteen knots, which is the good news, the less than good news being that a powerboat wobbles more than a sailboat, which in most winds is kept more or less steadily unbalanced. This is preferable to having to lean first to the right, then to the left, all day long, not counting when you lean over the side.

None of us had ever sailed off Venezuela, and we were especially beholden to Donald Street's *Cruising Guide to the Eastern Caribbean*. It was

Street who had confirmed our intuition that the Antilles, stretching from Puerto Rico in a 500-mile crescent—the Virgin Islands, the Leeward Islands, and the Grenadines—have become relatively crowded with the discovery of boat chartering. Besides, after twenty-five seasons of Caribbean cruising I had developed a curiosity for fresh exposures, and one day, quite by accident, I heard someone raving about "the offshore islands in Venezuela."

Keith the novelist and his wife, Laurie the actress, hadn't ever cruised before on a sailboat. Nor had Christopher the critic or his wife, Natalie the fuzzbuster (she is writing a book at the expense of J. Edgar Hoover), save for a brief cruise off the Maine coast twenty-five years ago, whereas my Pat has endured a great deal with me. She stops at accompanying me on my ocean passages, a diplomatic way of saying that she would rather die than cross the ocean on a sailboat and is unfailingly surprised when others manage this ("If you survive this, I'll kill you," she told me the first time I announced my intention to cross the Atlantic). But my companions were in an acquiescent frame of mind even when, on boarding the *Sealestial,* I told them that just to get started on the Venezuelan scene we'd have to strike out over a hundred miles. Captain Martin said he didn't mind at all sailing overnight; neither did the mate. Christopher and Keith and I volunteered to take watches. We would leave at 11:00 p.m., I said: No point in approaching Los Testigos too early. Isn't there a light to warn you against the islands' shoals? Yes, there is, but it does not follow that the light is functioning. Venezuela has its own priorities.

We slid by Los Testigos just after daybreak, passed by the island of Margarita, thirty miles farther, and put down only just before dinner at Isla Coche, about which one can safely say, forget it, unless it is convenient. And as much can be said about the Peninsula of Araya, thirty miles south, though the huge fort in Araya, completed in 1665 to defend one of the largest salt-gathering operations in the world, is bulkily impressive, even though it was shattered (by a hurricane) a century later.

You have the feeling, when you sail purposely in a premeditated direction, that something special lies ahead. On night four we nosed down to Puerto la Cruz, an explosively active oil port, where we submitted to Venezuelan bureaucracy, which is amiable, disoriented, and resolutely scattered about, thus customs being at one end of the city, immigration at the other, and the port authority in a well-concealed enclave somewhere in between.

It's odd, but I have found it so a hundred times when cruising: after three or four hours ashore, you find you can't wait to get back to your little sanctuary. And now, having got back, I suggested that we pull away from the dock and throw out the hook in the harbor, after which we swam, ate, and drank, and watched *Watch on the Rhine* on our VCR. After that, we would take another overnight sail, to La Tortuga, an offshore island about fifty miles away.

It was midmorning when we approached the island, bound for the northeastern point, Punta Delegada. About four miles away you begin to see a most striking blue, a light blue with a yellowish base, generating a rousing turquoise so compelling and so seductive that one needs to concentrate on the course to keep from heading toward it. We rounded the point and came in toward the sandy crescent, a beach a mile long, the shallow water its own shade of blue-green, and behind the sandbar and scrub the blue we had spoiled from such a distance, fingering the sandbar around. It is at La Tortuga that, ideally, a cruise should begin of the Venezuelan islands, which stretch into the ABCs (Aruba, Bonaire, Curaçao).

After lunch we explored the structures on the beach. There are three of them, all unoccupied. They exist, presumably, for the odd fishermen: utility havens. But the airstrip was visible, and lo! there was a Cessna 172 on it, and one minute later we found ourselves talking with a European in his mid-sixties who wore a straw fedora and was accompanied by a darkskinned woman of comely features and conformation. We spoke in Spanish until we ascertained, more or less at the same moment, that it was neither his nor my native tongue. A man of affairs, who had flown in to have a picnic with his lady and would return within the half hour to the Caracas airport, an hour's flight. "Who owns this paradise?" I asked.

The state.

Can people build houses here?

Only with permission, which they will not get.

Why aren't there more cruisers here?

There is an abundance of islands like this.

What is important—our Austrian friend showed beads of earnest sweat in telling us this—is to stay away from the coastline. "The coastline is dirty, dirty, dirty, garbage, refuse," His nose wrinkled in pain. "Where are you headed?" I had intended to head back to the mainland to do some coastal cruising. I changed my mind on the spot. "To Los Roques." He smiled.

We set sail toward the west—the trade winds are from the east and northeast—slipping away a bit from the island to accommodate the wind, then jibbing toward our destination. We had the sails down and were moving at three knots to round up into the little anchorage at eastern Tortuguilla.

And there we were, once again in the snugness of what felt like our own personal little aerie, never mind that it was at sea level, not on an Alpine peak. Again, a beach, only miniature in size this one, backed by stone that seemed to wish to cradle you. The moon was a few days old now and winked down at us as we swam and listened to music and reveled in Portuguese wine we had picked up at Funchal a month earlier. The men were fatalistically reconciled to another overnight sail, with watch duty. And the ladies, who had been grumbling, awoke to a glorious surprise.

When you approach Islas Los Roques from the east, you head for the southern tip, slide into a narrow entrance, and from there face twelve miles of northerly work, a long line of reefs on your right protecting you from any ravages of the sea, and on your left more reefs, only more elevated. You have a fairway ranging from fifty to one hundred yards wide. Immediately on your right you find an ex-cargo vessel that had obviously mistaken the wrong light for the right one and has sat there for several years, warning all passersby of the high penalty for carelessness. As the sun rises higher, the blues are once again illuminated and varied. Just at about noon you round past the tiny village into a shoal area with one of those splendid beaches. It was here that, ten years ago, Pat and I spent the weekend, and it is fine to note that no Chernobyl has happened to it since then. It might have looked exactly the same 500 years ago when Columbus came across the Atlantic for the first time. The utter vainglory of that much blue and chalk yellow. We were dazzled.

Until we examined the little harbor that quite by chance I elected to go to for the night, intending to make a little westerly progress. Imagine a horseshoe: the right leg, palm trees apparently rising from the sea itself; the bight, another perfect beach, maybe 125 feet long. And the left leg, fifty yards of what seemed like, and sounded like, a dozen streams pouring at night into our little harbor and rushing, the following morning, out of it. Reefs just barely covered by the water, which whirls through the interstices and sounds like an incubating Niagara Falls. There are heavenly places to stop in the Grenadines, but I nominate Sarqui in Los Roques.

Our westerly course took us to the Islas de Aves, once again semi-deserted—nubile little atoll-like beaches with surrounding reefs. There are two, twelve miles apart, Aves de Barlovento (Windward Birds) and Aves de Sotovento (Leeward Birds). There is a little Coast Guard station at the latter, and a he-man dinghy approaches you—would you like to trade a few cigarettes and Coca-Cola for a ten-pound grouper? (Answer: yes.) We set the spinnaker and ran the last thirty miles out of Venezuelan waters to Bonaire, which is the first of the Dutch islands, the "B" of ABC. Docking there is difficult because the harbor is so sheer—you go from depths of one-hundred feet to eight feet in the space of a few yards. But...you make out. Bonaire is not for cruising but is thought by some to be among the best places in the world for diving, and, of course, for snorkeling. A week after our return, one voyager in Bonaire reported in the *New York Times* a "dizzying profusion of marine life, all of it easily accessible not only by boat but also right off the shore," which is perhaps the good news, given the profusion of species. And then if, *par impossible*, you have tired of boat life, there is a casino there, and some of the cruise ships stop by.

As they do, most hectically, in Curaçao. Coming in there, after so much wilderness, gives the impression of moving from atoll to atoll to atoll, turning a corner and suddenly finding yourself in Walt Disney World. The bridge that needs to rotate to let you into the harbor is one long stretch of lighted festoonery, to get you into the spirit of this free port.

Opposite from where you dock is one of the *Princesses*. The next morning the Royal Viking *Sun* idles in, and you can't spot the name of the third passenger liner around the corner. There is the usual hectic four hours of shopping and paper clearing. We expected to spend the final night there in the harbor, but then one of those things happened that changes itineraries even as ours had been changed by the Graham Greene character in La Tortuga. This was a native sailor who came up to me—he had read one or two of my sailing books—and asked where we were spending the night. "—But why don't you go to Spanish Water?"

That is just ten miles southeast. If you aren't looking for the entrance, you aren't going to find it easily. In that respect it is like English Harbour in Antigua. Perfect for protection from stray pirates. You snake your way in and right away there is a beach, only this one is full of people and full of cast-off bikini tops. A half mile up is a pretty little yacht club, with mountains of green on either side, like New England in the summer. Where we anchored, we had perfect protection and the lights of a respectful distance, and the beach, now deserted, was within reach. The moon elected that night to stay with us through the evening, and ahead of our anchor, rising thirty feet as if to comply with a decorator's plan, a little navigating light, an eight-second flasher.

It is certain to happen that the Venezuelan islands will be exploited, but not spoiled, as they become protected nature centers. The trick is to get quickly to La Tortuga. To do this one you need a yacht broker. Offer him/her a deal: you and your friends will arrange for the boat at a marina in La Guaira, a half hour from the airport that serves Caracas. Perhaps a bareboat, though it is less likely you will find one until the demand grows. If not, a Venezuelan crewed boat. Dine aboard, then take off after dinner for La Tortuga and spend ten days, yielding up the boat in Curaçao, at Spanish Water. The boat's owner can worry about getting his vessel back to the Antilles. Or back, simply, to La Guaira, perhaps for another charter. Let the broker worry about that. Bring along your best friend, and he/she will plight his/her eternal troth. Bring along your worst enemy, and he/she will become your best friend.

Finale

Cruising World, October 1992

It was Tony, reaching around the lee strap to nudge me on the shoulder. Some sailors need protracted jolting to wake up for their watch. I don't, though I found myself grunting, "What time is it?"

"Six o'clock."

I had time for a star sight, though not much time. Getting dressed on a boat in the morning in balmy weather is an operation that consumes about three-and-a-half minutes if it is your habit as it is mine, to do your bathing in the late afternoon. That three and a half minutes even includes brushing your teeth.

By 6:05 (unbreakable force of habit checking the logbook comes before even a hop up to the cockpit to take in the general situation) I was staring at the page for December 4. At 24:00, before turning in, I myself had written: Log 2533, LOP on Sirius plotted. Fifty-eight miles to Barbados. At 01:00 I had written: DR plotted. Sunrise at 7:04. WAKE UP WFB AT 6AM. Light characteristics in Barbados: Fl 15s. 21m.

The Barbados light is supposedly visible twenty-one miles away when it is totally dark. It flashes a white light every fifteen seconds. The only log entry between then and now had been by Tony: 05:30 Course 270 Speed 8.1. Log 2580.

I went up on deck. The moon was very full, lighting up the horizon so much as to make star sights difficult. The wind was fresh and warm without being humid and my friends were taking turns with the binoculars. scanning west in hopes of seeing the Barbados light. I think of Columbus, and the grandiloquent sentences of Samuel Eliot Morison when he evoked the tension on that great night almost five hundred years before.

Anyone who has come onto the land under sail at night from an uncertain position knows how tense the atmosphere aboard ship can be. And this night of October 11-12 was one big with destiny for the human race, the most momentous ever experienced aboard any ship in any sea.

For us it would be momentous only if Barbados did not lie ahead.

The Spanish sovereigns had offered a substantial purse to the first sailor who spotted...the Indies, as Columbus thought them to be. And Columbus was already one week late, by his own reckoning and his journal expressed near certainty that one more day without a landfall would kindle the mutiny he had only just succeeded in quelling two days before. Morison imagines the scene:

Lookouts on the forecastles and in the round-tops talking low to each other...*Hear anything? Sounds like breakers to me—nothing but the bow wave you fool—I tell you we won't sight land till Saturday, I dreamt it, and my dreams—you and your dreams, here's a hundred maravedis says we raise it by daylight...* They tell each other how they would have conducted the fleet—*The Old Man should never have set the spritsail, she'll run her bow under—if he'd asked my advice, and I was making my third voyage when he was playing in the streets of Genoa, I'd have told him...* Under such circumstances, with everyone's nerves taut as the weather braces, there was almost certain to be a false alarm of land.

An hour before moonrise, at 10 p.m., it came. Columbus, standing on the stern castle, thought he saw a light, "so uncertain a thing that he did not wish to declare that it was land," (the words are those of Las Casas, who sailed with Columbus) but called Pedro Gutiérrez to have a look, and he thought he saw it, too. Rodrigo Sánchez was then appealed to, "but he saw nothing because he was not in a position where he could see anything"...The light, Columbus said, "was like a little wax candle rising and falling," and he saw it only once or twice after speaking to Gutiérrez.

Admiral Morison has great sport with his withering exploration of what the light was that Columbus had seen:

What was this feeble light resembling a wax candle rising and falling, which Columbus admits that only a few besides himself ever saw? It cannot have been a fire or other light on San Salvador, or any other island; for, as the real landfall four hours later proves, the fleet at 10 p.m. was at least thirty-five miles offshore. The 400,000-candlepower light now on San Salvador, 170 feet above sea level, is not visible nearly so far. One writer has advanced the theory that the light was made by Indians torching for fish. But Indians do not go fishing in 3,000 fathoms of water thirty-five miles offshore at night in a gale of wind. The sentimental school of thought would have this light supernatural, sent by the Almighty to guide and encourage Columbus; but of all moments in the voyage, this is the one when he least needed encouragement, and he had laid his course straight for the nearest land. I agree heartily with Admiral Murdock, "the light was due to the imagination of Columbus, wrought up to a high pitch by the numerous signs of land encountered that day." Anyone who has had much experience trying to make night landfalls with a sea running knows how easy it is to be deceived, especially when you are very anxious to pick up a light. Often two or three shipmates will agree that they see "it," then "it" disappears, and you realize that it was just another illusion.

Admiral Morison will not himself let us see land: not quite yet. The great moment requires full histrionic development:

At 2 a.m. October 12 the moon, past full, was riding about seventy degrees high over Orion on the port quarter, just the position to illuminate anything ahead of the ships. Jupiter was rising in the east; Saturn had just set, and Deneb was nearing the western horizon, toward which all waking eyes were directed. There hung the Square of Pegasus, and a little higher and to the northward, Cassiopeia's Chair. The Guards of Polaris, at fifteen degrees beyond "feels" told the pilots that it was two hours after midnight. On sped the three ships, *Pinta* in the lead, their sails silver in the moonlight. A brave trade wind is blowing and the caravels are rolling, plunging, and throwing spray as they cut down the last invisible barrier between the Old World and the New. Only a few moments now, and an era that began in remotest antiquity will end.

Rodrigo de Triana, lookout on *Pinta's* forecastle, sees something like a white sand cliff gleaming in the moonlight on the western horizon, then another, and a dark line of land connecting them. "*Tierra! Tierra!*" he shouts, and this time land it is.

I decided to shoot Jupiter. A line of position on it would run roughly east-west, and reassure me that I was headed toward the island, not north or south of it.

0650 Star (planet) sight plotted.

No more plotting sheets. I was now drawing the sight line directly on the sea chart, the left half of which contained the island of Barbados. We were, I figured—*eight* miles from shore.

"*Land ho*!" It was Allan, and a half minute after the words rang out, the cockpit was crowded.

I climbed the companionway, affecting total complacency. Good Bill Draper shouted out: "Three cheers for the navigator." Oh dear, what a sublime moment.

Calling American Airlines, Are You There?

November 25, 1993

It was a very nice Thanksgiving ornament, the telephone call from the president of the United States respectively to the head of American Airlines and to the head of the striking union. The president got them both to agree to submit their cases to binding arbitration. And then the trumpets sounded, and the airplanes sped off, and the public focuses on other problems.

Robert Crandall, the head of American, put it this way to an inquiring reporter. Bill Clinton "is the elected leader of the country. For any citizen or any company or any union to say, 'No, I won't do that' to the president requires an awfully good reason."

In fact, Crandall had an awfully good reason for saying "no" to the president. He might even have said: "Tell you what, chief. You give me back the money I'm going to be paying in extra gas tax, I'll turn it over to the attendants, and we'll fly!"

Now Robert Crandall is a tough *hombre*, and it is hard to criticize the airline industry for seeking the services of tough executives. Crandall has gone so far as to say that he would "never again" buy another airplane. What he was saying, in a profile published in the *New York Times* a few months ago, was that he can't see how the airlines can make money. And no industry that can't make money can continue to exist unless it is taken over by the government.

The classic relationship then becomes, of course, an employee group that knows that there is no bottom to the pockets of the owner, and accordingly the demands are exorbitant, and the waste inordinate. Air France spends 40 percent per passenger mile more than British Airways, the difference between them being that British Airways was privatized under Margaret Thatcher and needs now to make its own way.

If my arithmetic is correct, during the past ten years the airlines made a profit in 1984, 1985, 1987, 1988, and 1989 amounting to $4.095 billion. But in the other five years in the decade, the airlines lost $11.227 billion. And last year's was the heaviest loss: $4.028 billion.

That kind of pressure becomes quite simply unendurable, and what Crandall was saying, when he said he'd never again buy another plane, was to the effect that ten years from now, American Airlines may be a company engaged in manufacturing microchips, even as Chock Full o'Nuts is one of the few restaurant chains in which you can't get nuts.

That is one alternative, to swing into another business. A second alternative is to go the way of the new airlines, Southwest Airlines being the flashy prototype. These are the so-called no-frills carriers, and their specialty is to get an airplane to commute from one city to another, back and forth: no food, spare treatment, cheap fares.

Such service is useful if your needs are, say, to travel frequently between Phoenix and San Francisco. If you live in Sioux City, IA, you will have awakened in recent days to discover that the straitened condition of the airlines has left you without a single jet plane flying out of the city. "It's a real competitive disadvantage to us," complains Sioux City's mayor, understandably.

The cost of personnel to the airlines is 36 percent of their entire bill. The second highest item is less than one-half that—16 percent for fuel. Maintenance costs, aircraft leasing, food, and interest come in respectively at 12 percent, 11 percent, 4 percent, and 3 percent.

Now when arbitration was first suggested to Crandall, he said no, giving as the reason for it that it is inevitably the habit of arbitrators to look at the claims of one party, which are A, of the second party, which are Z, and come up, after much deliberation, with a finding of M.

But halfway between what the attendants want and what American Airlines wants has got to be closer to A than to Z, not equidistant, because the industry is ailing and something needs to be done about it. It is all very well to receive a call from the White House, but the cost of accepting the suggestion is likely to confront American with an insurmountable psychological load.

There is an ineluctability in the marketplace that does not respond to presidential calls. It would be nice if Clinton called every passenger on American Airlines to ask us please to contribute an extra $10 every time we fly in order to pull AA out of its hole.

But the passengers are looking for cheaper ways to travel, and as long as they hold out, something has to cave. American can't fly its routes spending less on fuel, or on maintenance, or on interest, or on airplane leasing. Maybe it should give up food, which would relieve the attendants of a burden. But then everybody would fly United.

Mr. James in Motion
Review of *Henry James: Collected Travel Writings* by Henry James
New York Times Book Review, December 12, 1993

It fair takes your breath away. Page after page, chapter after chapter; cities, towns, villages, churches, monuments, in country after country, described and probed by a belletrist with a mighty, enchanted *caduceus* in hand. He uses it to crown in elaborate liturgical ceremony the glories of man and nature, but also to squirt ice water on those aspects of the world and its inhabitants that are not, well, not according to Henry James. And, manifestly, he has all the time in the world at his disposal.

But then what accumulates is more than most readers have time for, even though we must all marvel at what we read. In 1897, when in his mid-fifties, Henry James complained of soreness in his wrist. This can hardly surprise us. (He thenceforward dictated to a secretary.) In 1909, he burned forty years' worth of letters and papers, and one can't seriously suppose that he found the time to reread them before burning them—not at the pace at which he wrote, and in the hours left over from his work. A year later, he spoke of having had "a sort of nervous breakdown." Might this have been a reaction to the consuming demands of his creative curiosity? Five years after that, he decided to make his expatriation official and so became a British subject. The following year, in 1916, he was dead, at seventy-two. A prodigious talent, and a most industrious artisan. Perhaps his biographer, Leon Edel, has calculated the size of his total output. The Library of America's two tightly formatted volumes of his *Collected Travel Writings* (*Great Britain and America* and *The Continent*) I estimate at about three quarters of a million words. Approximately the size of a nine-hundred-page issue of *Time* magazine, back when *Time* printed mostly text.

He was very famous, though not very rich. (Edith Wharton sneaked a few thousand pounds into his bank account.) He was the gregarious bachelor, fiercely conventional, who recorded that he had dined out 105 times in one London social season. During the Civil War, when he was studying law at Harvard, he grew a beard. When he was fifty-seven, he got rid of it, because it had turned white. He was close to his siblings; his brother William, the preeminent philosopher, was as famous as he. He spent time with Flaubert, Zola, Stevenson, Maupassant, Conrad, Browning, Kipling, Shaw, and Wells, and wrote enduring novels, including *The Wings of the Dove, The Portrait of a Lady,* and *The Ambassadors.* As a gift to celebrate his seventieth birthday, his friends gave him his portrait, done by Sargent. King George V gave him the Order of Merit, an award reserved for the very few, the mightiest in talent and achievement. His novels transformed the model, with their stream of consciousness and their literary *hauteur*—as much so as, a generation later, Hemingway's would do, in a very different mode.

What runs through the mind, then, of the reader of these travel pieces? Two things. The first is that nobody, except for Eagle Scouts in graduate schools, is going to read the entire text. The second? You can close your eyes and open either volume at any page and find yourself reading prose so resplendent it will sweep you off your feet. Yet after a while, after a long while, you will recognize that, really, you have to come down to earth because there are so many other things to do. And besides, if you stay with him for too long, in that engrossing, scented, colored, brilliant, absorbing world, you feel strung out, feel something like hanging moss.

For instance? In his incessant travels, one day he leaves Italy to go to Germany. Henry James does not gad about the world with his mind shut or his pen locked in his drawer. As he once put it, "I have it on my conscience to make a note of my excursion." So how does one square things with one's conscience upon traveling to Germany from Italy? One ruminates on the differences between the two countries. Read how Henry James does it, and abandon any hope of competing with him:

"A few weeks ago I left Italy in that really demoralized condition into which Italy throws those confiding spirits who give her unlimited leave to please them. Beauty, I had come to believe, was an exclusively Italian possession, the human face was not worth looking at unless redeemed by an Italian smile, nor the human voice worth listening to unless attuned to Italian vowels. A landscape was no landscape without vines festooned to fig-trees swaying in a hot wind—a mountain a hideous excrescence unless melting off into a Tuscan haze. But now that I have absolutely exchanged vines and figs for corn and cabbages, and violet Apennines for the homely plain of Frankfurt, and liquids for gutturals, and the Italian smile for the German grin, I am much better contented than I could have ventured to expect. I have shifted my standard of beauty, but it still commands a glimpse of the divine idea."

As one might put it today, "*That's* what I call being transported!"

James's little paeans are not easily duplicated, even those that are, so to speak, given *en passant*. Walking through the streets of Eton one summer in the 1880s his mind turns to Winchester, the home of another great public school. He recalls "the courts of the old college, empty and silent in the eventide; the mellow light on the battered walls; the great green meadows, where the little clear-voiced boys made gigantic shadows; the neighbor-hood of the old cathedral city, with its admirable church, where early kings are buried—all this seemed to make a charming background for boyish lives, and to offer a provision of tender, picturesque memories to the grown man who has passed through it." This little recollection, mind you, only for the purpose of reassuring us that "Eton, of a clear June evening, must be quite as good, or indeed a great deal better."

The contrasts are sharply drawn. There is the other face of England, as seen aboard a steamer cruising the "sordid river-front" in London. "For miles and miles you see nothing but the sooty backs of warehouses, or perhaps they are the sooty faces: in buildings so utterly expressionless it is impossible to distinguish. They stand massed together on the banks of the wide turbid stream, which is fortunately of too opaque a quality to reflect the dismal image...The river is almost black, and is covered with black barges; above the black housetops, from among the far-stretching docks and basins, rises a dusky wilderness of masts. The little puffing steamer is dingy and gritty—it belches a sable cloud that keeps you company as you go. In this carboniferous shower your companions, who belong chiefly, indeed, to the classes bereft of luster, assume an harmonious grayness; and the whole picture, glazed over with the glutinous London mist, becomes a masterly composition."

In 1904, Henry James had been away from America for twenty years. The death of his parents in 1882 was one reason for not returning; then, too, "the Atlantic voyage" could be counted "even with the ocean in a fairly good humor, an emphatic zero in the sum of one's better experience." And so, he gave us extensive impressions of what he saw ("If one is bent upon observation nothing...is trivial"). James is now acknowledged as an expatriate. He is a little bit disoriented: "It is of extreme interest to be reminded...that it takes an endless amount of history to make even a little tradition, and an endless amount of tradition to make even a little taste, and an endless amount of taste, by the same token, to make even a little tranquility. Tranquility results largely from taste tactfully applied, taste lighted above all by experience and possessed of a clue for its labyrinth."

Yet James's fondness for England, though vividly expressed, is not, I concluded after reading his tributes to New England, Italy, France, and Germany, by any means exclusive. But, then, wherever he travels, the critical eye is alert: "I had just come in, and, having attended to the distribution of my luggage, sat down to consider my habitation." And so there is, almost always, perspective, so often leavening. And he can be severe. About Geneva he writes that its "moral tone" is "epigrammatically, but on the whole justly, indicated by the fact, recently related to me by a discriminating friend, that, meeting one day in the street a placard of the theater, superscribed *Bouffes-Genevois*, he burst into irrepressible laughter. To appreciate the irony of the phrase one must have lived long enough in Geneva to suffer from the want of humor in the local atmosphere, and the absence, as well, of that esthetic character which is begotten of a generous view of life."

OK. But what about the Swiss in general? They have, we are informed, "apparently, an insensibility to comeliness or purity of form—a partiality to the clumsy, coarse, and prosaic, which one might almost interpret as a calculated offset to their great treasure of natural beauty, or at least as an instinctive protest of the national genius for frugality."

About the English, James was hardly the sycophant. In these travel writings he trains his eyes on national characteristics. He thinks it supremely a British endowment that they are a people disposed to let people alone. (Seventy-five years later, Anthony Burgess would leave England because, under socialism, he complained that they no longer left people alone.) James observes a political demonstration of a kind that, in countries of volatile temperament, would very likely have caused some consternation. Not so in England, because of this "practice of letting people alone," of "the frank good sense and the frank good humor and even the frank good taste of it."

He will permit himself in specific circumstances to be adulatory. In respect of the ancient rivalry between Oxford and Cambridge, Henry James might have instructed Solomon: "If Oxford were not the finest thing in England the case would be clearer for Cambridge...Oxford lends sweetness to labor and dignity to leisure. When I say Oxford I mean Cambridge, for a stray savage is not the least obliged to know the difference, and it suddenly strikes me as being both very pedantic and very good-natured in him to pretend to know it."

Since his formal mandate in these pieces, many of them written for *The Nation*, was to talk of travel, he talks of the people the traveler comes upon. He compares the Brit to the Yankee in what are, strictly speaking, sociological asides:

"The English have more time than we, they have more money, and they have a much higher relish for active leisure…A large appetite for holidays, the ability not only to take them but to know what to do with them when taken, is the sign of a robust people, and judged by this measure we Americans are sadly inexpert. Such holidays as we take are taken very often in Europe, where it is sometimes noticeable that our privilege is rather heavy on our hands."

Concerning the deportment of travelers, of "tourists," as we would now describe them, James is not unaffected by class prejudices, which is not to say that he should have been. On the one hand, he is easygoingly tolerant about young-blood licentiousness at the races at Epsom, commenting on "a coach drawn up beside the one on which I had a place," in which "a party of opulent young men were passing from stage to stage of the higher beatitude with a zeal which excited my admiration." However, on British women of another class than those who sat in coaches at Epsom getting drunk, he hands down opinions that achieve credibility by the authority with which they are stated. The reader doesn't think of James as motivated by snobbishness, and he is not condescending or in any way bent on inducing contempt. He is pronouncing on how people are. "She is useful, robust, prolific, excellently fitted to play the somewhat arduous part allotted to her in the great scheme of English civilization," he says of the working-class British woman, "but she has not those graces which enable her to lend herself easily to the decoration of life."

Elsewhere, he is, by his standards, blunt on the matter of some habits of the British on holiday: "You must give up the idea of going to sit somewhere in the open air, to eat an ice, and listen to a band of music. You will find neither the seat, the ice, nor the band; but on the other hand, faithful at once to your interest and your detachment, you may supply the place of these delights by a little private meditation on the deep-lying causes of the English indifference to them." Why? Well, he says, just think about it. "In such reflections nothing is idle—every grain of testimony counts; and one need therefore not be accused of jumping too suddenly from small things to great if one traces a connection between the absence of ices, and music, and the essentially hierarchical plan of English society. The hierarchical plan of English society is the great and ever-present fact to the mind of a stranger: there is hardly a detail of life that does not in some degree betray it."

James acknowledges his own preferences, his tastes, but he is not an epicurean or a snob, and, in any case, he was writing well before the age when tastes were transformed into social prejudices. But he unhesitatingly acknowledges a concern over human behavior and the implications of its neglect. Thus, on British tourists visiting Westminster Abbey: "When I reached the Abbey I found a dense group of people about the entrance, but I squeezed my way through them and succeeded in reaching the threshold. Beyond this it was impossible to advance, and I may add that it was not desirable. I put my nose into the church and promptly withdrew it. The crowd was terribly compact, and beneath the Gothic arches the odor was not that of incense."

Did this reaction disturb him? "You feel yourself at times in danger of thinking meanly of the human personality; numerosity, as it were, swallows up quality, and the perpetual sense of other elbows and knees begets yearning for the desert."

But in one essay Henry James, the great doctor of social manners, makes the definitive point. "It was, I think, the element of gentility that most impressed me. I know that the word I have just ventured to use is under the ban of contemporary taste; so I may as well say outright that I regard it as indispensable in almost any attempt at portraiture of English manners."

On his return to America, James isolated the special difficulty of American women of the affluent class in constituting a link in a social hierarchy. He observes that this is in part because they themselves lack truly institutional caste but also because there is a void in the next station up. American "ladies of the tiaras," lacking any access to royal courts, might instead settle for appearances at operas, "these occasions offering the only approach to the implication of the tiara known, so to speak, to the American law. Yet even here there would have been no one for them, in congruity and consistency, to curtsey to—their only possible course becoming thus, it would seem, to make obeisance, clingingly, to each other. This truth points again the effect of a picture poor in the male presence; for to what male presence of native growth is it thinkable that the wearer of an American tiara should curtsey?"

James is particularly rewarding in these copious travel writings when he engages his empirical strengths as an observer with his metaphysical imagination. He is, for instance, unable to discern the reason that affluent Americans at the turn of the century simply ignored the capacity of their clubs to accommodate that which clubs were so especially useful for, a neglect the clubs tended to share with the mansions of the wealthy:

"The American club struck me everywhere, oddly, considering the busy people who employ it, as much less an institution for attending to one's correspondence than others I had had knowledge of; generally destitute, in fact, of copious and various appliances for that purpose. There is such a thing as the imagination of the writing-table, and I nowhere, save in a few private houses, came upon its fruits; to which I must add that this is the one connection in which the provision for ease has not an extraordinary amplitude, an amplitude unequaled anywhere else." The American house, "with almost no one of its indoor parts distinguishable from any other is an affliction against which he has to learn betimes to brace himself."

Would he have said as much about contemporary arrangements? But, to begin with, there is very little club life in modern America, and the typical American who sets out to burn forty years of correspondence will not cause flame enough to heat a cup of tea.

Sometimes, whether plodding or coasting along these journals—and which of the two you find yourself reading can be a reflection as much of your own mood as of the caliber of James's performance—you might screech with impatience. As when you come upon constructions so periphrastic as to approach caricature:

"As for the author of that great chronicle which never is but always to be read"—it is not clear from the context whose journal James is referring to—"you may take your coffee of a morning in the little garden in which he wrote *finis* to his immortal work—and if the coffee is good enough to administer a fillip to your fancy, perhaps you may yet hear the faint reverberation among the trees of the long, long breath with which he must have laid down his pen."

Though one admires the filigree of it, if you wrap yourself in it too massively, you run the risk of choking. As in: "And what shall I say of the color of Wroxton Abbey, which we visited last in order and which in the thickening twilight, as we approached its great ivy-muffled face, laid on the mind the burden of its felicity?"

What we will say, Mr. James, is that you are a bloody genius, but sometimes you are too much. Too much in *this* day and age. Henry James's *Collected Travel Writings* are for long ocean trips and for monasteries, and for those happy to feel the great velveted halls of another, more deliberative age.

All At Sea
Town & Country, May 1994

Imagine a connection more harrowing, this side of real-life problems. You are in New York City. Your destination is Las Palmas in the Canary Islands, to catch the *Club Med 1*, setting out at 11:30 for the Caribbean. To get to Las Palmas, in November, from America, you need to fly all the way to Madrid, where you have just over one hour to make your connection. It's bad enough having to go 2,000 miles out of your way (Las Palmas–Madrid–Las Palmas) because Iberia Airlines, even though it flies over the same meridian as Las Palmas, en route to Madrid from New York, doesn't stop there. It adds humiliation to discomfort and expense to contemplate, after such an effort, missing the boat at Las Palmas. If you have spent a lot of time flying, you have had extensive, agonizing experiences with missed connections.

Since Club Med is the most obliging, customer-oriented organization on the face of the earth, you wonder why it scheduled a connection that tight. Well, the reason Club Med doesn't go to that trouble becomes obvious when you board and discover that you are the only passenger who set out from New York the night before. Come to think of it, there aren't many other Americans on board. And those who are there began the trip at its inception in Lisbon, seven days earlier. *Club Med 1* can berth 389 passengers. We took the same trip (Las Palmas–Martinique) a year earlier, the liner's maiden trip on that route, and were baffled to find only twenty-eight other passengers on board. On this trip there are 180. Most are French, and those who hadn't already boarded at Lisbon came in from European airports on early morning flights, arriving with two or three hours to spare.

But we made it. As the boat pulls out of the crowded harbor, minutes before lunch is served, you feel a light sensation of an ocean swell. The balmy wind of the sunny islands breaks through your jet phlegm; and you wonder how it can be that there is a single empty berth on this ship, embarked on so romantic a passage, taking the historic route that led to the discovery of the New World.

For my wife and me, this was a repeat trip. For our friend Schuyler Chapin, recently a widower, it was the first encounter with *Club Med 1*, an imposing vessel with five masts bearing 2,500 square meters of sail. It has eight decks, six of them recreational, the top deck exposed to sun and stars. You wander over to the high-deck dining room, idle by 150 different foods, cold and hot, exposed for you to choose from; and pledge to probe the question, Why isn't everybody here?

We would learn that our transoceanic passage is what they call in the trade a "positioning" cruise. It is required in order to position the ship in the Caribbean, where the winter business is done; even as another positioning cruise will be required to get the *Club Med 1* back to the Mediterranean for the summer business. And most vacationers aren't attracted to a positioning cruise. Their mistake, we agreed.

Nancy Lebel is a young, beautiful blonde. That is a flat, declarative, unimpeachable statement. She is a French Canadian whose English is perfect, as are her Spanish and her Italian. She sort of looks after you—Club Med gives you all the privacy you want, but there is always someone there gently looking out for you. They are called the *gentils organisateurs* (GOs). There are sixty-seven of them, young men and women, mostly handsome and pretty. They conduct their gym classes, preside over games, sing and dance at night, perform onstage as vamps, songsters, cancan exuberants, jugglers, ballet dancers; they smile at you warmly when you arrive, and the smile doesn't wear off when, nine days later, they bid you goodbye. The GOs are required to know English. Big deal—most of them know a third language. The officers are French, the kitchen staff predominantly Mauritian. The spirit of the GOs suffuses every employee on board.

So—I asked the captain the following day—why was his vessel less than half full? We conversed on the bridge, with its large, heavy-plated windows, forty feet above the water line, giving the on-duty watch a 180-degree view of the surrounding situation. The night before, sliding west of Tenerife at the fifteen-miles-per-hour speed we would maintain during most of the passage, we could discern the lights of little Gomera, from which Columbus had set out, on the big leg, 502 years ago, on a course pretty nearly identical to our own, except that when Columbus closed in on the Caribbean, he sailed north of the Antilles, and so missed islands that would have saved him the hard extra 600 miles to the Bahamas that very nearly caused mutiny. Why do so few people take the ocean passage?

Captain Gilles Bossard said that many people fear the sea. "When they cannot any longer see land, they become very nervous, quite afraid."

That is one explanation for the relative popularity of cruising on *Club Med 1* (as distinguished from making an ocean passage). The week-long cruises in the Caribbean begin and end at Fort-de-France, and either head south in the general direction of Grenada, touching in on five or six islands and ports, or head north in the direction of St. Thomas. Every day, on these cruises, the *Club Med 1* stops in at an island and the passengers go ashore, occupy the beaches, snorkel, shop, are back for dinner—and off the boat goes to the next anchorage, usually reaching it sometime in the night.

One thinks of this hectic vacationing as very American, maybe distinctively American. But only one-third of Club Med's passengers are Americans these days. Most are Europeans, who for years went no farther than to the Canary Islands for their winter vacation but are now heavy patrons of Caribbean cruising. The passengers, the captain said, are very energetic. "They are not accustomed to staying in a boat for more than a day or so." It is accordingly to be expected that they'd prefer the cruise over the ocean passage, allowing them every day to get away from the mother vessel, to explore fresh islands, beaches, lagoons.

But when summer comes around, most of the cruise ships, in search of patronage, leave the Caribbean. They head to the Mediterranean (and, a few, to the Baltic), where they do the same kind of thing, but putting in at Greek and Turkish islands and ports. For those fleeted few attracted to an ocean passage, the opportunity strikes only twice a year: once traveling west to the Caribbean, once traveling east to the Mediterranean. Positioning time. The western itinerary of *Club Med 1* gives the passengers a taste of cruising life. When the ship left Lisbon, it was to go the few miles to Cadiz; then on to Casablanca, Lanzarote, Las Palmas—only then, the long passage to Fort-de-France. What would be the itinerary on the passage back, in April?

The captain betrayed his disappointment when he said that "probably" the ship would go nonstop from the Caribbean to Casablanca, and from there across the Gibraltar Straits to Cannes. I registered dismay: such a course would take the ship directly into the trade winds, nullifying any use of the sails. Why not sail up to Bermuda (1,000 miles, three days), stop for a day, then go on to the Azores (1,900 miles, six days)? And then to Gibraltar (650 miles, two days)? He shrugged his shoulders. Yes, such a route would give good sailing, especially on the first leg, the trade winds coming in off the starboard beam. But that route would take four or five days more than the direct route—and commercial vessels don't choose itineraries that use up unnecessary time. Not unless there is a consumer demand. There is no such demand.

I spoke to Nancy about it. We were at the captain's table that one night and she was seated to my right, relieving me from speaking in my execrable French to the lady on my left, who had said to me that her English was very difficult for people to understand, documenting her point there and then, when I found myself asking her kindly to repeat what she had said. Is the allure of an ocean passage evanescent, in the age of jet travel? I reminisced that on our yearly retreats to Switzerland, beginning in the Fifties, my wife (and, in those days, our son) traveled regularly by ocean liner, to Southampton, or Le Havre, Gibraltar, Nice, or Genoa. You could pick and choose from a half-dozen countries' liners. They were joyous passages, exciting, action-filled, the January sea unruly, sometimes hostile. The older liners didn't even have stabilizers, and the heel and roll was heavy, causing on one occasion that comes to mind almost total absenteeism at mealtime. But always, on arriving, one had a sensation entirely different from what you get at the end of the little zigzagging associated with island-to-island cruising, which is what the *Club Med 1* does, as also her sister ship, *Club Med 2*, in the South Pacific, operating out of Noumea, New Caledonia.

But it has been many years since one could cross the Atlantic in a liner during the winter months from New York, with the exception of the *Queen Elizabeth 2*'s December crossing. And if the *QE2* ever retires from duty, one wonders whether any liner will do regular duty across the Atlantic. Wealthy, older people, Nancy reminded me, still take ocean passages, but they patronize those around-the-world trips undertaken in the winter by two or three luxury liners, notably the *QE2* and the Royal Viking Line. They are men and women who enjoy themselves, to be sure; but mostly one thinks of them as fully engaged in killing time.

Now, whether you are cruising on *Club Med 1* or doing an ocean passage, the routine is not substantially different. You can have your breakfast in bed, or take it up on the Gregolimano deck—anytime between 7:00 and 11:30. Beginning at 9:00, the organized activity begins, for those who want it. You can go to exercise classes, do gym work, swim in two pools, compete in bridge tournaments, study foreign languages. After lunch, there is relative quiet for an hour or two, then more of everything, including tea with a small band of swinging musicians. The casino is open in the late afternoon, and at night until the last player gives up. In every room there is a television with three or four channels, movies in various languages, as well as shipboard music from cassettes. A six-page newspaper brings you the day's heavyweight events, nicely compressed and printed. You can correspond with friends and family, but at $30 per page, the fax needs to be used discreetly, as does the telephone, at $15 per minute. The hell with it. It strengthens the idea of an ocean passage to be slightly out of touch.

Separate attention needs to be given to the cuisine. We had been on board a Club Med cruise in 1991, as well as on the transatlantic in 1992. Previously, we had marveled at the variety of the food served. But on the two other trips, one of them a cruise in the Antilles, the second a positioning passage like this, we were given house wines. They were okay, but not memorable.

On this trip, the cruise was advertised as "*gastronomique*," under the auspices of Paris's Serge Tchekhoff. It is boring to list what is on a menu, but for the curious, the first dinner is described below. It is relayed in French, for those who acknowledge no other means of properly conveying the delights of a cuisine: *Châtaigne de mer, mousseline d'oeufs brouillés aux langues d'oursins* (fluffy chestnut-flavored scrambled eggs laced with tongues of sea urchin). *Coquille St. Jacques rôtie tout simplement au beurre demisel; suprême de pintade fermière poêlée a l'os; pomme de terre grillées* (scallops, simply roasted; breast of young guinea hen, pan-fried, not deboned; grilled potatoes). *Crème tendre de chocolat* (soft chocolate cream). The wines: Champagne Ruinart, Bordeaux Graves Blanc "Cuvée Caroline," Grand Cru Classé St. Emilion Chateau Beausejour Becot.

It would be ungrateful to fail to mention breakfast, not merely because you can order whatever exotica you wish, on the assumption that no one of the 150 offerings on the buffet appeals to you, but because the display of fresh breads is very nearly exhibitionistic: twenty different combinations of croissants, sourdough, grain breads, sesame rolls, sweet rolls, French breads, whole wheats, in a display of bakery Walt Disney could not have improved upon.

You do need to remind yourself that, theoretically, you are riding on a sailboat. The sails on the *Club Med 1*, the captain swears, contribute about 20 percent of the effort to take this 617-foot megabark across the Atlantic. "If there were no power on right now," the captain says, pointing up at the 2,500 square meters of sail, "we would be traveling at six, seven knots." You are slightly skeptical but politely jot down the figure.

"Is the cost of the masts and the sails, and the computers that tell them what to do, worth it?" The answer you get is diplomatically oblique. It boils down to, *what gives passengers satisfaction is worth the cost.* Even if the sails were merely decorative, they'd be worth it for passengers looking for something that reminds them of life at sea, as it used to be. When you are seated in the dining room in the evening, and it is dark outside, the sheer motionlessness of it all removes from the senses any idea of the feat you are engaged in—moving across the ocean at about twice the speed Columbus managed with his little caravel, a real sailboat, which would fit between your table and the entrance to the dining hall.

The word passed quickly, just after 10:00, reaching even to the aftermost point on the lower sun deck, jostling the passenger lying topless, adoring the sun god. A sail had been spotted! Over there... About ten miles in front of us! The ship's company ogled as though we were approaching the *Titanic* getting ready to sink.

Details of the little sloop sharpened as we gained ground on it. It was forty, perhaps forty-five-feet long. Its spinnaker was flying, straining, up, over, down, as if determined to break free of its tethers. We couldn't yet see anyone at the helm, but we could almost feel the dizzying roll, pitch, yaw. Every minute the sloop would plunge into the water, veer to starboard, then hack to port: sometimes its hull would disappear entirely from view, obscured by the same waves that were unnoticeable to our mighty ship with its leveraged ballast and stabilizers. I fancied myself on board the sloop. Three years ago, I had made the passage, on a seventy-foot ketch. There are moments, in particular when you are attempting sleep, when you would give a year of your life for a few hours' stability; but just as one can get blasé about stability, so also the pitch and roll of the blue water sailboat somehow become... normal, as, one supposes, a Ferris wheel would feel normal after riding it for an hour or ten hours; and then too, one remembers with some smugness that the comfortably situated passenger on the liner will never experience the earned serenity you get on a sailboat when the wind eases up, or when the wind veers over, coming at you at a seakindly angle.

When we were abeam (the captain stayed clear of it by a quarter of a mile) we could make out several pairs of arms and hands waving at us, and then their horn went twit twit, and ours responded with a thunderous BURR BURR BURR BURR BURR. Since Club Med is high on protocol at sea, I made a mental note to look at my Chapman's, the sailor's bible, and find out what five blasts signify. Answer: five (or more) blasts is the "danger signal." Since neither the sailboat nor the superliner was in danger, I must assume that our emissions were simply exercises in HO HO HO: a translegal effusion of nautical *Gemütlichkeit*.

People approach boat life with varied social designs. Some, particularly young singles, are coiled in search of company. Before the day is out, they have made a half-dozen new friends. At the opposite end (in which we fell), there is the couple (in this case, a couple accompanied by the world's most amusing and entertaining companion) hungry for time alone, with a dozen books to catch up on, hobbies to indulge. (When it was hinted early on that they might wish to share a table with another couple or couples, they froze with shock at the mere thought of it; and, good old Club Med, nothing further was said on the subject, and our table for three was sacrosanct.) Schuyler had several hundred personal notes to write, acknowledging kindnesses in connection with the death of his wife. My wife Pat was robbed of a gin rummy partner but didn't want to forage for one, and satisfied herself with her hooks and the afternoon game of Russian Bank with her husband. He busied himself with correspondence to catch up on, Margaret Thatcher's book to read and review, and three infuriating celestial navigation systems he had brought along; they, and the sextant, and the endless trial and error, engrossed him, even after a lifetime's application.

Every morning I would eagerly report to my wife, and to Schuyler, what had been the distance traversed during the preceding twenty-four hours (about 300 miles) and they would look up and grunt something or other to placate me; sometimes they would merely grunt, continuing to read. I exhibited to anyone who would look my Ensign Trimble GPS, which, after a few minutes taking in the satellite situation above, tells you exactly where you are, how fast you are moving and how far you are from your destination. At night we could waddle from the dining room table to the casino. Schuyler and I would walk twice around the deck and wonder why, oh why, hadn't Club Med scheduled the trip a little earlier—or a little later—so that we might have some moon, visible now on the last two days of the trip. After our promenade in the black, we would look in on Pat at the casino, and dip into our collection of quarters, taken from a pot we pledged not to refill. It began with $100 and ended, of course, with zero. But nine evenings of a half-hour of casino life for a hundred bucks isn't bad, is it?

When I woke on Day Nine, I turned back the porthole night cover.

You would not have known from any sensation underfoot whether you were still at sea or docked. *We made it!* And the New World lies indeed where all my instruments tell us. That very night we were nestled into a bright New England winter snap, and it felt exactly right that, just a few days ahead, lay Thanksgiving.

A Lifetime of Jetlag
FYI, September 26, 1994

To be literal about it, you can't have had a "lifetime of jetlag" unless you were born in 1958, which was when the commercial jet age was born. There was jet conveyance before then, but only over short distances. Jet pilots in the Korean War didn't fly long distances, and, anyway, jetlag is probably the last thing to worry about when flying on do-or-die military missions.

In 1958 I was thirty-three, but it is true that I've had jetlag ever since I began flying in jets. I sometimes wake up at home and find myself reaching sleepily for the flight attendant's button. I remember asking one gregarious captain, at the end of what seemed a one-week-long, nonstop jet trip whether, like round-the-world cruising ships, his aircraft carried coffins for passengers who died on board. I have a creepy-crawly feeling that I'll have jetlag always, and maybe the time has come to explore the phenomenon in a fatalistic way, and pass along an experience or two, not so much to recommend it, as to say: Don't bother.

Like don't bother not to drink. Senator George McGovern, who is a fountain of wisdom on all matters not touching on public policy, told me one evening as we decompressed from a heated exchange with a bottle of beer that he was going the next day to Germany and didn't look forward to his schedule, because he would be flying all night and meeting in the morning, a couple of hours after arriving. I asked him if he heeded the counsel, "Thou shalt not drink on jet travel." No, he said. "I like to have a drink when I fly across the ocean."

That, really, is the simplest way to put it. I intend, Senator McGovern was saying, to have my Scotch and soda after take-off, and my glass of wine at dinner because it is a civilized thing to do, inducing relaxation and sleep. Senator McGovern made the other mistake, as renowned, but then as apparently incurable, as government waste. It is to make an appointment on the morning you arrive, eastbound across the Atlantic.

I remember an agonizing day. I was invited to Belfast to meet the brass and to write about the strife. This required flying to Scotland and connecting to Belfast, arriving a matter of minutes before our first scheduled visit with a cabinet minister. By the time of the fifth interview in mid-afternoon, I felt I knew something of the meaning of that form of torture that keeps the prisoner awake while questions are endlessly put to him.

Later in the afternoon, I was at the wheel of the rented car driving to Londonderry for an interview with the Catholic proconsul. My eyelids began to shudder, and I jammed my foot on the brake just in time to avoid one more violent death in that violent country.

The passenger traffic manager of the late Pan Am once told me that a reason (there are others) that the major carriers fly overnight instead of during the day across the Atlantic is that Americans are such Stakhanovite tourists, they don't want to forfeit one day of their fourteen-day vacation. "They don't know how awful they're going to feel the next day, when they have scheduled themselves happily to tour London, or Paris, or Rome."

Anyway, I agreed heartily with Senator McGovern, and we pledged never to communicate to each other any testimony from a longtime jet-lag sufferer, should one such burst into the room and say, "Yesterday, New York-Geneva, I had nothing to drink, and felt fresh as a daisy when I landed." The good news is that I haven't had to suppress any such testimony. Nobody around is telling me he did a long jet trip dry and it worked. Everybody says you should try it.

Then there are the noise nuts. We mustn't deny that jet noise is an irritant. Does it induce jetlag? The New York Times ran a story last October that began, "No, I didn't sleep. I can never sleep on airplanes. But after more than eight hours overnight from Kennedy International Airport I arrived in Vienna surprisingly rested and fresh."

You know what that man is telling you. No jetlag.

How come?

The gentleman had got hold of a NoiseBuster—"NoiseBuster reduces annoying noise electronically, using 'anti-noise' technology…" The product ($149) is manufactured by Noise Cancellation Technologies, Inc. So, I bought one, left New York, bound for Los Angeles with it on, took it off by the time the plane reached the George Washington Bridge—I figured it was a defective unit. A week later I was given a replacement, and set out for Paris. By the time I got to New Haven, I took it off and put on my 75-cent earplugs, which work five times as well as the NoiseBuster. However, the next morning I did not arrive surprisingly rested and fresh. I woke with jetlag.

Chemicals? I have had only a single conversation with Princess Diana, at the White House when she and the prince flew in for a state dinner. Finding myself alone with her, I thought it appropriate to comment on her flight that very day from London, and asked if she suffered from jetlag. But I didn't give her the time to answer, because I had a conversational gambit up my sleeve and rushed to spring it on her.

"You see," said I to the Princess, "what causes jetlag is, apparently, internal sweating caused by dryness. Now I have a friend who knows a doctor in London, and they were talking about jetlag, and the doctor said, 'Look, try this next time you go across the Atlantic. Take a heaping tablespoonful of salt and put it into a cup of coffee. Drink it and it will taste—awful! Five hours later, do the identical thing—but this time the salted coffee will taste like syrup! Why? Because your whole system is crying out for salt!'" I paused.

"Why don't you try that on the trip home?" She looked me square in the face, stuck out her tongue, clutched her throat, and made a gagging noise. It crossed my mind that she was having a bulimic attack, but no. She was reacting to the thought of drinking a cup of coffee with a tablespoonful of salt in it. Two days later, flying to Madrid. I tried it, gulping down the entire cup. It was the closest I ever came to looking like Princess Diana. The next day I had jetlag.

A friend reports that he has my jetlag answer, at least for flights to London and Paris. "The trouble is, I can't afford the Concorde." Now on that point, focus on these reservations: 1) Concorde flights are during the day, and no one questions that jetlag on most day flights is less acute. 2) What is it that persuades us that Concorde-speed travel diminishes whatever it is that causes jetlag?

Concerning the first point. On a round-the-world Concorde jaunt, our party flew on the last day Capetown-Monrovia, which is about 3,500 miles. (The Concorde is not permitted to fly overland, so it had to swing out to sea a bit to avoid disturbing the tranquility of Zaire.) There we refueled, and one hour later were off for London—another 3,000 miles plus. In London we had one hour to bathe, then a big farewell dinner. We had flown almost 7,000 miles in eight hours. On the other hand, our route was pretty well north—our watch time changed only one hour. Earlier in the trip, we had flown Acapulco-San Francisco-Honolulu, a shorter distance (less than 5,000 miles), but traversing sixty degrees of longitude; four time zones. Considerable jetlag. Our experience reconfirmed what we more or less know, that north-south trips don't do it to you, e.g., New York-Rio is pretty tame.

But on my second point, ask yourself this: Why is it that we should expect the Concorde to let us off lightly when crossing the Atlantic Ocean? Jetlag is supposed to result from affronting the sidereal order by traveling at a rapid speed across time zones. Well, shouldn't it follow that the slower you travel, the less the internal stress? I have crossed the Atlantic on a sailboat, averaging 175 miles per day—and there were no traces of jetlag. Why traveling at 1,350 miles per hour instead of at 600 miles per hour should your system absorb less, rather than more of the relevant distresses? Do you know the answer to that question? Good, because I do not, and no travel expert I've asked has the answer. I say: The primary reason some people don't get jetlag on the Concorde flights (I do) is that they are daytime flights. Why should flying overnight tax you more? This is a hypothesis, nothing more: you lose sleep, and fatigue is a primary generator of jetlag. For many years, my annual route in January was: New York-Paris-Geneva, leaving at 10:00 a.m. No jetlag. Since they eliminated the daytime flights, we have been forced to do New York-Geneva at night, landing at the New York equivalent of 1:00 a.m. Horrible jetlag.

Again, the rule-breakers: New York-Tokyo is awful, even though it is 1) daytime, and 2) a trip long enough to permit sleep for about as long as you like. But it is a fourteen-hour killer, in my experience. Roger Moore flies regularly Geneva-New York-Los Angeles. His prescription: swallow a tough sleeping pill as soon as you take off on the second leg, but one that wraps you up for only about three hours. Then, arriving at LA in the late afternoon (Swiss time, about 3:00 a.m.), kill yourself to stay awake through dinner and mild revelries after. Next day? You are fit to take on the Man with the Golden Gun.

My summary? If you want to avoid jetlag at all costs when heading for London, go New York-Buenos Aires-Capetown-London. Or wait till May and travel on the *Queen Elizabeth 2*. But do this at least: make no appointments on Day #2, and patronize any airline that flies during the day.

My Alta
Ski Magazine, November 1994

Three of us go to Alta, UT, every year, Wednesday through Sunday. Lawry and Milton come in from San Francisco. I come in from New York. When the three of us first skied with Utah powder legend Junior Bonous, which is like saying when we played tennis with Bill Tilden, Junior (who has grandchildren) referred to our Nobel Laureate as "Milt," which is the Mormon way in and around Utah. "That's like referring to Einstein as 'Al,'" I whispered to Lawry. When a half-hour later we found ourselves sharing a lift, I thought at least to pass along the word to Junior that our little (five-feet-two) companion had won a Nobel prize. "For what?" Junior asked. though I think he put the question to me to be polite—Junior doesn't really care if Milt got a Nobel prize for ichthyology; or, for that matter, that he got any prize at all. Junior cares only that Milton Friedman is a nice guy (he is) and that he is getting something out of what Junior is teaching him (he is). Alta, a half hour from Salt Lake City, is famous for its abundance of snow (500 inches every year) and for its saturated affability. It is quite another world, and that is probably why we've had seventeen reunions there.

My first visit to the Alta Lodge was in 1962. I had written an essay for *Esquire* entitled, "Why Don't We Complain?" and I remember complaining to my wife, who was with me, that it was awfully tough going, generating indignation in such a place as the Alta Lodge.

Just so nobody will think me sycophantic on the matter of the Alta Lodge and Alta, I leap to a couple of things that drive me crazy. We are 8,300 feet above sea level, and this is not an altitude you get used to in a couple of hours. As a matter of fact, in three days you do not get used to 8,300 feet of altitude. It's OK if you are sliding downhill, or walking on level ground—walking, say, over to Rustler's Lodge. It is a mean, draining bore when you have to walk up (or, for that matter, down) sixty-three steps, which is what it takes to go from where the car leaves you to where the Alta Lodge begins.

If you arrive, as some of us do, with five or six mounds of baggage, you look with genuine mortification at the young men in their late teens who are sent up to cope with several hundred pounds of disorderly weight. But year after year it is so: sixty-three icy wooden steps (covered, to be sure, but icy just the same), down and up.

"Do you know," Lawry said last time we were here as, climbing up, we paused for breath at a landing, "this stairway has really got to be an affectation." Lawry, a lawyer, author, and thinktanker, is of course right. It reminds one of climbing about at Machu Picchu; on the other hand, the Incas *had* to do it, because they never thought up the wheel. We take our usual vow never to return to the Lodge unless they get an elevator—and a silent vow to repeat that vow next year.

And then there is a complementary idiocy, only this one is the responsibility of the Alta Ski Lifts Company. In order to reach the two main base lifts, Collins and Wildcat, that take you to the area's 2,200 skiing acres, you need to climb up a steep little hill. It is a coincidence that sixty-three side-steps are (at my height) required to get up it. Why isn't there some sort of escalator to spare you this breath-consuming ordeal?

The answer to that question is that there is something just a little self-satisfied about Alta, and the humbling feature of the whole place is that it has pretty good reason for self-satisfaction. The good cheer is earned. It is the kind of thing you'd expect to find in the manner of the gardeners who tend the lawns at Windsor Castle. One gardener was asked by an American soldier during the war how one manages to cultivate so beautiful a lawn. He gladly gave his answer: First. the gardener said, you plow the lawn using a very shallow plow. Then you water it for 700 years.

Alta hasn't been around for 700 years, but then neither, as a sport, has skiing. Alta is, nevertheless, one of the oldest ski resorts in the West—meaning, really, it is postwar.

The Alta Lodge is fifty years old, but back then we were talking about a few rope tows, very different from today's eight chairlifts. triples and doubles, several with a vertical rise of about 2,000 feet. There was some concern a few years ago when the great Snowbird resort opened, just one mile away on the road to Salt Lake City. Snowbird includes a tram that will lift 125 skiers 3,000 vertical feet, and two or three floors of bazaars that sell everything; that, and a 600-room high-rise with gymnasia, suites, saunas, and everything. For that matter, if you head down toward Salt Lake, then do a turn and go back up on the other side of the range, you arrive at Deer Valley. "But you know," Chick Morton said to me—Chick was for many years the manager of Alta Lodge and remains a high potentate in the little cadre that runs Alta—"a lot of people come *here* to ski. Then they go back to Deer Valley for the nightlife and the fancy stuff." That troubles the Alta people not one bit: nightlife is for other ski resorts, and Snowbird has helped to reduce the traffic, which was just what Alta's owners wanted.

Onno Wieringa, who manages the lift association, is young, ever so perceptive, knows avalanches like Henry Ford knew automobile engines and incarnates bright self-satisfaction. He describes with some pride the new rope tow that pulls you a mile or so on the all-but-level slope that takes you back to the lodge from one of the outer runs. The objectives were to replace the old tow that required you to take your hand off when you came to each of the tow's dozen pylons with one that would permit the height of the rope to rise as required after last night's snowfall.

Last night's snowfall at Alta is not to be compared with that gentle little carpet that nestles down on Mr. Blanding's dream house on Christmas Eve. Four days before we arrived, in January, the day's snowfall was sixty inches. One night, a few years ago, the telephone rang in my room at 2:00 p.m. Would I kindly repair to the basement of the lodge? Half asleep, I wondered whether the lodge had come up with some concentrated *Gemütlichkeit* for its guests, and I found myself asking, "Is this compulsory?" The answer was a gentle but unambiguous "Yes." I read an issue of *Time* magazine from cover to cover in the cellar where the ski lockers are, in the company of fifty odd guests, whose impatience subsided when reminded that an avalanche the year before had swept away a wing of the lodge. But the science of preemptive, well-aimed artillery shells has diminished such climacterics, and I haven't been roused from my bed by avalanches since.

What is it like, a day at Alta, staying at the Alta Lodge? Life is absolutely unregimented, in sharp contrast, for instance, with life at Zurs in Austria. There, your ski-learning group is the center of life. You are appraised by the reigning ski czar who matriculates you in whichever of the twenty classes (1A, beginners; 10B, experts) for which you think your skills appropriate. At the end of the day, on his skis, the ski czar will stretch out his arm and point at you, his thumb either raised or lowered. And, accepting the finality of his judgment, you check in the following morning at the class next more advanced than where you were, or one class lower. Such a regimen would strike the folks at Alta as absolutely Hitlerian, which, as a matter of fact, it is.

At Alta you do as you like. What we do is convene at eight for breakfast, which is about as far removed from a continental breakfast as a breakfast can be. If you like, you can drink orange juice, take cereal with or without fresh yogurt, en route to a Spanish omelet with sausage and/or bacon to bide you until the French toast and pancakes arrive. Milton has his *Wall Street Journal,* Lawry his *USA Today,* I, the *New York Times.* We will convene at ten in the basement/avalanche room, put on our equipment, and make our way outdoors, skiing fifty yards down to the awful uphill slope, then up one of the two lifts up to Mt. Baldy. From there, there are combinations of every kind, including some very rough stuff (High Rustler), but most of it is perfect for intermediate skiers. (The runs were named when Stephen Vincent Benet was not around, e.g.: Mambo, Blitz, Taint, Stimulation, Warm-Up, Stone Crusher, Extrovert, Secret Access, Rabbit.)

At about 12:00 we are back at the lodge for lunch, where there is always a specialty, always satisfying. We knock off after lunch and reconvene about 2:30 and ski another hour and a half.

After skiing, we sleep, or read, or do our homework—correspondence, writing, editing. Lawry and I meet at the jacuzzi (there are two, one hotter than the other) at 6:30, and at 7:00 we congregate in my mini-suite for wine and pretzels, where we join in animated conversation on such questions as whether intellectual property is the cause or the substance of progress, what is generally missed about Lord Keynes' economics, how creepy-crawly are the ways in which the state regularly intervenes in more and more of the freeman's life, what is the point in the tax deductibility of mortgages, how is Lawry's thinktank doing, how is it that the *San Francisco Chronicle* consents to publish Lawry's atavistic copy, and how are Milton and his wife Rose sharing the duties of their ongoing memoirs.

After so many years of total immersion in one another's company, over a period of time so brief, it is remarkable what confidences one finds oneself willing to share. It is to be compared with night watches on a sailing boat: the intimacy is of the kind that generates true pleasure in one another's company. We eschew the lodge at dinner, occupying instead a booth at the Shallow Shaft Steak House, in tribute to which we undergo the sixty-three-step rite of passage, The conversation is unabated, and after dinner we walk a lazy half-dozen blocks in the cold, then wend our way down—Milton, generally, to his own room, Lawry to mine for a nightcap and maybe some music (I bring my own tapes). Lawry then goes off to his room, and the day is ended. Elsewhere at the lodge there is the Sitzmark Club, a television room where movies are shown, and the lounge. If fraternization is what you want, it is here abundantly.

I have previously remarked on the singular blessings of skiing for men and women getting along in years. It may well be that this advantage will become less noticeable as we begin to take skiing for granted, with the result that more and more Americans will be learning to ski at a younger age. It is as fruitful an investment in time as learning a language when you are six or seven. In skiing, absolutely no effort is required, and as we observe the skiers from the lift traveling up Mt. Baldy we distinguish instantly those who began young from those who began later on.

The demarcation is perfectly exemplified in our little group. Lawry grew up skiing in California, and his touch and style are expert. I began at thirty, Milton at forty. Lawry is ranked at, say, seventeen (on a scale of twenty), I'd come in at about thirteen, Milton at eight. I have observed that people do not need to give up skiing when they get older. All they need do is slow down, and do as much or as little as suits them. I had not observed, until my years with Milton, that it is also possible not only to improve in your seventies and eighties, but to do so dramatically. When Junior began giving us his yearly tips, Milt glowed with the satisfaction that comes from making observable progress. And then, one year ago, Junior asked, would we like to try the new skis? Milton is very conservative about trying out anything new, but he consented, as did I, and we were introduced to the Atomic Powder Plus Fat Boy skis.

They are, as is pretty widely known by now, one-and-a-half times as wide as ordinary skis, shorter, and they come in only two lengths. Milton tried the 163s, I the 183s. Junior said "Follow Me," and we looked at each other incredulously. Junior wafted down in powder at a relaxed pace through a dense forest. The very thought of engaging such snow in such conditions was, to us, preposterous—Milton avoids powder like poison ivy, and I submit to it once or twice every season to remind me of my fallibilities.

But Junior was not to be denied, so hesitantly I advanced on his trail, Milton on mine. And lo!—neither of us fell, and we found we could turn in every situation. It was a liberating experience, and this last year we arrived with rented Fat Boys. The skis are catching on, and the superstition that they are inadequate for *piste* skiing is just that, a superstition. Junior told us he would recommend against using the fat skis only to the skier who was bent on racing.

I asked Milton if he intended to race, before he puts down his skis? This was the week when it transpired that the person who smashed Ms. Kerrigan on the knee to keep her out of the competition was very close to Ms. Harding, who went on to win the US Nationals. I dropped a note to Rose to the effect that Lawry and I were thinking of engaging some hood in Salt Lake to come and have a go at Milton's knee before he outpaced us.

Well, I exaggerate; but I don't when I say that Lawry and I skied with someone who at eighty-one was three times the skier he was at seventy-eight.

Is there no end to these effronteries of skiing in orderly old age? The very first thing Milton did on Day One was report to the area ticket booth to get a free pass given out to skiers who are eighty or over. The lady at the desk chatted that Alta would probably have to suspend this perk for the elderly, given the number of people who were eligible today. "We're thinking," she said, "of giving the pass only to people over ninety." A voice behind Milton rang out robustly, "That wouldn't bother me. I'm ninety-two."

Every now and again, not often, Milton will observe that sometime in the future he simply won't be up to coming to Alta. I tell him the mere thought of a skier being superannuated is subversive, liberal-democratic-socialist hogwash, and if he brings it up again, Lawry and I will campaign for the Clinton Health Plan, and then everybody will die young.

Milton laughs, and the subject goes to sleep for another couple of years.

CHAPTER SEVEN

1995–1999

R.I.P. MGM

FYI, March 13, 1995

As I write, this news bulletin arrives by fax: "Kerkorian sells MGM Grand Air. The airline of the rich and famous—MGM Grand Air—is being converted into a cargo airline."

Well, there are more rich and famous out there than there were patrons of MGM.

Every morning dozens of passenger jet aircraft leave Los Angeles bound, nonstop, for New York City. Some of these planes were configured to house twelve passengers traveling first class, others as many as twenty-two. My guess is that hundreds of first-class seats were taken during those hours. Anyone flying within this period could, with minor modifications, have opted to fly on the 9:15 MGM flight. Some, indeed, were willing to make major modifications in their itinerary in order to fly MGM.

I did, some weeks ago. Seeking to return to New York, I rose at 5:00 a.m. to make the connections from Las Vegas to Los Angeles-New York. I had to walk a very long mile in order to fly MGM. I flew on it twenty-one times. What baffles is that on all those occasions, MGM flights were never even one-half full, let alone sold out. And yet MGM pegged its fare at *exactly* the sum you paid to fly on competing carriers, about whose space, food, and service let us agree to say nothing. My posthumous purpose is modest, which is to celebrate what is suddenly—a memory.

A brief bit of history. It was conceived eleven years ago as Regent Air. Its amenities were encyclopedic: a driver would pick you up at your office/house/apartment, drive you to JFK; and on arrival in Los Angeles, another driver would take you to your destination. On board there was a barber, in case you wished to trim your hair or beard. These rather ostentatious excesses ended after a little while. And when MGM took it over, after a year or so, the company experimented with an economy section on a trans-formed DC-8, aft of its regular first-class service. I did not examine it, but the word was that it was the equivalent of traveling first class on a con-ventional carrier. Then MGM ended the service, for twenty-one forlorn months, restricting the use of their sumptuous aircraft to charter parties, presumably for the Rolling Stones, their equerries, and other such folk, to ease their way from city to stupefied city.

At this point the great MGM Grand Hotel sprang up in Las Vegas. I do not know whether it is "great" as advertised, but evidently it is the largest luxury hotel in the world. I am unlikely ever personally to verify this, as I have zero desire to linger in the city it celebrates. But I prayed that MGM's Los Angeles-New York, NY-LA, (two flights each way, every day) would survive. The reported loss over a recent nine months was $2.64 million on revenues of $14.9 million. It was reasonable to assume that however deep the pockets of the operators, they would not persist in offering that service if less than a dozen persons patronized the flight, as was the case the last two times I flew.

How to abbreviate the experience? I have flown on Air Force One, have disported on the Concorde right around the world, on a dozen cor-porate jets, including a luxuriously appointed G-4 dispatched all the way to Geneva to bring me to Los Angeles. I suppose the Sultan of Brunei has a palace that flies about the world at 600 miles per hour, and I live utterly at peace with the conviction that I will never experience it. I depose that MGM's flights were accommodations less than the commuter-shuttlers charge for the sardine quarters on their airplane.

Why? What happened?

When my wife and I began the habit of spending February and March in Switzerland, we traveled on steam ships. There were several to choose from, and the delights of an ocean passage beckoned, year after year. But the liners were less and less full, and one day, about ten years ago, there were no more. Some gave up the ghost entirely. Others made their way to the Caribbean, to do the cruise business, stopping every night at an island to be exploited on the following day, with its beaches and underwater life. How many people cross the Atlantic in January and February by air? A million? A billion? In conversation with the traffic director of Pan American (R.I.P.) some years ago I asked why the airline had given up its daylight flights to Europe, so comfortable, so convenient, so (relatively) jetlag-free. There were two reasons, he said. The first is that an aircraft leaving at 10:00 a.m. and landing in Paris at 10:00 a.m. local time had, really, nowhere to go until the next morning, there being less than a hundred million Frenchmen set on boarding the flight at 11:00 p.m. to visit the Middle East or faraway India, or Mysterious Afrique. So, the planes would sit for twelve hours, waiting for passengers flying to America. The second reason? Americans, he said, will always seek to maximize the length of their two-week vacation. If they spend the first day traveling, why, *Pfft!*—they have diminished the length of their vacation by 5 percent. "They don't realize that traveling overnight they'll have jet lag and won't enjoy Day One of their vacation."

How is it that there aren't enough travelers, either the idle, or the retired, or the children with great big eyes that want to wonder at the sea, to sustain one liner during January and February, making four round trips? We are spoken of as the largest and most affluent community in the world, but we appear to disdain to patronize, or even to notice, the January liner, the overnight Pullman, the blissful MGM. Is it our Puritan roots? But people who sell clothes and jewelry and booze and $15,000 Mickey Mouse watches don't seem to have been hit by it, the strange insouciance to travel luxury.

For all that we live in cyberspace information-land, it is quite possible that you will live fifteen years without discovering that the best pizza in America is at the corner bakery. I love the marketplace, I swear eternal fidelity to its dispensations, though none at all to its sense of relative value (the marketplace knows everything about pricing, nothing at all about value). What hurts is when the marketplace passes a judgment based on public ignorance, which is what I call it when anybody who was willing to pay first-class fare, New York-Los Angeles, did anything other than call MGM and, on arrival, feel himself benumbed by the sensation of actually wishing the trip had been a little longer.

We don't have much patience with failed enterprises in America, but those of us who had the experience of MGM take thought, some of us, to attend the memorial service, and profess our sadness at the passing of so civilized an enterprise.

Travels with William F. Buckley
National Geographic Traveler, March-April 1995

Most people travel to reach some place, but sailors simply want to sail. The sea is the last area on earth where total spontaneity of movement is possible, and it's a glorious feeling to use the elements—the wind—as propulsion. Another benediction is the absence of noise on a sailboat, except for the amiable conversation of your friends and family.

An Atlantic crossing, however, is a different matter from a Sunday outing off Nantucket. When I proposed to sail from Florida to Spain, my wife, Pat, worried because my venture across the ocean would be undertaken in the same vessel with her only son and only sister. Pat informed me several times that she never expected to see me again. "If he comes through this thing alive," she told a friend, "I'll kill him."

I've been sailing since I was thirteen, and I know that accidents can happen. I remember my first voyage aboard the yacht on which I planned to sail the Atlantic—my beautiful *Cyrano*, sixty-feet long and built to an old fishing boat design. We planned a four-hour jaunt from Fort Lauderdale to Miami, with a crew of friends and family that included Pat and her mother, but about a quarter of a mile down a narrow canal, the engine suddenly stopped. Without power, we floated down the waterway with heavy boat traffic all around us. I instructed my son, Christopher, and his friend, Danny, to jump into the ship's dinghy and start the outboard engine to tow *Cyrano* back to the yard. Christopher gave a powerful yank on the starter. So powerful that the forty-horsepower outboard, which had not been properly secured, leaped up from the transom and dove to the bottom of the canal.

Just before our arrival in Miami that evening, after a rough passage through huge swells, Pat's mother looked at me and said, "Bill, dear, is there supposed to be a fire up there?"—pointing to the bow of the boat. (A kerosene lantern had fallen from the headstay onto a collapsed sail below.) When the blaze was extinguished, one of our passengers, who had never been on a sailboat before, asked if sailing trips were always like this. "Yes," said Pat, as calm as Ethel Barrymore. "Oh, yes. In fact, tonight's was one of the more peaceful sails we've ever had."

The *Cyrano*'s thirty-day crossing of the Atlantic did prove to be relatively peaceful, however, and full of the pleasures one takes aboard a sailboat on blue water. Yes, there were failures of equipment, including the barometer, a device as simple mechanically as a screwdriver. There was bad luck, such as when a wave weighing many more tons than our boat hit us during a spell of fifty-knot winds. But there was no failure of good-natured crew, friends, and family.

At sea there were magnificent evenings, sitting at dinner, sliding rhythmically over the water as if drawn by a cable. I can still smell the cleansing salt in the air, see the gray and the blue: our private ocean.

Our first landfall was the Azores. On the island of São Miguel there was a sixteenth-century church known for its tall tower and beautiful doorways, and the popular Hotel São Pedro. One night Christopher and Danny hiked up into a volcano on the island to camp with the hawks and the stars.

Then we sailed on, and when I spotted the southwest tip of Portugal, I felt a special excitement that comes after a transatlantic passage; then on through the Strait of Gibraltar to our final anchoring spot at Marbella.

To start in Florida and end up in Europe is an experience. I reflected that if I had moved my steering wheel five degrees to the right or left of where I was heading, we would have landed in Africa...or Norway.

This sense of accomplishment is one reason I like to sail. Another is that everyday life moves fast. A sailboat forces you to slow down; you become engrossed in the elements. I've noticed that an enormous number of airline pilots like to sail. Here you have an exaggeration of the polarities—people who never move slower than 550 miles per hour are absolutely *elated* to hit seven-and-a-quarter knots in a sailboat. Sailing a boat is a glorious sensation, and I expect to pursue it all my days.

Pity the Airlines
April 14, 1995

A recent issue of *Fortune* magazine carries a gloomy story about the airline business. The upshot is that it is a terrible investment but nevertheless continues to attract risk capital even as Broadway shows and presidential candidates attract speculators.

It is a glamorous business, yet it is hard to reconcile its apparently ineluctable growth (more people travel every year) with its dismal economic performance. In the past five years the airlines lost nearly all the money they earned since the first commercial flight in 1914 (St. Petersburg, FL, to Tampa, FL).

The writer notes the airlines' response to their economic plight, which is: frugality. Ten years ago, it was the cost of fuel that was said to be driving the airlines bananas. But the cost of fuel is down to normal and still parsimony reigns. The reason for this, we are advised, is the aggregate aspect of plane travel. In market situations, if you meet price resistance, you reduce incremental costs. You produce one fewer mousetrap. But one fewer passenger per flight can mean an aircraft running at a colossal loss.

The curse of the airline is the little competitor that hoves in with the round-trip fare to London for $199. The major airlines have no alternative but to match the price.

Well, yes, they do, and that is a complaint beginning to surface. Since you can't cancel the flight because you don't have enough paying passengers, what you can do is make them miserable. This is happening at a runaway rate.

Flying last week to Nassau, the Delta 727 stretch was completely full. A full plane isn't necessarily uncomfortable, but it can be made uncomfortable by the simple expedient of invasive configurations, the kind that give your knees one inch of space if you are five feet ten or less; no space if you are six-feet tall. When the seat tilts back, you have gained perhaps two inches of arc space.

For breakfast/brunch we were served one tiny, unbuttered, untoasted bagel with a tube of cream cheese and two jiggers of canned orange juice in a plastic saucer—that way you don't have to serve a plastic glass, get it? The traveling bar serves you with cold coffee and will sell booze, if you can bring yourself to escapist distractions at ten in the morning.

That was tourist class. USAir first class won't give you a drinking glass; you will need to use the wobbly plastic things, or else bring a glass from home. United Airlines' seats don't incline back far enough to spill a cup of coffee perched on top. And American—I almost forgot! Traveling first class from Chicago to New York at 8:30, your dinner is…potato chips.

The real challenge lies with the folk who write advertising copy for the airlines. What can they say? Not much else than that they will endeavor not to kill you.

The blame is, in part, the travelers'. Last December, MGM Grand Air terminated service on what was the finest flying service (transcontinental) in history: not enough passengers availed themselves of it—never mind that it charged no more than first class on the regular carriers.

Americans can be very odd about luxuries. We spend a trillion dollars or whatever on nonessentials, but refuse to sustain decent trains or transoceanic liners. It would be fine to experiment on, say, three major routes: New York-Miami, New York-Los Angeles, New York-Chicago. Four inches of leg room, seats that tilt back forty-five degrees, simple but good food: hot pastrami sandwiches and yogurt sundaes.

But that airline would need to cultivate its clientele, and these things take time. It would need to be distinguished by its absolute guarantee not to compromise its services—ever.

But what would it take to make such a guarantee, over a period of, say, three years? Enough to test the American traveler's consolidated appetite for non-gymnastic travel? To make that effort, the airline would need to come up with a ticket that costs one part of the leg you are now free to maneuver, but not the cost of the whole of a leg. Somewhere between APEX prices and business class prices.

But you would need enough capital to see you through the long trial period. MGM discovered that word of mouth isn't enough. You would need modest, nonsplashy advertising: constant reminders that air travel need not be an ordeal.

Then? Then if the buying public doesn't sustain it, why, we can always stay at home.

Definitive Vacations
Private Clubs, May–June 1995

There is an inbuilt problem with vacations, which is that when they are carefully planned—weeks, months, sometimes years ahead—they run the risk of losing the element of spontaneity that can give vacations that special lift. If you know at Christmas that you are going to take August 1 through 15 for a vacation touring the Carlsbad Caverns and the Painted Desert and the Grand Canyon you have, yes, the advantage of plenty of time to plan ahead, but also the disadvantage that during July you begin a countdown that makes the magic day when vacation begins just a little routinized, like when Gary Cooper polishes off the last of the badmen after shooting the first three.

My father led a very busy life, as so many Americans do, and when I was a boy confided to me his formula. "There is never a convenient time for a vacation," he said. So? "So take a vacation whenever you feel like taking a vacation."

Granted that's easy to say, less easy to execute. Obstetricians count nine months ahead and turn down patients for the appropriate period of their proposed vacation, their means of central planning. However completely you think you preside over your own schedule, there are always inflexibilities there. Inflexibilities which not even one of Ayn Rand's heroes could do very much about. If you have just been elected president, for instance, you really can't take a two-week vacation beginning on the 15th of January of the year ahead, though, come to think of it, nothing in the Constitution specifies where exactly you have to be standing when you take the oath of office. LBJ stood in the saloon of Air Force One on the ground at Dallas and presto! he was the thirty-sixth president of the United States.

One reads that Roman slaves had no vacations. If that is true, then their regimen would appear to defy what Americans take for granted as, quite simply, a metabolic requirement. The political prisoners at Gulag had no "vacation," but Aleksandr Solzhenitsyn, in his *One Day in the Life of Ivan Denisovich*, made mention of the ten-minute reprieve to celebrate Stalin's birthday a reprieve suddenly announced in the early morning after roll call, a ten-minute delay before the daily forced march to the frozen work area. *Ivan Denisovich* is about how a human being, living, eating, and working in circumstances almost unimaginably cruel, spots in his schedule little fireflies of hope and surcease: the day in which two extra ounces of bread secreted to him by a retiring guard bring a carnal joy almost orgasmic; an extra piece of coal stumbled upon on the march back from forced labor means that for an hour that night the cold of the barracks will be mitigated by a sense of almost voluptuous warmth. Such events are, in such circumstances, a "vacation" from the iron schedule of life.

We've gotten used to vacations, and indeed during the Forties vacations worked their way into the United Nations Covenant on Human Rights, which demands a vacation with pay for everyone. Some societies anticipated the United Nations by generations. Costa Rica, a touring political scientist counted a few years ago, had 187 vacation days every year, the accumulation of Sundays, Holy Days of Obligation, national holidays, and saints' days, plus personal vacation time.

In such situations one might even talk oneself into thinking of a day at work as a day on vacation, my thesis being that nothing kills a vacation more surely than endlessness. This, of course, is to round the corner, when the vacation suddenly looms as a great stretch of emptiness, which is what often happens, we are informed, when the very busy, very important man (seldom women—they are more resourceful) wakes up a month or two after his retirement party to realize that all that golf and leisure and Caribbean cruising have begun to cloy. Yesterday he was a divisional commander and what seemed like all the world was there for him to deploy, whether to bring him a cup of coffee or to launch an offensive against the enemy, and now, now—they keep him waiting on the f—ing phone! He can't find a porter at the airport! He forces himself to acknowledge a creeping indifference to his golf score.

The point, really, is that vacations are primarily there to interrupt the quiet, understated, indeed unacknowledged pleasure you take from work.

However routine, work is a fortifying experience, your intimate sense of your own productivity. Charlie Chaplin made himself grotesque in *Modern Times* standing by an assembly belt that moved faster and faster while he attempted to tighten a fleeting screw or whatever; and the movie about assembly-line work made all the world laugh, including men and women who stand for lifetimes at such automated assemblies and live full and happy lives. And for them, of course, there is the vacation, which in the past has included going to movies and seeing Charlie Chaplin in *Modern Times*.

Winston Churchill defined a vacation as "doing something different." He liked to paint, but no one who has painted has ever suggested that to paint requires less concentration than tightening screws on an assembly belt. An aspirant professional pianist will spend five or six hours every day at the keyboard. Here is a secret: the professional musician almost *never* plays for himself. He plays for *other* people. When he plays for himself, he is *practicing*—to play for other people. The vacation for Bach virtuoso Rosalyn Tureck means *not to play* the piano. What would be a vacation for the politician fully engaged in his profession? Cincinnatus twice left his farm to fight for his country but happily turned his sword into a plowshare when the fighting was over. He was not a very good politician, by modern understanding.

They don't all come that way. Hubert Humphrey's sadness came only after the public narrowly declined to make him president. He had never really taken a vacation before, hurtling from mayor of Minneapolis to senator to vice president to presidential candidate. Some friends, colleagues, and observers speculate that if he had permitted himself the experience of a vacation he might have lived longer and might have served more effectively in competition for high office. For some legendary people the very idea of a vacation is somehow alien. Charles de Gaulle building a sand castle on the beach? In exile at the forlorn island of St. Helena ("*ce rocher damnable!*"), Napoleon would lie five hours in his iron bathtub dictating to his amanuensis stuff nobody ever after read. For the glory mongers, there are no vacations.

For others, there is nothing like them. I have coveted my share of this and that in life, but nothing so much as what kept me awake as a thirteen-year-old at night at boarding school in England for weeks before it would happen. Vacation! It would mean joining my two sisters, coming in from their own boarding school nearby, and being driven to Southampton to catch the majestic *Normandie*, a five-day passage to New York, then one month at home over Christmas! Two weeks before sailing there was the rumor, communicated to me by the headmaster: a threat of a strike. If it materialized, that would mean cancelling the passage and—I'd learn from my father's London agent—there was no other steamship on which we could secure passage in December, 1938.

The suspense was all but unendurable, but the ship did leave on time. You feel it still, the sudden relief from what you did yesterday and the day before and the day before. You are Antaeus, the Greek god whose strength dissipates menacingly until, at intervals, he touches his feet down on the ground, getting from the mere touch that jolt of life and energy that make bearable his muscle-bound mission on Earth.

But I am carried away. In need, obviously, of time off. Of a vacation.

Airplane Crosstalk
March 22, 1996

Those Americans condemned to spend hundreds of hours every year on airplanes are remarkable, some would say, for their stoicism; others would say for their docility.

The Marriott hotels make it a point to ask their overnight customers if they found anything wayward in the service given; if so, please specify what it was. One has to suppose that after going to such pains to research customer complaints, some people, somewhere, meet to reflect on them.

If there is ever—anywhere—a meeting by airline executives to reflect on what they impose on traveling Americans, one wonders where and how they have collected their data. Have you ever been handed a slip of paper soliciting your reactions to airline procedures?

I tend to travel first class, thanks to the hospitality of my own clients, combined with hedonistic inclinations cultivated with great sweat over a period of many years. The primary difference between first-class and tourist-class travel is the increasing differential in price. If the price increase were happening *pari passu* with increased amenities, that would make economic sense.

But exactly the opposite is happening. The quality of the food diminishes, legroom straitens, and scheduling is progressively bizarre.

One might simply ignore the whole business on the grounds that compared to other world problems—starvation, plagues, and landslides—it's so-what time. But what edges into the consciousness isn't so much the discomforts as the sense of creeping social docility.

In 1961 I wrote an article for *Esquire* called "Why Don't We Complain?" It is the only thing I ever wrote that has been anthologized a dozen times. It evidently occurs to many editors that the question of American lassitude is a phenomenon worth reflecting upon, even as American resignation. Less than one-half of us bothered to vote in 1992.

I am sitting first class on USAir, a flight from San Antonio to Pittsburgh. I'm not going to Pittsburgh, but to Cleveland, but there aren't any direct flights to Cleveland, not one. Two days ago, I traveled New York to San Antonio. The travel time was just a few minutes longer than the flight last week from New York to Geneva, Switzerland.

The schedule proclaimed a stop in Dallas, and then on to San Antonio. But forsooth! After landing in Dallas, it transpired that there were only three of us going on to San Antonio. Suddenly the airplane developed mechanical problems and we were offloaded onto a flight to San Antonio leaving an hour-and-a-half later.

On this flight to Pittsburgh, the departure time was 9:15. At 10:00 a.m. the passengers were served breakfast. Now there are, here and there, strict religious sects with odd dietary laws governing when you can and when you cannot eat. But they don't affect most Americans, and I would bet my favorite pooch that not two—not one—of those passengers on that plane had foregone breakfast before they boarded.

Perhaps they ate (as I did) at 7:00 a.m. a little juice, coffee and a breakfast roll. Customarily, human beings would next feel the impulse to eat something again not sooner than noon. But USAir serves its full breakfast not at noon but at 10:00.

And most people simply eat it. They don't say: Why are you stuffing a second breakfast down my throat when you can readily deduce that I have already eaten breakfast? They don't say: This is a two-and-one-half-hour flight; why not wait at least until the final hour, not the first half hour, to offer me more food?

I do request a cup of coffee. It arrives in a paper cup. I had forgotten that USAir is famous for this draconian economy. You pay first-class fare and you get coffee in a receptacle MacDonald's would go out of business after a month if caught using.

Why doesn't USAir, which is charging $400 for this flight leg, give its clients the option of paying $402, in return for which they get served coffee in a real, genuine cup? The only alternative, under the circumstances, is to make a note to carry a mug in your briefcase whenever you can't avoid flying on USAir.

My seat is 1D and my legs are just about perpendicular, for the simple reason that any attempt to stretch them out a few inches is barred by the bulkhead. If you are less than five feet tall, you might be comfortable seated in 1D.

Where do you put your reading matter? On your lap. Because the bulkhead's magazine pouch has space only for the airline magazine and, at that, is situated where your leg might rest if you sought to nuzzle it forward an extra inch or two, seeking space.

Why don't they put receptacles for your traveling paraphernalia four feet higher, where they would get in nobody's way, occupying space otherwise unused? Perhaps because no one has ever suggested it.

Why is there no nonstop service, San Antonio-New York, if there is traffic enough for San Antonio-Pittsburgh? A very good question, and conceivably one that no one has ever asked. American air travelers are a supine class.

Down Amsterdam Way
June 14, 1996

AMSTERDAM, The Netherlands—The story has been around for a while. Still, it's a striking experience. They are called "coffee shops," and you bump into the first of many verbal games here, like the confusion between "legal" and "illegal." In formal logic, the law of contradiction specifies that something can both be—and not be at the same time. Not so in Amsterdam, as witness the coffee shops. They are illegal and protected by the state.

You are led in and the appointments are tidy-seedy. The wooden counter must have looked secondhand when it was built. The walls are undecorated. The six or eight tables are for four people; the chairs utilitarian.

You ask for (you have been coached) the "menu," and are given a handwritten page splotchy in appearance that lists twelve items. The first two are for hashish. The ensuing are brands of marijuana, the one at the bottom designated "Spunk." It is the newest and evidently most popular.

The price schedule works through your mind, translate gilders into dollars. You ask questions of your three guides, two of them officials from the health department. It translates to about $2 for a joint.

How much of the stuff can you buy and take out with you? "Legally, five grams, which means three of the above." Actually—legally, thirty grams.

See if you can follow this: if anybody should stop you on the street (extremely unlikely) and you have more than thirty grams on you, the presumption is that you are engaged in marijuana trafficking, rather than merely in using the stuff for yourself and the kids. What happens? You are at least warned.

There is an Orwellian shade drawn over the whole scene.

There are complicated reasons why the Dutch don't just go ahead and say it's legal, period. There are international covenants to be worried about. And the authorities like to have a sanction in the closet, in case they want to get tough.

To get served in the coffee shops you have to be seventeen. If you sell to a sixteen-year-old, the authorities can take away your license. How threatening is this? Not very; it doesn't happen much.

Yes, there is a looming threat to reduce the number of coffee shops in Amsterdam, talk even of cutting the number (450) in half. That would hurt the individual proprietor because the typical coffeehouse takes in $150,000 per year. Not a gold mine—call it a silver mine.

But the attitude of the governors of all this business is very far from flippant. They are wholly dedicated to the proposition that drugs are a very grave health problem but not a problem-best dealt with by criminal sanctions. The Dutch draw an entirely plausible line between the soft drugs (the marijuana family) and the hard drugs (cocaine, etc.).

They are fastidiously concerned with the data. The director of the health center in charge of the hard-drug center is a doctor, and he has been in the business for eighteen years. The official guess is that the authorities know 85 percent of the hard-drug users, who have no reservations about identifying themselves, at least not because they fear criminal prosecution. What they get if they turn themselves in or are caught is treatment.

While talking in the corridor to the man behind the windowpane, the conversation is interrupted. A middle-aged man of weather-beaten appearance, Arabic in skin and features, comes in, gives the woman behind the desk a number. She enters it instantly into her computer and in a nanosecond hands her client a vial, which there and then he pours into his mouth, drops the container into a bin and leaves. Methadone.

What happens down the line? Half of them respond to treatment and kick the hard-drug habit. The other half? "After fifteen years, if they don't make it, we stop the methadone. Hard on the lungs. We administer the drug," the director says.

What is the large view of this? Well, the drug users are getting treated, and have no need to engage in criminal activity to support their habit.

The big picture?

The most encouraging datum: in 1985, 28 percent of hard-drug users were younger than twenty-six years old. In 1995, 4 percent were under twenty-six. Meaning? Hard-drug experimentation is rapidly declining among the young.

Another datum: crime by drug users is down.

The people tackling the problem aren't to be confused with the types one finds here and there who are simply soft on drugs. The anointed in the counterdrug culture would consider it heaven on earth if after the next ten years drug consumption were down to zero.

It won't be, because these graphs are asymptotic, never reaching the goal line. But there is no appetite to stick people in jail. For robbing or killing, yes. But not for being stupid, which is what drug users mostly are.

Barbuda
Islands, August 1996

Sailing with my wife and me were older brother Jim and older sister Priscilla. I had told them about cruising life in the Antilles and its special delights, among them the endless beach of Barbuda. This wasn't like taking the kids the first time to Disney World: my siblings have been around. Jim was in the Navy during World War II and knew all about beaches because he served aboard an LST, which was designed to come up on a beach to disgorge troops, tanks, and spare parts. Priscilla had wandered with me for several days in the Tahitian islands, including the fabulous Bora-Bora, and, once before, we had sashayed around what I insist are the most beautiful islands in the world—the Azores. But the Azorean beaches suffer from dusky gray sand, in contrast to the white-white beaches of the Antilles. (I remember speculating on whether the old trick of the ad-man in the Thirties might work to sell the Azores to the tourist world. He was hired—remember?—by a fishery trying to unload an aberrant million pounds of snow white salmon. He came up with the slogan, "Guaranteed Not to Turn Pink in the Can!")

Our approach to Barbuda was restricted, when the skipper of our chartered Swan 65 advised me, with heroic equanimity, that the noise I had heard during the preceding half hour, as we bounded under sail from Antigua toward Barbuda in a happy easterly, had meant that the engine mount had "collapsed."

"How long would it take to repair?" I asked.

"Well, certainly not less than one week." But his young face brightened: "With the course you've set, we can sail all the way, and the generator's working just fine."

Who needed an engine?

But this meant that our tack toward the anchorage area, about a hundred yards from Barbuda's spectacular beach, had to end before the outermost reefs began, which left us a half mile from land. Yet we needed to press on, not only because of the special allure of the famous three-mile-long beach but also because we had our social obligations. My wife's old friends Arthur and Francisco were staying at the K-Club and had asked us to dine with them during our cruise. And at the south end of the beach was Coco Point Lodge, founded and run by Bill Kelly, a college friend whom brother Jim had promised to visit.

"How old is the Coco Point Lodge?" I asked Jim as the sails came down. He didn't remember exactly but said that if I could remember when

Princess Margaret Rose was married, that was when the lodge opened, because she had honeymooned there. Well, I didn't remember exactly when Margaret Rose and Antony Armstrong-Jones had married, only that it was many *anni horribili* back for the royal family.

But we were anchored off the K-Club, where Arthur and Francisco awaited us. The captain said he would take the dinghy in to the beach and advise me what was involved in stepping ashore.

A half hour later he was back. "There's something of a...swell," he cautioned. "But we can handle it."

Since my wife, Pat, has frail hips, thrice operated on, Jim and I decided to do a dry run in order exactly to evaluate the difficulty in landing on the island with our dinghy.

We approached, and the swell seemed quietly and nicely to subside. We were only feet away when a rogue wavelet crashed in, and we tumbled out in crotch-level water. Pat, it was now clear, would not be visiting this island, but I would attempt to discharge minimal social obligations, and Jim would visit a half hour with Bill Kelly.

With my cellular phone I told Francisco at the K-Club that we had arrived and were standing in the loamy sand within eye distance of his hotel.

Minutes later Francisco was, as always, breathlessly describing the amusements and vexations of life in general and life in particular. As we trudged up toward the clubhouse, he gave us two data relevant to our plans.

Concerning the destination of brother Jim, we should know something about the "problem" of the north part of the beach, the K-Club, and the south, Coco Point Lodge. Both are luxury resorts, he said, but the relations between the two owners were straight-out Hatfield-McCoy.

"It's like North Korea and South Korea," Francisco explained. The resorts do not have contact with one another, "so we'll have to make special arrangements," he said to Jim, "to get you from here to Coco."

And then, he chatted on, as we approached the lightly screened, aquamarine-and-white clubhouse (all but demolished three months earlier by Hurricane Luis but miraculously rebuilt in time for the season), there was the problem of Princess Diana.

We had been at sea a few days and were ignorant of what the society pages of every tabloid in the world were evidently whispering, namely that Di was on the island of Barbuda, staying at the K-Club.

"Alone?" I found myself asking, without malice aforethought, just spastic journalistic curiosity.

"She has her lady-in-waiting," Francisco explained. "They spend the entire time at the swimming pool."

I found this odd, given the lascivious wonders of the beach and also the two floodlit tennis courts, the nine-hole golf course, the snorkeling, the sailing. On the other hand, there isn't actually that much to do on a beach, is there?

Arthur, who is a famous architect, had joined us—we were now sitting in the lounge across from the bar, Jim having made off across the DMZ to Coco Point Lodge—and nodded in vigorous agreement, because when he goes to the beach, he said, he goes in order to get a lot of reading done, whereas Francisco is a beach-nut who stretches out hour after hour, sun-worshipping. Beaches, Arthur and I agreed, are splendid to look at, not to plop down on.

They were enjoying the K-Club and its 250 acres on an island with 1,500 inhabitants. Barbuda, I was told, had a gruesome distinction: it was an island on which for more than 100 years slaves were *bred*. Thirty-five years ago, when the Coco Point Lodge was established, the island was completely undeveloped. Today 60 percent of its income is from tourists, and now it had the crown jewel, Princess Diana.

Her arrival had caused great commotion. Poor dear, she slipped out of Heathrow a day or two after Christmas, with her lady-in-waiting, onto a commercial flight to Antigua, using an assumed name.

But, of course, one of the dogs of the press spotted her, and by the time her private plane (Antigua-Barbuda flight time, fifteen minutes) had landed, a great legion of paparazzi had gathered, intending to make her stay on the island as exposed as possible.

To thwart this, the authorities in Barbuda had rallied. Among other things, they closed off a half mile of the great beach. This was not accepted without complaint. Francisco cited the owner of a local grocery store who was quoted in the papers as saying that "legally, we can access the beach and sit right next to her. I totally object to anybody shutting off what is public property."

Nor had Diana made time for the locals. On being asked to appear at a ceremony to present medals to people who had played key roles in restoring the island (95 percent of roofs had been damaged by the hurricane), she simply declined the request—not what was expected of someone who only weeks before had told the world she hoped to be thought of as the Queen of Hearts. On the other hand, the Princess obviously sought isolation, given that she had chosen to stay in a club that excludes children under the age of twelve, which meant that William and Harry wouldn't have been admitted, even if they could have been wrenched away from the prince, the queen, and the imperial guard at Sandringham, where they spent New Year's.

I was called to the telephone. It was my brother, speaking to me from across the DMZ. He reported that Bill Kelly suggested that I contact the captain aboard our vessel and warn him not to approach our designated rendezvous point, where we had landed forty-five minutes before, because, night having fallen, he might hit one of the barely submerged reefs.

But there was no way to reach the captain. I didn't have a radio with me, and the captain was not monitoring any channel. Very well then, Jim would meet me in fifteen minutes, as previously arranged.

As I returned to my hosts and my rum collins, a crew-cut, middle-aged man in casual dress addressed me.

"I'm Ken Follett," he said, "and Ed McBain is also staying here. Now that is a coincidence, isn't it—you, me, McBain?"

I told Mr. Follett I thought *The Fist of God* was one of the best suspense/espionage novels I ever read, and he said, thanks, but he didn't write it.

I plunged into another title, but he hadn't written that either. I told him I still winced at the review he had given one of my thrillers in the *Listener*, but he said he hadn't written it.

The only thing I could do under the circumstances was to congratulate Mr. Follett on whatever it was he had written (*The Eye of the Needle*; the *other* author is Frederick Forsyth). We wished each other a happy New Year.

The time had come, and Francisco and Arthur came with me to the beach, where we could make out the dinghy. We waited for Jim. He was almost ten minutes late. He had been stopped, after getting out of the Coco car and walking out to the beach, by the secret service guarding Princess

Di's privacy. Jim was once a senator and is now a senior judge. He positively emanates sobriety. Not even Ken Follett would cast him as a terrorist.

Then it was back over the reefs to report to wife and sister all the news of the captivating island of Barbuda.

Air War
October 11, 1996

You hear from time to time about the deterioration in airplane travel, less than one ought to hear about how routinely bad it has become. The old saw is that you can become accustomed to anything. Presumably if the strength of the sun were to diminish by one candlepower every day, odd things would begin to happen. Not all unwelcome, I say, writing in Phoenix where the weather, reaching 103 degrees, set a record for mid-October the other day. But then one day we'd find that much more electricity was being used, and lights were going on earlier and earlier.

But most travelers would say that airline performances are losing month by month, year by year, the equivalent of a million candlepower units every year. One needs, obviously, to go from personal experience.

Last week traveling to Dallas from Newark, NJ, on Continental, the schedule was tight, and so when it took a half-hour for the flight to climb to the head of the takeoff line, heart palpitations began. But then just before the captain was scheduled to take off, he announced calmly that he would need to return to the terminal because there was something wrong with the back-door entrance to the airplane.

Back we went, forfeiting our half-hour. Whatever was wrong with the back door took a mere fifteen minutes to fix. Back in line, and we began flying, about one hour and ten minutes behind schedule.

I would learn from a savvy fellow passenger that what happened was that the companionway on which you used to climb to get inside the plane from the rear was hanging out. Apparently, nothing on the dashboard advises the captain that such has occurred. What apparently happened was that another captain, on another airplane, inching forward toward takeoff, noticed that the plane in front of him had a staircase open and inviting. He evidently radioed the captain, who pulled out of line and went back to find somebody who would shut his staircase.

What, I asked breathlessly of my veteran companion, if the plane had taken off with the companionway lowered?

"A lot of shaking around, wind resistance, that kind of thing, and of course he'd have had to return in a hurry."

When we were finally flying, I tilted back my seat as far as it would go, which was an inch or two further than on American. Hold your left hand rigid pointing up, your palm facing to your right. Now bend the fingers so that they are horizontal. That would be the inclination of a bed, or of a chair that bends to fully horizontal, the kind of thing they advertise now on Air France and Singapore Airlines. Well, American Airlines' seats go, I'd guess, about 10 percent of the way. It is only barely noticeable.

Some people don't care. Some care very much, I being one of these. I care when I am working with my laptop and care when I am reading. But American, presumably to succeed in inserting one more file of seats, sacrifices all comfort that has to do with body posture. On Continental, the lean-back is not extravagant, but at least twice what American gives you.

I was busily at work when I felt a shaft of ice-cold air trained on my neck. I reached up and slightly redirected the air nipple above the gentleman seated just behind. He leaned up and said to me, would I please raise my seat, because where I had it, he was very nearly immobilized.

I struggle quite consistently to be obliging when asked to do anything short of nodding my head at sophistry. Look, I said, there is exactly one reason why I am flying Continental to Dallas right now. It is that I flew American to Dallas last week and was excruciatingly uncomfortable because the seats wouldn't recline. You are asking me to forfeit the entire purpose of going to Newark just to ease the situation down where your knees are.

He understood. The passenger ahead of me was a stoic, who held his seat upright. But when lunch was served, I had to turn my book almost sideways, my head correspondingly, to attempt to read.

On and on the story goes. Last year (I write once every year about airline service) I wrote about dreadful USAir, which gives you drinks in paper cups, pretzels only if a dividend has been declared. The only solution to it,

I was told by someone on the ground, is to fly first class. But I have been totally faithful to a vow I took early in life to fly first class, and the vicissitudes I mention occur precisely in first class.

The only alternative left for those whose businesses require us to fly continuously is to practice stoicism. It has great rewards, not least economic. My learned friend Count Erik von Kuehnelt-Leddin, the Austrian aristocrat, aged eighty, remarked once that he was asked, getting off at the rear of the train, why he traveled third class. "Because there is no fourth class," he said.

A solution might be to make airplanes, head-to-toe, more comfortable on all competitive lines. Then pass the word around. Then see whether intense and loyal patronage will always give you a full plane, leaving the others for the contortionists and those who, hard though they try, fail to achieve stoicism.

Maritime Traveler
Yachting, November 1996

You arrive in Baddeck on the Bras d'Or Lakes in Cape Breton, Nova Scotia, Canada, to pick up your chartered yawl and you spend an endless hour trying to find out why your cellular telephone doesn't work. (Answer: in Canada the protocol that acknowledges your PIN number is different. Don't let it confuse you: just proceed.) Cellular phones at sea, when you are, within tower-hailing distance, in coastal cruising, which is almost all the time, have all but displaced the Oscar-Whiskey-Delta radios that have always been burdensome ("Where are you, Oscar-Whiskey-Delta?") But there are always those initial exasperations before cruising.

They were quickly forgotten last July as we set out on an eight-day cruise in exotic waters in and around the Maritime Provinces of Canada. We scheduled a modest start; overnight, ninety minutes down the lake at Boulacet Harbour, en route to St. Peter's Channel into the sea. A tranquil evening, marred only when a bad knot (tied by me) permitted the water thermometer to fall into the sea. I felt a special attachment to that particular thermometer and in a flush of Me-Tarzan heroism, dived fully-dressed to retrieve it. Too late. I succeeded only in incapacitating my cellular telephone, inadvertently left in my pocket. I have institutionalized it as a legend. No cruise begins without the finger of fate wagging reproachfully, making you pay earnest money on the special overhead of life at sea.

There are a few things wanting on board *White Mist*, e.g., mosquito repellent and candles (indispensable to the right atmosphere at night). The forward starboard bunk houses my personal indispensables, including grapefruit juice, cookies, flame-makers, three boxes of tapes, portable cassette player, compass, barometer, night glasses, binoculars, camera, knife, computer, alarm clock, inverter, extension cord, and peanut butter.

The Bras d'Or Lakes are a delight. We have cruised in them twice before. Our objective this time is to pull out of Cape Breton and head to Prince Edward Island and the Madeleine Islands up north, returning to Cape Breton at the end of a week. Michael Fuller is on board as first mate and general factotum ("What do you want him to do?" his father, owner of *White Mist*, asked over the telephone. "Cook, clean, and help on deck.") Michael is in college and spent last summer in Central America, mostly on horseback on a ranch. He is ruggedly bearded (tough, outdoor look) but his gentility creeps through.

It was a fifty-mile leg to Port Hawkesbury. We had up jib and jigger for a stretch or two, but the wind was resolute in its determination to stay on the nose, no matter which way we headed. You pull out of the Bras d'Or Lakes at St. Peters, into the Atlantic Ocean. You turn right to head up the Lenox Passage separating Cape Breton from Nova Scotia proper. The channel is adequately, though not abundantly, marked. I was reminded of the inexpressible joys of GPS by looking down from time to time at the slender little Magellan perched alongside the compass whenever there was ambiguity, projecting the longitude on the chart with the eye. It would be useful if a boat gadgeteer came up with a plastic little overlay with parallel lines corresponding to those on standard charts, so that you could position them and trace your coordinates more or less exactly. Early in the afternoon we lost the sun, the first step in the capitulation of everything around us to the terminal exasperations of Hurricane Bertha.

We reached Port Hawkesbury, where we had agreed to meet up with my friend Peter on his thirty-eight-foot *Astraea*, to journey together for the cruise. He had set out three days earlier from Nantucket in thick fog and would arrive triumphantly after 600 miles of sailing. He was there when we arrived, *Astraea* snugly tied up on the dock. We all went to his boat, eight feet shorter than our own, but vast in internal dimension thanks to the expansion in boat beams between 1950 (when our *White Mist* was built) and 1992, when Hood's *Astraea* was launched.

They had had two of those golden days at sea, the wind on the quarter, sailing wing and wing at hull speed. The only little cloud on the passage was when a young crew member, instructed to inflate the dinghy, inflated instead the life raft. Peter's serenity was interrupted when he saw his huge Avon engulfing what seemed the entire boat ("You know, it takes like $700 to recommission those things!" he told me as we trudged off to church.) We were glad not to have been aboard when that happened. Mercifully, Peter's great ires quickly dissipate.

There was a problem. The Coast Guard was telling us Bertha would bring strong winds, very strong winds, gusting up to seventy kilometers per hour (that's forty-two knots), and that the wind would travel from the southeast clockwise and that the rainfall would accumulate up to seventy millimeters, (which translates to about two inches). I had a road map of the entire area, on which Henry Fuller, owner of the boat and of the Cape Breton Boatyard at Baddeck, had traced a suggested itinerary. From Hawkesbury we would set out through the Canso Causeway for the easternmost point of Nova Scotia, about twenty-five miles, then gird the Gulf of St. Lawrence to Prince Edward Island and begin the coveted trip up the coastline, and up to the Madeleine Islands. But there would be no point in scheduling our departure, or for that matter, our exact destination, until the following morning, when Bertha would reveal her final hand.

The hard rain began at midnight. Twenty-four hours later we were still tied up with winds blowing at about fifty-six knots, the energies of the little boat community feverishly engaged with lines and hawsers and fenders and car tires to prevent, or mitigate, damage.

A word must be said about the Port Hawkesbury Yacht Club. It is one large room with broad tables of the kind one associates with a bridge tournament or a bingo game. The large sign outside reads: "P-H-Y-C, BOATS WELCOME, SHOWERS. TEN DOLLARS PER NIGHT, SHOWERS $2." Sometimes there is an attendant, often there isn't. There is a slot at waist level into which you deposit your money. No one bothers to see that you do. A tall, young, blond lady occasionally appears, giving advice on all matters. If you want a beer, you simply fetch it out of the refrigerator, potato chips from the unattended kitchenette.

I have a half-dozen times sailed in and out of Halifax and to the Bras d'Or Lakes and if I have failed to remark the universal geniality of the people in these Maritime Provinces, I have been remiss. They are the most pleasant breed of men and women I have encountered in a lifetime of pretty hectic travel. You wonder, at Port Hawkesbury, what it is that causes the middle-aged man coiling a large hose from whom you inquire where the public telephone is, to drop what he is doing and physically lead you to it. He worries that you might not have found it on your own, as it is thirty yards distant.

We experience a very long sail to Georgetown, sheer joy in a steady wind of only slightly immoderate force. Prince Edward Island is not to be confused with Bermuda. Both are islands, both are surrounded by water, and both were developed and colonized in the seventeenth century.

For the visiting yachtsman, P.E.I. (as everyone refers to it) is easily exploited: it has more navigable harbors and inlets than Bermuda. What is conspicuously missing in P.E.I. is natural or architectural charm. In Bermuda, the concern is mostly for the tourist and charm becomes a physical trademark. One does not go to Bermuda to farm potatoes (P.E.I.'s principal product), and the shopping is not easy. In the capital city of Charlottetown, we sought out a ship's chandlery, intending to buy a large snap hook and a length of yellow floating line. As ever, everyone was anxious to help. We were directed to someone working on a powerboat that sat on a cradle ten feet above the water. Lying on his back, bearded, wearing a baseball cap, he heard us out.

The kind of snap hook we wanted he would need to send off for; the floating line he had in stock in his shop. How far away? Oh, three miles— he would fetch it up for as soon as he was through putting the boat he was working on in the water. The offer sounded like a noontime promise to deliver your sandwich sometime in late afternoon. We completed the tour of the non-memorable town, whose most recent architects have not broken with tradition, which demands that buildings be stolid and featureless.

The fields are green, here and there engaging, but far removed from the tidy lushness one finds on either side of the St. John River, just a hundred miles west in New Brunswick; or in Horta, 1,900 miles east, in the Azores. There are here-and-there odd interventions in the natural featurelessness. The Brudenell Golf Club, just past Georgetown on the east coast, is a luxuriously appointed hotel/club with individual, domed cabins in weathered gray slate. Once again, the hospitality: visiting yachtsmen who desire to shower need do no more than turn the water on. Everything else is provided, with a smile.

Fortune Bay, halfway up the island, has a restaurant justly renowned. The chef, who personally instructs those who wish it on his "tasting" menu, advises you that nothing is served that was not grown on the island—there is even a Prince Edward wine, though others are offered. The site is spectacularly pleasant, overlooking the river and the bay. The food is superbly prepared, but if you order the tasting menu, allow three hours.

A mere fifteen hours sailing takes us from Brudenell Yacht Harbor to Ile du Havre Aubert, the southernmost of the Madeleine Islands. It is all downwind, but we have no spinnaker pole and can't handle wing and wing, so we jibe and jibe and jibe.

Aubert is the southernmost of islands that strung together, go sixty miles northward, connected by causeways. The impact on pulling in at Havre Aubert is instantly reinvigorating. The young man who materializes at the dock to help us tie up ($40 per day) speaks only in French. We make our way to a restaurant for a late dinner. I have the faintly dizzy sensation one slides into after a long sail, instinctively bending one knee, then unbending it as the other knee begins its complementary cycle, seeking body equilibrium as the imaginary boat beneath heaves and weaves and pitches and tilts this way and that. To walk now on level surfaces that stay level confuses the brain.

We made it to the cafe, bristling with people bristling with talk, mostly in French. Some of us ordered snow crabs, a specialty of the region. Nice, but you burn up as many calories wrenching them from their shells as you ingest eating them. The table wine, a Portuguese vino verdhe, is stupendous.

What to do the next day? There are 18,000 year-round inhabitants of the Madeleine Islands and 100,000 summer visitors. Where do they come from, and how? There is a five-hour ferry from Souris in P.E.I. You can come in by ocean liner from Montreal (a two-day passage), or from Carlton in Quebec (just north of New Brunswick)—or fly, once a day, on Air Atlantic from Halifax.

The facilities at Havre Aubert marina are fine (no fuel—just water). A small restaurant, Maree Haute, is pedestrian in appearance but not to be missed. Unpretentious, superb food, reasonably priced. Walking back to the boat you pass the little jail, with its outdoor exercise court, next door to a local painter who exhibits his art and does not leave the island during the winter. Across are the hardware store and grocery, and a small shop in which boats are actually built. The entire structure of this enterprise is about the size of one Chris Craft.

Our schedule is once again affected by Coast Guard radio. There is a boisterous gale, thirty-six hours off, against which the southeasterly return to Cape Breton would be unpleasant. The alternative? An overnight sail to the northeast point of Cape Breton (Cape North), then four hours south to the waterway that will take us back to Baddeck.

There is something to be said for sailing on long courses in the ocean. Whatever the weather does, you simply plow on, making your course as best you can. When you are traveling point to point you huddle by the Coast Guard broadcast and decide what is the adroit thing to do...So, we would sail all night. When we left the restaurant every cloud had gone, the temperature was at seventy degrees, and ten minutes after we pulled out the voluptuous sun kissed the horizon good night.

Alas, no wind. Snatches of it appear ten hours later, after rounding Cape North, sixty miles off, but mostly we drone on. We stopped for lunch in the Great Bras d'Or Channel—primarily to rest our ears. And then another four hours of power, plodding against the wind toward Baddeck. Prompted by a thirst for sail, I decided impulsively to treat ourselves to an eight-mile sail downwind away from Baddeck on the St. Andrews Channel. The wind was very strong and we needed only the genoa to coast down at seven knots. The stillness is quite wonderful, isn't it, when the noisy engine closes down?

And then the quiet, candle-lit dinner below, Michael improvising a no-meat no-fish dinner, steaming hot and nourishing, Ella Fitzgerald on the cassette, and early to bed.

We would pay dearly for our little downwind sleigh ride because the wind was at thirty-five knots, relentless, rain-driven. At times we were making less than two knots headway. We arrived at the Cape Breton Boatyard wet and cold, ready to go home. It is a marvelous cruising area, the Bras d'Or Lakes, the Bay of St. Lawrence, Prince Edward Island, the Madeleines, and back. About 300 miles, a piece of cake…But of course that isn't quite true. Cruising is never just chocolate-malted milk. I expect we all know that and probably wouldn't have it any other way, except when the wind and rain are doing their misanthropic worst to make life miserable and the engine sounds like the devil's tom-tom on the Day of Judgment. But you always know that, just ahead a bit, the sea and the skies are smiling.

One Thousand and One Days on the Orient Express
FYI, Spring 1997

I'm sure it has happened to you, the invitation—however conveyed—to a trip, perhaps even to an adventure. You stare at it for a little while then pull up an Uzi and blast away at your calendar, leaving not one living trace of what had been commitments trivial and solemn, some of them months old. It had happened to me three times before: once the invitation to come along as a guest of the Argentine navy aboard its 400-foot cadet sailing ship (Santo Domingo to New York). Again, when I was asked: Would I like to travel to the South Pole with the Secretary of the Navy? And then the phone call: Would I like to travel down in the little deep-water sub to ogle the *Titanic*?

The brochure from Yale University now described a trip on the "Nostalgic Istanbul Orient Express Via Trans-Mongolian and Trans-Siberian Rail Lines." Breathlessly, I showed the brochure to my wife, declaring my intention to go. She scanned it, and shook her head in disbelief.

Three months later, twenty-four hours after boarding the Russian train, I wrote these sentences.

Just in case I should forget, though I won't: don't even consider taking your wife/husband on the luxury Trans-Siberian railway trip, Beijing-Moscow or vice versa. It is hard enough on one person, even of moderate agility. They tell you these are luxury compartments— designed and built, to be sure, in the 1930s. When I read that, I nodded my head acquiescently. Nine nights on such a train? So? What could be so austere about the 1930s Orient Express? The swells who traveled about the world with their valets didn't really notice Wall Street suicides or the grapes of wrath. These were trains designed for them to enhance their pursuit of luxury. Indeed, the word is formally used on their stationery: "Orient Express/Luxury Private Train."

The temperature in the compartment, as I write, is 89 degrees. There is no air-conditioning. There is no toilet (there is one toilet per sleeping car, i.e., for nine compartments). There is no hanging locker. There are no drawers. In the bathroom, which is a sink, there are two ledges, one eight inches across, the other, four inches: enough to hold one tenth of your (my) toiletries. (There is ten times more vertical wall space, but it goes unused.) Above the electrical socket is printed, "110V, Razor." You have anticipated a need for an alien plug and you confidently whip up, from your kit, the appropriate one. Nothing happens. You call the Russian attendant. "Oh yes, the electric outlets. Well, they don't work. Don't work. anywhere on the train." You pull out your laptop computer to situate it on the little desk-table, which only just accommodates it. You look about for convenient spaces to place such sundries as pens and paper clips and diskettes, but the window ledge is without a fiddle. (A fiddle is the guardrail that keeps objects like eye glasses or ashtrays from tumbling over.) Forward of the table, at waist level, there are two tiny ledges that do have fiddle-protection. But they lie athwartship. Since railroad cars, when they tilt, do so from side to side, not from back to front, these fiddles are useless; and anyway, they are out of reach when you are sitting (the only place you can sit). Although there is no hanging locker, you are given hangers. They are usable on the steel webbing of the luggage racks overhead. Everything you hang—jackets, pants, over coats—dances about in the kinetic frenzy of your luxury private cabin.

SHUT UP! What *dumb* things to fret over, freshly embarked on a 5,300-mile trip across Eurasia with sights to see—great plains, tundra, mountains, lakes, rivers even the Great Khan never saw! The Voice I hear is dead right.

So, you crumple up your disgruntled notes and look for the waste basket. *Only you can't find one.*

So, you uncrumple your notes and try to sleep in the heat. The little electric fan does work, and in your misery, eyes closed, you force yourself to wonder what it must be like for the wretched outside, the herdsmen of the Gobi Desert, dry, menacing, sullen from wasted history. Meanwhile it is difficult, with the seeing and sawing, to read your book. You have the distinct impression you are racing down the tracks at 110 miles per hour. Actually, we never go over 55 mph. How do I know? Because I do not venture outside without my Global Positioning System, and I can stick it out of the window and get speed and geographical location. Sleep eventually rescues you.

It is a pretty overpowering thought, to do the great trip on the fabled rail route completed as recently as under Czar Nicholas II. The first night of travel, after three days in a Beijing hotel, we would spend on the Chinese-Siberian train. It operates on a narrower gauge than the succeeding Russian train. I would learn from Alan, a fellow traveler from Palo Alto who knows quite simply everything, that the reason different countries have different gauges is to discourage invasion. (When the Spaniards set out to rebuild their railroad system they intentionally selected a different gauge from the French, to guard against another Napoleon.)

After the first night's train travel we would arrive in Mongolia, about whose vivid history we would hear vividly from Professor Hal Kahn of Stanford. He told us about the Khan's genius as a warrior and organizer, and of the awful, conventional brutality of life and times under him and his successors (defiant cities under siege were often made an example of by simply killing, after the city was taken, all its men, women, and children). At

Erlian we boarded the Russian-gauged Nostalgic Orient Express, arriving on Day Three at Ulan Bator, the capital city.

Depending on the seniority of your application, you are berthed next door to the bar car and three dining cars; or as many as nine cars away, in which case you must be prepared for three alpine expeditions every day. The little aggravations dog you. The electrical outlet in the compartments having failed, you needed to find juice for your computer and there is only one live plug—in the shower car, in the same little office from which the tour guide and the lecturers address you, once or twice or more every day. But in order to hear them, you have to leave your cabin and stand in the narrow passageway, because there are no speakers inside the cabins. After coping the first time with the computer problem, on Day Two I trudged on to the bar car and ordered a gin and tonic. No ice. Why? Because, sir, the water in Mongolia is not pure. You ask why they don't use non-Mongolian water to make the ice? No answer. The air in the bar car is impossibly fetid. You think—never mind: I will swallow my lukewarm gin and tonic and have a little smoke and forget it all; but you can't smoke. *In a bar car in central Mongolia you cannot smoke a cigar!* You take your warm drink to the dining car. Surely there will be candlelight, indispensable to your vision of choo-chooing in the night across vast dark spaces. No. Only bright over-head lights—you might be dining at one of those buffets in Penn Station still open at 3:00 a.m. for staff and stray travelers. It is dismally hot and you ask why the windows aren't raised. You try to understand exactly what the Russian tells you. It has something to do with the absence of a crank handle, without which those windows simply stay shut. You sit down, and close your eyes, and say to yourself, repeatedly *I am on the Luxury Trans-Siberian Express beginning a 5,300-mile romantic expedition covering ground it took Marco Polo a lifetime to traverse. I am just now in Mongolia, where the great Khan found himself, in the thirteenth century, master of practically the entire known world. Think about it!* If you don't succeed in prolonging the enchantment of the entire venture in your fancy, you…will…go…nuts.

At Ulan Bator we saw the museum, viewed and heard some native song and dance, and ended the afternoon visiting a yurt ("a circular domed portable tent used by the Mongolian nomadics in Central Asia"). Once inside we had succor from the sudden biting cold, a wind that shrilled in from the mountains to the west. The little fire burned sheep dung. We had been warned by management not to eat or drink anything proffered us, under pain of instant death, and so had to cope with the diplomatic problem: we accepted bits and pieces of the hard gruel especially prepared for us by the patient, heavy woman in the little tent, her four children at her side. Surreptitiously and with much evasive action we disposed of them, in my case in the deep pocket of my parka. It was at Ulan Bator that we lost Mr. Metcalfe.

Having been almost three days without any news, except from Professor Kahn of happenings 700 years ago, we were riveted to learn that when time came just now to pull away and head towards Russia, a quick poll of the sixty-eight passengers revealed that Mr. Metcalfe was simply not there. Earlier in the afternoon he had elected to forego the yurt excursion, but when Mrs. Metcalfe, his PhD wife, returned with the rest of us, he was not there. She supposed him gone out for a ten-minute walk. A frantic forty-five-minute search was undertaken, of the railroad station and points of conceivable interest in the immediate vicinity; but soon a desperate Mrs. Metcalfe was informed by management (the principal official on the excursion was Mr. Amstutz from Zurich, superintending the Swiss owned train) that there was no alternative to simply going on. Our train's track reservations are hallowed, negotiated with Peter the Great, or whomever, and there is no way a thirteen-car train can just dawdle some place waiting for Mr. Metcalfe. So, Mrs. Metcalfe grabbed an overnight bag and went off in the night in central Mongolia looking for her husband.

The business about the rigidity of the train's scheduling was forcefully communicated to us the following morning when, as told to do, we awaited a knock at the door of our compartments at "about 4:00 a.m." It came, and one of the three uniformed customs officials handed me a form. Our instructions were to complete it and await a second call about a half hour later, when we would give the Russian officer our passports. One hour later, approximately, there would be a third knock: our declaration form, stamped, was then returned, with our passport.

I remember remarking at breakfast to Sam, my dear old friend who occupied the compartment next door, that if I had the resources of the *New York Times*, I would assign a cub reporter to explore the question: Why do the Russian immigration and customs people put trans-Siberian passengers through that early morning ordeal? Are the officials all otherwise occupied before 4:00 a.m. and after 6:00 a.m.? Or is it just a Marxian twitch, *déranger le bourgeois*? After all, you can arrive at the airport in Moscow and do Immigration and Customs in a half hour, so why on the Mongolian border two hours? And before dawn? But Sam and I were becoming listless. He had contracted a dogged stomach disorder, while I tried, as it happened unsuccessfully, to subdue an energy-consuming cold. But there were no complaints on board. We had been thoroughly chastened, and then, too, we had Metcalfe to worry about.

Siberia. In the mind's eye it is primarily the vast frozen part of the world that Stalin thought providentially designed by God for forced labor camps. Much of it is permafrost, too cold, in the higher latitudes, ever to let the ground thaw out. To contend with Nature's oppression, some of Siberia's factories are built on stilts. Shrewdly cut fissures are exploited as canals for the heavy east-west traffic. Siberia is immense, larger than the United States, though its population (around 31 million) is roughly that of California's. Its natural resources are huge: fuel, gold, timber, diamonds, furs, all together accounting for one half of Soviet hard-cash receipts (in 1988, for a net of $20 billion). Its citizens are, we learn, bitterly resentful of Russian exploitation (we Siberians writes Valentin Rasputin, are "a barge moored to Russia that brings in its wealth of goods and then is pushed away from the shore"); but from all appearances they are resigned to at least another millennium or two of satellite status.

Everything about Siberia is huge. We paused at Ulan-Ude. Its most immediately memorable feature is the largest extant head of Lenin (twelve feet, nape to pate). The Russians have a difficult time coping with Lenin. On the one hand they know he is a not-so-good historical character. On the other hand, without him somewhere in the picture they are ugly historical ducklings. In Moscow, before the happy events of 1991, there were sixty-two statues of him, reduced now to eight—it is an asymptotic exercise, the intersection (zero statues of Lenin) never quite taking place. The day is yet unknown when all of imperial Russia will be clean of any monumental memory of V.I. Lenin, whose cosmetic remains we would view a week later in Moscow.

From Ulan-Ude we went on and dallied at Lake Baikal, traversing it by hydrofoil, learning that the lake is 400-miles long, one-mile deep, and that there is as much fresh water there as the entire world consumes in five years. It nicely reflects the Siberian metabolism to hear that the lake widens by one inch every year. "So we only measure it every seventeen years." We would spend five days before reaching the Urals, which separate Europe and Asia, and my memory is of day after day of large open areas clotted with birch trees, thinly populated and unsupervised, yet here and there transmuted as if tended acre by acre, making great British gardens, with *soigné* fur trims and decorative finger lakes. Our passage over Siberia was as long as coast-to-coast travel in the United States.

Irkutsk, the gold capital of Eastern Siberia, is a great cultural and scientific center. It sprang neatly to shape early in the nineteenth century, though only after some prodding—it was for a while disorderly, in the tradition of gold towns. In 1808 a governor brought in forced labor and filled in the muddy streets. They looked around for a professional engineer to oversee what more needed doing, but there wasn't one around. Nature abhorring a vacuum, one Gushya, an exiled convict, took over. "He terrorized the house holders, especially when their wooden buildings failed to conform to the new street plan," our guidebook informed us. "If a corner or wall stuck out too far, he would have it chopped off, causing some half-sawn-off rooms to be left open to the elements, sometimes for years. By 1822, Irkutsk had a new look, with 15,000 citizens and 2,000 houses." City planning, direct approach.

It was at Irkutsk that we learned that Metcalfe lived! A native had gently directed him to the US Consul, to whom Mrs. Metcalfe was subsequently directed, and by the time we had news of them, they were flying home; to be sure, without their baggage, which continued to travel with us on the Trans-Siberian Express. I remembered that our tour instructions had included advice on how to secure insurance against missing out on the trip for whatever reason, in the case of Mr. Metcalfe, a little inopportune vagueness.

We had yet ahead of us Novosibirsk, the great industrial center, with its opera house and prodigious local market, which stretches out for acres. We were being taken now to the Church of the Holy Cross. Its life had more than once been threatened. At one point, soon after he exercised total power, Stalin had decreed that all churches and synagogues should be razed, and many were. But many also remained standing, some of them put to secular use, as granaries, or whatever. Approaching the church, using the loudspeaker in the bus, our guide Olga described the once-threatened church as if it were a member of her family. At one point in the Thirties an emissary to Moscow was conscripted to travel to the Kremlin and plead for the church's survival. He had been carefully prepared: he was instructed not to make any mention of any spiritual concern for the church. He was to express his wish for its survival only because of the church's antiquity and its ornamental importance to the city. It was truly a miracle, Olga said, though there had been a downside to it all. The church was spared; the emissary, alas, disappeared.

We entered it, high-ceilinged, the walls crowded with paintings and statues, the glass stained. And immediately on closing the church door we heard music seemingly divine: one woman's voice, one man's, with organ at the background, it turned out to be. Three bearded priests were at the altar, saying the Orthodox Mass. I sidled over to the nave to observe the musicians more closely. He was perhaps thirty, not older; she, with her unerringly pitched *bel canto*, in her mid-thirties. The priests were all three of them young men. The parishioners (it was not Sunday) were about twenty, at least half of them young. There were more people at Holy Cross that day than we found waiting to view Lenin, five days later.

Some of us were ready for a little culinary diversion. The food was always substantial, but not much more could be said for it. At one market stand I tried to make headway, but failed to get my request over to the smiling young woman on duty. Unaccountably, a word flashed into my mind from the Russian vocabulary list passed around that morning at breakfast, and I found myself saying: "*ikra?*" Instantly she ducked down under the counter and bounded up with two round tins—400 rubles. I shot a covetous and triumphant glance at Sam. "*Tonight we shall feast on caviar,*" I solemnly announced. To which end we roamed the market and collected sour cream and onions and lemon and an aromatic high-priced vodka and great cylinders of fresh bread. That night I handed the cans to the waiter to take back to the kitchen, open and serve. I sliced the onions, poured the vodka, exchanged toasts with Sam and waited for the plate of black gold. The waiter came back and placed our booty down on the table. We stared down at globs of emetic raw sturgeon. We tried to give it away, without much success. Do not order *ikra* behind the Iron Curtain.

Our travel companions were about one half of them associated with Yale, the other half with Stanford. They were mostly, like Sam and me, of a certain age. With no exceptions they were genial men and women. Social energies were, however, pretty well consumed after a day's travel and sight-seeing, and the pianist who performed in the bar car found it unattended most of the time after nine o'clock (time changes were eccentric and incessant—we traveled through ten time zones). We passed by Ekaterinburg, where Lenin exhibited his Bolshevik manhood by ordering soldiers to pump lead into four girls and a little boy, as well as into their parents, Nicholas and Alexandra. So now we had reached the Urals, which semi-officially separate Europe and Asia. And, on the same long day before reaching Moscow at midnight, Yaroslavl, leafy and old and self-confident astride the Volga River, with pre-civil war mansions and a professional choir of thirty singers who performed for us, stupefying in their discipline and musicianship; then on to Moscow.

Bobby and his wife, Candy, both much younger than I, were progressively fatigued by our exertions and those of the train, and when we got to Moscow, Bobby stormed United Airlines for two seats on the nonstop to New York, where their own Lear would pick them up and return them to Dallas. His dogged perseverance kept him away from much of the last-night-together banquet (in the exquisite dining room of the Savoy Hotel with, however, overhead lights more appropriate to an operating room). But he came back finally to rejoin the group, a triumphant smile on his face, and whispered out his exultant news. By heavy exertion, he had succeeded in reducing by one day the itinerary of the Trans Siberian Luxury trip.

The Nth Vacation: Where to Go, What to Do?
July 1, 1997

I have been on vacation (one week), and feel that diffident whiff one gets on reopening the typewriter after letting it rust for a week.

The notion of a vacation has had difficult times, especially with wrought-up journalists who seem to think that if anybody needs a vacation, it is the world, not the journalist. That's true, of course, but the welfare state has never gotten its hands on the globe, which spins along impervious to parietal conventions of earthlings.

But I am tempted to pass along some wisdom in the matter, which when I read it forty years ago left me numb with shock and amazement.

The profile was of lexicographer Bergen Evans, who with his sister, operating mostly out of Northwestern University in Chicago, brought out volume after (readable) volume on correct English usage. Evans was a splendid scholar with a terrific ear, and though he lacked the colorful bite of Fowler, he is endurably useful.

What Evans said about vacation travel was that as he got on in age, he consulted with his wife, and they determined that they would not spend their vacation traveling.

Now any such declaration sounds insurrectionary, so much is travel associated with vacation. But Evans was saying something Americans have a difficult time confronting. It is that the thrill of a great production of nature or of art can indeed be safely taken for granted in the mind's eye.

Suppose your house were situated a few blocks from Niagara Falls. Would you view the falls routinely—or, more likely, only when a visitor came around who said, "Please show me the falls"? Evans was saying that the pleasure of travel derives primarily from exposing the myriad accomplishments of nature and of art. But he is saying more: namely, that he needs not to revisit the Parthenon in order to delight from what is there.

He is claiming something of the photographic memory the poet or the lawyer might have, allowing him to pull from memory the exact words put together by a genius. Ludwig von Beethoven lost his hearing, but no one questions that he "heard" the music he wrote. Running his eyes over a score would give him exactly what the blind man's fingers would have after running them over a passage in Braille.

Curiosity of another order has got to activate a fifth trip to Hong Kong, wouldn't you say?

This time around was from Istanbul to JFK, the little chart on the airplane telling you it's 5,009 miles. Is the sensation of boarding in New York and disembarking in Istanbul sufficient to activate those juices that lead you to take vacations? Or are you likelier, at a certain point, to say: The flight itself is of zero interest; indeed, of negative interest. The arrival takes me to see things I have seen and have exploited to the extent I am inclined to exploit them. Therefore—Bergen Evans is not easy to answer on this point—what you most get from your vacation is 1) the pursuit of your own work; and 2) collateral reading.

If Patrick O'Brian does not get the Nobel Prize for literature, I'll lend my name on any call to boycott it. It was bad that it missed Ezra Pound and Jorge Luis Borges and Vladimir Nabokov, but O'Brian is quite simply the most original, most resourceful, most word-gifted entertainer since Dickens, and I owe to my vacation the reading of two of his thirteen books on the life of Jack Aubrey, post-captain, and Stephen Maturin, his surgeon, naturalist, and philosopher.

Then, too, I began Edward Gibbon's *The Decline and Fall of the Roman Empire*. How can you begrudge a vacation that introduces us to "a more sober and accurate language" in dealing with the size of Rome?

The reader "may impress a juster image of the greatness of Rome, by observing that the empire was above 2,000 miles in breadth, from the wall of Antoninus and the northern limits of Dacia, to Mount Atlas and the Tropic of Cancer; that it extended in length more than 3,000 miles from the Western Ocean to the Euphrates; that it was situated in the finest part of the Temperate Zone, between the twenty-forth and fifty-sixth degree of northern latitude; and that it was supposed to contain above sixteen-hundred-thousand square miles, for the most part of fertile and well-cultivated land."

That's the tiniest hunk of *The Decline and Fall*, but enough to remind us that, after a while, vacations begin at home.

Did You Pack Your Own Bags?
April 17, 1998

The warning is very ancient. It says that the true enemy of a loss of liberty is the diminution of the nervous reflex that spots creeping tyranny.

There are many examples, but none better, surely, than the idiotic ritual one is required to submit to at airports. Everyone is familiar with the routine, but it has become so habitual, we go through it without giving it any thought.

You present your bags and your ticket and are asked for "an ID." This is generally a driver's license or a passport. You pull the driver's license from your wallet and the porter or gatekeeper pretends to look at it. All right, let's say he actually does look at it. Looks for what?

He looks for the name of "Adam Berlin," which is what you are ticketed as: "A. Berlin," Rochester to Atlanta. He nods.

Why is he nodding? Because he sees a picture that resembles you. What he has established is that a driver's license was at one point issued under the name "Adam Berlin," which is the same name that appears on a travel ticket presented by a man who looks like the picture of him on the driver's license.

Next point: name one saboteur, or for that matter one killer or mugger or rapist, who did not have a driver's license. Since you need no identification to buy a ticket, all that needs to be done is to have a driver's license with a photographic likeness of you on it. If you want such a license under a name that is not your own, send $5 to any bookstore and ask it to send you a copy of "A Children's Guide on How to Spy."

But that is only the first thing, of course. Then come the questions:

Have you been separated from your suitcases since they were packed? (No.)

Did anyone other than you pack the suitcases? (No.)

Are you carrying inside the suitcases any packages for anyone that were not packed by you? (No.)

You feel embarrassed for the poor porters or ticket collectors who have to ask such rote questions when the chance of their uncovering foul play is much less than your chance of going down in flames on their airplane. If you are engaged in mischief inside your suitcases, you are not going to reveal this to the baggage porter.

The whole sequence is inherently stupid and humiliating, requiring as it does liturgical questions and liturgical responses by great big grown men and women who should resent it all. There are 1.5 million people who fly every day; times 365 makes almost 550 million per year. That comes to about half-a-billion times per year that somebody is asking silly questions demanding of somebody else meaningless responses.

During the days when people worried about security at immigration points of entry, a middle-aged French intellectual with practically no knowledge of English heard the immigration examiner ask, "Do you believe in overthrowing the United States government by force or violence?" "Er," he replied, in agony exactly to understand the question, "preferably by force." That stopped the assembly line until it was explained to him that the purpose of the question hadn't been to ask him whether he *preferred* force to violence; rather to ask him simply to say no as a comprehensive answer.

If there is anybody out there who defends the baggage-question ritual, he has not been heard from in any public forum. On what comes after the bags are checked, it is not widely divulged how much contraband is picked up by those X-ray machines that survey our briefcases and hatboxes and carry-on miscellany. Here it is a little easier to understand why the show nevertheless goes on. It goes on because who can say how many people are (gainfully?) employed to carry on those searches. If God were to grab a thunderbolt and aim it down on humankind, forever extirpating any temptation to commit mayhem or plunder in the air—what would we do? I mean, there we'd be with what, 50,000 people serving no purpose whatever?...Could that be why nobody thinks to ask: Are they in fact serving any purpose? Do people really try to board planes when carrying hand grenades in their briefcases?

But the other fraternity, the people who ask you if you packed your own bags, have other important things to do, which are quite vital. We can't know whether, if relieved of the security questionnaire, there could be downsizing and a reduction of the overhead of air travel. But shouldn't we worry over a creeping servility to bureaucratic make-work?

Go Away, Admiral
July 17, 1998

When you read this, steel yourself, as this reader had to do. We learn from the current issue of *Yachting* magazine that the Coast Guard is thinking of—has thought of?—issuing a regulation that would require all boaters to wear life jackets at sea.

This is very different from the law requiring us all to stow life jackets on a boat in case of emergency—that rule has been around since the *Titanic*, and quite right. Perhaps Captain Smith should have made his rounds wearing a life jacket. And who knows, if the logic of the madman in the Coast Guard who is ventilating this proposal takes hold, Leo and Kate would have been wearing life jackets even when having at it in the hold of the boat—no compromise; they are on a boat and they must wear life jackets.

We learn that the Coast Guard floated this proposal just after Memorial Day and asked for comments. There are an estimated seventy million boys, girls, men, and women who go out on the water. In the best of all possible worlds, the Coast Guard would have had seventy million letters wondering whether that venerable institution had gone quite batty. The Coast Guard reports getting only 416 letters, which is testimony either (a) to mortal inertia in the seagoing public, or (b) high confidence that such a surrealistic suggestion isn't going anywhere, so it is safe just to ignore it.

But that isn't right. *Semper paratus*, the Coast Guard (along with the Boy Scouts) teaches us, but let it here be recorded that it is preposterous to propose the wearing of a life jacket in all situations. This dissenter began sailing at age thirteen and has more or less never stopped, and has never once worn a life jacket while at sea, using instead, in pitchy situations, a lifeline, which is different.

If the Coast Guard were to proceed with the proposal, I, and surely a hundred thousand others, would respond to the challenge as H.L. Mencken did to the edict in Boston in the Twenties that forbade traffic in the *American*

Mercury. He appeared in the Boston Common ostentatiously reading the magazine and went happily off to jail with a ton of publicity that caused publishers to lust for a "Banned in Boston" stamp to affix on new fiction.

The Coast Guard is a splendid service, but the gentlemen there should rein in those whose design is to take all the pleasure out of going to sea. California is where goofy things most often happen (and where from time to time they are most dramatically corrected). But we learn now of a proposal that would make smoking in the home illegal if—get this—there is anybody else living at home who does *not* smoke. You can follow the analytical trail, can you not? If you light up, you release smoke. Smoke is a carcinogenic substance. It will contaminate anyone else in the household who isn't himself/herself a smoker. So?

A fine article was published in *The Weekly Standard* by Jewish theologian and talk-show host Dennis Prager on "The Soul-Corrupting Anti-Tobacco Crusade." In a niftily worded essay about what I classify as the shower adjusters ("No, Elmer, the water should be *two degrees cooler*"), he discusses those who want to get themselves and their firehoses into any situation in which someone wants just to sit down and have a smoke.

In that article, in passing, Prager cites as an authority for the ruling that environmental smoke is *not* a health hazard the views of Dr. Philippe Shubik. Dr. Shubik's publication is published at Oxford University and is called "Teratogenesis, Carcinogenesis, and Mutagenesis," and anybody who has a magazine called *that*, commands from me full, unquestioning obedience.

Now I like to think that the Coast Guard will never succeed in stripping from an hour on the water the pleasure of spontaneity and unencumbrance of life and limb. And I doubt that even in California they will get around to telling Erastus Corning Jones that he can't light up because Mrs. Jones doesn't smoke. But we must repay their awful feints against our diminishing freedoms with massive retaliatory rebukes, this being my humble contribution to that end.

Full Sail on the New England Coast
Hemispheres, August 1998

I know—everybody knows, there's no arguing about it—the most beautiful part of the world is wherever you grew up, so there's the egalitarian formality. Now let me tell you about the most beautiful part of the world, which is the New England coastline. Writing about it isn't to exclude New England's inland, but you can't have both at the same time and if you pull in at Saybrook, CT, and resolve to stick to the shoreline until it runs out, you'll be traveling by car or by boat (preferably by boat) all the way to the easternmost tip of the United States in Eastport, ME, which is opposite Campobello, where Franklin Delano Roosevelt was stricken with polio—but we have to leave history out of it; otherwise you'd never get any farther than Boston.

Coastal New England begins in Connecticut, in Greenwich. Before you reach the eastern end of the state, you have passed by more harbors than the whole of California gives you along its 1,200-mile coastline; it's as if New England were beckoning to you, at every possible moment, to come on in out of the rain.

We're talking about the same coastline our way-back fathers happened upon and proceeded to colonize. In Plymouth, the old burial ground is still there, which tells us who really did come in on the Mayflower. You have glided by the old white churches and the fishing nests of Gloucester and New Bedford, and the Cape Cod Canal that saves you fifty miles of roundabout travel if you are headed Down East. You can take in a thousand inlets and little havens and major ports of New England, cold and luminously green in spring, challengingly hot in midsummer, and then, in fall, comes the premonitory little pulsations of cold in the early morning. And then is when the leaves begin to turn and you know what the forests would look like if they were painted by all the fauvists in France, using googols of red and orange and yellow and traces of green and yellow umber. At York Harbor, where Maine begins, was the great inn that opened its 300 rooms for only ten weeks, after the reluctant spring, and before the autumn freezes. It wouldn't be fair, one starstruck old-timer said, to let New England's coastal season last any longer—nature has to give other people a little time of day.

So, you sail up the coast making a major daily stride or two (twenty or thirty miles) and fuss a little with wind and tide and every day resolve to immerse yourself in the ocean, with water temperatures as cold (in midsummer) as 60 degrees. Then, perhaps in midafternoon, perhaps later, you noodle into one of those great bays. You can linger as long as you like at

Casco and Muscongus, Penobscot and Frenchman, framing Mount Desert Island, famed for great summerhouses and overnights for tourists. There are deep waters and sheer promontories, great rocks and pine woods, and the little villages whose settlers, during the century and a half after the pilgrims came, struggled to make snuggeries where life could be sustained, drawing on the ocean to one side, the soil and wildlife and forests to the other. They dreamed a great deal but could not have anticipated that on top of taking care of the problems of Indians, the British king, hunger, and cold, they were also bending the great natural resources of coastal New England to give passing pleasure to all who come to experience, and lifelong pleasure for those who come in out of the rain there permanently.

The Pilots Are Really Sick
April 16, 1999

The judge who ruled against the Allied Pilots Association was very weepy about where the dictates of his conscience took him. "What my oath requires me to do makes me sick to my stomach because a lot of decent men and women pilots are going to be hurt by this."

Thus said Judge Joe Kendall of the federal District Court in Dallas in his ruling that American Airline pilots should come up with $46 million to reimburse the airline for damages done in ten days last February when, lo! they all got a mysterious illness that kept them from duty.

The ruling of the judge rates special attention for several reasons, one of them that the union has to pay $46 million, which is $8 million more than it has in assets. As the chief union officer defiantly commented, though one supposes his eyes were moist when he said it, the day in which money would actually be taken from the union to the company was a long way off.

The plans, of course, are to begin with an appeal. But if that should fail, the union might be tempted to turn to the company and say something on the order of, Do you really want $46 million from us? In that case, add $146 million to the demands we will be making at the end of the present contract.

Still, the judgment is a milestone of sorts in the history of union accountability. It is one of the largest fines ever assessed. And the sentencing judge endeavored to make it clear that he was acting only out of a sense of duty, that he had nothing against the pilots themselves.

Yes, what about the individual American Airlines pilot?

"Joe, this is the Allied Pilots Association, LA branch. You're scheduled to pilot Flight 804, LAX to JFK, tomorrow at ten o'clock. Well, you can't take that flight."

"Why not?— Is this Al calling?"

"No. This is Henry. Al's sick."

"Gee I'm sorry about that. Why don't I fly tomorrow?"

"Because you're sick too."

"Me sick? I never felt better in my life!"

"You're sick and you are not flying until I tell you you are no longer sick."

So, the judge is genuinely sorry for Joe, who failed to show up in time to fly the Lockheed to New York because he was told to call in sick. Three hundred passengers assembled at the Los Angeles airport were also made sick. Some of them were less sick than others. Some had to wait only an hour or so to catch the TWA flight. Some missed a connecting flight to Rome. One got to New York too late to say goodbye to her mother, who was terminally sick.

The judge had issued a restraining order after four days, and that order had the effect of making the bug positively virulent, causing a sickness that resulted in the cancellation of 6,600 flights, derailing 600,000 passengers. The arithmetic done by the judge had to do with revenues lost by American Airlines after the restraining order was handed down. Nobody attempted to measure damages done to the disrupted plans of 600,000 people.

The judge may be sad about having to hand down the judgment but, really, he shouldn't be. The disappearance of accountability is a phenomenon of an age in which fewer and fewer people are held responsible for what they do. The list of those delinquencies is topped by the father who refuses to acknowledge his child or tries to duck the expenses of rearing him. In politics, accountability can be exercised on election day, but there is a gross incongruity in what the voters can do to the politician and what the politician can do to the voters. Sometimes the very idea of accountability is moot. The voters will not again have a chance to "punish" William

Clinton even if his Kosovo war ends with American casualties, added to the Kosovar casualties.

This has been the season for exhibitionist mooning in front of the law, in protest against the New York police and the mayor. The idea is to participate in an illegal demonstration—illegal because it ties up traffic, or whatever; then to get photographed while engaged in bravery; then get booked at the police station, making sure they spell your name right; then leave the station with no bail and no future date set for arraignment. One has visions of political luminaries calling their secretaries to book them an illegal act for the p.m. on the understanding that it will all be over in time to meet their dinner dates.

Some people guess that American Airlines pilots think it humiliating to affect to be sick when they aren't sick. They're right. It is humiliating, and it should also be costly.

CHAPTER EIGHT

2000–2004

Gstaad and the New Rich
March 17, 2000

GSTAAD, Switzerland—This is my fortieth "winter" (six weeks in February/ March) in Gstaad, the twin purposes of coming here with my wife, back when it all began, being to work and to ski. *Mens sana in corpore sano* stuff.

Providence has a way of disarranging people's pretty little life programs, in this case an early and severe accident that ended my wife's skiing life. But work and skiing for me went on year after year. The first book I undertook here in 1959 was *Up From Liberalism*. Just now I have completed a novel called *Elvis in the Morning*.

Now, Gstaad is much written about in the society pages, its dominant scribe being Taki Theodoracopulos, a feisty, amusing, well-read cosmopolitan who dearly loves to inveigh against objectionable features of life, including the *nouveaux riches*. Taki clears the way for his philippics (regularly published in London's *Spectator*, in the *New York Press*, and here and there) by reiterating his own weaknesses, among them a spell in a British prison for carrying cocaine while sashaying through customs in the London airport. He is the heir to a shipping fortune, whence his self-designation as "the poor little rich boy." He gambles to articulate excess and, if he is to be believed (which he is not), he is drunk every night. Cut that in half.

But for all the bluster, he is avidly read not only by socialites who peep into his columns and draw deep breaths of relief on the days they escape

Taki's scrutiny, but also by others who are amused and instructed by him. He is acknowledged as a serious commentator with a high-alarm cant-detector system who treads dispositively on hypocrisy and exhibitionism.

He too has been in Gstaad many seasons and writes from time to time on the new rich, though he confesses the difficulty in defining exactly how one qualifies for the title. Bill Gates is certainly a *nouveau riche* in the taxonomical sense, but the term is supposed to tell you something more than that a poor little Harvard boy pulled out and a few years later found himself a multibillionaire. There is the added complication that some people with old money (i.e., their grandparents were rich) can't refrain from exhibitionism. Taki correctly distinguishes between huge expense done for private pleasure and huge expense done to attract public notice. He is withering at the expense of the latter.

Consider, at Gstaad, the Eagle Ski Club. It used to be quite exclusive, in the sense that more people wished to get in than were wished in, allowing for a certain choosiness. But antiquated ski-lift facilities reduced the patronage of the Eagle Club, and management maneuvered by raising the admissions fee, a form of recapitalization. The results are as Taki might have predicted.

Consider. The habit at the Eagle Club is to post conspicuously a clipboard hanging on a surface that you necessarily run into climbing the stairs into the dining room. It is a large ledger, ballpoint pen attached. On this, individual members write their names and indicate the sum of money they authorize the club to bill them as season's gratuities for the dining room staff. A typical annual contribution, forty years ago, would have been 100 Swiss francs. One club member, seeking attention back then, wrote out his name in bold letters and gave 300 francs. David Niven retaliated by writing, just under the public philanthropist's name, *500* francs, and listing his name as: Anon. That was a high rebuke. Willing to be generous, not willing to advertise your generosity.

This year, because of straitened club life, the typical gratuity listed has grown to SF 500 (US $300). But lo!—halfway down Page One, a member comes in for SF 5,000! And, ten or fifteen names below, comes in a *second* name, giving $5,000. Now understand this: we are talking about a *lunch* club. Maybe these donors patronized it ten times during the season. That's high tipping. Taki would call it the mark of a *nouveau*, which, as noted, has less to do with which progenitor accumulated the money than with civilized habits of distributing it.

Taki (he is universally so referred to) was schooled in America, is truculently pro-American, and is discreetly near to spendthrift-generous. After his encounter with the law in Great Britain, there was some throat-clearing by management on the question whether he should be readmitted to the Eagle Club. John Kenneth Galbraith, who has wintered in Gstaad most of his adult life and made it a practice to scorn the Eagle Club, nevertheless thought to intervene in the matter of Taki by writing a public letter to a director, noting that Taki's singular disadvantage over other members was that he had been caught in social malefactions, unlike the typical Eagle members. Taki returned.

Gstaad, meanwhile, goes along, a radiant Alpine sanctuary, pausing in a languid spring to reenter the scene in the summer with music, tennis, and golf. The language is German, though almost everyone is a polyglot, and the sense of the place is that Swiss culture, not easily defined, will make its way through historical vicissitudes with some self-confidence, but a mature self-confidence, not the kind Taki speaks of when scorning the ways of the new rich.

Security in the Air
November 13, 2001

It is instructive to catch the emotions on the fly. They do not always yield self-esteem. You furtively hope the bullet will hit the *other* guy, not you. The airplane crashes, and instinctively you hope it wasn't a terrorist who did it. But a moment later, you start thinking about statistics. Maybe it would be *better* if it were a terrorist strike. Fleeting thoughts go down memory lane.

How many casualties have come to us through terrorism in the last twenty years of flying? The civilian victims of September 11 can't be counted because, like nuclear bombs, they overwhelm the picture. So, you ask, how many planes have met death on account of terrorist activity? The four spectacular planes of 9/11. Then you need to go back to the Egyptian plane whose copilot decided to commit suicide and took everyone down to the sea. On the other hand, that wasn't exactly terrorism, was it? But, of course, the big one was Lockerbie, 270 dead from terrorist action on a Pan American flight headed for the US. And one Air India plane off Ireland in 1985.

The thought materializes: If Monday's New York accident comes in as a terrorist episode, that's bad, but less bad than if it is a maintenance act. Because in the world of data, the chances of losing your life in flight on account of terrorist activity are lower than on account of mechanical failures. These are very low, and tend to diminish every year. At last year's rate, you could fly, say, one million flights before finding yourself on the plane with the marginal vulnerability. But (the statistics are raging through the mind), you could fly *twenty* million flights before you'd find yourself on a plane struck down by terrorists.

Besides, you say to yourself, there is a full-blown war going on against terrorist activity. At the level of mechanical safety, it can be said that there is constant concern to avoid critical problems in the air, but that is a steady kind of thing, not to be compared with the explosion of concern triggered by 9/11. One commentator on the Jim Lehrer show was asked whether it was easy for a skilled mechanic so to disrupt a jet engine of the type carried by the fatal Airbus to make it fall off. Yes, he said. For a skilled mechanic, very easy. However, he said: It was flatly inconceivable that it should happen, given airplane security procedures. It is one thing to let somebody slip by who is carrying a knife in his briefcase, another to permit someone four hours in an airplane engine with a dozen screwdrivers and filaments of explosive.

So—the thinking is, on Tuesday—the problem was mechanical. The implications of mechanical imperfections work their way into the thinking of the irresolute. Back at school when, teaching basic economics, professors tried to impress on us the importance of the marginal consumer, they'd say something on the order of: *If the Ford Motor Co. produces two million automobiles in a year, they lose a lot of money. If they produce two million and one automobiles, they'lll make a billion dollars.*

The model is exaggerated, but the point survives. The airlines are doing about 25 percent less business than before 9/11 and are losing their shirts. The marginal passenger on an airplane costs (virtually) nothing; his absence costs economic survival. The *Los Angeles Times* writes of Eugene and Nikey Key of Palm Desert, CA, scheduled to fly on Delta Flight 136 Monday morning from LAX to New York. They've been around the world by plane and ship six times. They canceled. "His wife said she was simply afraid."

So, we read of futuristic devices. Take that useful prefix going the rounds—"bio"—and stick it up before "metrics." Biometrics! Consider this possibility: arriving at New York's La Guardia Airport, an American Airlines passenger proceeds to the nearest kiosk. After swiping her smart card through a machine, she presses her index finger on the pad attached to the device in order to confirm that she's the authorized holder of the card and her boarding pass is printed. At the gate, she puts her finger on another reading device to reconfirm her identity, then steps onto the plane.

Yes, and with biometrics we make progress on security of the kind they worried about on Monday. But that doesn't bring us security against mechanical failures. For that, you need countergravitational devices, and they are out of this world.

Yes to the Railroads
June 14, 2002

The scare headlines popped up here and there, intensifying last week. We were told that Amtrak would cease services unless... Exactly.

And Congress will, we soon learned, and inevitably expected, come through with $500-odd million, sufficient to give Amtrak another six months of life. And, in Congress, something more than a stopgap measure is taking on steam. That would be Sen. Fritz Hollings' bill, a grand design of $59 billion to give us, coast to coast, a modern system. Sen. Hollings is a shrewd legislator. Drawing deep on the fragrance of 9/11, he has called his bill the "National Defense Rail Act."

Now the argument against federal financing of rail travel begins with the axiomatic rule: let the rail passengers pay for their own conveniences. A pretty fair rule, but it's not a violation of it to remark the complexities.

The first of these is, of course, that the government is heavily involved in subsidizing traffic of every kind. The motorist can hardly drive around the block without driving over asphalt primarily financed by town and county, but also with contributions coming in tangentially from the federal government. When you debouch from I-95, you travel from road surface 100 percent paid for by the federal government, down the ramp to cutoffs toward the construction of which the feds made a lesser contribution, but a contribution nonetheless, onto roads paid for by the state, and by lower echelons of government, county, and city. It takes hardy pioneering into highly exclusive warrens before the user runs into the driveway he actually paid for himself.

The same holds true for the airlines, an intimation of whose problems was given us by US Airways last week when management said that service could not continue until $1 billion was raised.

There are other entwinements. The railroad, for instance, carries mail and postal packages. These, of course, are paid for by fees. Arriving at the right figure for such fees is an intricate assignment. What would it cost to ship the same package via the competition? Well, that would mean a truck. Trucks travel on federally paid-for roads.

And then, railroads have to pay for rights-of-way. Some own their own tracks, some do not. How do you allocate the capital expense of servicing these tracks? And how to factor in the national need for adequate transportation facilities? When President Eisenhower launched the great highway program in 1956, he had partly in mind the need to increase the facilities for transcontinental defense—a coast-to-coast Panama Canal, so to speak.

Now where the question gets itchy is the factor of relative convenience. There are a thousand towns in America with no rail service at all, where inhabitants who want to travel have to make their way by automobile or bus or airplane. These are people many of whom seethe at the thought of northeast-corridor Americans getting around between Boston and Washington on a fleet of trains that are losing money.

Fifty-two percent of travel between New York and Washington is done by railroad. Can the situation be rectified by simply charging more money? Experience shows that it can't. For some people, the demand for train travel is inelastic, but not for a lot of people. If you doubled the rail fare, you would not double the revenue.

This is a pretty universal experience, there being no railroad service in any industrial country that pays for itself. Do we have here an example of an organic exception to the rule that services should pay their own way? That may be in fact the case, but in any event, conservatives need to climb onto a higher level from which to seek a broader perspective. The urbanization of America and the volatility of American travel need to be accepted as a part of the American culture that shouldn't be constrained, let alone aborted, by dogmatic enforcements of otherwise useful rules of procedure.

The plan of Sen. Hollings is significantly to improve and to increase the availability of railroads, and he needs to justify doing this, at a cost of more than $5 billion per year, by persuading Congress and the public that however uneven the usufructs of rail travel to different parts of America, a national endowment is economically defensible, culturally desirable, and tangentially useful to the common defense.

On the Water: Destination Dalmatia

Yachting, January 2003

The resolve to return one day to Dalmatia was twelve years in gestation—we cruised the area in 1990. One is choosy about whom to spend seven days with in tight quarters, not that that's entirely fair to say about *Ynot* (Yes. As in Why Not?) The eighty-foot French-built sloop is truly grand, and tightness is experienced only on leaving the master head after a shower. The door opens inward, and egress requires a deep, stomach-intaking breath. Why did designer Bruce Farr do this to his commodious sloop? My fantasy is that the owner, seeking self-discipline, instructed the designer to come up with a fit that would deny him passage out of the shower into the rest of the ship and the great outdoors the day his girth increased by a single inch. Why not?

But that is a digression. Our objective was in three parts. The first was to locate a boat that would really move under sail while also providing the comforts aboard that fastidious people want who don't want to cruise in powerboats. The next objective was to effect yet one more reunion of three couples whose steadfast friendship found us sharing a sailboat over the millennium. The third objective was to see again the Dalmatian coastline and the villages alongside, which have resisted great human efforts by kings and warriors who could do everything to Croatia except diminish its beauty and allure.

The six of us arrived in Split from various parts of the world and made our way to the boat. I met Van Galbraith when we were both freshmen at Yale, in 1946. Three years earlier I had shared a single room at prep school with Alistair Horne. Van, fast recovering from a serious illness, has been busy in Brussels, providing for the common defense. He is, this time around, assistant to the secretary of defense for Europe, having served under President Reagan as ambassador to France. In between, he practiced law and banking. Alistair was in British intelligence, spending time in postwar Dalmatia. He went then to journalism and, soon, to the writing of history. When we joined up at Trogir he had just sent off to his publisher a massive history of Paris, for which he will certainly receive yet another award. I in turn had just completed a novel based on Ayn Rand (author and founder of Objectivism) and other difficult people. I was feeling hugely sorry for myself because, in August, pneumonia had set in, keeping me from my annual ten-day New England cruise aboard my beloved thirty-six-foot sloop *Patito*, about which I have written that the boat is perfect for four people, and five people is three too many.

Ynot lay, captivating, on the waterfront promenade of Trogir, only five kilometers from the airport. If Disney had undertaken the job of jolting travel-weary passengers dusty from routine and uncertain health into another world, he'd have achieved, on a very good day, Trogir. The walled town has the waterfront and aboard the boat the late afternoon sun shot across the Kameriengo Fortress, on one wall of which is a huge red smear, red as in blood. I remember thinking that Disney was going a little far in historical melodrama—but there it was. And highlighted just forward of the boat a palace of sorts, one of a half dozen prominent features in the fifteen acres of gnarled narrow stone streets. And, of course, a cathedral—fourteenth century—and a second church. Alistair is a historian and drinks it all in. Others, raised in the non-Byzantine history of the new world, are willing to forget or to ignore who it was that the Apaches were quarreling with, back when Kotor was fending off the Turks. The modern tourist is free simply to walk about in the close streets, peer into the churches and castles, and maybe pause to wonder whose blood it was that was shed in defending, or assaulting, the Kameriengo fort. How long do bloodstains last? Was the blood Illyrian? Croatian? Venetian? Roman? Maybe Lady Macbeth was at Trogir once—everybody else seems to have visited here, and we were exultant to be among them.

Everyone who has chartered a boat and boarded it before nightfall wants to get under way. The itch to go is easy to understand when you arrive at your boat tied up in a marina in a thistle of a hundred other boats. But even pulling away from our royal single-boat quay at Trogir, there is the excitement of a boat springing to life. Van and I, who have crossed oceans four times together on my own boats, were especially curious to see *Ynot* under sail and the captain proposed a short (twelve kilometer) excursion to Milna, on the island of Brac. That leg would permit us, in the southwest wind, to hoist sail and feel our great steed in action. No boat I had ever owned or chartered before had power winches, so I stared rapt at the scene where, without any hand pulling on any line or turning any winch handle, the mainsail crawled up to the top of the mast, and the great genoa unbound. It was as if the industrial revolution was taking place right there in the Splitski Kanal, before my very eyes.

We were in Milna in a couple of hours, and walked about the fishing village with its soft yellow lights arcing over the horseshoe-shaped harbor front. We must move on or we won't have time to visit Vis or Havar or Korcula or Peljesac or Kotor—let alone Dubrovnik.

We ate dinner on board, resourcefully prepared by the captain's wife, Ann, helped by Nicky Moss, a young woman bent on seafaring, and by veteran seaman Randy West, resident of St. Barths. There was a novelty in our dinner arrangements. I have chartered boats every year since 1959, and was never before given the *Ynot* option. The captain's proposal reached us during the summer, via agent Julie Nicholson. Traveling, as you intend to do, from Split south to Kotor and back up to Dubrovnik, he wrote, you will find yourselves every night in attractive Dalmatian villages with varied and attractive local restaurants. If you decide you want to eat ashore one night, or more, Ynot Inc. will reimburse you $30 per person, per meal.

We found the option attractive, and exercised it every night, except for this first night at Milna. The fare uniformly stressed the fish from surrounding waters. Veal in its various forms is always there, but most memorable, the mussels, heaping onto plates burning hot oil and butter and herbs. The Croatian wines are famous (Zinfandel is said to have begun there), and we liked especially the Radonic and Plegivica). The first restaurant was candle-lit, the service good, the waiters, English-spoken; seating arrangements there, as almost everywhere, permitted diners to sit outside. The $30-a-plate subvention proved just about right, covering most of the cost of dinners, good and not so good. This isn't a serviceable idea for cruising just everywhere. You wouldn't want to find yourself dependent on finding an attractive local eating place in stray Grenadine islands, or in Baja California, or, for that matter, in every Greek island or Turkish harbor.

We had fine weather every day but a disappointing lack of sailing winds. We had the sails up going southwest to Vis, but they flopped about, the genoa brought in after only an hour or two. Vis has the allure of the forbidden island. It was a military base for the former Yugoslav army. Josip Broz Tito hid out there during the war, discreetly protected by intermittent sallies of the British air force. At Komiza, on the western side, is a picturesque harbor, with vendors along the wharves and fishing boats tending to their concerns. Tourists are welcome and greatly needed. Tourists came in abundantly before the war, ten million per year to Croatia, and the trade is almost back to normal, but although Vis is acknowledged as one of the most beautiful of the coastal islands it isn't heavily visited, and indeed, up until 1989, was off-limits.

The most alluring phenomenon is just off the island at Bisevo, where the Blue Grotto holds forth. We were there a dozen years ago, and Van swam into it at just the right moment, when the sun's rays penetrate an underwater opening and flood the interior in an intense, ephemeral (the sun rays are admitted, then blocked after just one hour) blue illumination that gives the sensation of occupying your own personal grotto. Below you (this is snorkel time) is Dalmatian water, unsparing in its clarity. You are inside the grotto and the water is protected, so the surface is flat as a mirror, the rocks a stuttering pink and yellow.

We didn't swim a whole lot on this trip. The water temperature is fine, the first week of September at Latitude 43 North, Longitude 16 West. But bear this in mind, you aren't there for beach life. There is everything beautiful and intriguing in the rocks and coves, but enticing beaches are rare, their surfaces crusty. I remember several sailing trips in my beloved Azore Islands, which have everything except sandy beaches. They are gray. The man in charge of tourism for Vis and Korcula would profit from the initiative of the fabled advertising agency in the Thirties, hired to help unload a huge supply of salmon from British Columbia, unaccountably and dismayingly snow-white. The agency came up with the label, "Guaranteed Not to Turn Pink in the Can." Yugoslav beaches are guaranteed not to turn white on you.

I found myself especially eager to see Kotor again, though the islands en route are, each one, worth visiting and exploring. At Korcula we met for dinner Alistair's friend, Veronica Maclean, the learned widow of Fitzroy Maclean. Herself an author, she elected to continue to live, in the summers, in the house just behind the cathedral in the glamorous walled city liberated from the Nazis by Tito, the dashing author, politician, soldier Maclean alongside. The temperature of our animosity to Tito, tyrant, has cooled since the bloody dissolution of the amalgam he held together for thirty years. Rounding the point to enter Korcula I was summoned from below. My wife reported a sea battle going on. And, indeed that was so, with 5,000 viewers lined up along the city walls, booing and applauding. It is an annual spectacle, a half dozen wooden ships with sails and oars in thirteenth-century dress, with great smoke issuing from whatever synthetic ammunition they had got hold of. It was the famous sea battle between the Venetians and the Genovese. The prize? Marco Polo himself, captured there, and imprisoned in Genoa. He sat down in jail and wrote his memoirs.

The schedule on this cruise was easygoing. Breakfast whenever individual passengers rose to have it. Then for two or three hours we'd wander about the town we were visiting, or stay aboard and read (Sheelin Horne did watercolors, Bootsie Galbraith took photos). Sometime around noon, we would start the day's journal, lunch served while under way. The sail that took us along the island of Peljesac, around the estuary, then up the Stun canal was perfect, *Ynot* showing her grace under wind pressure of eighteen to twenty knots. At Ston there was the great wall to see, kilometers, the longest fortification in Europe built to protect the critical salt supply.

We headed southeast, sliding by the tip of Croatia up—in Montenegro territory now—into the two-mile-wide bay that winds north, then east, then north again, and yet again cast, eight miles of this with mountains and pastures and villages, and you are in Motor. We got in just as dark fell. We had had then, powering smoothly down Kotorski Bay, an hour of straitening daylight and the flickering on of land lights, decorating the darkening mountain ranges like candles at the base of vaulted cathedrals. We reached, at the bay's end, the city that withstood the Turks and preserves its lively Old Town, encircled by a 2.8-mile wall. Etched over the stone entrance portal is a magic date: November 21, 1944. That was the day the Nazis, who had succeeded where the Turks had failed, were finally routed.

We were eager to revisit the two, picture perfect little islands, side by side, off Perast, discerned only faintly yesterday in the falling light. They are staunchly there. Our Lady of the Rocks, about the size of two tennis courts, still has its baroque church and a museum now, with a guide to take you about. Gospa od Skprjla, the companion island, is fifty yards separated, the church dwelling set off by giant cypress trees. We approached it gingerly by dinghy. A dozen years earlier we had touched down there into the company of two reclusive nuns who tended the little seminary and the little garden and the trees. Would they still be there?

We walked toward the entrance door on the north side. Rounding the corner we stared down at a sunbather. Her eyes were closed, her bra lay at her side. She proved slow to rouse from her sleep, then amiably informed us that the ancient property, abandoned, had been acquired by a family in Serbia who left the building locked, opening it only for special occasions. Our informant, we learned, arrived by swimming the 300 yards from Perast. There was nothing more to see than what lay before our eyes. Legend has it that the island had been nothing more than a small reef and that on June 22, 1452—one year before Christopher Columbus was born—two brothers fishing on the spot came upon an image of the Madonna. In veneration, they filled the reef with rocks and built the church. The nuns we spoke with in 1990 told us that life had been hard, that during his reign, Tito had executed

450 clergy. There is no one left, at Gospa od Skrpjela, to persecute, and worship there is of the sun.

Retracing our passage out of Montenegro, destination Dubrovnik, we looked diligently with binoculars hoping to find the Club Med facility we had paused at (Van was a director of Club Med) when it was newborn. It had been thriving with vacationers, and we passed an hour with three Dubliners celebrating the end of their medical school. They were loving it there, at the San Marco Club, though it was a little Spartan, offering no electricity in the individual huts. As we approached today, we could discern more than fifty of these eggheaded thatch huts. Coming in closer, we saw that the entire camp had been abandoned. Three natives were chatting in trunks at the old wharf, one of them a polyglot who advised us that we were free to address him in any of six languages. He told us that the Club Med had closed down during the war, and never revived after the cease-fire. We walked about the spooky ruins. The outdoor dining hall still has its tables, decomposing now, and behind is a crestfallen stage where old posters and rosters and vestiges of exuberant outdoor life hang.

A mere nine years had brought on the near total disintegration we surveyed. The church we had just left had had life for 550 years, and will survive in brick and mortar, whereas the San Marco Club four miles distant will no longer be traceable, unless you arrive with a GPS fix. If you are looking for it, you will find what is left of it at 18 40.6 N, 42 24.2 W.

We powered (no wind) northwest, having decided to spend the final night on *Ynot* in Cavtat, which is, incidentally, right by the airport used when flying into and out of Dubrovnik. It is a harbor shaped as if replicating the end of a wrench, and provided security against everything except the noise of aircraft traffic. We'd leave the fabled Dubrovnik, which is all but entirely repaired from what it suffered during the war, for the end. Cavtat suffers from a huge modern hotel, overlooking the harbor and indeed Dubrovnik. It is so hideous we debated walking over to it to learn who had designed it, desecrating that view of the harbor. Perhaps another war will dispose of it. Until then, one can only look away.

Last nights together encourage a little rumination. Everyone pledged to do it all again, on that particular boat, if lucky, with the same crew. Afterthoughts? I had a couple. In the general flurry of departure, I had forgotten to bring a few items critical to my complete contentment when cruising. Never leave without your own GPS, which gives day-by-day, sometimes hour-by-hour satisfaction as you fuss over the charts and sight that mountain peak. Bring your own binoculars—why not? There was only a single pair on board, and we were ten people, including the crew. Finally—and this is a little cumbersome—bring a radio-cassette player (I've used a yellow Sony Seamaster for thirty years), which will let you adjust the volume from where you are sitting. Central volume controls operated in the main saloon aren't good enough. And bring then thirty tapes or CDs of the kind of thing you especially like. All of the above can be crammed into one accommodating briefcase. And of course—and this one, none of us neglected—bring your own friends.

That night everyone wrote out checks to reimburse the treasurer their share of expenses. The basic cost of *Ynot* is $3,000 per day. Merely to mouth the figure brings on shudders, but then also heightens the enjoyment; anything so costly had to be special. There is the ensuing deconstruction of the gross figure, in search of reassuring perspectives. It boils down to $500 per person per day, which sounds a lot more digestible, and in turn invites reassuring thoughts on comparative indulgences, like a day and night in Hong Kong, or on a luxury liner, or—what the hell. Five hundred doughnuts at $1 apiece.

Moral? Work hard, and disinherit your grandchildren.

Tycoon Class
September 12, 2003

The airlines plead that they continue to lose money, though they had a reassuring quarter. There has been a lot of talk about a passengers' bill of rights, and it is true that the airlines are indifferent to substantive complaints of their customers. Yes, they will attempt to give quicker service when asked about flights and departure times, relying fruitfully on the Internet. What they studiously avoid discussing is the piracy that attaches to business-class travel.

Regulation of airfares is effected by competition, which is as it should be. What is largely unnoticed is that in business class there is practically no competition. All airlines opportunize on the customer who craves uncramped travel.

Getting the price of an air ticket is something akin to shopping in a Chinese bazaar, one traveler recently commented. It is true that there are services—one thinks of Expedia.com—which will line up airfares from Point A to Point B with marvelous speed, permitting you to give your preferences for date and time of departure, and to opt for nonstop. But if you want business class, the fares are pretty uniform. Uniformly high.

An example, only one week old. To travel Washington to Phoenix to New York is $600, economy. By business class it is $2,800. To travel New York to Geneva by economy is $500, by business, $3,000. The penalty, in the first instance, is about 450 percent. In the second, 600 percent. It's easy enough to divine the undisclosed reason for the high penalty fare—the airlines find people who will pay the price. What is hard to find is an objective reason for the larceny. There is more leg room and hip room in business, but not six times as much.

The perpetual quarrel over the regulation of air traffic eased off after 9/11, in part owing to the sharp decline in air travel. Air travel was severely affected and some airlines had to put a part of their inventory of planes into cold storage. The traveling public sensed that the travails of travel, which include baring one's feet in order to establish that there is no hidden nitroglycerine under your sole, are accepted as part of the price we pay for travel in the Age of Terrorism.

The airlines apparently ignore the resentment felt by those, especially older people, who yearn for the relative comfort of travel in business class accommodations but can't afford the tariff. Of if they can afford it, are resentful at their complicity in the piracy. The traveler to Geneva by business class is accepting a surcharge of about $475 dollars per hour of travel. To pay $475 per hour to permit you to stretch your legs or to lean back in your seat an extra fifteen degrees is resented as idolatrous indulgence. It is the equivalent of paying not $200 for a hotel room, but $1,800, because it is 25 percent larger. "Why do you travel third class?" I once asked an urbane Austrian intellectual who bridled at self-indulgence. "Because," he said, "there is no fourth class."

The late William Rickenbacker, the inventive and witty son of the war ace and president of (the late) Eastern Airlines, proposed forty years ago a sensible way to permit the traveler a range of choices and the airlines their deserved profit. The ongoing mistake, he reasoned, is the airline's serving simultaneously as carrier and as marketer. The way to go, he counseled, is for the airline to auction its space in great blocks. "Who will pay $20 million for space on 5,000 Eastern Airlines flights, New York to Miami, Jan. 1 to July 1?...Do I hear $22 million? Going for $21.5 million, going...gone."

Let the wholesaler then sell the tickets for whatever price he can get, which takes into account the urgency of the flight and the comfort level. That broker would send you business class to Geneva for $100—if the seat you occupy would otherwise go empty.

The wholesale broker could, without inflicting pain, vary the price of an airplane passage, taking into account all relevant factors. As it stands now, the traveler burns with resentment at being asked to pay six times the cost of the lesser ticket.

But the problems of the business-class traveler aren't likely to arrest the attention of our governors, and elderly people are difficult to organize. Perhaps this is one for the AARP.

The Angel of Craig's Point
Miles Gone By, 2004

I sold *Cyrano* in 1978, *Suzy Wong* in 1981, as the problems of maintaining wooden boats and of making them pay their way in the charter business became too demanding. But not having a boat of my own was not an option, and so I commissioned Christo (Christopher Buckley) and Danny to look for a smaller boat, made of relatively carefree fiberglass.

They quickly came up with *Patito*, a thirty-six-foot sloop, and I have loved the little boat. For our inaugural cruise on *Patito*, we chose the St. John River in New Brunswick. Christo and Danny and I were joined by an old friend, historian Tom Wendel.

Our last day on the river, after sailing briskly downwind with only the headsail for two or three hours, during which we lunched, we thought to take a little exercise—a good walk—and, while at it, to get rid of two sackfuls of garbage, neatly tied up in plastic bags and riding in the dinghy we were towing.

I spotted a little private wharf on Craig's Point and glided in toward it, intending to ask the owner's permission to use his garbage container and perhaps even to tie up the boat on his dock for an hour while we walked. As we approached the dock, Christo leaned forward, a docking line in his hand ready to toss to the man in his early sixties who approached us. We assumed he was doing so in the usual manner in which boats are approached when coming in for a landing—i.e., prepared to receive the bowline and to cleat it to the dock. I signaled Tom to make the request from amidship. He said, "Is it okay if we tie up here for a few minutes? We'd also like to get rid of the garbage, if that's all right."

To our astonishment, the man answered, "It's is not all right. Go away. This is private property."

I intervened. "How far from your house is the public road?"

He pointed in the general direction of his own house. "It's back there."

"Well," I said, "Could we just walk across your property to find a public place to leave the garbage?"

"You may not. Go away."

To put it calmly, sailors are not used to being treated that way. To begin with, our anxiety to put the garbage on an assembly line to the city dump presumptively indicated our concern for the cleanliness of the water that ran by Craig's Point, where the gentleman lived, not Wallacks Point, where I live, 300 miles away. But, of course, there was no alternative but to retreat from his dock area. We consulted hastily, calculated the probable extent of his shoreline property, went safely beyond it, and threw out a hook, and three of us went ashore. At least we could get our walk. The garbage could continue to accumulate until we reached the yacht club the next morning.

After our walk we sailed another hour, spotted a seductive mini-cove nestled among tall cypress trees, and let down the anchor for our last meal aboard *Patito* on that trip. Christopher and Danny set about preparing a gourmet dinner while Tom played an entire Bach toccata on the Casio portable keyboard. I felt an ungovernable urge, and reached for my typewriter. Before we sat down to dinner, I announced that I wished to read to my crew a letter I had written to the editor of the afternoon paper at St. John. I had intended a catharsis for the unpleasant experience at Craig's Point, and achieved it.

Four days later, back in New York, my secretary, Frances Bronson, told me that the editor of the *Telegraph-Journal* of St. John, NB, was on the line and wanted to speak to me.

I was stuck. Journalists should always take calls from other journalists (my rule). But I knew that there was no way I could take this phone call and speak the truth without undermining my own enterprise. So, I instructed Frances to tell the editor, "Mr. Buckley has nothing to add to the letter he addressed to your paper a few days ago at St. John, and sends his best wishes."

A few days later, someone sent me in the mail a copy of the *Telegraph-Journal* for July 16, 1982. On the right, there was a large picture of me, smiling. The headline read:

"BILL BUCKLEY LOVES HOSPITALITY IN NB"

An editor's note began the story...

(Editor's note: William F. Buckley, editor of *National Review*, a conservative magazine published in New York, and host of the popular *Firing Line* program on the educational television network, was in New Brunswick recently with his family. They had a few problems but were delighted with the help they received. And he wrote to us to say so.)

Dear Sir:

Indulge, if you will, a vacationing American journalist with Canadian connections (my wife, even after thirty years' marriage, is obstinately Canadian) a word or two about our recent voyage in my small sloop with three companions, from Stamford, CT, to St. John, via Nantucket.

1) Near Lepreau Point, west of St. John some twenty-five miles, we ran out of fuel—and there was no wind. My son and his compan-

ion took the dinghy, approached the nearest house, and explained our predicament. The gentleman conveyed them to the nearest gas station, where they filled two five-gallon containers, returned them to the beach, wished them Godspeed, and rejected most amiably a proffered bottle of champagne.

2) At St. John, while waiting for the current's equilibrium in order to make the passage across the falls, a resident volunteered to drive us in his work truck to the restaurant where we lunched. En route he spotted our five-gallon container, ascertained that we intended to buy some diesel fuel, and volunteered to do so for us while we lunched, and to place the container in our dinghy; where, an hour later, we found it, together with the receipt from the gasoline station.

3) The following day, heading up the river, I radioed to my office to ascertain whether the details had been completed involving the ferry crew retained to bring my sloop back to Connecticut. After the telephonic exchange had been completed, the operator said to me: "Excuse me, sir, but I heard your secretary give the telephone number of the hotel where she booked your crew. She gave you an area code of 709. That is the area code for St. John's, Newfoundland, not St. John, New Brunswick." I quickly called back to New York, explained the confusion, and thanked the marine operator whose merciful intervention spared us a geographical solecism that would have qualified for the annals of, well, something.

4) But I must close by mentioning the man my shipmates have come to refer to as "The Angel of Craig's Point." That may really be overstating it, but the gentleman who owns the house on Craig's Point, at latitude 45 degrees 23.5, longitude 66 degrees 12.3, is certainly very special. We had accumulated some garbage, and went by dinghy to the gentleman's little wharf, where he met us with open arms, guiding us to a disposal point, complimenting us effusively on the thought we took to preserve the ecological purity of your beautiful river. Such ardent attention he gave us that we soon gathered that he devotes himself substantially to welcoming any yachtsmen or passersby who have garbage or any form of detritus to dispose of. Such heartening concern

for nature, and such hospitality evidenced to strangers, prompt me to send a copy of this letter to the editor of the famous *A Cruising Guide to the New England* (and Canadian) *Coast*, so that future editions will assure that no yachtsmen will pass by Craig's Point without paying respect to its Angel, and leaving him their garbage.

We are very much in debt to the citizens of St. John for your hospitality.

WILLIAM F. BUCKLEY JR.

NEW YORK, NY

The following day I received a copy of the *Telegraph-Journal* of St. John for July 17, 1982. The headline was too good to be true.

"THE ANGEL OF CRAIG'S POINT STRIKES BACK"

On the left of the boxed story, another headline:

"MORE ABOUT BILL BUCKLEY'S GARBAGE BAGS"

Then:

BY JIM WHITE
Associate Editor

Where is William F. Buckley's garbage?

That's the big question facing residents of the Craig's Point area on the St. John River north of Westfield.

Mr. Buckley, the well-known American writer and editor of the *National Review*, wrote a letter to the editor of the *Telegraph-Journal* which was published yesterday, complimenting New Brunswickers on their hospitality during a recent visit.

But the vituperative Mr. Buckley struck out at one resident of

Craig's Point in a seemingly innocent passage, and that resident wants to set the record straight once and for all.

Mr. Buckley in his letter referred to the "Angel of Craig's Point," who assisted him in disposing of his accumulated "detritus" from his "small sloop."

Mr. Buckley went on further to suggest passing yachters should not miss the opportunity to deposit their garbage at Craig's Point.

But the so-called "angel" has an entirely different recollection of the encounter.

Aubrey Pope, a retired St. John businessman, remembers the July 1st encounter with Mr. Buckley's party very well.

The Buckley sloop had spent the night in the shelter of a cove off Craig's Point, Mr. Pope said.

The next morning, Mr. Pope's wife noticed "three chaps in a rubber dinghy heading toward the shore."

Mr. Pope, who is well known up and down the river, went out to greet the landing party.

By the time Mr. Pope arrived at the shore, one of the men was standing on the wharf and the others were handing out two boxes and a couple of bags of garbage.

"If they had only asked permission, I would have been happy to give them a hand," Mr. Pope said.

But the party arrogantly went about their work and told Mr. Pope they were going to dump the garbage beside the road.

When Mr. Pope told the group there was no roadside pickup they insisted they wanted to get rid of their unseemly cargo.

At this point Mr. Pope informed them they were trespassing on his private property and were no longer welcome. They could pick up their garbage and return to their boat.

"They got in their boat and rowed into the river," Mr. Pope said. "Then they put into shore a little way's down river. They walked ashore with the boxes. I don't know where they dumped it, but they didn't have their garbage when they came back to the boat."

Attempts to get through to Mr. Buckley at his New York

office failed. But Mr. Buckley's assistant, Frances Bronson, said Mr. Buckley had submitted the letter for publication and had no further comment.

Kempton Pope, son of the owner of Craig's Point, said the rudeness of the Buckley party was what really riled his father.

"If they had introduced themselves we probably would have been proud to have Mr. Buckley's garbage," he said with a chuckle.

It had been ages, Tom Wendel wrote me from California, since he had seen such a farrago of misinformation as that given to editor White by Aubrey Pope. But we had had our laugh, and I resigned myself to living with the consolation that misrepresentations of *Patito's* behavior were limited to a modest circulation centered on Craig's Point, NB.

Not so.

On September 6, *People* magazine (circ. 2,854,000) ran an item in its Chatter column, written by Josh Hammer.

"DUMPING ON THE LOCALS"

After a recent cruise down New Brunswick's picturesque St. John River, writer-skipper William F. Buckley Jr., sent a letter to the St. John *Telegraph-Journal* praising a fellow whom he dubbed "the Angel of Craig's Point." According to Buckley, the man had helped his crew dispose of its shipboard garbage. Aubrey Pope, 67, a local businessman, recognized his description but surfaced with a somewhat different version of Buckley's tale. As he told it to an editor at the *Telegraph-Journal*, three of Buckley's crew members had indeed sought to unload their trash—by dumping it all on Pope's private dock. Pope happened to intercept them and ordered them off. "I'm not very big, but I can get ugly," he said, adding that he "would have been glad to help"—if it hadn't been for their "arrogant attitude." Buckley's response was to dump his trash without permission at a scenic spot farther down river and then fire off his sarcastic missive, in which he "thanked" Pope for his help, gave the exact location of his dock and advised mariners passing through not to cruise by Craig's Point "without paying respects to its angel" by dropping off their garbage there.

Oh dear, I thought. It was all really getting out of hand. Not only had we obstreperously arrived at Mr. Pope's dock, landed on it without his permission, and (in effect) threatened him, we had actually thrown our garbage into a scenic spot next door. So, of course, I needed now to write to *People*. I did so, patiently straightening out the story. *People* did not publish the last half of the sentence that began, "It would not occur to us to dump garbage on private property without permission"—which sentence went on to say, "or to publish a story to the effect that Mr. Hammer had done so, without first calling him up and asking him whether so bizarre an allegation was correct."

And then, on top of all that, I had a pleasant letter from Roger Duncan, the editor of *A Cruising Guide to the New England Coast*, the bible of New England sailors. I hadn't actually sent him a copy of my letter to the St. John paper, but somebody else had done so. And now he was writing to thank me for thinking to send him such random information about cruising experiences as I was collecting. He advised me that his own experience with Canadians, like mine, reaffirmed that they were the most hospitable breed of people on earth. He finished:

> I appreciate your thinking of the *Guide*. It is only with the help of cruising men who write in their experiences of various harbors that we can possibly keep the book current. I visit a great many harbors and so does (my associate) John Ware, but we could never accomplish the project without help. Any other information of interest to cruising yachtsmen will be welcome, either now or later.

I needed to straighten Mr. Duncan out in a hurry.

And then, on reading the correction published in *People*, the editor of the St. John paper wrote to remind me that he had tried to reach me over the telephone but I had not taken his call. He added that Mr. Pope was now asserting that his own story of what had happened was confirmed by someone who had used binoculars from the other side of the river. I replied:

Dear Mr. White:

Thank you for your amiable letter. You will perhaps have reflected on the reasons why I did not take the telephone call from you that day in July. Obviously, my letter, while composed three parts of genuine praise of Canadian hospitality, was composed one part of sarcasm at the expense of Mr. Anti-Pope. I could hardly have talked with you over the telephone without giving away the show, and obviously I wouldn't have wanted to do that.

On the astonishing point that there was a live witness via binoculars: that would suggest, given that the verbal exchanges with Mr. Pope were exactly as described by me, that the binoculars disposed of facilities for picking up the sound of human voices several hundred yards away. Since to my knowledge such powers as these are limited to the CIA and KGB, then you have more to worry about than my inaccessibility. If your reporter advised you that we proceeded to dump the garbage ashore, why he is just plain wrong, and if it were necessary to prove the point, you could have four sworn affidavits. My own guess has been that Mr. Anti-Pope is industrious in elaborating circumstances that vitiate his rudeness. I note that *People* magazine edited my letter, leaving out the last sentence, which was the only trenchant remark on their own misbehavior. Ah well. Could it be that journalists are also human?

Exactly one year later, Tom Wendel, Danny, Christo, and I found ourselves once again on the St. John River. We had planned to cruise to the Bras d'Or Lake in the northern part of Nova Scotia, but a tight schedule plus head winds rerouted us, and now we were at anchor within sight of the Angel's spread, a few hundred yards upstream. We had consumed, with dinner, a magnum of fine Bordeaux, a cruising gift from a friend, which greatly animated us. Accordingly, we typed out a note, stuck it in the bottle, corked it tightly, and let it float downstream. The note read:

IMPORTANT . . . REWARD . . .

The finder of this bottle can claim a fifty-dollar reward by presenting
the bottle to Aubrey Pope, Esquire, at Craig's Point, Morrisdale, NB.
The reward will be payable on saying to Mr. Pope, "This bottle rep-
resents the gratitude of the Canada Beautiful Society, Ltd, Garbage
Collection Division, W. F. Buckley, Corresponding Secretary, Care
Editor, St. John *Telegraph-Journal*."

Somewhere in the oceans of the world that bottle is floating about.
That, or else it has been presented to the Angel for the promised reward.

Aweigh
Atlantic, July–August 2004

Consequential decisions can be triggered by inconsequential causes. She
leaned over, picked up the phone—and I knew then that I'd be filing for
divorce. But later, introspective curiosity sets in. And the search for self-jus-
tification. So we poke around dormant gray matter trying to bring out a
plausible teleological narrative. All this has been happening to me since I
decided to sell my boat.

Selling a boat one has spent happy decades on is, in a way, a fateful
decision. It can be likened to a decision to stop skiing or playing the piano,
if one has skied a lot or played the piano a lot. The sequence here is critical
to the effort to explain a self-inflicted privation. What brought it on? It
wasn't that I decided to do away with my boat after narrowly surviving the
storm I took it through. I wasn't making a gesture of despair and remorse
after losing a companion overboard.

Dramatic forerunners engender sequels that are self-explanatory, most of
the time. There was none such here to account for my decision. If there had
been a catalytic event, you would be looking for something quite simple, on
the order of resolving to file for divorce after finding your wife in bed with
another man—a banality. It was the *inconsequential* factor that I searched for.

What did happen is that Michael, a first mate I had retained—as I
regularly did—to crew for me one day every summer week and ten days
in August, had had to pull away. A mortal cancer had seized his mother,

quickly killing her. Of course, he would leave me for a period, to be back in Canada with his father; I expected his return after two or three weeks, but then he reported that he had contracted an episodic malady of sorts that would keep him away for the balance of the sailing season. He would be returning directly to Yale to get on with his graduate work in molecular biology. My summer schedule was put awry.

A few weeks later, my plans reconstituted, I was sailing on *Patito* with three very old friends off Cape Cod. I blurted it out to them at dinner, on the fourth night, that I had decided to sell my boat—on which, as on its predecessors, they had all sailed with me over many years, and to distant places. Their stupefaction was gratifying, in that it confirmed the felt gravity of my decision. I had acted on impulse—but not, I tried to explain to them, impulsively.

In September of 1938 two of my sisters and I received distressing news, relayed to us by our governess. It was that two weeks hence we were to embark for England, where for one academic year we would attend English boarding schools. This disruption of happy lives, home-schooled in northwestern Connecticut, we found unbearable. My father, who had thus struck us down, was at the time visiting Europe with my mother and other siblings. He had given no reason for this arbitrary move, beyond saying that the experience of foreign schooling would be educational for us; never mind that we had all already been to British schools five years earlier, when we were living in Europe. Age twelve, I wrote to him resignedly (there was no alternative to complying with my father's decisions) about the impending extraterritorialization, and took sly and arrant advantage of his predictable defensiveness—he owed us one, and he had a very tender heart. I told him with a letter that I pined to have a sailboat when we got back from the English ordeal.

And so, nine months later, in June of 1939, I beheld my own sailboat on the neighboring lake. It was a torrid affair from the moment I sighted her. I thought it a filial gesture to name my boat *Sweet Isolation*, reflecting my father's political leanings in the pre-war years. My little (seventeen-foot) conventionally rigged Barracuda (sailing class extinct) took me around the triangular course on Lakeville Lake twice every Wednesday, Saturday, and

Sunday, mid-June to Labor Day. I contended in the no-handicap marathon against six other boats of different designs, all of them captained by aged men and women in their twenties and thirties. We all struggled hugely to acquire the trophy. You needed to win it three times before taking permanent ownership. An exact replica of it could be found at the local hardware store, on sale for $21.

I would rise early on racing days to gauge the wind's preliminary dispositions, and to contemplate a strategy for that afternoon. I would be driven the five miles to the lake, arriving an hour before race time so that I could practice my starts and coach my crew (usually one of my siblings). We had three summers of this before the Wononscopomuc Yacht Club races became a casualty of Pearl Harbor; they did not revive after the war. The spring-fed lake, one mile square, is still there, and from it, when the winds are still and the sun is low, you can discern the brick profile of the Hotchkiss School. On the opposite rise, in the low Berkshires, Wanda Landowska could view the lake from her house where, for RCA, she recorded her historic harpsichord renditions of *The Well-Tempured Clavicord*. On the afternoon of the recording session, after beginning to play, she stopped. She advised the state police, by telephone, that they must close the entire road east of the lake to traffic, so that she could have the total stillness she needed. No one had ever before made such a request; no one else ever will; but the police, dumbfounded by the high Teutonic voice of the lady whose face had graced *Time* magazine, complied.

There was no sailing for me during the war, but I was discharged from the Army in May of 1946 and had *Sweet Isolation* back in the water a week later. In July, I contrived a cradle on a four-wheel trolley. Attached to the station wagon, it took my boat to Edgartown. We sailed, my sisters and the childhood friend I'd be sharing a room with at Yale a month later, in those glamorous waters. One afternoon, off Chappaquiddick, the mast was disabled in a strong wind and my sister Tish was swept into Nantucket Sound. For harrowing minutes, as we struggled desperately to bring the boat about, we knew she was at risk of drowning. A Coast Guard vessel spotted her flailing arms and picked her up; then it fetched us and my crippled boat, and towed the bedraggled lot back to a marina.

That night, silent, we looked at the dinner menu at an inn overlooking the harbor. We were woozy from the afternoon's trauma, and unstimulated by alcohol (I wasn't yet twenty-one, and management would not serve me a beer). My eyes idled over to the cruising boats slipping into the harbor, their red and green running lights twinkling off the cozied water. There was shelter here from the heavy winds that continued to roil the sound outside. One vessel, especially imposing, was identified for our benefit by the waiter, a college student doing summer work and crewing in the afternoons on one of the racing boats. That boat going by—he pointed—was the *Manxman*, a surviving Class J boat, 136-feet long, created to compete for the America's Cup in the 1930s. I counted twelve or more crew members in the dimming light, fastening down sails, two or three of them, wearing yellow jackets and khaki shorts, crowded around the skipper. The sight of that long dark beauty, and of the sloops and yawls and cutters and schooners nestling in the harbor, many of them secured now on their moorings, paralyzed me with longing. A cruising sailboat! That was now the object of my desire. For several years I read the yachting magazines as a window-shopper, praying that one day I would put my foot in the door, and sail into Edgartown Harbor as the captain of my own boat.

I did that in 1954, having conscripted my brother-in-law, who had never before sailed, into a joint purchase of *The Panic*, the name we gave to our Dutch-built forty-two-foot steel cutter. It was the most misbalanced sailing vessel ever created. In a hard wind, making way close-hauled, you needed the strength of both arms to hold the tiller to the desired angle.

But she was all ours, including the tiny captain's cabin, not much bigger than the berth it housed, and we gave it an enormous ice box in which, for long hauls, we could store as much as 250 pounds of ice. We laughed a lot on *The Panic*, cruising, on most summer weekends, my wife, Pat, presiding over a remarkable cuisine that evolved from three Sterno stoves that hung from individual fixtures. Multi-gimbaled, they were indifferent to any motion of the boat, fore and aft or side to side. One night in Maine, Pat's imaginative dinner was prolonged in preparation. I announced that in order to celebrate appropriately the wind, the sun, the stars, the moon, and the harbor in Maine (there is always reason to celebrate aboard a boat), I would pour myself a third drink, and I went to the bottle of pre-mixed margaritas she had brought on board. I wondered whether, having already drunk two, I would be courting tipsiness with a third, but I poured it anyway. I thought to ascertain the strength of the drink, and so tilted the kerosene lamp to read the fine print on the label. It described the ingredients and then gave directions: "Pour two ounces over ice. Then add tequila." I had been near tipsy from drinking lime juice—causing my crewmates and my wife to be tipsy with amusement.

Cruising in October to Bermuda, we had to make our way through the eastern end of a hurricane. After a very hard day's combat using only the storm jib and trysail, I finally hove to for a long night of furious wind. This capitulation at sea is achieved by adjusting the reduced sails to vie against one another in such fashion as to induce relative immobility.

The next day the crew, shaken after the struggle of the day before and the shriek of the wind against the shrouds during the sleepless night, was somnolent and detached. The dishes were unwashed. No one had moved to make breakfast. There was cloud cover, and we were too far from the island to take radio bearings on Bermuda's commercial radio station. I had to tell them that I simply didn't know where we were. Demoralization was setting in. I revived the crew by serving hardtack and port. The sweet alcoholic potion revived their spirits, and the chewy hardtack gave sustenance. The sun soon crept out, giving me a sight, and on we slogged in a forty-knot wind, eleven hours close-hauled on a starboard tack, ocean water taking up one third of the cubic space of the cockpit, arriving finally in that tipsy boat at St. George's Harbor.

Earlier the same year we had raced *The Panic* with the Newport fleet to Bermuda. On arriving, I learned at a festive cocktail party the hairy tale of the metallurgist. He had raced in his brand-new thirty-eight-foot Swedish-built aluminum boat, on which, forty-eight hours out, was heard a thwack unrelated to the conventional creaks and groans of boats hard pressed under way. The thwack came again forty minutes later. The metallurgist took a professional interest in what was happening. He disclosed after the fourth thwack—they were coming at decreasing intervals—that when the interval was down to one minute, the vessel would have at most one remaining minute to stay afloat: an entire aluminum bulwark on the port side would at that point simply fall away. His boat arrived in Bermuda when the thwack-time interval was at four minutes. The owner sold the boat and never sailed again.

For all that his was a singular experience, his decision to get rid of the boat after undergoing it is hardly inexplicable (never mind that the Swedish builders flew in an engineer, and presumably a lawyer, to cope with the derelict). I would soon learn the psychological impact of a boat loss, not only on the owner but on others. *The Panic* was destroyed by a hurricane in 1961, in my back yard, so to speak. It was uprooted from its mooring at the Stamford Yacht Club and splayed across the stony breakwater at the harbor's entrance. The shock of its loss was felt by others who knew the boat. Hugh Kenner, the aseptic critic, let out a full-throated jeremiad. Here was the end of a boat that had "done much for her friends, in the summers before her side was stove in," he wrote to me.

> She had taken them all around the Sound and along the New England coast, and even to Bermuda (thrice), and shown them Wood's Hole, and the Great Fish that eats taffrail logs, and the Kraken, and the strange men of Onset with their long faces, and perfect Edgartown; and lapped them at night gently to rest; and given them the wind and sun and made for them a place of adventure and refreshment and peace; and taught them this, that beyond illusion it is possible to be for hours and days on end perfectly and inexpressibly happy.

Boat owners tend to upgrade, and I now had the insurance money. I very quickly bought, sight unseen, a forty-foot Sparkman & Stephens yawl of illustrious design (Nevins 40) from its four owners in Miami. It was offered with a piquant story. The sailors had served together in the Army in Japan and, aged twenty to twenty-two, had dreamed of owning a sailboat and taking it around the world. They could put together only enough money to buy the bare boat and engine from the American boat company in Hong Kong. It was all teak—teakwood was cheap in that part of the world. They flew there joyfully upon their discharge, men with varied skills learned as civilians and in the Army. They sanded and painted the hull, mounted the rigging, installed the plumbing and electrical systems, and finished the deck. Two months later the boat was ready, and they set out, westward, for Miami, arriving eighteen months later, flat broke, and happy. They calculated that they had spent $1.75 per person per day. That updates to about six dollars. I paid them $30,000 for the *Suzy Wong*, and sailed her for sixteen years, some weekdays, most summer weekends, here and there cruising on blue water, running two races to Bermuda and one to Halifax, very contented until I found the *Cyrano*, a sixty-foot schooner with an eighteen-foot bowsprit—a big upgrade, though bought for the same $30,000 I realized on selling the *Suzy*.

There was much to do to make that schooner habitable—indeed, to transform it into the dream boat that I sailed for ten years, and took across the Atlantic, Miami to Bermuda to the Azores to Gibraltar, with my son, my sister-in-law, sailing friends, a cook, a hand, and a mate. I built a dodger (this shields the deckhouse from the wind) and installed a circular sofa whose center could be raised and stripped of its cushions to form a circular table; with the center level on the springs, its cushions in place, four or even five flopped-out sailors could rest or read, and when it was lifted eight people could dine. Two long berths at either side of the navigation table proved handy, and now the rudder could be electronically controlled when the helmsman sought shelter. Protective canvas could be rolled down on all sides to seal in the entire area.

While standing in the navigation well, examining the almanac, the ship moving in a moderate following wind, I spotted the Pico light off Horta. Landfall after eleven days of sailing. I shouted back to my son, Christopher, at the wheel. His childhood friend Danny Merritt, who has sailed with me since he was a teenager, was sitting alongside on the taffrail. He stood up and peered excitedly in the direction I signaled. I wrote a book (*Airborne*) about that passage.

But the next year, sailing the *Cyrano* from Fort Lauderdale to Cozumel, again with my son and Danny, I reflected hard on the running costs, tucked into my briefcase by my bookkeeper. The figures spoke to me unanswerably: I had to sell the boat. There was only that single reason for doing so, but it was decisive. The *Cyrano* cost too much to maintain, my grand plan to subsidize it through chartering having failed after nine years of trying. If anybody (rich) is looking for a perfect boat, track it down, and live happily ever after.

It was then that I bought the *Patito*.

I left the purchase of the new boat in the hands of Christopher and Danny. It was they who thought to call it *Patito*, which is the Spanish diminutive for "duck," a term I use when addressing my wife, and she when talking to me. I knew that they would find the right boat, this time in fiberglass, to succeed the old wooden boat they had wearied of maintaining. I beheld the *Patito* for the very first time after giving a lecture at Trinity College and then driving for almost two hours to Essex. I arrived at the dock in cold April weather at about eleven, and my new boat was there, lit up below with candlelight, a flicker or two of snow falling into the cockpit, the salon well warmed with a kerosene heater. Christo and Danny, in high spirits, had a bottle of wine open. The *Patito* is thirty-six feet, and the most intimate of my boats. I have written about it that it is perfect with four aboard, and that five are three too many. The *Patito* has been with me full-time. I have been faithful to it except for three transoceanic sails on the *Sealestial*, a boat I skippered but did not own.

The *Sealestial* is a seventy-one-foot ketch. On transoceanic runs the rule was that I and my friends would do the sailing, and the (paid) crew would do the maintenance. It was a good arrangement, giving us, at work and at play, eating and sleeping, a privacy beyond even the gross privacy of living on a little boat in great oceans. On a 3,000-mile Pacific run, Hawaii to New Guinea, we did not once in thirty days see another ship at sea or a plane overhead. Such apparent alienation sharpened the miniaturization of it all. I calculated that from the starting point, in Hawaii, I could have directed the boat to land in Japan instead of New Guinea by altering the rudder a mere four degrees—one ninetieth of the orbit of possibilities. On that passage we had the run of experiences at sea, recounted in a book I wrote, *Racing Through Paradise*.

It was good that my sea books featured the same friends, given that one's memory of a boat incorporates the company aboard it. That essential factor of human pleasure—a small crew, mostly with repeat companions—

struck me most vividly when, walking past the fleet that had just completed the Annapolis-Bermuda Race, I spotted and spoke to a friend who had crewed aboard what they call a "maxi"—a boat longer than the seventy-two feet permitted during my racing years. I asked if he had got on with the rest of the crew. He replied that half of them (there were eighteen) he had not even met during the passage.

The convention involving the *Patito* did not change. The operative day each week was Friday. We would gather at my house for a drink, and sometimes a look at the Weather Channel, though we could see the waters of Long Island Sound by looking out the window. The mate would have the boat ready, and soon after 6:30 p.m. we would set out for Long Island, usually Eatons Neck or Oyster Bay. In a hard southeaster we would sail east to Norwalk, or west to Greenwich. Depending on the wind, the sail would take an hour-and-a-half or two hours. We had gotten used to a dry martini on arrival. Music was instantly at hand. "The Entertainment Committee never sleeps" was my mantra as I slid in a tape of Dick Wellstood or Claude Debussy. A half-hour later the meal began to arrive, prepared at home but cooked by the mate. The mates changed every year, handily recruited mostly from nearby Yale—young men who lived in the area, knew how to sail, were anxious to do so, and welcomed the stipend. They were quickly integrated into a Friday routine that usually ended with a game of poker and a swim.

The *Patito* ventured out from the sound from time to time—to Bermuda (twice), to Nova Scotia and Cape Breton, to Saint John River in New Brunswick and thereabouts—but the Friday-evening sail, twenty years of it, was simply an organic part of my home schedule, and of my life, and the binds to friends deepened.

What happened when Michael told me he couldn't persevere with his duties was that everything I had correlatively planned for the August sail changed. I could not ferry the boat east, where I had thought to pick it up and sail in Passamaquoddy Bay and over to Digby, in Nova Scotia, and back to Saint John and up the enchanted river.

Piano playing (at normal speed and for normal lengths of time) is not a physical exertion; and as the master and commander progressively off-loads the physical work at sea, exertion is minimal except when visibility attenuates, and wind and seas assert themselves. Then there is concentrated work and thinking to be done, and a measure of anxiety. But these aren't physically taxing, unless I have missed something that Freud *et al.* passed along. I resist the word "tedium," because sailing can have so many rapturous moments, and there are accompanying pleasures. When you are in a harbor, there may be four congenial people around the table, eating and drinking and conversing, listening to music and smoking cigars, the wind and the hail and the temperature outside faced up to and faced down. Here, in your secure little anchorage, is a compound of life's social pleasures in the womb of nature. So, deciding that the time has come to sell the *Patito* and forfeit all that is not lightly done, and it brings to mind the step yet ahead, which is giving up life itself.

Index